THE PHILOSOPHY OF SIMONE DE BEAUVOIR

T0335347

HYPATIA

THE PHILOSOPHY
OF SIMONE
DE BEAUVOIR

CRITICAL ESSAYS

Edited by Margaret A. Simons

INDIANA UNIVERSITY PRESS
BLOOMINGTON AND INDIANAPOLIS

This book is a publication of

Indiana University Press
601 North Morton Street
Bloomington, IN 47404-3797 USA

http://iupress.indiana.edu

Telephone orders   800-842-6796
Fax orders   812-855-7931
Orders by e-mail   iuporder@indiana.edu

The paper used in this publication meets the
minimum requirements of American National
Standard for Information Sciences—Permanence of
Paper for Printed Library Materials, ANSI Z39.48-
1984.

Manufactured in the United States of America

Library of Congress Cataloging-in-Publication Data

The philosophy of Simone de Beauvoir : critical
essays / edited by Margaret A. Simons.
       p. cm. — (A Hypatia book)
    Includes index.
       ISBN 0-253-34722-X (cloth) —
ISBN 0-253-21840-3 (pbk.)
       1. Beauvoir, Simone de, 1908–   I. Simons,
Margaret A.   II. Series.
       B2430.B344P45 2006
       194—dc22   2005029149

1 2 3 4 5 11 10 09 08 07 06

In Memory of Linda Singer and Kate Fullbrook

CONTENTS

Contents

Acknowledgments

This volume is dedicated to the memory of two inspiring Beauvoir scholars who contributed much to our understanding and appreciation of her philosophy: Linda Singer and Kate Fullbrook. Linda Singer was one of the first to challenge the traditional Sartrean reading of Beauvoir's ethics; she did so in an article published in my 1985 special Beauvoir issue of *Hypatia*. In their 1994 book, *Simone de Beauvoir and Jean-Paul Sartre*, Kate Fullbrook, with her husband, Edward Fullbrook, effectively demolished the claim that Beauvoir's novel, *She Came to Stay*, was an application of Sartre's philosophy in *Being and Nothingness*. I will be forever grateful to Linda and Kate for their personal encouragement and for the critical insights they brought to Beauvoir scholarship.

Nancy Tuana and Laurie Schrage have my sincere gratitude for the invitation to edit the 1999 special issue of *Hypatia* on Beauvoir's philosophy that forms the basis of this volume. Yolanda Patterson, as the head of the Simone de Beauvoir Society, has been a vital force in encouraging Beauvoir scholarship through the society's conferences, as well as the publication of the *Simone de Beauvoir Society Newsletter* and *Simone de Beauvoir Studies*, now in its twenty-second year. It gives me great pleasure to express my appreciation for her work. I am also grateful to Elizabeth Fallaize and Ursula Tidd, who organized the wonderful 2001 conference of the society at Oxford University.

I would also like to thank Claudia Card for her wise counsel, Marybeth Timmermann for her editorial assistance, Shannon Mussett for introducing me to a new generation of Beauvoir scholars, Dee Mortensen for her encouragement, and all of the contributors to this volume for their patience over the years as the Beauvoir Series preempted my time. Finally, I would like to express my sincere appreciation to the Southern Illinois University Edwardsville Graduate School for their years of encouragement and to acknowledge the support of the 2004 Lindsay Research Professor Award, without which the completion of this project would not have been possible.

THE PHILOSOPHY OF SIMONE DE BEAUVOIR

INTRODUCTION

Margaret A. Simons

Simone de Beauvoir (1908–86), a trained philosopher and author of a graduate thesis on Leibniz, was well known to American philosophy students in the 1950s and 1960s as the existentialist author of *The Ethics of Ambiguity* (1946) and *The Second Sex* (1949). But both her existentialist ethics and her essay on women were usually presented as the application or development of a philosophy originated by her companion, Jean-Paul Sartre. Beauvoir's philosophical work was held in such low regard that by the late 1960s her name had largely disappeared from American histories of French existential phenomenology (see Simons 1999, 101–14), a situation that would change with the rebirth of feminism as a political movement.

Feminist activists/theorists such as Shulamith Firestone in *Dialectic of Sex* (1970) and Kate Millett in *Sexual Politics* (1971) modeled their radical feminism on *The Second Sex*, and feminist philosophers, encouraged by the formation of the Society for Women in Philosophy (SWIP) in 1969, took up Beauvoir's critique of the philosophical canon and began to challenge her exclusion. But integrating Beauvoir into the canon proved problematic. Existential phenomenology was hardly a feminist philosophical tradition: Sartre's descriptions of the female body in *Being and Nothingness*, often cited as the philosophical foundation of *The Second Sex*, were filled with disgust; and Beauvoir herself rejected efforts by feminist philosophers to define her position as philosophically distinct from Sartre's. By the mid-

1970s and the arrival of feminist identity politics, Beauvoir had become the target of intense feminist criticism.

But scholarly research on Beauvoir's philosophy continued. The Society for Phenomenology and Existential Philosophy scheduled their first program session on Beauvoir's philosophy in 1978, with the American Philosophical Association following soon afterwards. An important early impetus for research came from the 1979 New York University conference organized by Jessica Benjamin to celebrate the thirtieth anniversary of the publication of *The Second Sex*. Publications about Beauvoir began to appear as well. Interviews and articles on Beauvoir's philosophy were published in a 1979 issue of *Signs* (vol. 5, no. 2) and in the 1979 and 1980 issues of *Feminist Studies*. In 1985 the new feminist philosophy journal *Hypatia*, which was then part of *Women's Studies International Forum*, published a special issue on Beauvoir and Feminist Philosophy (WSIF vol. 8, no. 3), drawn from the 1984 University of Pennsylvania conference on *The Second Sex*.

The resurgence of interest in Beauvoir's life and work following her death in 1986, the growing influence of feminism in philosophy, and the posthumous publication in 1990 of Beauvoir's diaries and letters to Sartre launched a renaissance in Beauvoir scholarship among philosophers, rejecting the disparagement of her work and challenging the traditional interpretation of Beauvoir as merely Sartre's philosophical follower.[1] Papers on Beauvoir's philosophy have been presented at the Modern Language Association, in conferences of the Simone de Beauvoir Society, at the Center for Advanced Research in Phenomenology at Florida Atlantic University, at the World Congress of Philosophy and the Symposium of the International Association of Women Philosophers, and at program sessions of the Beauvoir Circle. In 1999 conferences in Paris, Köln, and Eichstätt, and at Penn State University celebrated the fiftieth anniversary of *The Second Sex*.

Nor has the interest in Beauvoir's philosophical work been limited to the scholarly community. When *Time* magazine selected the top ten nonfiction books of the twentieth century, they included *The Second Sex* (1949), "Simone de Beauvoir's philosophical treatise on the condition of women in modern life" (June 8, 1998). *Life* magazine named Simone de Beauvoir one of the one hundred most influential people of the millennium: "She developed existentialist philosophy in novels and nonfiction, . . . and wrote the most influential feminist book of the twentieth century."

The articles in this volume present some of the most exciting scholarly work on Beauvoir's philosophy. Framed by a 2001 address by the French feminist philosopher Michèle Le Doeuff, the articles range widely over the genres and eras of Beauvoir's writing life, including discussions of her unpublished diaries from the 1920s, her autobiographical writings and novels, and her essays in existentialist ethics, as well as *The Second Sex*. Themes in the volume include Beauvoir's philosophical relationship with Sartre and the question of influence; her ethic of the erotic; her views of marriage, motherhood, and female friendship; and her analysis of oppression and liberation. The authors read Beauvoir in the context of numerous philosophers, including Husserl, Merleau-Ponty, Heidegger, Rousseau, Foucault, Sartre, Hegel, Descartes, Levinas, and feminist philosophy.

Calling for a critical engagement with Beauvoir, Michèle Le Doeuff reminds feminist critics that Beauvoir was not our imaginary mother, nor our Savior, but a real woman whose work is to be discovered among other women's work. According to Le Doeuff, Beauvoir's critics, uncomfortable with this "hyperrealist bearer of bad news," have sought to rewrite her words and retouch her image, beginning with the mistranslation of her books but also including an effort to carve out a narrow, conformist body of Beauvoir's work unrelated to feminism. Le Doeuff calls for a questioning of the ready-made categories through which Beauvoir's work is understood, and she issues a Nietzschean challenge: Are you capable of supporting the reading of Beauvoir such as she is? Reading Beauvoir's philosophy in historical context, questioning traditional interpretations, and engaging critically with her most politically radical and feminist work, the authors in this volume take up these challenges posed by Le Doeuff.

Sara Heinämaa, in "Simone de Beauvoir's Phenomenology of Sexual Difference," questions the traditional reading of Beauvoir as a literary writer and follower of Sartre and argues that Beauvoir's phenomenological description of sexual difference in *The Second Sex* makes an important and original contribution to philosophy. Heinämaa points to Beauvoir's autobiographical writings and ethical essays for evidence of her rich philosophical life and deep engagement with Husserlian phenomenology. Rejecting the standard model of the philosopher as solitary system builder, Beauvoir, according to Heinämaa, instead accepts phenomenology's radical Cartesian model of philosophizing as questioning, self-criticism, and dialogue. Beauvoir thus aligns herself philosophically with the Husserlian Maurice Merleau-Ponty rather than with Sartre. Heinämaa reads *The Second Sex* as a Husserlian problematizing of the question of woman's way of being, that is, about femininity, otherness, and subordination.

Edward Fullbrook, in "*She Came to Stay* and *Being and Nothingness*," also challenges the traditional interpretation of Beauvoir as Sartre's philosophical follower, addressing the claim that Beauvoir's metaphysical novel *She Came to Stay* (1943) was merely a literary application of Sartre's philosophy in his essay *Being and Nothingness* (1943). Fullbrook draws on analyses of Beauvoir's novel by Merleau-Ponty, Hazel Barnes, and Elizabeth Fallaize in documenting the philosophical correspondence of Beauvoir's novel and Sartre's essay. After reviewing Beauvoir's method based on a description of concrete experience, Fullbrook compares the theories of intersubjectivity, embodiment, temporality, and appearances in *She Came to Stay* and *Being and Nothingness*. He then provides evidence from the two philosophers' letters and diaries to show that Beauvoir wrote her novel before Sartre wrote his essay and that the distinctive ideas and arguments that the two works share originated with Beauvoir.

Contesting Heinämaa's rejection of a Heideggerian influence on Beauvoir, Nancy Bauer, in "Beauvoir's Heideggerian Ontology," discusses Beauvoir's use of Heidegger's philosophy and his concept of *Mitsein*. Rejecting the popular interpretations of *Mitsein* as a broadly ethical concept or a primordial human fellowship, Bauer also rejects the claim that Beauvoir's use of the Heideggerian *Mitsein* is incompatible with her endorsement of Hegel's idea of the fundamental hostility of human consciousness, a claim made by Sartre in *Being and Nothingness*. For Beauvoir, unlike Sartre, Bauer explains, the fundamental hostility of consciousness does not rule out non-hostile human relations. Like Hegel, Beauvoir explicitly keeps open the possibility that people may achieve reciprocal recognition. But according to Bauer, unlike Hegel, Beauvoir identifies a gender difference in the desire for recognition, with men and women desiring to forgo different aspects of their ambiguous existence as free subject and object for the other.

In "Marriage, Autonomy, and the Feminine Protest," Debra Bergoffen addresses a question that Le Doeuff argues is left unresolved in Beauvoir's work: the question of autonomy and the emotional life. Criticizing the traditional view of marriage as betraying the ethical meaning of the erotic, Bergoffen also criticizes feminism for its rejection of marriage in the name of autonomy. Bergoffen finds in Beauvoir a recognition of the ambiguity of marriage as both a political institution and an intimate relationship based on an ethic of the bond and the erotic gift. Beauvoir contrasts this concept with the ideal of autonomy evident in the concept of marriage in the social contract tradition. Drawing on Rousseau, Bergoffen argues that politics is the work of relational subjects living out their need of and vulnerability to each other. In a post-patriarchal society, according to Bergoffen, the ethical meaning of the bond will prevail, and one will become fit for citizenship only in recognizing the "lie of autonomy."

Andrea Veltman continues the discussion of the feminist critique of marriage in "Transcendence and Immanence in the Ethics of Simone de Beauvoir," where she challenges the feminist critique of Beauvoir's transcendence and immanence dichotomy in *The Second Sex* as a remnant of Sartrean metaphysics. As early as the 1944 essay, "Pyrrhus and Cineas," according to Veltman, Beauvoir's concept of transcendence refers less to the movements of an intentional conscious subjectivity and more to constructive activities that situate and engage the individual with other human freedoms. Arguing in 1944 against such authors as Epicurus, Pascal, and Gide, Beauvoir rejects the claim that engagement in the world leads to unhappiness. Beauvoir's concept of transcendence takes on an ethical dimension in *The Second Sex*, where she contrasts it with immanence, referring to the passive submission to biological fate and the largely uncreative labor necessary to maintain life. Veltman argues that Beauvoir's dichotomy has the unrecognized potential to critique continuing inequities in motherhood and marriage.

Eva Gothlin returns to the question of autonomy and the emotional life in "Beauvoir and Sartre on Appeal, Desire, and Ambiguity," where she traces the development of Beauvoir's ethical concepts and, contrasting them with Sartre's concepts, challenges the traditional assumption of Beauvoir as Sartre's philosophical follower. In *Ethics of Ambiguity*, Beauvoir describes the fundamental ambiguity of human existence as consciousness and body, as a separate subject and interdependent with others. In *The Second Sex*, Beauvoir describes woman as embodying more explicitly than man this human ambiguity, as in pregnancy and in the relationship with her child. Beauvoir's description in *The Second Sex* of woman's unique sexual desire as an appeal is another instance, according to Gothlin, in which Beauvoir characterizes women's experience in terms of an ethical concept, in this case the concept of appeal as a will to communication and intersubjectivity. Contrasting Beauvoir's concepts with those of Sartre from the same period, Gothlin notes that unlike Sartre, Beauvoir places sexuality, femininity, and the body not outside the sphere of ethics but at the center of it.

Shifting the focus from marriage and heterosexual relationships, Julie Ward argues in "Reciprocity and Friendship in Beauvoir's Thought" that Beauvoir finds a resolution to the problem of the conflict of subjects in female friendship. Taking her lead from an episode recounted in Beauvoir's autobiography, Ward analyzes Beauvoir's 1927 diary, where she finds in Beauvoir's description of her female friendships an alternative to the problem of the opposition of self and other, which Beauvoir defines as a central philosophical theme. Beauvoir's 1943 metaphysical novel, *She Came to Stay*, and her 1949 essay, *The Second Sex*, complicate Beauvoir's earlier depiction of the opposition between self and other by introducing narcissism as a line of force parallel to that of masochistic fusion. In *The Second Sex*, Ward finds an implicit answer to Beauvoir's question of how a genuine mutual recognition between subjects can arise under patriarchy in Beauvoir's discussion of lesbian relationships, where, according to Beauvoir, the experience of mutuality can break the dilemma of narcissism or masochism.

Suzanne Laba Cataldi, in "Sexuality Situated: Beauvoir on 'Frigidity,'" continues the exploration of Beauvoir's ethic of the erotic and her philosophy in *She Came to Stay*. Relating scenes from Beauvoir's novels to her views of female eroticism and frigidity in *The Second Sex*, Cataldi reads Beauvoir's construction of frigidity as a symbolic means of rejecting male sexual dominance. Criticizing Fullbrook and Fullbrook (1994) for imposing a Sartrean analysis of bad faith on Beauvoir's famous example of frigidity in *She Came to Stay*, Cataldi sees the example instead as a form of protest by the female character against her companion's bad faith treatment of her as a thing. Cataldi argues that by situating sexuality in the context of women's oppression, Beauvoir provides a social and historical approach to understanding frigidity that is lacking in the medical diagnosis.

In "Beauvoir's Parrhesiastic Contracts: Frank-speaking and the Philosophical-Political Couple," Laura Hengehold also takes up Le Doeuff's challenge to address the problem of emotional autonomy. Focusing on interpersonal relationships capable of strengthening someone's soul by putting them in relation to the truth, Hengehold draws on Foucault's notion of a "parrhesiastic contract," a mutual commitment between two or more people to speak frankly and to risk hearing the truth. Beginning with Beauvoir's student diaries and analyzing her novels and essays, Hengehold traces Beauvoir's descriptions of women's "parrhesiastic" practice as they strive to create and preserve their souls amid shifting circumstances. In her theoretical works, Hengehold argues, Beauvoir develops an ontological and sociopolitical explanation for the parrhesiastic promise of sexual relationships as well as their dangers and disappointments. For Beauvoir, Hengehold concludes, women must take erotic and emotional risks and also work on the world apart from their partners if they are to be subjects of truth rather than its objects.

In "Beauvoir's Idea of Ambiguity," Stacy Keltner focuses on Beauvoir's essays in existentialist ethics. Keltner argues that Beauvoir, in "Pyrrhus et Cineas" and *The Ethics of Ambiguity*, uncovers the fundamental ambiguity of our social and temporal being, an ambiguity masked by traditional philosophies of pure inwardness or pure externality. The technological innovations of late modernity have dramatized the paradox of human mastery of the world and possibility of world destruction, thus highlighting the historical paradox of ambiguity. Drawing critically on concepts from Heidegger, Jasper, and Sartre, Beauvoir constructs an existentialist ethics of ambiguity and the project based on a description of human existence as materially, socially, and historically embedded. In understanding ethics as a movement toward freedom, Beauvoir's aim is to develop certain "precepts" for action that preserve temporal ambiguity. Similarly, Beauvoir is critical of any conception of the social bond that evades the ambiguity of our separation and connection. Finally, according to Keltner, Beauvoir argues that an existentialist ethics must respond to the historical "appeal" from the past that makes us responsible for concrete political action in the present.

In "Simone de Beauvoir: A Feminist Thinker for the Twenty-first Century," Karen Vintges challenges the dismissal of *The Second Sex* as irrelevant by arguing that it can be taken as the paradigm of contemporary feminism. Against the charge that Beauvoir is an old-fashioned modernist thinker, Vintges presents evidence of Beauvoir's conception of a self that is emotionally sensitive and situated, rather than purely rational. Nor does Beauvoir defend a modernist concept of a fixed self. According to Vintges, she anticipates, in her ethics as "art of living," the postmodernist critique of identity. Vintges argues that although limited by its assumption of its past, Beauvoir's concept of the self remains open to the future and thus does not imply a closed identity. Beauvoir's autobiographical writings, according to Vintges, represent a self-technique wherein she sought to shape, not an essential, unitary self as an effect of introspection, but a coherent identity as an effect of stylization and practical philosophical self-creation. In her criticism of all essentializing of women and in her presentation of positive ideals as contingent choices, Beauvoir maintained a pluralistic agency of feminism and created a new ethos as a woman without speaking in the name of woman as an essential subject.

Ursula Tidd, in "The Self-Other Relation in Beauvoir's Ethics and Autobiography," contributes to both the exploration of the problem of emotional autonomy and the focus on Beauvoir's autobiography. In this chapter, Tidd examines how some of Beauvoir's ethical notions about the self-other relation explored in her theoretical philosophy of the 1940s were developed in her subsequent autobiography. Tidd argues that Beauvoir represents reciprocal alterity in these autobiographical texts through a testimonial engagement with autobiography conceptualized as an act of bearing witness for the Other, through the privileging of various interlocutors and privileged others with whom "the real" is experienced, and through a negotiation with the reader. Contrasting Beauvoir's philosophy of the Other with that of Levinas, Tidd also explores the wider question of how Beauvoir's engagement with autobiography might constitute a mode of ethical engagement with the Other.

Gail Weiss, in "Challenging Choices: An Ethic of Oppression," rejects the tendency noted by Le Doeuff of separating Beauvoir's moral philosophy from her feminism in an attempt to integrate it into an academic canon. Focusing on the example of mothers who murder their children,

Weiss argues that the experience of oppression challenges traditional ethical theories such as those in Sartre's philosophy and Beauvoir's *Ethics of Ambiguity* that presuppose a rational, autonomous moral agent. In *The Second Sex*, however, Beauvoir sets the stage for an alternative concept of morality that is not grounded in freedom. Beauvoir's analysis of the oppressive institution of motherhood, according to Weiss, can render these women's actions intelligible as responses to situations over which they felt no control, thus restoring their humanity as moral agents operating outside the realm of choice and possibility. Weiss finds an alternative concept of the moral life for the severely oppressed in a simple "will to endure" that is founded, as the feminist ethics of care has shown, in the ability to enter into relations with others, an experience of intercorporeality that precedes choice. Focusing on relations with others rather than on choices, Weiss argues, allows us to see moral failures as failures of relation rather than merely failures of the individual in question. Freedom and choice thus become goals to strive for rather than foundations for morality.

In "Between Generosity and Violence: Toward a Revolutionary Politics in the Philosophy of Simone de Beauvoir," Ann Murphy identifies another aspect of Beauvoir's philosophy that has been ignored: her contribution to the French philosophical discourse on violence. Murphy argues that Beauvoir's discussion of violence, which organizes her thinking on the relationship of ethics and politics, is linked with the theme of generosity in her *Ethics of Ambiguity*. Noting the critical politico-philosophic focus on the ambiguity of gift giving and generosity, beginning with Mauss and continuing to Derrida, Irigaray, and Cixous, Murphy points to Beauvoir's and Sartre's interests in the ways in which generosity could be alienated and enacted as a type of violence and subjugation. Understanding the way Beauvoir consistently theorizes generosity and violence together also complicates the investigation of generosity in Beauvoir's ethics, which has been contrasted with Sartre's early descriptions of the hostility of human relationships. According to Murphy, Beauvoir's *Ethics* takes issue with the embrace of altruism and generosity as political strategies and entertains the possibility of violence in revolutionary politics.

Shannon Mussett, in "Conditions of Servitude: Woman's Peculiar Role in the Master-Slave Dialectic in Beauvoir's *The Second Sex*," proposes a new interpretation of Beauvoir's use of Hegel's master-slave dialectic in

The Second Sex. Arguing against the view that woman escapes the master-slave dialectic with man because of her exclusion from a life-and-death battle for recognition, Mussett provides two grounds for claiming that, for Beauvoir, woman is trapped in the master-slave dialectic. Beauvoir's woman, like Hegel's slave, inhabits the peculiar position of mediator for man, according to Mussett. Furthermore, woman's absolute negativity in relation to man means that woman undergoes the same education as Hegel's slave. Lacking any positive expression of self, woman is forced to confront the absolute negativity of self-consciousness, even without a violent confrontation with man.

The authors in this volume thus provide a model for new Beauvoir scholarship. Challenging the traditional reading of Beauvoir as Sartre's philosophical follower, situating her work historically in the larger phenomenological tradition, exploring the links between her ethics and her feminist work, and taking up the unresolved question of autonomy and emotional life, the authors exemplify the critical engagement with Beauvoir's work called for by Le Doeuff in her opening address.

NOTE

1. Recent books on Beauvoir's philosophy include: Kristana Arp, *The Bonds of Freedom: Simone de Beauvoir's Existentialist Ethics* (2001); Deirdre Bair, *Simone de Beauvoir: A Biography* (1990); Nancy Bauer, *Simone de Beauvoir, Philosophy, and Feminism* (2001); Debra B. Bergoffen, *The Philosophy of Simone de Beauvoir* (1997); Claudia Card, ed., *The Cambridge Companion to Simone de Beauvoir* (2003); Penelope Deutscher, *Yielding Gender: Feminism, Deconstruction and the History of Philosophy* (1997); Elizabeth Fallaize, *The Novels of Simone de Beauvoir* (1988) and *Simone de Beauvoir: A Critical Reader* (1998); Kate and Edward Fullbrook, *Simone de Beauvoir and Jean-Paul Sartre* (1993) and *Simone de Beauvoir: A Critical Introduction* (1998); Ingrid Galster, ed., *Simone de Beauvoir: Le Deuxième Sexe* (2004); Sara Heinämaa, *Toward a Phenomenology of Sexual Difference: Husserl, Merleau-Ponty, Beauvoir* (2003); Eleanore Holveck, *Simone de Beauvoir's Philosophy of Lived Experience* (2002); Michèle Le Doeuff, *Hipparchia's Choice* (1991); Eva Lundgren-Gothlin, *Sex and Existence: Simone de Beauvoir's The Second Sex* (1996); Toril Moi, *Simone de Beauvoir: The Making of an Intellectual Woman* (1994); Wendy O'Brien and Lester Embree, eds., *The Existential Philosophy of Simone de Beauvoir* (2001); Margaret A. Simons, ed., *Feminist Interpretations of Simone de Beauvoir* (1995), ed., *Hypatia* special issue, "The Philosophy of Simone de Beauvoir," vol. 14, no. 4 (Fall 1999), and *Beauvoir and The Second Sex: Feminism, Race, and the Origins of Existentialism* (1999); Ursula Tidd, *Simone de Beauvoir, Gender and Testimony* (1999); and Karen Vintges, *Philosophy as Passion: The Thinking of Simone de Beauvoir* (1996).

ENGAGING WITH SIMONE
DE BEAUVOIR

Michèle Le Doeuff

TRANSLATED BY NANCY BAUER

1

Let us congratulate Elizabeth Fallaize and Ursula Tidd! They have produced a title for this conference that couldn't be more timely. For "to engage with Simone de Beauvoir," to wish to establish a relationship with her that does not bypass the critical mode, to look, on the contrary, for elucidation (with respect to her and, on the way, with respect to ourselves, with respect to that with which she sustains us), to agree to "get in gear" with her, is to recognize that she has a reality and a theoretical validity, to recognize a significance for ourselves as well, and, thanks to the dialogue that is thereby engaged, to set out to find a meaning that perhaps goes beyond her and ourselves.

That we ought to take such a step is far from obvious. Certainly, during these past few years some excellent studies of Beauvoir's work have been published; but I would like to speak of a more surreptitious problem, one at the boundaries of this work: of commentaries heard here or there, emanating often from people who twenty years ago would simply have disdained Beauvoir, when it was more chic to call her passé [*passée*] or surpassed [*dépassé*]. Peg Simons would tell you the same: at a conference held at New York University in 1979 ("The Second Sex: Thirty Years Later"), very few papers focused on Beauvoir herself. I still remember the contribution of a celebrated French colleague that was dedicated to the beauty of cockroaches (I am not making this up), without a single reference to Beauvoir—the best way, no doubt, to evince contempt for her or to offer to replace her, as though there were not enough room for more than one woman in this world.

Times have changed. We have changed them. It is no longer possible to claim, in the light of a certain New French Feminism, that Beauvoir is obsolete. We have properly installed her existence, including in the academy. And so we see new women and men coming into contact with her: students who are likely to encounter her as an author on a syllabus, seasoned colleagues, adolescents, journalists . . . Now, in the nascent interest that is theirs, we don't really see a true "engaging with," a dialogue or "getting into gear" with Beauvoir. From the outset, you are largely going to hear that she is not as they had expected, thus not as she really should have been. And why didn't she have children? How can one conclude *The Second Sex* with the word "fraternity"? Did you see the horrible description she gives of breast cancer in a letter to Algren, thereby launching a negative and cruel way of seeing the illness? Etc. These are all questions I end up hearing, not as intellectual or political criticism, but as protestations— Why doesn't she offer herself as the ideal bosom for me or my daughter? Did she love me enough in advance, me, her sister by gender?—as if they were expecting her work and her life, which was a part of her work, not to be work but something else. And they are astonished to see that some people—that is to say, we—have taken such pains to keep this work alive. You and I know that this astonishment and the questions from which it stems do not constitute good method. We must, however, remind ourselves that these reactions reveal the context in which our work takes on, or doesn't take on, meaning.

Moreover, I sometimes catch myself responding and defending Beauvoir on this turf. No children, ah! that has to do with Sartre's having had mumps when he was a student. Besides, you don't need to know that; reading Beauvoir attentively is enough to grasp that her childlessness was due to a twist of fate more than a decision. But why would it be necessary to harp on this question indefinitely? Her letter to Algren describes not breast cancer but a treatment for it that was being administered during that era, in 1950. An epistolary discourse on a medical practice does not create that

practice—don't hold her responsible for what doctors did, which was ap-
palling, and which she denounces. But when you grumble about this letter,
do you want to say that she shouldn't have been the hyperrealist bearer of
bad news that she was? In that case, she should never have written *The Second Sex* or *A Very Easy Death*. As for the term "fraternity," if it shocks you,
could it be that the beginning of the sentence on the "natural differentia-
tions" between women and men pleased you more, or that the previous
pages, which conjure up a singular eroticism, a sexuality, a sensuality, a singular sensibility, seemed to herald something else?

If there is reason to think that this is not a suitable way to approach
Beauvoir's work, one must at the same time try to understand why she is so
often approached in this way. If you establish so primal a relationship to
her work, you are not at all "in gear" with her but are treating the work as
so many ink blots in a Rorschach test: you project onto it your own tastes,
your own fears, or the social values that are currently in the air. Our societies have ideological preferences that we might schematize thusly:
"Women are not like men; every woman is potentially a mother; and let us
not talk of the equality of the sexes." To judge Beauvoir's work by the standards of the dominant ideology would be to play with her as with a projec-
tive myth—an imago of the imperfect mother, a mother but imperfect—
whereas she ought to have been this bosom so sweet that one forgets that it
also exists for itself. Beauvoir did not love us perfectly in advance; she was
a real, singular woman, anterior and exterior to the expectation that is ours,
and so always to be discovered. Her work exists among other women's
works, not as the Book in some absolute sense. To establish a dialogue with
a body of work, whether it be written or artistic, requires first of all that you
see it as exterior to our subjectivities, beyond our fantasies, as the unforeseeable that it is. Let us give her a chance to tell us what we perhaps do not
already know, to provoke us to change to a greater or lesser degree our vision of the world.

Still more, when we express dissatisfaction about Beauvoir, aren't we
mistaking her not only for an imaginary mother who should magically
have told the world to be just as we expected it to be, but also for a Christ
in the feminine, a Christ whose word should have redeemed the world and
healed the crippled? There is no place for a magic word in the work of the
most austere of our authors. On Beauvoir's view, there is the world, a real

world, unhappy, full of oppression and suffering, but whose very unhappiness is rendered invisible: ideologies justify its being as it is, habits of thought hide its problems from consciousness. Even though this world and the representations that hide it, legitimize it—or, on the contrary, reveal a fragment of its truth—have been produced essentially by men, there is still a fundamental difference between the world and the representations. And then, as a third pole, there she is, a critical subject who seeks to untangle the facts from the myths, a thinking subject, a woman at work who cannot offer anything other than what she indeed does offer: a reflection that at least invites us to extricate ourselves from the myths. When you insist on the fact that she was a terribly disappointing icon or saint (and this sort of thing is, I think, the deep reaction of those who wonder at the importance that we have given her), you reinforce the idea that she should have or could have been a saint, which is absurd. She has nothing to do with shamanism, which seeks to improve things for you on the plane of the imaginary while distracting you from a painful real; and this is why she never tried to exalt the value of her work by claiming to have the purest or most loving of hearts. Auto-apologetics was not her strong suit. It's the postmodern atmosphere that incites us to look for ideas that would never be found under her pen. The idea that there are nothing but representations, thus that it is salvific to produce "healing" representations that are suited to being presented as issuing from a kindhearted or marvelous person, even to flirt with the idea of "becoming divine"—all this reflects a perspective that is the antithesis of the critical problematic that was hers.

This is no doubt obvious. And yet as a result of this misunderstanding, instead of striking up an "in gear" dialogue with Beauvoir's works, and if possible as they were written, the tendency has seemed to be rather to rewrite her words and retouch her image. In the English-speaking world, as Peg will confirm, it began with the (mis)translations of her books.[1] The translators felt free to modify her words as they pleased, to construct a Simone who was more to their tastes.[2] In the standard American translation of the scene in the Luxembourg gardens, when Sartre is attempting to annex her, she did not "struggle" [*se débattre*] with Sartre but "discussed things" [*débattre*] with him . . . It is no doubt prettier, nicer this way (all you need for a woman to capitulate is one little discussion), but a kernel of truth disappears, concerning a moment of extreme violence that she had the courage to relate. And here one would be tempted to issue a Niet-zschean challenge: Are you capable of supporting the reading of Beauvoir such as she is? You will guess that I am out to lend support to the project of retranslating her works: this Nietzschean challenge must first be issued to the editors: Would you blush at being editors of Beauvoir such as she re-ally was?[3]

The French-speaking world is far from being spared from rewritings. A letter arrives from a colleague who describes herself as "not a specialist on Beauvoir"; she has nonetheless supervised a Ph.D. thesis, just about fin-ished, on our Simone: would I agree to sit on the jury? Having had some misadventures previously, I asked to read a little bit, even in draft form, be-fore committing myself and was sent the opening section of the thesis. On the first page, a note announces that feminist commentaries on the author have not been taken into account, since although the feminists tried hard to enlist her in their ranks, Simone de Beauvoir always refused to let herself be enrolled. As a result, not much was actually left of the potential bibliog-raphy; as far as possible references to the original works were concerned, they also would be lacking. Do not take this as laziness: it has to do with a profound sort of rewriting aimed at creating an acceptable Beauvoir for a university milieu that the candidate no doubt saw as more anti-feminist than it really is. True, this is a proof of the importance of our author: were she devoid of importance, one would not set out to adapt her work to a politics that would in every way have preferred that she had never existed at all. One simply wouldn't speak of it at all. No more would one seek to substitute legitimate descendents for a group of readers who have fought for her. One would not strive hard to retouch the persona by giving it to be understood that she herself resisted feminism.

Some scholars maintain that the preaching that became the Gospel has reached us in expurgated and rewritten form, notably on the question of women, but not exclusively. In the history of philosophy, we commonly employ an opposition between "Athens" and "Alexandria": the Alexandrian commentators and grammarians may well have manipulated the textual heritage of Athenian philosophy, as happens when compilers, commenta-tors, or writers of introduction are in charge of original works—that is to say, all the time. It is therefore necessary to maintain a methodological dis-tance between that which could have been "Athenian" and that which the

Alexandrian editors did to it. It is the standard course always to return to the original texts when one can, whether we are talking about Descartes or Beauvoir, as opposed to the interpretations, interpretations of interpretations, or knowledge by hearsay.[4] Still, Alexandria is always there. Explicitly or implicitly, the successive waves of commentators make selections and choose bits and pieces of the work. Even for Beauvoir it is possible, after having read only some non-feminist commentaries and reading selectively from her works, to produce the contours of a body of work unrelated to feminism, a body of work that is narrow and thin, at any rate not very significant and meant for some extremely dutiful students.

If Beauvoir has become, potentially at least, a bone of contention, including from a political point of view, it is important to understand these tensions insofar as they shape interpretations; and if one asks oneself what there is to discuss, for example from a political point of view, we must start by distinguishing between the work and the multiple discourses that are produced around or about this work. Political and ideological choices reveal themselves more and better in the commentaries, the commentaries on the commentaries, the production of commentaries being precisely the place where political choices are produced, attacked, and defended. I would propose this rather than a pastiche of the 1970s, when some students insisted that "Philosophy is class struggle in the domain of theory." Come on—can we consider Beauvoir herself as "sex struggle" in the domain of theory? Granted, when she notes in a critical way that women do not revolt against oppression, one might think that she precisely is inventing a "sex struggle," which would be reciprocal; but this is rather an evasion of the oppression that she had in mind. Granted, too, liberty or independence constitutes the central value of her work, which is fundamentally a political choice; the project of autonomy that she champions nevertheless comes to a halt and recedes when the question of the emotional life is evoked, that which might indicate what remains for us, ourselves, to think through. And yet we wouldn't know how to draw up as simply the program for that which Beauvoir, faults and all, can stimulate in us. For the most precious thing, in my eyes, is that a philosophical text produces in the minds of its readers, in each one, female and male, experiences or creative shocks that the author (or whoever) could not predict, and that take on at once cognitive and therefore political value. A value variable to infinity, since it is the meeting of an individual and a body of work.

The testimony of Lydie Dooh-Bunya, a Cameroonian, at the conference "Simone de Beauvoir: From Memory to Plans," is particularly important.[5] She recalled how in 1954, when she was 21, she got hold of *The Mandarins* and *The Second Sex:* "And then, what a shock! In my original world, colonialism had established a system in which colonists of both sexes had set themselves up as superior beings. I was, therefore, far from understanding that within their own society there held sway a strict sexual hierarchy in which the French women, these colonists' wives with their haughty ways, the majority of whom terrorized their indigenous employees, were second-class citizens! And this is how, my friends, through reading *The Second Sex* I discovered in my own way can you imagine? Re-la-ti-vi-ty!" A shock all the more keen since Lydie's mother had created an "Association of Women Who Expose Men's Lies." Reflection on the sexual hierarchy and its ramifications also existed in Cameroon, but we should note: the shock, for Lydie, was to discover that the same thing went on in France.

This, I think, is what it is to genuinely engage with Beauvoir. Lydie does not rewrite *The Second Sex;* she witnesses to a personal experience that is also deeply political, generated for her by the reading of Beauvoir, an experience that was in the first place cognitive and theoretical and that took place in the meeting of two minds. Later on, when she had settled in Paris, Lydie was to found MODEFEN, the Movement for Black Women's Rights (*le Mouvement des Droits de la Femme Noire*). It is for her to say if the meeting with Beauvoir, which was linked for her with the memory of her mother's "Association of Women Who Expose Men's Lies" in Cameroon, and perhaps other experiences as well, counted for something in the initiative she took to found MODEFEN.

The precious value of the works of Beauvoir lies is this capacity they have to produce unforeseeable experiences, productive shocks large or small, which are not necessarily all pleasant. (*The Woman Destroyed* can provoke a feeling of the sublime more than of pleasure.) At the end of the day, what is political is that we be able either to enter into dialogue with the work, recounting the experiences that it engenders or, on the other hand, imagining that we have a hold on her, to endeavor to set her right by constructing a more conformist version of it. In any case, this is about us as well as about her. But when we strive to dialogue with her, it is a "self" in becoming that is mobilized; when we rewrite her, it is our fixation, institutional or personal, that is revealed.

For twenty years now, as an engaged commentator who does not seek to be everyone's cup of tea, I have reconciled myself to this: whether I am seeing straight or making a mistake, when I try to construct a theory based on explications of texts that are as precise as possible, I have been aware, even when I am arguing with Simone, that third parties will then intervene on my reading and that the major opposition will be conformism. This conformism comes back to me in the form of commentaries on my commentaries (your turn, listen up: each of your commentaries inaugurates a debate): "You shouldn't have spoken ill of Sartre!" for it just isn't done, criticizing a "great philosopher," and above all, of course, a French one! The question of knowing whether a woman can appear critical toward a philosophical man remains both a political and an intellectual one. Even the fanatics of deconstruction hardly like it when a woman deconstructs the figure of the "great philosopher" or simply neglects to take it seriously, thus forgetting that by right it must be spared a certain scrutiny.

I hear this less and less—in twenty years, the tide has turned. I hear rather: "What a pleasure to see you putting Simone higher than Sartre!"—something that was not perhaps my intention, or was it? What I have also noticed lately is a negation [*négation*], not to say a denial [*dénégation*], of the conflicts, biographical and intellectual, between Sartre and Beauvoir. As if acknowledging that this couple had a history that was also conflict-ridden just isn't done. As if, politically speaking, it wasn't acceptable to know that between a couple there can be discord—and sometimes even violence.

The scene in the Luxembourg gardens was at first translated absurdly in English, and now I am reproached for having commented upon it as a scene of violence. So I will conclude this way: you have a choice; you can think that on this page of the *Memoirs*, as on so many of the others, Beauvoir had the courage to speak a difficult truth, upsetting for the received image of love—something that moreover could constitute a welcome warning for her little sisters and ours. Or else you can call psychoanalysis to the rescue, along with the notion of gender, to rub out the problem and to declare that this scene was one of pleasure for Beauvoir as a woman, just as it was for Sartre as a man. Basically, they found themselves: she found herself as a woman, in her defeat; he found himself as a man, in bringing her down.[6] The choice between these two readings, mine and that which replies to it in the name of psychoanalysis, is certainly political. It is also a choice between two assessments of what is at stake in autobiographical writing. Hence, my final question today: Would it not be time to have a debate with yourself, a dialogue specifically engaged with yourself on the occasion of all dialogue with Beauvoir? Would not reading Beauvoir also be a perfect opportunity to put in question for yourself the ready-made categories through which a body of work is understood? What is a book that makes good sense, if not an occasion for the person who reads to change? Not by "influence" but because it stimulates self-reflection and puts your mind to work.

NOTES

This chapter was the keynote address at the Ninth International Simone de Beauvoir Conference, Oxford, July 2001. It was originally published as "Nouer avec Simone de Beauvoir, Oxford, juillet 2001," in *Simone de Beauvoir Studies* 18 (2001–2): 1–8.

1. See Margaret A. Simons, "The Silencing of Simone De Beauvoir: Guess What's Missing from *The Second Sex?*" *Women's Studies International Forum* 6, no. 5 (1983). Reprinted in Margaret A. Simons, *Beauvoir and* The Second Sex (Lanham, Md.: Rowman & Littlefield, 2000).

2. Beauvoir's case is far from unique. Compare the way the translators of Vivès during the sixteenth century enthusiastically bludgeoned the text of *De Institutione Feminae Christianae,* a piece of work that though authored by a man concerns the education of the Christian woman. (See part II of my *The Sex of Knowing* [New York: Routledge, 2003].)

3. In May 2000 a complete, scrupulous Swedish translation of *The Second Sex* by Åsa Moberg, Adam Inczèdy-Gombos, and Eva Gothlin was published by Norstedts—an event that it is important to hail.

4. It would be a mistake to think that sexism is the only force capable of distorting texts. Let me take the liberty of referring you to my study of the avatars of Descartes' "provisional" morality, "In Red in the Margins," in *The Philosophical Imaginary* (New York: Continuum, 2003), originally published as *L'Imaginaire Philosophique* (Paris: Payot, 1980).

5. The conference took place at the Sorbonne in 1989.

6. See one of the contributions in the volume *Michèle Le Doeuff: Operative Philosophy and Imaginary Practice,* edited by Max Deutscher (Amherst, N.Y.: Prometheus Books, 2001).

SIMONE DE BEAUVOIR'S PHENOMENOLOGY OF SEXUAL DIFFERENCE

Sara Heinämaa

2

Simone de Beauvoir is not usually considered a phenomenologist, and her works, including *The Ethics of Ambiguity* (*Pour une morale de l'ambiguïté*, 1947) and *The Second Sex* (*Le Deuxième sexe*, 1949), are not usually studied as philosophical.[1] Beauvoir is read as a novelist and essayist, and her nonfictional works are taken as sociohistorical studies—popular rather than scholarly, moral rather than ethical.

This common view is fundamentally mistaken. I argue that Simone de Beauvoir is a philosopher and that she herself considered her work to be philosophical. Her understanding of philosophy was specific, however, and this specificity is the leading theme of my paper.

My claim is that the philosophical context in which Beauvoir operated is the phenomenology of body that Edmund Husserl initiated and Maurice Merleau-Ponty further developed.[2] So I argue against the traditional understanding according to which Beauvoir's philosophical notions stemmed from Jean-Paul Sartre's works, but I also question the more recent argument that Beauvoir based her views on Martin Heidegger's work. I want to show that at the core of Beauvoir's writing about sexuality and ethics is a particular understanding of the philosopher's *practice and task,* and that she shared this understanding with Husserl and Merleau-Ponty.

In the case of *The Second Sex*, I argue that Beauvoir's main interest is not in explaining women's subordinate position or in defending their rights. Instead of putting forward a sociohistorical theory or a liberalist thesis, Beauvoir presents a phenomenological description. The phenomenon that she describes is the reality named *woman*, and her aim is to analyze the meanings involved in this reality. Her work includes a radical problematization of our ideas of femaleness, femininity, and women's subordination as well as those of sexuality, embodiment, and the self-other relationship.

To realize the phenomenological nature of Beauvoir's problem setting, it is necessary to understand the nature of phenomenological philosophy— its tasks and methods. I thus begin with a short excursion into phenomenology as presented by Husserl and Merleau-Ponty.[3]

PHENOMENOLOGY: A FOUNDATIONAL SCIENCE

Husserl defines *phenomenology* as a study of phenomena, that is, the ways in which the world appears, or presents itself, to us in experience. It is often claimed that phenomenology, thus defined, is a return to introspective philosophy, but this is a gross misunderstanding. Husserl argues again and again that phenomenology is not about the internal processes or activities of the human mind. It is about the ways in which we *relate* to the world and its beings.[4] The phenomenologist takes a *step back* from the world, suspending his belief in the reality of the world and its beings. The aim, however, is not to examine oneself, but to become aware of one's involvement in the reality of the world, that is, in the constitution of the *meaning of reality*, and one's attachments to this reality. Merleau-Ponty's description of the phenomenological stand is illuminating: "Reflection does not withdraw from the world towards the unity of consciousness as the world's basis; it slackens the intentional threads which attach us to the world and thus brings them to our notice" (Merleau-Ponty 1993, viii).

In *The Crisis of European Sciences* (*Die Krisis der europäischen Wissenschaften und die transzendentale Phänomenologie*, 1954), Husserl gives a set of genetic phenomenological problems for future study: he refers to the problems of death and birth, the problem of the unconsciousness, and the problems of historicity and social life (their "essential forms"). And then,

21

he states, "there is the problem of the sexes" (Husserl 1954, 192). The phenomenologist's task is to study the meanings of these phenomena, their constitution as different kinds of realities and objectivities, that is, entities, occurrences, processes, events, facts, and so forth. So the questions concerning death, for example, are not What is death? How does death happen? What is its mechanism? Rather, the question is How does it happen that we experience death as an occurrence *(Vorkommnis)*? Similarly, we can ask, Why is the sexual relation experienced as a difference and an opposition? Is this necessary? Can the experience have some other structure? The relevant experiences to be studied are not just erotic desires but all actions and passions in which the other is perceived as a man or a woman (Fink 1988, 274).

Husserl's phenomenology involves a strong view of the relation between philosophy and the empirical sciences. Philosophy, understood as phenomenology, is a foundational science in that it studies the basis of the empirical sciences, the ideas that empirical sciences need to rely on: the ideas of nature, history, society, and humanity—mind and body.

This does not mean that philosophy is independent or autonomous. Husserl points out that the sciences and philosophy have a common root in the theoretical attitude that suspends the practical interests of everyday life and studies the universe as a whole. The scientist-philosopher is interested not just in the actualities (the present) but also in the possible. When he constructs a theory of sexuality, for example, he does not describe merely this or that sexuality but tries to grasp sexuality in all its complexity and variation. His description should aim at including all possible sexualities as well as the actual forms of our sexual life.

The important difference between the scientist and the philosopher is in the radically critical nature of philosophy. Husserl characterizes this difference by saying that the task of philosophy is to ask the ultimate questions. The philosopher turns back to investigate the foundations of the theoretical enterprise, the hidden assumptions and engagements that it depends on. His task is to pose the radical questions about the conditions of the possibility of scientific thinking, about the ideas of truth, reality, objectivity, and universality. The interest of his study is thus not practical or purely theoretical but critical.[5]

The philosophical questions cannot be answered in the same way as empirical questions can be answered. Instead of being solved, they might lead us to new problems and paradoxes (Merleau-Ponty 1996). This does not entitle us to bypass them. Although there are no final solutions, philosophical questioning is indispensable: it alone can make us conscious of our involvement in the constitution of reality, of the meanings of *being* and *real* (Merleau-Ponty 1964, 142).

BEAUVOIR'S PHENOMENOLOGICAL STARTING POINTS

When studying Beauvoir's relation to phenomenological philosophy, the most interesting sources are the philosophical sections of her autobiography and her ethical essays.[6] These texts show that Beauvoir not only studied Husserl's texts in detail but also found his notion of philosophy appealing.

Beauvoir gives significant information about her relation to phenomenology in her autobiography. In *Prime of Life* (*La Force de l'âge*, 1960), she tells us that, when studying Husserl's lectures on time consciousness, she felt that she was "getting closer to truth than ever" (1995a, 231). Moreover, she explains her relation to phenomenological philosophy by comparing her own attitude to that of Sartre:

> Sartre claimed that I comprehended philosophical doctrines, that of Husserl among others, faster and more accurately than he did. In fact, he tended to interpret philosophies according to his own schemata; for him it was very difficult to forget himself and to adopt without reservations a strange point of view. But I did not have such resistance to fight; my thoughts adapted immediately to the thought I tried to understand. I did not accept it passively; even when I agreed, I also noticed gaps and incoherencies, and explored possible elaborations. If a theory convinced me, it did not remain exterior to me, it changed my relation to the world, colored my experience. In short, I had a sound capacity to adopt, a critical sense to develop; for me philosophy was a living reality. (1995a, 254)

Beauvoir's ethical essay, *The Ethics of Ambiguity* (*Pour une morale de l'ambiguïté*, 1947), testifies to her capacities and engagement. It shows that Beauvoir's understanding of the aims and methods of Husserl's phenomenology was deep and fruitful. This is clear in Beauvoir's comparison between her ethical stance and the phenomenological attitude. She follows Husserl and Merleau-Ponty in insisting that the aim of the phenomenological suspension is not to turn toward oneself but to become conscious of our true existence, that is, our relations with the world and others (1947, 20–21). Furthermore, Beauvoir emphasizes that the suspension does not "contest" the reality of the world; it only refuses to take this reality as an absolute and unproblematic given. She explains that the phenomenologist does not reject the facts and events of the world but questions its "mode of reality" *(mode de réalité)* (1947, 21).

The most direct evidence of Beauvoir's phenomenological engagement is found in *The Second Sex*. There she tells us that the basic concepts of her work—the concepts of body and sexuality—are taken from the phenomenological tradition of thinking. She emphasizes repeatedly that her discussion of sexual difference is based on the concept of the living body *(Leib, corps vivant, corps vécu)*.[7] Husserl first introduced this concept in his lectures on objectivity and spatiality, *Thing and Space (Ding und Raum)*, in 1907. Six years later Husserl gave it an extensive explication in the second part of his *Ideas (Ideen)*. This work remained unpublished for a long time, but Merleau-Ponty studied it in the Husserl archives in Louvain in 1937, and he refers to it repeatedly in his *Phenomenology of Perception* (*Phénoménologie de la perception* 1945) when developing his notion of the body.[8]

The core of Husserl's concept of the living body *(Leib)* is that it differs essentially from the material objects *(Körper)* that we manipulate in our everyday dealings and scientific practices. Husserl makes this far-reaching distinction by pointing out that the body presents itself to us in two different ways: as the starting point of all our activities *(Leib),* and as a passive or resistant object *(Körper)*. He then argues that the living body is primary and that it appears essentially as the expression and instrument of the spirit. It is not a separate reality, but it is the horizon of all our activities, both everyday dealings and scientific idealizations (Husserl 1952, 157, 281; Merleau-Ponty 1993, 106–13).

The existentialists applied and developed further Husserl's analysis of the living body. Merleau-Ponty in particular submitted the living body to an extensive and thorough study in the first part of his *Phenomenology of Perception*. Beauvoir knew this work well; she reviewed it for *Les temps modernes* in 1945, and she refers to it repeatedly when presenting her understanding of embodiment in *The Second Sex*.

Beauvoir starts her review of Merleau-Ponty's phenomenology by writing: "One of the great merits of phenomenology . . . is in its abolishing of the opposition between the subject and the object. It is impossible to define an object apart from the subject by whom and for whom it is the object; and the subject reveals itself only in relation to the objects that it is engaged with" (Beauvoir 1945a, 363). These statements may sound trivial, Beauvoir remarks, but they have far-reaching philosophical implications: one can develop a genuine ethics only by taking the phenomenological understanding of the subject-object relation as the basis (363). According to Beauvoir, such an understanding is necessary for a sincere and total ethical commitment.

Beauvoir sees the main value of Merleau-Ponty's work here. For Merleau-Ponty, she writes, the personal consciousness "is not a pure for-itself, nor a gap in being, as Hegel wrote, and Sartre repeated, but it is 'a curve, a folding that can be unfolded'" (1945a, 367). She explains further that Merleau-Ponty rejects Sartre's opposition between the for-itself and in-itself and describes the bodily subject in its concrete existence; her sympathies are clearly with Merleau-Ponty (1945a, 366). For her, Merleau-Ponty's phenomenological descriptions of the body, its spatiality, movement, sensations, speech, and sexuality are a "rich" and "convincing" source. Their additional merit is that they are not "violent": on the contrary, they suggest that we should adopt the movement of life itself (367).

The review testifies to Beauvoir's commitment to phenomenology. It also shows that Beauvoir clearly saw the difference between Merleau-Ponty's and Sartre's interpretations of Husserl's work and that she considered Merleau-Ponty's nondualistic modification more promising on account of its ethical implications (1945a, 367).

Beauvoir's original and far-reaching innovation was to pose the question of sexual difference within and in terms of a phenomenology of body.[9] *The Second Sex* gives us a rich description of the living sexual body, its bodily and spiritual aspects, and its relations to other bodies and to the world as a whole. Thus it implies the fundamental question of the sexuality of philosophy itself. In Beauvoir's understanding, sexuality is not a detail of being but an element that runs through our whole existence—including our philosophical reflections.

THE PHILOSOPHER AND THE WRITER

We may wonder why so many interpreters have neglected Beauvoir's explicit philosophical statements. One reason for this neglect is that Beauvoir's works are usually studied in the context of her personal life, and her personal life is almost always reduced to her relationship with Sartre.[10] Here the common comparison is between "Beauvoir—the novelist" and "Sartre—the philosopher." Such representations usually refer to an interview that Beauvoir gave in 1979, where she stated: "Sartre is a philosopher, I am not" (Benjamin and Simons 1979, 330–45). The prevailing conclusion is that Beauvoir did not have any philosophical—or for that matter, phenomenological—interests, and that her works can be interpreted and evaluated without any reference to philosophical concepts or methods.

This conclusion is a mistake. Beauvoir's relation to philosophy is much more complex than such simple oppositions lead one to believe. In her autobiography, she characterizes her philosophical interests and activities in several different sections. She clarifies her philosophical engagements by rejecting certain approaches and affirming others. She gives a clear picture of her intellectual abilities and her weaknesses, and she expresses her enthusiasm and her love (see, for example, Beauvoir 1997b, 220–22, 324). Moreover, Beauvoir explains how her novels take part in the philosophical discussions of the self-other relation and the relation between universals and particulars (1997a, 92–98; 1995a, 625–29). The simple picture of the female novelist and the male philosopher ignores the rich evidence that Beauvoir offers of her philosophical life.

But what is more problematic—at least philosophically more problematic—is that the picture is based on a naïve notion of philosophy, and worse, one that Beauvoir herself did not approve: the philosopher is seen as a system builder, as an original inventor and creator who works independently of the intellectual tradition or even against it.

Beauvoir presents a different view of philosophizing, an alternative notion of philosophy. In her writing, philosophical activity is seen primarily as the search for truth and evidence, and as questioning and communication with others. Her autobiography makes this notion quite explicit and argues for it. When describing, for example, how she tried to study Hegel's system and finally started to comprehend it, Beauvoir is careful to distinguish between comprehension and affirmation:

> I went on reading Hegel, and started to understand him better; the richness of details dazzled me, and the system as a whole made me feel giddy. . . . But the more modest movements of my heart refuted such speculations: hope, anger, expectation, anxiety asserted themselves against all such transcendings [*dépassements*]. The flight to the universal was only a passing episode in the personal adventure of my life. I went back to Kierkegaard, which I had been reading with passion; the truth that he asserted defied doubt as victoriously as the Cartesian evidence. Neither System, nor History could, any more than the Malicious Demon, cancel the living certainty of "I am, I exist, at this place and this moment, me." (Beauvoir 1995a, 537)

Beauvoir contrasts the Hegelian system to her own passions. This is not a rejection of philosophical thinking; it is a challenge to a certain understanding of philosophy: Beauvoir questions Hegel's and Sartre's philosophical doctrines by appealing to the evidence of her living experience (see also Beauvoir 1997b, 341; 1995a, 498–99, 627–28; 1947, 104–105, 158–59).[11] We should not take the statement as testifying to a focus on her own personal life or on everyday affairs. By challenging philosophical systems in the name of intuition and passion, Beauvoir presents a philosophical statement, a statement about the nature of philosophical thinking. She affirms the Cartesian notion that gives priority to present evidence, and this leads her to reject all philosophical theories and all "finalities of history" that fail to justify themselves with such evidence (Beauvoir 1947, 145–46).[12]

The context of Beauvoir's work is in the Continental tradition of philosophy, which gives much credit to René Descartes' radicalism. In this tradition, Descartes is not just criticized as a dualist but also appreciated as a critic of habitual thinking. The most relevant sources are Descartes' methodological text, where he suggests that we must—at least once in our lifetime—question all our convictions. The point is not to become involved in criticizing others; rather, the aim is to question one's own preconceptions, to take responsibility for one's own beliefs and convictions through such self-criticism.

When specifying her philosophical attitude, Beauvoir refers to Søren Kierkegaard, Husserl, Merleau-Ponty, and Heidegger, who all developed further the Cartesian notion of philosophy as radical thinking. In the phenomenological-existential movement, Descartes' idea of philosophical radicalism is intensified so that it becomes the requirement of recurrent self-criticism. The philosopher's work is never completed; he/she has to return from the clear and distinct focus of his/her reflection to its ambiguous, dark margins. This radical Cartesianism is the core of Beauvoir's idea of philosophical activity and practice.

In addition to criticism and evidence, Beauvoir emphasizes the role of language. She sees philosophy as an attempt to reach for truth by radical questioning, but she does not think that this can be accomplished or even practiced in solitude. Thinking is not an internal monologue; it is cooperation, and as such it depends essentially on others, on their thoughts expressed in words and texts. For Beauvoir, philosophy means a dialogue, a discussion with others by means of speech and writing. In her autobiography, she states that writing is the only place in which intersubjectivity and transcendence can be realized (1995b, 242; 1996, 498). Thus the contrast Beauvoir makes between philosophy and literature is not a rejection of philosophy for art, but a rejection of philosophies that do not pay attention to living experience and its expression in language.

To summarize, Beauvoir did not think that the most important aspect of philosophy is realized in solitary system building. Instead, she emphasized the role of questioning, problematizing, and dialogue. When she states that she is not a philosopher, she means that she is not a system builder or a theory constructor. This does not imply that her work lacked philosophical interests. On the contrary, Beauvoir tried to realize in her own writing the open self-critical attitude that she considered the living core of all philosophy and that she found in the phenomenological tradition of modern thought.

This is my interpretation of Beauvoir's idea of philosophy. In what follows, I argue that we should take the idea seriously and use it as our key when trying to unlock Beauvoir's complex work on sexuality. The following sections offer a close reading of the first pages of *The Second Sex,* where Beauvoir lays out the conceptual and methodological basis for her study. My aim is to show that Beauvoir starts her work by posing a series of phenomenologico-philosophical questions. She is not putting forth an empirical investigation, nor is she interested in declaring rights. Instead, she wants to question the basic ideas that we presuppose when we discuss and argue about sexual relations.

THE QUESTION ON WOMAN

Beauvoir begins *The Second Sex,* not by putting forth a thesis, but by posing a question. In the first words of the book, she tells us that for a long time she has thought about writing a book on woman, but instead of starting by defining and describing her subject matter, she then asks what the question should be, how it should be posed: "What is the problem, is there one?" (Beauvoir 1993, 11).

The accepted interpretation assumes that Beauvoir takes the notion of woman as given and proceeds to explain the existence and situation of this being called "woman." But in fact, Beauvoir starts by problematizing the topic of feminist and antifeminist arguments. She notes that the question of woman is not a well-defined problem; it has different meanings, and even its sense and relevance can be doubted. The formulation of the question is thus part of the problem to be studied, and this is why we must start by examining different questions.[13]

First, Beauvoir presents a series of questions about being and existence. Are there women, really? she asks. And furthermore, Do women still exist, will they always exist, and is it desirable that they should exist? (1993, 11). We can take these questions as ordinary factual questions about subjects in the world, and then we can answer them by "yes" or "no," depending on our experiences, interests, and use of words. We can also take Beauvoir's questions in a philosophical sense, as questions about the meanings of being and reality, and I suggest that this was part of Beauvoir's purpose.[14] She is not attempting to prove (or disprove) the reality and existence of women, but aims primarily at posing fundamental questions on woman's way of being: How does she exist? Is her being real? and What is meant by reality when it is stated? If we follow this line of thinking, then the problems cannot be solved simply by referring to our experiences; we must also study the basis and meanings of experiences.

So the first pages of Beauvoir's book present us with questions about being but leave them unsolved: the reality of women is neither affirmed nor denied. Thus, the focus is shifted to fundamental ontological inquiries into the meaning of being. Beauvoir proceeds by asking for a definition of woman, namely, What is meant by this reality?

But not even this question is answered directly. Instead of defining her subject matter, Beauvoir goes into studying the possibility of different definitions. First, she distinguishes among three different realities—femaleness, femininity, and womanhood—and introduces a provisional definition: "Not every female human being is necessarily a woman; in order to be a woman, one must participate in the mysterious and threatened reality which is femininity" (1993, 11).

This amounts to claiming that femaleness is necessary but not sufficient to make a woman. In addition, one must have the vague quality of femininity. So the question becomes, What is the nature of this quality? And is it a quality at all, or rather some other kind of reality? It is important to get this question straight. Beauvoir is not searching for the *content* of femininity; she wants to study its ontological status: how does femininity exist, how does it present itself to us, what is its mode of being? Here again, Beauvoir considers several alternatives. She asks if femininity is a product of the imagination or an ideal reality. Or is it a model or a goal for action and behavior? (1993, 12).

It is sometimes stated that Beauvoir denies the reality of femininity. But if we study her book carefully, it becomes clear that this is a misinterpretation. Beauvoir formulates most of her questions and descriptions in terms of feminine existence. Instead of referring to women's writing, to women's sexual experiences, or to women's world, she speaks about "feminine literature" (*la littérature féminine,* 1993, 30); "feminine eroticism" (*l'érotisme féminin,* 1991, 176); and "the feminine world" (*le monde féminin,* 1993, 30). When she sets out her descriptive task, she uses the concept of feminine existence *(existence féminine),* not the concept of woman: "The point here is not to proclaim eternal verities, but rather to describe the common basis that underlies every singular feminine existence" (1991, 9; see also 1993, 13).

The introduction to the book sets the question of the nature of femininity in terms of the controversy between universalism and particularism. Beauvoir presents the medieval alternatives of conceptualism and nominalism and hints also at the Platonic solution. She does not, however, consider these alternatives as philosophically satisfying. The book is an attempt to defend a mediative view that does not postulate eternal unchanging essences but also does not fall into particularism or nominalism (1993, 13). Beauvoir does not reject the reality of femininity even though she does not accept it as a static, unchanging essence. She thinks about it in dynamic terms: to be a woman—to take part in the common, general reality of femininity—is not to be subsumed under a concept or a general rule, and it is not to instantiate an eternal idea or a Platonic essence. To be a woman is to have become a woman (1993, 25). For Beauvoir, woman "is not a fixed reality but a becoming" (1993, 73).[15]

We can understand this idea only if we take seriously Beauvoir's commitment to the phenomenological understanding of the living body. As shown above, for Beauvoir the body is not a thing but a way of relating to things, a way of acting on them and being affected by them. It is "our grasp upon the world and the outline of our projects" (1993, 73).

As such, the body is an opening, more like a melody than a stable solid structure. Its earlier realizations do not determine its future manifestations, but they do suggest and motivate different alternatives and open up horizons of possible actions. Beauvoir emphasizes that the human condition is indefinite and ambiguous: it allows for different variations and modifications (1995a, 21). Its generality is not that of a concept or a fixed idea; it does not reside within the particulars or above them but resides in the relations between the particulars. In *Force of Circumstance* (*La Force des choses,* 1963), she states her view quite explicitly: "The dimension of human enterprise is neither finite nor infinite but indefinite: this word cannot be enclosed within any fixed limits, the best way of approaching it is to follow [*divaguer sur*] its possible variations" (Beauvoir 1997a, 97–98).

For Beauvoir, feminine bodies and masculine bodies are not two kinds of entities but different variations of human embodiment. They both realize and recreate "in their different ways" the human condition, which is characterized by fundamental ambiguity (1947, 11–12). In the end of *The Second Sex,* she writes: "To tell the truth, man, like woman, is flesh, and therefore a passivity. . . . And she, like him, in the midst of her carnal fever, is a consenting, a voluntary gift, an activity; they live in their different ways the strange ambiguity of existence made body" (1991, 658; see also 1947, 11–15).

Understood in this way, femininity is like a musical theme: it is not determined by its earlier performances but is living and evolving in the environment created by them. It does not reside in any specific organs, persons, or practices but resides among them. So it manifests and develops in the whole of actions and passions, and its specificity is in its mode of changing.

OTHERNESS AND SUBORDINATION

We have seen that Beauvoir starts her book with a series of radical questions, fundamental ontological questions, and questions of definition. But this is not all. The discussion of femininity is followed by a series of new questions, questions about questioning. Who is she to pose the question of woman? Beauvoir asks. Why is she asking the question? What is her motivation?

These self-critical questions lead Beauvoir to introduce and study the notions of otherness and subordination. She notes that a man would never write a book on "the particular situation that males have in humanity" (1993, 14). Thus, the relation between man and woman is not symmetrical. Man represents both the positive and the neutral aspects of humanity; woman represents only the negative (1993, 14). Man describes himself in his theories and histories of humanity; woman remains in silence. He stands both for the normal and for the ideal; she, for the deviant. Beauvoir comments by putting forth her well-known thesis: "He is the Subject, he is the Absolute, she is the Other" (1993, 15).

Beauvoir's statement is usually taken as an affirmation of the Otherness of women.[16] But if we read carefully, keeping in mind her philosophical interest, we can see that her discussion involves a radical problematization of these basic notions, both the idea of women's Otherness and the notion of their subordination. In the following paragraphs, I follow her discussion and study these ideas separately. I first focus on the way Beauvoir problematizes the idea of woman's Otherness and then discuss her notion of subordination.

When studying Beauvoir's notion of sexual difference, it is extremely important to notice that the paragraph that describes woman as Other is not Beauvoir's last word on the subject. She adds a footnote to explain that this is a definition given by a man (1993, 15–16, 403). She refers to a particular text, Emmanuel Lévinas's *Time and Other* (*Le temps et l'autre*, 1947), where Lévinas suggests that "otherness reaches its full flowering in the feminine, a term of the same rank as consciousness but of opposite meaning" (Lévinas 1947, 77). Beauvoir answers this critically by arguing that Lévinas overlooks the fact that woman, too, is a consciousness for herself. She summarizes: "Man defines woman not in herself but as relative to him" (Beauvoir 1993, 15).

To understand this argumentation, we must once again return to Husserl's texts because Lévinas's discussion of femininity is largely based on Husserl's work. It is a critique of the analysis Husserl presents in his fifth *Cartesian Meditation* (*Méditations cartésiennes*, 1931; *Cartesianische Meditationen*, 1950) of the self-other relation. There Husserl studies the simple case of perceiving the other. He points out that to see another conscious being, another person, is to see somebody who is able to see you, somebody who is similar to you in his/her seeing. So reciprocity, according to Husserl, is a necessary condition for relating to the other: to see the other requires that you see him/her as seeing (Husserl 1950, 122).[17] Beauvoir repeats this idea in her analysis: "There can be no presence of an other unless the other is also present for himself: which is to say that true alterity is that of a consciousness separate from mine and identical with mine" (Beauvoir 1993, 237).

When Lévinas asks if there is a case of absolute Otherness, he is asking if it is possible to experience the other without presupposing the identity of activities, for example, seeing. And when he states that femininity represents the absolute Other (to him) he suggests that sexual difference is a specific relation in that there the other is experienced without any possibility of identification. The sexual relation is a third kind of way of relating to the world: the other is not perceived as a material object, totally without experiences, actions, and passions; but it is not experienced as an alter ego either, with activities similar to our own. The sexual other is different in a way that is qualitatively specific.

Beauvoir attacks Lévinas's analysis: "He deliberately takes a man's point of view, disregarding the reciprocity of subject and object" (1993, 16). Here she seems to misinterpret at least part of Lévinas's claim. For her, Lévinas denies feminine subjectivity and reduces the feminine other to the status of object and matter (1993, 17).[18] But Lévinas's statement can be understood in the opposite way: instead of compromising the difference between two sexual subjects, it exaggerates the difference. The feminine is experienced as an other but not as an alter ego, not as another consciousness, a different species of the same genus. Rather, the feminine appears as radically and forever unknowable.

My aim here is not to take a stand on the controversy between Beauvoir and Lévinas. I only want to make it explicit and to show its indebtedness to Husserl's phenomenology. Beauvoir does not accept Lévinas's idea of radical sexual difference. For her, women and men are two variations of human embodiment.

This leads Beauvoir to the questions of reciprocity and subordination: How is it that the similarity and reciprocity of the sexes has not been recognized? How is it that one of the contrasting terms is set up as the sole essential, and the other is defined as pure Otherness? "Whence comes this subordination in the case of women?" (1993, 18).

What follows is a discussion of the nature of woman's subordination. It is remarkable and important that Beauvoir does not proceed by presenting causes or effects. Instead, she focuses on the nature of the phenomenon and clarifies it by pointing out that it is not a result of any social change, nor is it an effect of any historical occurrence or event *(événement)*: "Throughout history they [women] have always been subordinated to men, and hence their dependency is not the result of a historical event or a social change—it was not something that occurred [*arriver*]" (1993, 18).

Beauvoir's point is not to deny subordination. She does not claim that subordination "did not happen," but she suggests that its reality is not in the order of happenings and events. So it is not as if Beauvoir first posits women's subordination as an event and only then denies its reality. Instead, she questions its status as a happening, as a contingent, accidental event. She points to the specific, peculiar nature of this subordination, its "seeming" necessity and naturalness (1993, 18). Women's subordination is not a contingent fact or a necessary structure; its way of appearing, its ontological meaning, is somehow between these two extremes.

Here again, Beauvoir refers to Merleau-Ponty's *Phenomenology of Perception*. There, in the end of the chapter on sexuality, he writes that "human existence requires us to revise our ordinary ideas of necessity and contingency because it is the transformation of contingency to necessity by the act of repeating" (Merleau-Ponty 1993, 199; Beauvoir 1993, 39–40). He explains further: "Existence has no fortuitous attributes, no content which does not contribute towards giving it form; it does not admit any pure fact because it is the movement by which facts are drawn up" (Merleau-Ponty 1993, 198).

Merleau-Ponty argues that sexuality cannot be described as a fact because it characterizes our existence already on that basic level of experience that functions as the foundation for the constitution of facts. According to him, sexuality is as fundamental to human existence as mortality or embodiment. Beauvoir accepts this, but she argues that the sexual relation does not need to have the structure of subordination or even difference (1991, 189). These forms of experience are not necessary in the same way, or in same sense, as mortality and embodiment. This is because, she states, it is easier to imagine "a society that reproduces parthenogenetically or consists of hermaphrodites" than to think about an immortal or disembodied human being (1993, 40).

The context of this discussion between Beauvoir and Merleau-Ponty is in Husserl's method of imaginary variation *(freie variation der Phantasie)*. The phenomenologist starts from a particular example and aims at unveiling the necessary, essential structures of all experience. According to Husserl, this can be carried out by varying the experience in the imagination and by studying its relation to other cases, actual and possible. Here the phenomenologist gets help from the descriptions of historians and artists. Husserl notes that especially the poet can help the phenomenologist imagine unusual, extraordinary possibilities (1913, 16–17, 163).

Beauvoir and Merleau-Ponty agree that sexuality is a basic structure of human existence, comparable to mortality. Merleau-Ponty suggests that every experience of another human being is an experience of a man or a woman (cf. Fink 1988, 274). Beauvoir, on the other hand, points to the possibility of imagining a society without sexual differentiation *(différenciation sexuelle)* (1993, 40). Here the aid given by literature is indispensable: science fiction and anthropological studies help us detach ourselves from our own experience and imagine strange possibilities.[19]

Sexual difference might be more deeply embedded in our experience of persons and human beings than, for example, skin color or other "racial" differences. One could at least argue for this by pointing out that societies exist that do not make the distinction between black and white, but there is no known culture that does not make the distinction between women and men. Nevertheless, Beauvoir seems to be right in insisting that not all experience of personhood needs to involve sexual differentiation.

In summary, Beauvoir offers us three definitions when introducing the problem of woman. First, she presents the idea that being a woman means both being female and being feminine. Secondly, she states that woman is the Other. Thirdly, she introduces the idea of subordination. So her work clearly involves definitions, but it is crucial to realize that it does not affirm any of them: all defining terms—femininity, Otherness, and subordination—are further problematized. Thus, the accepted interpretation that reads the introduction of the book as a definition of woman is based on a misunderstanding. Later in her work Beauvoir makes her attitude quite clear when stating that "in her core, she [woman] is even for herself quite undefinable" (1993, 400). *The Second Sex* does not offer us a general theory of women or a definition of them. Its main interest and merit is in its uncompromising attempt to question and test all definitions and theories.

Beauvoir writes: "The fact is that she would be embarrassed to decide what she is; the question has no answer; but this is not because the hidden truth is too vague to be discerned; it is because in this domain there is no truth" (1993, 401).

NOTES

I am grateful to Juha Himanka, Morny Joy, Timo Kaitaro, Johanna Oksala, Martina Reuter, Marja Suhonen, and Dan Zahavi for their critical insights and helpful suggestions.

1. Please note that I cite only the contemporary reprint dates for texts; in the reference list I provide dates for the original French and German texts. I give my own translations in this paper because prevailing translations are often misleading and even false.

2. A more detailed argument is presented in Heinämaa (2003).

3. I have argued for Beauvoir's phenomenological background in my earlier work (Heinämaa 1995, 1996a, 1996b, 1997), but I develop my argument further here by focusing on Beauvoir's idea of philosophy. For a more detailed argument, see Heinämaa (2003); for other interpretations that indicate or explicate Beauvoir's phenomenological interests, see Simons (1983), Butler (1986), Kruks (1990), Vintges (1996), and Bergoffen (1997).

4. The retreating or arresting movement of the phenomenologist is sometimes described as *detachment*. Husserl, however, used the German term *ausschalten*, which has the meaning "separation" but can also be understood as "switching off" (1913, 65–66). When the word is taken in the latter meaning, then the phenomenological step does not require that we break off our connections to the world but only that we interrupt our natural and habitual activities.

5. For a more detailed presentation of Husserl's notion of philosophy and science, see Heinämaa (2003).

6. See *Pyrrhus et Cinéas* (Beauvoir 1944) and *Pour un morale de l'ambiguïté* (Beauvoir 1947). On the philosophical and ethical relevance of Beauvoir's novels, *L'invitée* (1943), *Le Sang des autres* (1945b), and *Tous les hommes sont mortels* (1946), see Beauvoir (1995a, 618–29; 1997a, 92–100) and Merleau-Ponty (1966).

7. The German noun *Leib* is related to the verb *leben*, which means "to live." The term has been translated into English in several different ways. David Carr uses "living body" in his translation of *Krisis;* for *Körper* he uses both "body" and "physical body," depending on the context (Husserl 1988, 50). Richard Rojcewicz and André Schuwer use the term "Body" (capitalized) for *Leib,* and the term "body" for *Körper,* in their translation of the second part of Husserl's *Ideen* (Rojcewicz and Schuwer 1989, xiv).

Merleau-Ponty's discussion of *corps vivant* or *corps vécu (Leib)* is often translated "lived body." I do not follow this convention because my intention is to illuminate the methodological and conceptual connections among Husserl, Merleau-Ponty, and Beauvoir. So I follow Carr's procedure and use the term "living body" for both the German *Leib* and the French *corps vécu.*

8. On Husserl's discussion of the living body, see Zahavi (1994).

9. Some feminist thinkers claim that Merleau-Ponty's phenomenology of body is androcentric (Butler 1989, Grosz 1994). For a counterargument, see Heinämaa (1997), Stoller and Vetter (1997), Waldenfels (1998, 186–95), and Stoller (2000).

10. For a wider view, see Simons (1986), Le Doeuff (1991), Kruks (1990, 1991), Lundgren-Gothlin (1992, 1995), Heinämaa (1996b).

11. On Beauvoir's relation to Hegel's philosophy and its different interpretations, see Lundgren-Gothlin (1992), and O'Brien-Ewara (1999).

12. In *The Second Sex,* Beauvoir argues against Sigmund Freud's system on similar lines: "The [Freudian] idea of 'passive libido' is disconcerting, since the libido has been defined, on the basis of the male, as a drive, an energy; but one would do no better to think a priori that the light could be at once yellow and blue—what is needed is the intuition of green" (1993, 92–93). Beauvoir's argument here is methodological: she points out that Freud was unable to understand woman's desire *(désir femelle)* because he defined sexual desire a priori as a purely active principle. Beauvoir's phenomenological critique is that instead of sticking to traditional concepts, Freud should have relied on what he saw and heard, that is, on expressions of a different kind of desire (green), not analyzable in terms of activity and passivity (yellow and blue). This is discussed in length in Heinämaa (2005).

13. Nancy Bauer (1997, 2001) argues interestingly that Beauvoir's radical questioning and her critical argumentation is analogical to Descartes' in his *Meditations on First Philosophy.*

14. Phenomenological research starts with the distinction between factual questions about reality and being, on the one hand, and phenomenological questions about

the meanings of reality and being, on the other hand. Eugen Fink argues in his "Die phänomenologische Philosophie Edmund Husserls in der gegenwärtigen Kritik" (1933) that phenomenological reduction is not a solution to precedent problems or a method of solving them but a starting point for a new way of questioning.

15. I have argued elsewhere that the accepted view that identifies Beauvoir's notion of becoming to the process of socialization is mistaken (Heinämaa 1996a, 1996b, 1997).

16. The terms *other* and *otherness* are capitalized when used in Lévinas's absolute sense, which excludes reciprocity. It is remarkable that critics do not question the basis of this interpretation even when it leads them to state that Beauvoir was guilty of simple contradictions. See, for example, Hekman (1990, 74–76), and Chanter (1995, 48, 73).

17. On Husserl's understanding of the self-other relation and intersubjectivity, see Zahavi (1996a, 1996b).

18. It is, of course, possible that there is a genuine disagreement, not a misunderstanding. Beauvoir was arguing for atheistic humanistic ethics, and in this paragraph she might be just rejecting the theistic model that Lévinas was developing for otherness on the basis of the Judeo-Christian tradition (Beauvoir 1993, 242–43, 295–96).

19. Beauvoir ends her essay on Sade by writing: "The supreme value of his testimony lies in his ability to disturb us. It forces us to re-examine thoroughly the basic problem which haunts our age in different forms: the true relation between man and man" (1990, 64). For other disturbing descriptions of sexual difference and non-difference, see, for example, Woolf (1998) and Garreta (1986).

References

Bauer, Nancy. 1997. Recounting woman: Simone de Beauvoir and feminist philosophy. Ph.D. diss., Harvard University.

———. 2001. *Simone de Beauvoir, philosophy and feminism.* New York: Columbia University Press.

Beauvoir, Simone de. 1943. *L'invitée.* Paris: Gallimard.

———. 1944. *Pyrrhus et Cinéas.* Paris: Gallimard.

———. 1945a. La phénoménologie de la perception de Maurice Merleau-Ponty. *Les Temps modernes* 1 (2): 363–67.

———. 1945b. *Le sang des autres.* Paris: Gallimard.

———. 1946. *Tous les hommes sont mortels.* Paris: Gallimard.

———. 1947. *Pour une morale de l'ambiguïté.* Paris: Gallimard.

———. 1991 [1949]. *Le Deuxième sexe II: L'Expérience vécue.* Reprint, Paris: Gallimard.

———. 1993 [1949]. *Le Deuxième sexe I: Les Faits et les mythes.* Reprint, Paris: Gallimard.

———. 1990 [1951]. Must we burn Sade? In *The Marquis de Sade, The 120 days of Sodom and other writings.* Trans. Annette Michaelson. Reprint, London: Arrow Books.

———. 1995a [1960]. *La Force de l'âge.* Reprint, Paris: Gallimard.

———. 1995b [1972]. *Tout compte fait.* Reprint, Paris: Gallimard.

————. 1996 [1963]. *La Force des choses II.* Reprint, Paris: Gallimard.

————. 1997a [1963]. *La Force des choses I.* Reprint, Paris: Gallimard.

————. 1997b [1958]. *Mémoires d'une jeune fille rangée.* Reprint, Paris: Gallimard.

Benjamin, Jessica, and Margaret A. Simons. 1979. An interview with Simone de Beauvoir. *Feminist Studies* 5 (Summer 1979): 330–45.

Bergoffen, Debra B. 1997. *The philosophy of Simone de Beauvoir: Gendered phenomenologies, erotic generosities.* Albany: State University of New York Press.

Butler, Judith. 1986. Sex and gender in Simone de Beauvoir's "Second Sex." *Yale French Studies* 72: 35–49.

————. 1989. Sexual ideology and phenomenological description: A feminist critique of Merleau-Ponty's "Phenomenology of Perception." In *Thinking muse: Feminism and modern French philosophy,* ed. Jeffner Allen and Iris Marion Young. Bloomington: Indiana University Press.

Chanter, Tina. 1995. *The ethics of eros: Irigaray's rewriting of the philosophers.* London, New York: Routledge.

Fink, Eugen. 1933. Die phänomenologische Philosophie Edmund Husserls in der gegenwärtigen Kritik. *Kant-Studien* 38 (3/4): 229–383.

————. 1988. *VI. Cartesianische Meditation: Teil 2: Ergänzungsband, Husserliana: Dokumente: Band II/2,* ed. Guy van Kerckhoven. Dordrecht: Kluwer Academic Press.

Garreta, Anne. 1986. *Sphinx.* Paris: Éditions Grasset & Fasquelle.

Grosz, Elizabeth. 1994. *Volatile bodies: Toward a corporeal feminism.* Bloomington: Indiana University Press.

Heinämaa, Sara. 1995. Sukupuoli, valinta ja tyyli: huomautuksia Butlerin ja Beauvoirin ongelmanasettelun yhteyksistä. *Tiede&edistys* 20 (1): 30–43.

————. 1996a. *Ele, tyyli ja sukupuoli: Merleau-Pontyn ja Beauvoirin ruumiinfenomenologia ja sen merkitys sukupuolikysymykselle.* Helsinki: Gaudeamus.

————. 1996b. Woman—nature, product, style? In *Feminism, science and the philosophy of science,* ed. Lynn Hankinson Nelson and Jack Nelson. Dordrecht: Kluwer Academic Publishers.

————. 1997. What is a woman? Butler and Beauvoir on the foundations of the sexual difference. *Hypatia* 12 (1): 20–39.

————. 2003. *Toward a phenomenology of sexual difference: Husserl, Merleau-Ponty, Beauvoir.* Lanham, Boulder, New York, Oxford: Rowman & Littlefield.

————. 2005. "Through desire and love": Simone de Beauvoir on the possibilities of sexual desire. In *Sex, breath & force: Sexual difference revisited,* ed. Ellen Mortensen. Lexington Books, forthcoming.

Hekman, Susan J. 1990. *Gender and knowledge: Elements of a postmodern feminism.* Cambridge: Polity Press.

Husserl, Edmund. 1913. *Ideen zu einer reinen Phänomenologie und phänomenologischen Philosophie, Erstes Buch: Allgemeine Einführung in die reine Phänomenologie, Husserliana, Band III,* ed. Walter Biemel. Haag: Martinus Nijhoff.

————. 1950. *Cartesianische Meditationen und pariser Vorträge, Husserliana, Band I,* ed. Stephan Strasser. Haag: Martinus Nijhoff.

————. 1952. *Ideen zu einer reinen Phänomenologie und phänomenologischen Philosophie, Zweites Buch: Phänomenologische Untersuchungen zur Konstitution, Husserliana, Band IV,* ed. Marly Bimel. Haag: Martinus Nijhoff.

———. 1954. *Die Krisis der europäischen Wissenschaften und die transzendentale Phänomenologie: Eine Einleitung in die phänomenologische Philosophie, Husserliana, Band VI,* ed. Walter Biemel. Haag: Martinus Nijhoff.

———. 1973. *Ding und Raum, Vorlesungen 1907, Husserliana, Band XVI,* ed. Ulrich Claesges. Haag: Martinus Nijhoff.

———. 1988. *The crisis of European sciences and transcendental phenomenology: An introduction to phenomenological philosophy.* Trans. David Carr. Evanston, Ill.: Northwestern University Press.

Kruks, Sonia. 1990. *Situation and human existence: Freedom, subjectivity and society.* New York: Routledge.

———. 1991. Simone de Beauvoir: Teaching Sartre about freedom. In *Sartre alive,* ed. Ronald Aronson and Adrien van Hoven. Detroit, Mich.: Wayne State University Press.

Le Doeuff, Michèle. 1991 [1989]. *Hipparchia's choice: An essay concerning women, philosophy, etc.* Trans. Trista Selous. Reprint, Oxford, Cambridge: Blackwell.

Lévinas, Emmanuel. 1947. *Le Temps et l'autre.* Paris: Quadrige/PUF.

Lundgren-Gothlin, Eva. 1992. *Kön och existens: Studier i Simone de Beauvoirs "Le Deuxième Sexe."* Göteborg: Daidalos.

———. 1995. Gender and ethics in the philosophy of Simone de Beauvoir. *Nora: Nordic Journal of Women's Studies* 3 (1): 3–13.

Merleau-Ponty, Maurice. 1993 [1945]. *Phénoménologie de la perception.* Reprint, Paris: Gallimard.

———. 1996 [1953]. Éloge de la philosophie. In *Éloge de la philosophie et autres essais.* Reprint, Paris: Gallimard.

———. 1966. Le roman et la métaphysique. In *Sens et non-sens.* Paris: Gallimard.

O'Brien-Ewara, Wendy. 1999. Expanding the tradition: "The Second Sex" and the legacy of French Hegelianism. Paper presented at Cinquantenaire du Deuxième Sexe 1949–1999, 19–23 January, at Sorbonne, Paris, France.

Rojcewicz, Richard, and André Schuwer. 1989. Introduction to *Ideas pertaining to a pure phenomenology and to a phenomenological philosophy, second book: Studies in the phenomenology of constitution,* by Edmund Husserl. Trans. Richard Rojcewicz and André Schuwer. Dordrecht: Kluwer Academic Publishers.

Simons, Margaret A. 1983. The silencing of Simone de Beauvoir: Guess what's missing from "The Second Sex"? *Women's Studies International Forum* 6 (5): 559–64.

———. 1986. Beauvoir and Sartre: The philosophical relationship. *Yale French Studies* 72: 165–79.

Stoller, Sylvia. 2000. Reflections on feminist Merleau-Ponty skepticism. *Hypatia* 15 (1): 175–82.

Stoller, Sylvia, and Helmuth Vetter, eds. 1997. *Phänomenologie und Geschlechterdifferenz.* Wien: Universitätsverlag.

Vintges, Karen. 1996. *Philosophy as passion: The thinking of Simone de Beauvoir.* Bloomington: Indiana University Press.

Waldenfels, Bernhard. 1993. Interrogative thinking: Reflections on Merleau-Ponty's later philosophy. In *Merleau-Ponty in contemporary perspective,* ed. Patrick Burke and Jan van der Veken. Dordrecht: Kluwer Academic Publishers.

———. 1998. *Grenzed der Normalizierung: Studien zur Phänomenologie des Fremden 2.* Frankfurt am Main: Suhrkamp.

Woolf, Virginia. 1998 [1928]. *Orlando*. Reprint, Harmondsworth: Penguin.

Zahavi, Dan. 1994. Husserl's phenomenology of the body. *Études Phénoménologiques* 19: 63–84.

———. 1996a. *Husserl und die transzendentale Intersubjektivität: Eine Antwort auf die sprachpragmatische Kritik*. Dordrecht: Kluwer Academic Publishers.

———. 1996b. Husserl's intersubjective transformation of transcendental philosophy. *Journal of British Society for Phenomenology* 27 (3): 228–44.

SHE CAME TO STAY AND BEING AND NOTHINGNESS

Edward Fullbrook

3

Since the time of Kierkegaard, existentialists have used fictional characters to convey their philosophical views. Presumably their reason for doing so was the belief that the total living individual is both the subject and the object of philosophy and *that the principles of a philosophy of existence can be expressed only in a concrete setting.*

—Barnes 1961, 15; italics added

The American philosopher William McBride recently observed in *The Chronicle of Higher Education* that "most of the Sartre scholars in this country tend to be sympathetic to the claim that Beauvoir should be taken seriously as a philosopher, that there was a lot of exchange of ideas between the two of them" (Heller 1998, A23). This sympathy is new. Traditionally, Jean-Paul Sartre scholars have tended to treat Simone de Beauvoir only as an eyewitness to the life (thought) of her man. Against this background, Kate Fullbrook's and my *Simone de Beauvoir and Jean-Paul Sartre: The Remaking of a Twentieth-Century Legend* appeared in 1993. Our book outlines and emphasizes the philosophical content shared by Beauvoir's *She Came to Stay* (1984) and Sartre's *Being and Nothingness* (1956) and calls attention to the fact that Sartre's and Beauvoir's recently published letters and journals show that: (1) Beauvoir wrote most or all of *She Came to Stay before* Sartre had even begun to write *Being and Nothingness;* and (2) many of the philosophical ideas credited as originating with *Being and Nothingness* did not appear in Sartre's journals and other writings until *after* he had read the second draft of *She Came to Stay.*

This seemingly "preposterous" thesis—that at important junctures in their intellectual partnership Beauvoir, not Sartre, was the originating philosophical force—quickly attracted attention. We have since written numerous essays further exploring the genesis of the ideas shared by the couple as well as a book devoted to explication of Beauvoir's philosophical writings (E. Fullbrook and K. Fullbrook 1995, 1998, 1999, 2001; K. Fullbrook and E. Fullbrook 1995, 1996, 1997; K. Fullbrook 1998). But we have not returned to a general consideration of the overall philosophical indebtedness of *Being and Nothingness* to *She Came to Stay.* Now, however, with weakening of the psycho-cultural resistance to Beauvoir-as-philosopher and, more importantly, to women-as-philosophers, the time seems right for a fresh look at the still-accumulating evidence surrounding the fascinating origins of these famous works.

But optimism is tempered by the controversy over the relative philosophical contributions of Beauvoir and Sartre, which remains deeply rooted in social history. By normal standards of scholarship, the terms on which this debate is conducted are rather unorthodox. So far as I know, no evidential case has ever been made for the hypothesis that the body of ideas in dispute originated with Sartre rather than with Beauvoir. Belief in Sartre as the source of the couple's ideas voiced in common predates the time when the words *woman* and *philosopher,* even less the words *woman* and *major philosopher,* could be comfortably conjoined. Credit for these ideas accrued wholly to Sartre as part of *normal social process.* Recognition of philosophical achievement was apportioned between the two, not on the basis of a determination of who contributed what, but instead, like so many things, on the basis of gender.

This history of the received wisdom on the relative roles of Beauvoir and Sartre precludes direct critique. No scholarly text exists that purports to establish Sartre's priority. This makes arguing Beauvoir's case like arguing against a ghost. In the continuing absence of any serious effort to establish the legitimacy of the claims for Sartre, all one can do for the case for Beauvoir is to point to the facts again.

What follows falls into four sections. The first and longest identifies the philosophical arguments found in *She Came to Stay* that also appear in *Being and Nothingness*. The second considers whether these arguments originated through concrete analysis or apriority. The third examines the journal and epistolary evidence regarding the dates of authorship of *She Came to Stay* and *Being and Nothingness*. And the final section combs the same sources for evidence of which philosopher contributed what to the set of ideas the two works share.

THE PHILOSOPHICAL ARGUMENTS

A shortcoming of *Simone de Beauvoir and Jean-Paul Sartre: The Re-making of a Twentieth-Century Legend* (K. Fullbrook and E. Fullbrook 1993) on the Beauvoir/Sartre partnership is its neglect of works by Maurice Merleau-Ponty (1964), Hazel Barnes (1961), and, more recently, Elizabeth Fallaize (1988), which identify various philosophical arguments running through Beauvoir's *She Came to Stay*. I draw on these readings so as to put to rest the charge that our reading of *She Came to Stay* is idiosyncratic. Novel philosophical theories shared by the two works include theories of appearances, temporality, embodiment, the division of reality between immanence and transcendence, a theory of intersubjectivity encompassing a solution to the problem of the Other, the concepts of the Third and of the Gaze or Look, and a typology of concrete relations based on a subject/object polarity.

I begin with intersubjectivity—or, as it is called in *Being and Nothingness*, Being-for-Others—for two reasons. First, this topic takes up the most important third of Sartre's treatise. And second, in *The Literature of Possibility: A Study in Humanistic Existentialism* (1961) Barnes introduces Beauvoir's treatment of this material in a way that brings into focus not only the controversy with which I am concerned but also, and more importantly, the ambiguity of the developmental relations between the two works. Barnes, the English translator of *Being and Nothingness*, writes:

> For our study of bad faith in human relations we are fortunate in having both Sartre's formal analysis in *Being and Nothingness* and de Beauvoir's *She Came*

to Stay (L'invitée), a novel which follows so closely the pattern outlined by Sartre that it serves almost as a textbook illustration. (Barnes 1961, 113)

Then, following a lengthy summary of Sartre's analysis of the Other, Barnes turns to Beauvoir's of the same:

This emotional labyrinth is all faithfully illustrated for us in Simone de Beauvoir's novel, *She Came to Stay*. Although this book and *Being and Nothingness* were published in the same year (1943), the similarity between them is too striking to be coincidence. As with all of de Beauvoir's early fiction, the reader of *She Came to Stay* feels that the inspiration of the book was simply de Beauvoir's decision to show how Sartre's abstract principles could be made to work out in "real life." (121–22)

However, Barnes significantly appends to this the following footnote:

I do not at all preclude the possibility that de Beauvoir has contributed to the formation of Sartre's philosophy. I suspect that his debt to her is considerable. All I mean in the present instance is that the novel serves as documentation for the theory, regardless of who had which idea first. (122)

"[I]t is only after finishing the book," says Barnes about Beauvoir's novel, "that one notes with amusement its *step by step correspondence* with Sartre's description of the subject-object conflict" (385; italics added). Barnes's book traces much of this correspondence, which includes an argument for the existence of others' consciousnesses. The history of this philosophical problem and "Sartre's" solution take up the first of the three chapters devoted to Being-for-Others in *Being and Nothingness*. Whereas previously philosophy had relied on an argument from analogy—she behaves rather like me, therefore she must be conscious like me—Beauvoir and Sartre base theirs on the phenomenological event of experiencing oneself as the object of another's consciousness. The sudden flush of shame or pride a person experiences when made the object of another's disapproving or admiring glance provides the archetypal case. Only another consciousness, goes the argument, could cause this transformation in one's own consciousness.

But for Beauvoir and Sartre, the subject/object relation matters not so much because it answers an old philosophical question as because they believe it structures many personal and sociological relations. In *She Came to Stay*, Beauvoir identifies three fundamental "procedures" or "attitudes" that one may take up regarding the subjectivity or consciousness of the Other. Persons may seek to experience themselves as the Other's object; they may seek to guard their subjectivity by making the Other their object; they may seek a reciprocity with the Other, whereby each treats the other as both subject and object, as equal freedoms and sources of value. Of these three fundamental attitudes to intersubjective relations, *Being and Nothingness* omits reciprocity but devotes its third chapter on intersubjectivity to analyzing the other two. For the first attitude, where one exploits one's possibilities as an object, Sartre describes two categories of concrete relations: love and masochism. For the second attitude, where one seeks to protect one's subjectivity, Sartre describes four categories: indifference, desire, hate, and sadism. He closes his account of intersubjectivity by considering how the introduction of a third person ("the Third" or the formation of a "triangle") affects the subject/object relation and gives rise to subject and object groups.

Barnes's book shows how not only Sartre's essay but also Beauvoir's novel develop all the material just outlined. Sartre's translator's reading of *She Came to Stay* identifies the correspondence at such length that here I can give only the barest outline. The novel has five important characters: Françoise, a writer through whose consciousness most of the story is told; Pierre, a young theatrical actor-director who has a long-term relationship with Françoise; Xavière, an alluring child-woman who disrupts Françoise and Pierre's relationship; Elizabeth, Pierre's sister who is an unhappy but successful painter; and Gerbert, Françoise's appealing younger assistant.

With these characters, Beauvoir creates a set of shifting triangles that, through the principle of the Third, structure the work as a whole. Xavière is "the apex of the first triangle," which includes Françoise and Pierre (Barnes 1961, 123). "Relations at the beginning," notes Barnes, "are on the plane of indifference" (123). For Sartre and Beauvoir this means pretending that another person is only an object. This is how Françoise relates to Xavière when she first enters her and Pierre's life. "She does not see Xavière as a self-determining subject or as an Other who might in any way affect Françoise's life. She is but the material for one of Françoise's projects" (123). But, notes Fallaize in *The Novels of Simone de Beauvoir*, "Xavière is simply a representation of the implicit challenge that all other consciousnesses constitute to our own" (Fallaize 1988, 29), and gradually she forces Françoise to become aware of her subjectivity. According to Barnes,

> Xavière's emergence as a subject threatens Françoise in two ways. In the first place she forces Françoise to become aware in a new way of her self-for-others and to see her whole life in a different and dubious light. . . .
>
> The second threat is to Françoise's relation to Pierre. In part this is simply the Sartrean disintegration of a dual relation under the Look of a Third. . . . Now the difference in their [Françoise's and Pierre's] evaluation of Xavière makes her see Pierre as an opaque being with whom she can no longer feel an absolute unity. (Barnes 1961, 124)

Beauvoir treats the physical desires that soon emerge between Xavière and Françoise and Xavière and Pierre with restraint because, says Barnes, of "her resolve to document Sartre's statement that, whereas all human relations are implicitly sexual, they do not have sexual intercourse as their specific goal. De Beauvoir gives full weight to both parts of his theory [of desire]" (1961, 127). Later, Pierre "becomes the pure embodiment of the Sartrean project of love (love in bad faith, of course). In loving Xavière he wants to *be loved* by her. He wants her to choose him as the center of her existence. Recognizing the intensity of her will to be the subject in any relationship, it will be the supreme conquest if she voluntarily chooses him as the limit of her freedom" (127). Meanwhile Françoise's relation to Xavière becomes "a project of love in which she is almost snared in the object-state with which she has hoped to fascinate Xavière's freedom; it is love on the masochistic side" (129). "True masochism," however, "is represented by Pierre's sister," and her relationship with a married man (128). For these and other concrete relations, Barnes's critique calls attention to the ontological structures that Beauvoir's phenomenological analyses reveal. She also shows how Beauvoir's novel works its way through the different categories of concrete relations as enumerated in *Being and Nothingness*. For example, Barnes writes: "So far we have seen, in terms consistent with Sartre's analysis, exemplifications of indifference, of two projects of love, and of masochism. In Xavière we see a portrayal, in very delicate terms, of sadism" (1961, 129).

As the plot progresses, Françoise, who for Beauvoir represents philosophy's traditional unawareness of the existence of a direct relation between human consciousnesses, experiences herself objectified in front of Xavière's consciousness with increasing frequency. Commenting on one of these episodes, Barnes writes:

> In this passage de Beauvoir has compressed the essence of Hegel's conflict of consciousness and of Sartre's idea that the emergence of another consciousness effects an internal hemorrhage of my world. The keyhole example soon follows. (Barnes 1961, 132)

Both Beauvoir's novel and Sartre's essay use the sudden flush of embarrassment experienced by someone caught spying thorough a keyhole as an illustration of a subject-object reversal effected by an Other's look, from feeling oneself as wholly a subject to experiencing oneself as an object in a world organized by another consciousness (Beauvoir 1984, 307–10; Sartre 1956, 259–63).

By this point in her novel, Beauvoir, notes Barnes, still "has not examined quite all of the philosophical implications of being-for-others. There still remains the exploration of hate," the last of the categories of concrete relations found in *Being and Nothingness* (Barnes 1961, 134). This is effected through Françoise's decision to kill Xavière, "a metaphysical murder rather than a real one," and that "is but the dramatic conclusion of a philosophical proposition" (135).

Thus far, by focusing on Barnes's reading and with a little help from Fallaize, we have found in *She Came to Stay* all the major ideas and arguments found in two of *Being and Nothingness*'s three chapters on being-for-others. The material from the third chapter, "The Body," is best correlated to Beauvoir's text in conjunction with the topics of temporality, bad faith, and the division of reality between immanence and transcendence or, as Sartre calls it, between being-in-itself and being-for-itself.

Merleau-Ponty identifies the hypothesis that human reality divides between immanence and transcendence as central to Beauvoir's novel. In "Metaphysics and the Novel," his essay on *She Came to Stay*, he writes:

> Her book shows existence understood between two limits: on the one hand, there is the immediate closed tightly upon itself, beyond any word and any commitment (Xavière); and, on the other, there is an absolute confidence in language and rational decision, an existence which grows empty in the effort to transcend itself (Françoise at the beginning of the book). (Merleau-Ponty 1964, 39)

The novel begins with Françoise (whose metaphysical reflections we witness) acting as an experiential stand-in for two philosophical deficiencies or myths endemic to Western philosophy: that no direct relation exists between individual consciousnesses, and that consciousness can be treated as independent of body. Beauvoir sees the experience of the Other and the embodiment of consciousness as paired, and both as related to the immanence/transcendence divide in human experience. Her choice of fiction as her philosophical medium permits her to analyze the two issues concurrently, while discovering their roots in the concrete. She centers the plot on Françoise's progressive disabusing of herself of the traditional philosophical views—whose foolishness becomes manifest when subjected to the context of lived experience—and the formation of new ones. Fallaize astutely brings out this dimension of Beauvoir's text.

> As happens so often in the text, the metaphysical and the psycho-sexual again come together here; Françoise's lack of awareness of her being-for-others, of how she appears to other people in the world, is damaging to her awareness of herself as a sexual and gendered being. To think of herself as "no-one," as "a naked consciousness in front of the world" (SCS p. 146) is to fail to perceive herself as body and as a woman. As the crisis intensifies, and Françoise is gradually forced to recognize her existence in the world on the same terms as other people, she begins to see that "whether she liked it or not, she too was in the world, a part of this world. She was woman among other women" (p. 146). The juxtaposition of these two statements is striking. The discovery of being-for-others, of her social existence, is a rediscovery of corporality, and hence of sexuality and gender. Françoise's illness at the end of the first part [half] of the book signals the re-emergence of her awareness that she is not pure consciousness, that she also has a corporal existence—but here she experiences the temporary preeminence of the body in passive terms as she retreats with relief into illness. (Fallaize 1988, 33–34)

Likewise, in "Metaphysics and the Novel" Merleau-Ponty writes as follows on Françoise's metaphysical conversion at the time of her illness and confinement to a clinic:

> Henceforth, Françoise can no longer know herself from inner evidence alone. She can no longer doubt that, under the glance of that couple [Pierre and Xavière], she is truly an object, and through their eyes she sees herself from the outside for the first time. And what is she? A thirty-year-old woman, a mature woman, to whom many things are already irrevocably impossible—who, for example, will never be able to dance well. For the first time she has the feeling of being her body, when all along she had thought

herself a consciousness. She has sacrificed everything to this myth. (Merleau-Ponty 1964, 33)

As one might expect, Merleau-Ponty also takes keen interest in how Beauvoir's phenomenological descriptions demonstrate the wrong-head-edness of mechanistic explanations of perceptual experience. The situational nature of fiction enables her to show how the body, with its organs of perception, and the subject, with its consciousness, are intertwined. The body is subjective, and the subject is embodied. In the real world objects reveal themselves only to consciousnesses that are individually and materially situated. Perceptions are conditioned by variations in the state of one's embodiment and structured by the stories one tells and hears told about one's past and future. This individualized structuring extends, according to Beauvoir, Sartre, and Merleau-Ponty, even to elementary space and time.

Early in *She Came to Stay*, Beauvoir sketches her theory of temporality through Socratic dialogues between her characters (1984, 51–52), arguing that perception of time is primarily about projected futures. Later, this argument emerges more fully developed from her account of the gradual demise of Françoise's "world" (113–26, 161, 171, 180), culminating with Françoise's apparent loss of Pierre to Xavière, her confinement to a hospital bed, and her contemplation of existence from this new vantage point (178–212). It is this exemplification on which Merleau-Ponty focuses his summary of Beauvoir's theory of temporality:

> things retreat beyond her grasp and become the strange debris of a world to which she no longer holds the key. The future ceases to be the natural extension of the present, time is fragmented, and Françoise is no more than an anonymous being, a creature without a history, a mass of chilled flesh. . . . There was a unique pulsation which projected before her a living present, a future, a world which animated language for her—and that pulsation has stopped.
> . . . A feeling is the name conventionally given to a series of instants, but life, when considered lucidly, is reduced to this swarming of instants. . . . One can escape the crumbling of time only by an act of faith which now seems to Françoise a voluntary illusion. (Merleau-Ponty 1964, 33)

I want to conclude this necessarily incomplete and sketchy discussion of the philosophical material common to *She Came to Stay* and *Being and Nothingness* by looking at the way both of these works begin, the "striking and ingenious" means by which they both launch their philosophical endeavors. These projects initially faced a major obstacle. Beauvoir and Sartre wanted to take individual consciousness as their ontological starting point while also taking up the position that things exist independently of anyone's consciousness of them. This stand presented them with a well-known problem with no known satisfactory solution: if the only access to things are their appearances to human consciousness, then how does one show that those things exist except as appearances *to* someone's consciousness? As Arthur Danto observes about Sartre's writing of *Being and Nothingness*, "it was therefore imperative that he solve the problem of appearance in order to save his view that we are conscious of real independent things. His analysis is striking and ingenious" (Danto 1991, 42). Roughly, that analysis goes like this. When we interrupt our usual goal-directed intercourse, we become aware of facing beyond our current field of vision a horizon of possible appearances whose number "is, loosely speaking, infinite, or at least indeterminate" (Danto 1991, 43). We experience each appearance as part of a series of potential appearances, a series that must be infinite, given (according to our perceptions) the infinite points of view space and time afford. But it is impossible for a mortal human subject to be conscious of an infinity of appearances. Therefore, there must exist a world of things outside the world of human consciousness.

Being and Nothingness, in its difficult "Introduction," begins by presenting this solution to the problem of appearances. But so too does *She Came to Stay*. Merleau-Ponty, after explaining the use of fiction as a philosophical method, begins his analysis of *She Came to Stay* with the following passage, which refers to the opening of Beauvoir's novel:

> There is a perpetual uneasiness in the state of being conscious. At the moment I perceive a thing, I feel that it was there before me, outside my field of vision. *There is an infinite horizon of things to grasp surrounding the small number of things which I can grasp in fact.* The whistle of a locomotive in the night, the empty theatre which I enter, cause to appear, for a lightening instant, those things which everywhere are ready to be perceived—shows performed without an audience, shadows crowded with creatures. Even the things which surround me exceed my comprehension, provided I interrupt my usual intercourse with them and rediscover them, outside of the human or even the living world, in their role as natural things. (Merleau-Ponty 1964, 28–29; italics added)

Beauvoir presents her argument for the existence of things independent of consciousness by the same method she uses for her argument for the existence of other consciousnesses. We have examined how Beauvoir uses Françoise's bad faith regarding the existence of the Other to demonstrate the basis of our belief in the existence of other consciousnesses. Françoise also begins the novel committed to believing, as she informs Gerbert, "that things that don't exist for me simply do not exist at all" and that "[o]nly her own life was real" (Beauvoir 1984, 6, 3). But of course, as Merleau-Ponty notes: " 'Elsewhere' and 'other' have not been eliminated; they have merely been repressed" (Merleau-Ponty 1964, 30). Beauvoirean/Sartrean bad faith requires awareness of what one is denying, and it is through Françoise's perception of the reality to be repressed that we as readers are confronted at the phenomenological level with Beauvoir's theory of appearances.[1]

The novel begins: "Françoise raised her eyes" (Beauvoir 1984, 1). Interrupting her work with Gerbert on a script late at night in her theatre office, she takes in the appearances that present themselves to her in the room. But as she non-instrumentally perceives these things, the feeling that these appearances hook up to a whole series of appearances outside her field of vision makes her uneasy. "Outside was the theatre . . . with its deserted corridors circling a great hollow shell" (1). She tells Gerbert that she is going to fetch some whiskey, but we are told that really "it was the dark corridors which were the attraction" (1). Her theatre walk then reveals each appearance as part of the well-known series of appearances comprising a theatre: the corridors, the half-light, the red carpet, the auditorium, the stage, the safety curtain, the rows of seats, and the deserted theatre's solitude and sense of expectancy. Against this expanding series of appearances, Françoise notes the finitude that embodiment and temporality impose on her consciousness and hence on her capacity to perceive these appearances. "She would have had to remain there forever in order to" exhaust this series of potential appearances that the theatre alone offered to her (2). Furthermore, in the theatre "she would have had to be elsewhere as well: in the props-room, in the dressing-rooms, in the foyer; *she would have had to be everywhere at the same time*" (2; italics added).

Beauvoir then expands the horizon of things that Françoise perceives. She steps outside the theatre, where the "houses all round the square were sleeping," where a quick step echoes on the pavement, a truck rumbles along the avenue, and where she thinks of provincial towns and later of Pierre moving through the night on a train, and finally, of "all those icy mountains and crevasses" on the moon (1984, 5). Beauvoir uses this process of invoking the phenomenology of Françoise's lived existence and of drawing concrete examples to remind the reader repeatedly that Françoise will "never be able to see more than one thing at a time" (6) in an infinite or inexhaustible series of appearances. In this way, Beauvoir's narrative, at its very beginning, establishes the transcendence of a realm of being vis-à-vis Françoise's and, by implication, all human consciousness. Françoise

> felt very strongly about this; the corridors, the auditorium, the stage, none of these things had vanished when she had again shut the door on them, but they existed only behind the door, at a distance. At a distance the train was moving through the silent countryside which encompassed, in the depths of the night, the warm life of her little office. (6)

This section, of course, is radically incomplete as a survey of the philosophical content of *She Came to Stay*. But my intent, rather than to offer an overview of Beauvoir's early philosophical thought, has been merely to identify the book's main lines of philosophical argument paralleling those in Sartre's *Being and Nothingness* and to document the fact that distinguished writers have previously identified them. But of these, Barnes's and Merleau-Ponty's readings of *She Came to Stay* differ in one highly significant and interesting respect. Unlike Barnes, Merleau-Ponty does not once suggest that Beauvoir's book might owe anything to Sartre. Why their mutual friend and colleague apportioned credit in this way becomes clear when the journal and epistolary evidence is examined.

WHICH CAME FIRST: ANALYSIS OF THE CONCRETE OR ABSTRACT PRINCIPLES?

The three passages from Barnes's *The Literature of Possibility: A Study in Humanistic Existentialism* (1961) quoted at the beginning of the previous section brush silently against a matter of pivotal importance for understanding "the formation" of what tradition labels "Sartre's philosophy," and for shedding light on "who had which idea first." Barnes's manner of paralleling the two works suggests, but never quite makes explicit, a key question: Which comes first for Beauvoir and Sartre, the "pattern" or the "illustrations," the "abstract principles" or the "real life" cases, the "theory" or the "documentation" and analysis of concrete examples?

Philosophers working in philosophy's a priori mainstream typically begin by choosing from the common fund a set of general propositions, which they then weave together to arrive at conclusions that, finally, they may or may not exemplify with worldly examples. In this tradition, "illustrations," "real life cases," and "documentation" function merely as icing for the cake. But the phenomenological/existential tradition reverses this order of procedure: it draws ontological, metaphysical, and general statements from descriptions of the particular and the concrete. Mary Warnock explains this other philosophical method as follows:

> The existential philosopher, then, must above all describe the world in such a way that its meanings emerge. He cannot, obviously, describe the world as a whole. He must take examples in as much detail as he can, and from these examples his intuition of significance will become clear. *It is plain how close such a method is to the methods of the novelist, the short-story writer.* (Warnock 1970, 136; italics added)

In one of her first essays, Beauvoir identifies this method as her way of doing philosophy and explains her preference for deploying it in the context of a novel. In "Littérature et métaphysique" (1948), which first appeared in *Les Temps modernes* in 1946, Beauvoir argues that a novel that employs "pre-established theses" is a "mystification" (109). She maintains that the basic requirement for an "honestly written" philosophical novel such as *She Came to Stay* is that its philosophical content must not predate the novel itself. Rather than illustrating preexisting philosophical ideas, the novel must be executed as a piece of original philosophical "research" that generates (by the method Warnock describes) its philosophical content. Each of its ideas must be for the author "a living discovery" (109).

So, as Fallaize observes, the process at work, or at least that appears to be at work, in *She Came to Stay* is "psychological phenomena giving rise to a rationalised philosophical discourse" (Fallaize 1988, 41). And for forty years, Beauvoir remained adamant that this was, indeed, the true process by which her novel developed. *She did so even in the presence of Sartre.* Sharing a platform with him in Japan in 1966, Beauvoir gave a lecture later published as "Mon expérience d'écrivain" (1979) in which she explained the process by which she wrote *She Came to Stay*. She identifies a personal "concrete psychological experience" as having led her to awareness of an ontological opposition, but which does not preclude the possibility of a reciprocity, between consciousnesses. She also describes her search for the means that would allow her "singular story to take a universal dimension":

> Briefly, I discovered something that everyone knows: the consciousness of others exists; another is a subject for himself as I am for myself; in his world I am an object which he arranges more or less as he pleases and which he may regard as hateful, unpleasant. So I had had a concrete experience and which was first of all situated on the psychological plane. But as long as one remains on the psychological plane, that is to say anecdotal, the book does not write itself. The book began to design itself in my head when I found a way of passing from this singular experience to a universal; I expressed it to myself, as I do before you, when I understood that it was the problem of others, the relationship to the consciousness of others which tormented me. (Beauvoir 1979, 440–41)

Like many radical twentieth-century philosophers, Beauvoir had serious reservations about the nature of the philosophical enterprise and sought to distance herself from orthodox practice. But unlike her innovative male counterparts, this rebellion has often been turned against her as evidence that she was not a philosopher and therefore depended on Sartre for her ideas. From her earliest essays (Beauvoir 1944, 34–35, 58; 1948) to her late interviews (Simons and Benjamin 1979), she disdained philosophy that took the form of that "lunacy known as a 'philosophical system'" (Beauvoir 1965, 221). Noting women's insusceptibility to this madness, she reserved the word *philosopher* for those who were—and she openly cited Sartre as an example—"prone to obsessions of this type" (Beauvoir 1965, 221; Simons and Benjamin 1979, 337–38). But Beauvoir has paid a heavy price for this usage. Those wishing to deny the existence of Beauvoir-the-philosopher have found it rhetorically effective to quote out of context her remarks about not being a "philosopher."

In 1979, by which time the myth that Beauvoir was simply Sartre's philosophical handmaiden was already firmly established, Margaret Simons and Jessica Benjamin pressed Beauvoir over the origins of her theory of the Other in *She Came to Stay:*

> M. S.: Sometimes, it is difficult for me to understand correctly your relationship with Sartre, your autonomy. Your ideas of the woman's situation, and of

> the Other, are really your own creation. And yet sometimes, in your own statements, it sounds as though you are saying the ideas came from Sartre....
> S. B.: Oh! No! Absolutely not.... No, these ideas are my own, indeed ... when I wrote my novels, I was never influenced by Sartre because I was writing from my lived and felt experiences.
> J. B.: So when you wrote in *L'invitée* (*She Came to Stay*) that Françoise says what really upsets her about Xavière is that she has to confront in her another consciousness, that is not an idea that particularly came [from] Sartre ... ?
> S. B.: It was I who thought about that! It was absolutely not Sartre!
> J. B.: But that is an idea which it seems to me appears later in *his* work.
> S. B.: Oh! Maybe! (Laughter) In any case, this problem ... of the other's consciousness, it was my problem. (Simons and Benjamin 1979, 338–39)

In the final months of her life, Beauvoir was still struggling against the popular view that the philosophical thought in *She Came to Stay* was Sartre's. In an interview in September 1985, Simons, referring to the time when she started her studies with Beauvoir, remarked: "But a lot of people told me, 'Why are you working with her? Why not the man himself? She is just a follower.'" Beauvoir replied:

> My books are completely personal. Sartre never interfered. *She Came to Stay, The Mandarins,* all of that is mine. (Simons 1992, 37)

But people do sometimes misrepresent what they have and have not done. As Hazel Barnes's remarks indicate, it does not necessarily follow that Beauvoir's novel, with its essential embeddedness in the concrete and the particular and its ostensible development of philosophical arguments from this base, is the original source of those arguments. Sartre's *Being and Nothingness* also sometimes appears to develop its arguments by the method Warnock describes. So it could have been that for forty years, Beauvoir was adamantly falsifying her account of how she wrote *She Came to Stay,* although Sartre never contradicted her. It could have been that Sartre had already developed its philosophical discourse (or some part of it), and beginning with that, Beauvoir looked around for phenomena that would illustrate it and then created the illusion—and novelists are illusionists—that the novel's philosophical insights initially emerged from the phenomena examined. This theoretical possibility of a double-barreled deception by Beauvoir, and the deep-seated cultural tendency for women not

to be believed in such matters, is why the two thinkers' journals and epistolary material is so crucial to settling this issue of origination.

WHICH BOOK WAS WRITTEN FIRST?

Sartre's biographers divide over whether he *began* to write *Being and
Nothingness* in late July 1940 or in the autumn of 1941. Contat and Rybalka, Thompson, and Beauvoir favor the later date, whereas Gerassi and
Hayman say that in July and August of 1940 Sartre wrote upwards of a
tenth of his essay before putting the project aside until more than a year
later. (See Contat and Rybalka 1974, 82; Thompson 1984, 48; Beauvoir
1965, 501; Gerassi 1989, 168; Hayman 1986, 164.) Both of these dates,
however, come after Beauvoir had *finished* the first and most, if not all, of
the second draft of *She Came to Stay*. Furthermore, Beauvoir had completed the final revisions to her novel several months before Sartre began or
recommenced writing *Being and Nothingness* in autumn 1941 (Beauvoir
1965, 369, 485). Indeed, in October 1941 Beauvoir submitted *She Came to
Stay* to the publishers Gallimard (Beauvoir 1979, 45). In January 1942 they
agreed to "publish it as it stands" (Beauvoir 1965, 519).

Extensive, diverse, and incontrovertible documentary evidence exists
detailing Beauvoir's progress with the writing of *She Came to Stay* and also
Sartre's reading of it. In *The Prime of Life* (1965), her second volume of autobiography, Beauvoir says that after a false start on *She Came to Stay* in late
1937, she began it anew the following year and finished with the final revisions in the late spring of 1941 (369). But much more detailed and con-
temporaneously recorded information on the writing of her novel appears
in her letters, in her war journals, and also in Sartre's letters and journals.
And all of these sources tell the same story. Briefly, it is as follows.

On September 2, 1939, Sartre left Paris and Beauvoir for military service. During their separation they exchanged letters nearly every day until
Sartre was taken prisoner on June 21, 1940. Both also kept journals (Beauvoir 1990; Sartre 1984). In Sartre's absence, Beauvoir threw herself into
writing her novel, and naturally in her letters to Sartre she told him about
its progress. More than thirty of her letters from this period contain such
references (Beauvoir 1991). When Sartre left Paris, her novel's first draft

appears to have been only about half written, but by early December she had another 300 pages. On December 7 Beauvoir wrote to Sartre:

> Since yesterday, I've been revising the novel from the beginning. I've had enough of inventing drafts; everything's in place now and I want to write some definitive stuff. I'm enjoying it enormously, and it seems terribly—quite seductively—easy. (1991, 200)

Her letters report that of this new and "final draft" she had 60 pages by December 29, 80 pages by January 3, and 160 pages by January 12. On January 17, anticipating Sartre's return on leave, she wrote, "I really think you'll heap me with praises when you read my 250 pages (for there'll be at least 250 . . .)" (1991, 258). Beauvoir's journal says that on February 5, the morning after Sartre arrived on leave, he occupied himself reading *She Came to Stay* (1990, 270). Her journal mentions seven more reading sessions that he had with her novel before he left on February 15 (270–83).

Sartre's first letter to Beauvoir after returning to military life concludes: "*Vous avez écrit un beau petit roman*," suggesting that he had read more than just the revised first half of her novel (Sartre 1983, 70). And three days later, on February 18, he writes to Beauvoir about the philosophical meaning of an episode that comes near the end of *She Came to Stay* in chapter 7 of part 2 (Sartre 1993, 61; K. Fullbrook and E. Fullbrook 1997, 15). Further references to his reading of her novel follow in his letters. Meanwhile, in his own journal, Sartre's entries are now replete with references to *She Came to Stay*, and these bring us to this essay's final question.

WHO THOUGHT WHAT FIRST?

Although it is now certain that *She Came to Stay* was written before *Being and Nothingness*, it is not absolutely proven that the original philosophical ideas and arguments that the two works share did not originate with Sartre. It remains theoretically possible that these were all Sartre's ideas, which he privately communicated to Beauvoir, who then built her novel around them and who then made up a false story about how she wrote *She Came to Stay*, a story she held to for the next forty years. To some people this possibility may appear so implausible that it does not seem worth pursuing, but the cultural bias (in which women as well as men have been socialized) against crediting the woman in such cases is so strong that even this implausible possibility must be eliminated if Beauvoir-the-philosopher is to receive her due.

Since the publication in France of Sartre's *War Diaries* in 1983, scholars have identified these journals, which he kept during the war prior to his capture, as the place where he first developed many of the philosophical ideas that were to form the framework of *Being and Nothingness* (1984). It is important to emphasize and document just how widespread is the agreement among Sartre scholars that his emergence as an original philosopher took place in his writing of these wartime diaries. In his introduction to the English edition of the *War Diaries* (Sartre 1984), Quintin Hoare notes that "the prewar years seem in retrospect to have been but an apprenticeship" and the "excitement of the notebooks" comes partly "from the fact that they represent the essential transition from that apprenticeship to the full flowering of Sartre's talents . . . as an original philosopher, in *Being and Nothingness* (1943), drafts for many of whose key passages will be found here" (Hoare 1984, x). Sartre biographer Ronald Hayman also identifies this as the period in which "Sartre's existentialism was beginning to take shape" (Hayman 1986, 149). Another Sartre biographer, Kenneth A. Thompson, writes: "It was also in these notebooks [the *War Diaries*] that he outlined his morality and drafted his philosophical reflections that were to find their definitive form in *Being and Nothingness*" (Thompson 1984, 43). Thomas Flynn observes that in these notebooks "we discover reflections that will find their way into *Being and Nothingness*" (Flynn 1992, 215). William McBride finds in the journals "an anticipation of some of the principal themes of *Being and Nothingness*" (McBride 1991, 32). Likewise, for Andrew Leak, the *War Diaries* "constitute an important *avant texte* for *L'Être et le néant*" (Leak 1995, 58).

This "flowering" of Sartre as a philosopher with his own ideas, however, does not manifest itself until after his leave to Paris in February 1940 and his many reading sessions with *She Came to Stay*. As Sartre himself noted in a letter to Beauvoir on January 9, 1940:

> I have reread my five notebooks, and they don't please me nearly as much as I had expected. I find them a little vague, too discreet, even the clearest ideas are little more than rehashings of Heidegger's: in the end, all I have done since September . . . is only a long re-elaboration of the ten pages he devoted to the question of historicity. (Sartre 1984, 19)

Anna Boschetti, referring to the period just before Sartre's February leave, confirms Sartre's reading of himself. "The philosophy we see coming to birth almost from day to day in his letters and notebooks," she writes, "is still much closer to a rewriting of *Being and Time* [Heidegger] than to an outline of the ethic implicit in *Being and Nothingness*" (Boschetti 1988, 55). Similarly, Leo Fretz, writing of the "confrontation between Sartre's philosophical positions from before and after 1940," speaks of "the turnaround of 1940," when Sartre becomes "Sartrean" in the sense that his concept of consciousness "becomes endowed with a *personal* structure" (Fretz 1992, 70, 77, 71).

The simple truth seems to be that following his protracted engagement with Beauvoir's text in Paris, Sartre returned to camp metamorphosed into a dynamo of philosophical originality. For the two weeks that followed, his notebooks, offering occasional acknowledgment to Beauvoir, make the generation of philosophical ideas look as easy as picking apples from a tree.

Between the 17th and the 27th of February, Sartre appears to have set down in his notebooks as much of the philosophical content of *She Came to Stay* as he could remember (Sartre 1984, 196–262). Many, but not all, of the ideas and arguments he records are the same as those that caught the attention of Merleau-Ponty, Barnes, and Fallaize. Sartre begins in good faith. He introduces the concept of unrecognizables (not discussed in this essay) and acknowledges that it comes from Beauvoir's novel (1984, 197), although in *Being and Nothingness* he treats it as his own (1956, 527–31). In his entry the following day, February 18, Sartre turns to Beauvoir's theory of temporality. In retrospect, the passage that opens his exposition is one of the most shocking in twentieth-century philosophy. It shocks, not because it mentions neither Beauvoir nor his recent experience of reading her novel, but because Sartre seems to be as set on deceiving himself as he is his readers. "I feel strangely bashful about embarking on a study of temporality. Time has always struck me as a philosophical headache" (1984, 208), he writes before briefly reviewing his numerous past failures in this field, including in his novel *Nausea* (1965) and in his lectures. "But all that wasn't yet ripe. And, behold, I now glimpse a theory of time! I feel intimidated before expounding it, I feel like a kid" (1984, 208–209). Glimpse, indeed! What follows is pure Beauvoir, some of it little more than paraphrases of dialogues from *She Came to Stay* (208–10).

Sartre continues to take possession of Beauvoir's theory of temporality on February 19 (1984, 210–15). On the 22nd and 23rd, he takes up Beauvoir's view (not discussed in this essay) of consciousness's continuous need for objects as the ultimate basis of all forms of desire. Then on the 27th, in seven impressive pages, he sketches out a large part of Beauvoir's theory of intersubjectivity (255–61). Without ever quite making explicit the idea of the Gaze or Look, he makes a good job of explaining the basic subject/object polarity (258). But he does not connect this analysis—as Beauvoir does repeatedly in her novel—with the philosophical problem of the existence of other consciousnesses. His effort's strong point is its treatment of concrete relations with the Other. He covers love (255–56, 261), sadism (256–57), indifference (258–59), and desire (259–60), but he missed masochism and hate. Nor do I find evidence that Sartre had yet taken in that concept of Beauvoir's that he later termed the Third. But this and other material from *She Came to Stay* could have been in his lost Notebook 13, which runs from March 1 to March 5, 1940.

Finally, there is the matter of Merleau-Ponty's treatment of the philosophical content of *She Came to Stay* as originating with Beauvoir rather than with Sartre. Merleau-Ponty knew beyond doubt that Beauvoir's book was written well in advance of *Being and Nothingness*. Her letter of December 23, 1940, to Sartre begins: "It's very cold this morning throughout Paris and particularly in the Dôme. Merleau-Ponty's here, a few steps away, busy reading my novel" (Beauvoir 1991, 356).[2]

Notes

The author expresses his thanks to Kate Fullbrook for her editorial advice.

1. The first chapter of the Moyse/Senhouse translation of *She Came to Stay* (Beauvoir 1984) has a short series of interconnected errors that do not enhance the intelligibility of Beauvoir's presentation of her theory of appearances. Central to Beauvoirean/Sartrean thought is the distinction between the appearances of nonconscious being and the way conscious beings organize those appearances. Beauvoir and Sartre generally refer to an instance of the latter as a "world." Thus, in her novel's opening chapter, Beauvoir distinguishes repeatedly between *la terre* and *le monde* (Beauvoir

1972). But in several places, the English translation (Beauvoir 1984) does not honor this distinction, having translated *terre* as "world." It appears that the translators have acted to save Françoise from her bad faith regarding existence of "elsewhere." The ellipses in the following passage form part of their translation.

> On the other side of the window-panes, the small, secluded square was asleep under the black sky; and, some way away, a train was moving through an empty landscape . . . And I am there, I am there, but for me this square exists and that moving train . . . all Paris, and all the world [*terre*] in the rosy shadows of this little office . . . and in this very instant all the long years of happiness. I am here [*là*], at the heart of my life. . . . (Beauvoir 1984, 4–5)

Similarly, when Gerbert asks Françoise to identify her regrets, she replies: "Having to live only in my own skin when the world [*terre*] is so vast" (5).

2. In her letter of January 5, 1941, Beauvoir, after explaining a broken engagement, writes: "I telephoned M. Ponty instead, met up with him at the Dôme, and spent the evening with him. He paid me vast compliments on my novel (the 1st part), telling me it was 'great': in spite of everything, that really did encourage me" (Beauvoir 1991, 364).

REFERENCES

Barnes, Hazel E. 1961. *The literature of possibility: A study in humanistic existentialism.* London: Tavistock.

Beauvoir, Simone de. 1944. *Pyrrhus et Cinéas.* Paris: Gallimard.

———. 1946. Littérature et métaphysique. *Les Temps modernes.* 1 (7): 1153–63.

———. 1948. Littérature et métaphysique. In *Existentialisme et la sagesse des nations.* Paris: Nagel.

———. 1965. *The prime of life.* Trans. Peter Green. Harmondsworth, UK: Penguin.

———. 1972. *L'invitée.* 1943. Reprint, Paris: Gallimard.

———. 1979. Mon expérience d'écrivain. In *Les Émtcrits de Simone de Beauvoir,* ed. Claude Francis and Fernande Gontier. Paris: Gallimard.

———. 1984. *She came to stay.* Trans. Yvonne Moyse and Roger Senhouse. London: Fontana.

———. 1990. *Journal de guerre.* Paris: Gallimard.

———. 1991. *Letters to Sartre.* Trans. Quintin Hoare. London: Radius.

Boschetti, Anna. 1988. *The intellectual enterprise: Sartre and Les Temps modernes.* Trans. Richard C. McCleary. Evanston, Ill.: Northwestern University Press.

Contat, Michel, and Michel Rybalka. 1974. *The writings of Jean-Paul Sartre.* Vol. 1, *A bibliographical life.* Trans. Richard C. McCleary. Evanston, Ill.: Northwestern University Press.

Danto, Arthur C. 1991. *Sartre.* London: Fontana.

Fallaize, Elizabeth. 1988. *The novels of Simone de Beauvoir.* London: Routledge.

Flynn, Thomas R. 1992. Sartre and the poetics of history. In *The Cambridge companion to Sartre,* ed. Christina Howells. Cambridge: Cambridge University Press.

Fretz, Leo. 1992. Individuality in Sartre's philosophy. In *The Cambridge companion to Sartre*, ed. Christina Howells. Cambridge: Cambridge University Press.

Fullbrook, Edward, and Kate Fullbrook. 1995. Whose ethics: Sartre's or Beauvoir's. *Simone de Beauvoir Studies* 12: 84–90.

———. 1998. *Simone de Beauvoir: A critical introduction.* Cambridge, UK: Polity, and Malden, Mass.: Blackwell.

———. 1999. The *absence* of Beauvoir. In *Feminist interpretations of Jean-Paul Sartre*, ed. Julien S. Murphy. University Park: Pennsylvania State University Press.

———. 2001. Beauvoir and Plato: The clinic and the cave. In *The existential phenomenology of Simone de Beauvoir*, ed. Wendy O'Brien and Lester Embree. Amsterdam: Kluwer.

Fullbrook, Kate. 1998. Simone de Beauvoir and the intellectual marketplace. In *Writing: A woman's business: Women, writing and the marketplace*, ed. Judy Simons and Kate Fullbrook. Manchester: Manchester University Press.

Fullbrook, Kate, and Edward Fullbrook. 1993. *Simone de Beauvoir and Jean-Paul Sartre: The remaking of a twentieth-century legend.* London: Harvester.

———. 1995. Sartre's secret key. In *Feminist interpretations of Simone de Beauvoir*, ed. Margaret A. Simons. University Park: Pennsylvania State University Press.

———. 1996. Leveling the field/tampering with the icons: On "Refining and remaking the legend of Beauvoir." In *Simone de Beauvoir Studies* 13: 13–24.

———. 1997. Beauvoir's literary-philosophical method. *Simone de Beauvoir Studies* 14: 29–38.

Gerassi, John. 1989. *Jean-Paul Sartre: Hated conscience of his century.* Vol. 1. Chicago: University of Chicago Press.

Hayman, Ronald. 1986. *Writing against: A biography of Sartre.* London: Weidenfelf and Nicolson.

Heller, Scott. 1998. Scholars seek to rank Simone de Beauvoir among leading 20th century philosophers. *Chronicle of Higher Education*, 4 September, A22–23.

Hoare, Quintin. 1984. Introduction to *War diaries: Notebooks from a phoney war*, by Jean-Paul Sartre. Trans. Quintin Hoare. London: Verso.

Leak, Andrew. 1995. Writing and seduction: Sartre's *L'Être et le néant* I. Actaeon. *Sartre Studies International* 1 (1, 2): 57–76.

McBride, William L. 1991. *Sartre's political theory.* Bloomington: Indiana University Press.

Merleau-Ponty, Maurice. 1945. Le Roman et la métaphysique. *Cahiers du sud* 270.

———. 1964. Metaphysics and the novel. In *Sense and non-sense*. Trans. Hubert L. Dreyfus and Patricia Allen Dreyfus. Evanston, Ill.: Northwestern University Press.

Sartre, Jean-Paul. 1943. *L'Être et le néant: Essai d'ontologie phénoménologique.* Paris: Gallimard.

———. 1956. *Being and Nothingness: An essay on phenomenological ontology.* Trans. Hazel E. Barnes. New York: Philosophical Library.

———. 1965. *Nausea.* Trans. Robert Baldick. Harmondsworth: Penguin.

———. 1983. *Lettres au Castor: Et à quelues autres.* Ed. Simone de Beauvoir. Paris: Gallimard.

———. 1984. *War diaries: Notebooks from a phoney war.* Trans. Quintin Hoare. London: Verso.

————. 1993. *Quiet moments in a war: The letters of Jean-Paul Sartre to Simone de Beauvoir 1940–1963.* Ed. Simone de Beauvoir. Trans. Lee Fahnestock and Norman MacAfee. New York: Scribner.

Simons, Margaret A. 1992. Two interviews with Simone de Beauvoir. In *Revealing French feminism: Critical essays on difference, agency, and culture,* ed. Nancy Fraser and Sandra Lee Bartky. Bloomington: Indiana University Press.

Simons, Margaret A., and Jessica Benjamin. 1979. Simone de Beauvoir: An interview. *Feminist Studies* 5 (Summer, part 2): 330–45.

Thompson, Kenneth A. 1984. *Sartre: Life and works.* New York: Facts On File.

Warnock, Mary. 1970. *Existentialism.* Oxford: Oxford University Press.

BEAUVOIR'S HEIDEGGERIAN

ONTOLOGY

Nancy Bauer

4

In the very last sentence of the "Introduction" to *The Second Sex*, Simone de Beauvoir says that her aim in the book is to help her readers understand why it is so hard for women to *"participer au mitsein humain,"* that is, "to participate in the human *Mitsein*." But this is my translation. Howard Parshley, the hapless translator of the English version of *The Second Sex*, has Beauvoir saying instead that she will help us see why women have trouble when they try to "aspire to full membership in the human race."[1]

Parshley's tendency to obscure the philosophical roots of Beauvoir's thought is by now well known.[2] But Parshley is not the only reader of Beauvoir who has declined to take seriously her use of the Heideggerian neologism *Mitsein*, or in English, "being-with." Despite a surge of philosophical interest in *The Second Sex* over the last decade or so, a surge consisting overwhelmingly of investigations into the book's philosophical roots in the thought of figures such as Husserl, Merleau-Ponty, and Hegel, commentators have had scarcely anything to say about the significance of Beauvoir's copious use of Heideggerian terminology—not just *"Mitsein,"* but also *"Dasein,"* "authenticity," the "call" or "appeal," the idea of human beings as "grasping" the world, and "disclosedness."[3] The critical silence appears to signify that, at least in the main, Beauvoir's philosophical readers find her use of these terms gratuitous. Thus, "human *Mitsein*," for instance, would just be a fancy way of saying something like "human *community*"; and we might presume that Beauvoir recurs to the Heideggerian term simply because she wishes to exploit, more or less cannily or innocently, what she regards as Heidegger's philosophical cachet, at least in 1949, at least in France.[4]

This idea—that Beauvoir's indulgence in the philosophical argot of a forebear merely *idles*, philosophically—is not new. Indeed, it has always controlled the reception of *The Second Sex*. Beauvoir's references to other philosophers are characteristically regarded as incidental to her aspirations and achievements in the book, which at the level of philosophical substance tends to be viewed as a lackluster pastiche of the thought of her partner, Jean-Paul Sartre. In the last decade or so, however, more and more feminist philosophers have called for a "return to Beauvoir" and have taken pains to bring to light not only the pronounced philosophical distance separating Beauvoir from Sartre but also the central importance of her use of other philosophers' concepts in *The Second Sex*.[5] One might well wonder, then, why philosophers interested in reviving philosophical interest in the book are evidently reluctant to take its Heideggerian bearings seriously.[6]

In the present essay I will suggest two reasons for this reluctance, reasons that come to light upon an examination of Beauvoir's appropriation of the concept of *Mitsein*.[7] First, I will suggest, we have been too quick to attribute to Beauvoir a popular but, I think, unconvincing reading of *Being and Time*, Heidegger's magnum opus, a reading on which *Mitsein* is to be interpreted in the main as some sort of broadly *ethical* or *normative* concept. The idea, very roughly speaking, is that an absolutely, ontologically basic feature of being human is experiencing oneself as part of a *fellowship* about which one is bound to *care*.[8] On this interpretation, one might naturally read Beauvoir's claim that women "aspire to participate in the human *Mitsein*" as suggesting that what women want, and rightly enough, is to join a literal *fellow*ship, that is, a preexisting community of men, one that already exemplifies what it is, and means, to be human. But this view is bound to disturb revisionist readers of *The Second Sex*, for it dovetails with a longstanding and common understanding of the book as inaugurating contemporary feminism in an insidiously "masculinist" way, one in which men are held up as exemplifying the standard women must strive to meet in order to achieve full humanity.[9] It is therefore no wonder that revisionist readers, who aim to encourage feminist philosophers to revisit *The Second Sex,* are loathe to draw attention to Beauvoir's use of *Mitsein*—so understood.

On my view, however, though the notion of *Mitsein* may turn out—indeed *does* turn out, at least in Beauvoir's hands—to have broadly ethical ramifications, its main function in both *Being and Time* and on Beauvoir's reading of that book is not to exalt some notion of human community but rather to further Heidegger's central project of laying out a challenge to the Cartesian epistemological tradition and its threat of solipsism. This challenge, as I shall argue, raises its own set of epistemological (and, farther down the road, ethical) problems, having to do, not with the human being's vulnerability to the temptation to doubt, à la the Cartesian tradition, the existence of anything outside of his or her mind, but, quite the contrary, with the endless temptation to *lose oneself* in the *Mitsein.* And these problems are of singular importance, or so I shall argue that Beauvoir claims, for women.

A second factor that I imagine accounts for a certain hesitancy to take Beauvoir's use of Heidegger's idiom seriously is that doing so appears to generate a tension in Beauvoir's ontology. On the one hand, there is her manifest commitment to a Hegelian way of understanding what it means to be a human being. Throughout *The Second Sex,* she clearly endorses the idea, patently appropriated from Hegel's master-slave dialectic, that (as she puts it in the introduction to the book) "we discover in consciousness itself a fundamental hostility toward every other consciousness" (*TSS*, xxiii; TA; *LDS* I:17). If we take the word "fundamental" here seriously, then it may seem hard to understand how Beauvoir could simultaneously be committed to the idea that we are fundamentally "with" one another in the Heideggerian sense, at least on the broadly normative reading of *Mitsein.* Even if you see Beauvoir as arguing that we can, as it were, domesticate our fundamental hostility toward one another and thereby achieve what she and Hegel call "reciprocal recognition," it will be hard to square the idea that human beings are fundamentally hostile to one another with the idea, implicit in the concept *Mitsein,* that they are by definition always *from the start* "with" one another. And so there seems to be no place for Heidegger in Beauvoir's ontology.

Indeed, the idea that at the level of ontology one could be both a Heideggerian and a Hegelian is explicitly dismissed out of hand by Sartre in Part III of *Being and Nothingness*. Sartre brands Heidegger a failure as an ontologist precisely on the grounds that you cannot get the Hegelian "problem of the other" off the ground if you start with the notion of *Mitsein*. On Sartre's understanding of Heidegger, *Mitsein* is a kind of "solidarity" (333), a paradigm for which is the coordination of a set of well-trained rowers: "It is," Sartre writes, "the mute existence in common of one member of the crew with his fellows" (332).[10] Heidegger's idea, Sartre thinks, is that somehow we are fundamentally in synch with one another, fundamentally pulling our oars together. Sartre, to the contrary, wants to say that any synchronicity between us is something that gets established at the level of the everyday or, in Heidegger's parlance, the "ontic," and not at the level of the ontological. But if we grant for argument's sake the Heideggerian idea that we are *ontologically* with one another, we see, Sartre argues, that we then cannot explain why we perceive others to be other at all. That is, if we imagine that we are fundamentally "with" one another, then it's hard to see why and how we are clearly *not* steadfastly in solidarity with one another in an everyday way. If you are interested in the problem of the other, as Beauvoir manifestly is, then according to Sartre you are obliged to reject the Heideggerian notion of *Mitsein*. Indeed, he says this flat out: "The relation of the *mit-Sein* can be of absolutely no use to us in resolving the psychological, concrete problem of recognition of the Other" (334).

But this consequence follows only if Sartre has got the concept of *Mitsein* right. And I do not think that he has. More importantly, I think that Beauvoir would agree with me. Furthermore, it is clear that Beauvoir's appropriation of *Hegel* is considerably different from Sartre's. A careful reading of *The Second Sex* reveals that the idea that human beings harbor "a fundamental hostility toward every other consciousness" does not entail for Beauvoir—as it does for Sartre—the impossibility of non-hostile human relations. Indeed, Beauvoir borrows this idea from Hegel's famous "master-slave dialectic," which ends optimistically enough with the promise, fulfilled later on in *The Phenomenology of Spirit*, that human beings have the capacity to negotiate their mutual hostility and to achieve what Hegel calls "reciprocal recognition," a state in which, to simplify the idea, each party acknowledges the fundamental humanity of the other. For Sartre, Hegel's optimism is misplaced: ultimately, Sartre claims, I am destined either to threaten or be threatened in my relationships with other people. But like Hegel, Beauvoir explicitly keeps open the possibility that people may come to achieve reciprocal recognition. In the conclusion to *The Second Sex,* for example, she writes,

> To emancipate woman is to refuse to confine her to the relations she has with man, but not to deny them to her. In positing herself for herself [*se pose pour soi*] she will not continue less to exist *also* for him: mutually recognizing each other as subject, each will yet remain for the other an *other* . . . (*TSS,* 731; TA; *LDS* II, 662)

As this quotation hints, Beauvoir does not adopt Hegel's understanding of reciprocal recognition wholesale. On Hegel's view, the initial encounter between the master-to-be and the slave-to-be immediately provokes in each party a desire to be recognized by the other as essentially "for-itself," as, in other words, essentially different from a mere *object*, from something that has a certain set of static properties, from what Hegel calls the "in-itself."[11] Each party wishes to be seen as having only one static property, namely the property of not having any static properties. On Beauvoir's view, the wish Hegel articulates tends to be peculiar to *men*.[12] For a woman, she claims, the desire for recognition tends to take the form of wishing to be confirmed as *essentially* in-itself, as essentially, in an object-like way, having a static set of specific properties. And unlike Hegel, Beauvoir sees reciprocal recognition, that is, the foregoing of both sorts of wishes, as requiring an acceptance both of the reifying (objectifying) nature of one's own judgment of the other and of the inevitability of one's being judged, in a reciprocally reifying way, by that other. To put the point another way, the risk required for the consummation of reciprocal recognition, according to Beauvoir, is the risk of allowing both the other and oneself to be and be seen as *genuinely* other, which turns out to entail the risk of, paradoxically, claiming a certain *freedom* from him—or her. And the significance of Beauvoir's appropriation of the concept of *Mitsein* is that it shows us why my establishing genuine human relationships with other human beings requires that I insist not on joining some primordial fellowship but on allowing for, or even putting a certain distance between, others and myself.

In what follows I lay the groundwork for this reading of Beauvoir's Heideggerian bearings, first by offering a way of understanding what Heidegger means by *Mitsein* via a set of claims about the central aims of *Being and Time,* and then by positioning my own interpretation of Beauvoir's use of *Mitsein* against the pertinent claims of two other revisionist philosophical readings of *The Second Sex.* The point of this essay is not to construct a knock-down argument for my way of reading Heidegger. Nor do I aspire to conduct an exhaustive investigation into Beauvoir's use of the concept *Mitsein,* let alone her appropriation of Heidegger's more general project. I seek only to suggest that we have good reason to take seriously, as we have for the most part yet to do, the Heideggerian ontological bearings of *The Second Sex* and to explore their intimate connection with Beauvoir's manifest investment in the idea of reciprocal recognition.

HEIDEGGER'S *MITSEIN*

On my reading of *Being and Time,* Heidegger introduces the notion of *Mitsein* to combat a philosophical picture—specifically, a Cartesian picture—in which the individual mind, groping to pin down with apodictic certainty the existence of something outside itself, must bridge some sort of metaphysical gap between itself and other people. That is to say, Heidegger wants to help us escape from a philosophical paradigm that would have us forget that, phenomenologically, my world is not anchored in some solipsistic vanishing point, bounded at its limits by a transcendental "I," but rather "is always the one that I share with Others" (see §26 of *Being and Time*). *The* great theme of *Being and Time,* on my understanding of the book, is that philosophy, particularly in its modern incarnation, has succumbed to a temptation to operate with a false ontology, the hallmark of which is the claim that there is a fundamental separation between consciousness and the world.

For Heidegger, the seductive lure of this false ontology has been enhanced by philosophy's understanding of itself as a kind of science, and specifically as a mode of inquiry that needs to wrench its objects from their natural contexts in order to reveal their true nature. Some form of wrenching is ordinarily part and parcel of isolating a scientific problem. A chemist who is, say, analyzing the nutritional content of an apple ought not concern herself, qua the task at hand, with the question of how the apple tastes or what sort of people will buy it or how much it costs; she simply removes herself and the apple to the lab. Similarly, Heidegger suggests, the scientistic philosopher is inclined to ignore the roles that the objects of his inquiry play in everyday life and to study these objects in isolation, under, as it were, a philosophical microscope. But while the chemist's special way of attending to an apple will, if all goes well, result in a clearer picture of the apple's chemistry, the philosopher's scientism is fundamentally *distorting* and provides him with something quite different from what he set out to understand.

To get an intuitive grip on the difference here, let's look at an example. Consider the metaphysician who espouses a version of reductionistic physicalism on which nothing other than microphysical particles (or waves or forces) genuinely—"literally," as the reductionist is wont to say—exist. On this view, only these microphenomena are causally efficacious, and talk of composite phenomena is talk about things that are causally inert and do not—again, "literally"—exist. Cian Dorr, a metaphysician who endorses this view, recognizes that it entails that "if there are any people, they are all epiphenomena." And he acknowledges that it follows that

> if there are epiphenomena, then they are of no importance to me; whereas if I exist, then I am of great importance to myself. But if I exist, then I am an epiphenomenon. Hence I do not (strictly and literally speaking) exist. The activities I used to ascribe to myself—thinking these thoughts, feeling these feelings, and so forth—are not performed by any single thing: rather, they are jointly performed by those things I used to call "the particles that compose me." If I want to say things that are strictly and literally true, I had better stop using this word "I" all the time, since it doesn't refer to anything. Instead we—we particles, that is—should say "we."[13]

Now, Heidegger would not want to deny that people's bodies are made up of particles or even that one day we might be able to provide an exhaustive causal explanation at the level of microphysics for why composite objects, even people, behave as they do. What he *would* want to deny is that *philosophy* makes any serious progress by approaching the question of existence in the way that Dorr approaches it. The problem is not that Dorr's specific view is *wrong;* it's that what Heidegger would see as his fixation on a highly particular—and thereby distorting—way of looking at the question of what it is for a person to exist prevents him from attending to what it is to *be* a person. This is not a problem that Heidegger sees as particular to (highly controversial) views such as Dorr's. It is a problem for any philosopher who fails to attend to what he is studying as it, in his natural dealings with it, *is*. And for Heidegger, what something *is* invariably has to do with the role it plays in human lives.

So a Heideggerian ontological investigation forbids the wrenching of the object of study from its context, or contexts, of human meaning. Heidegger dramatizes this point in sections 15 and 16 of *Being and Time*, where he considers the simple example of a hammer.[14] One way to investigate what a hammer is would be to do a molecular analysis of it. Or we could examine how exactly its head fits onto its handle. Or we could go to a hammer-maker to learn how to make a hammer from scratch. And so on. But Heidegger's point is that none of these investigations would tell us the most important thing about what a hammer *is*—namely, something that people use to get nails into things or pull nails out of them or bonk would-be criminals on the head (since hammers *are* blunt objects). Someone living many centuries from now who unearths a hammer during an archeological dig and wants to know what it is will be asking a question about what role hammers played in our lives. One might be inclined to object that it matters that a hammer is a human artifact: not all phenomena with which philosophers concern themselves are *meant* for human use in the way such objects are. But, at least as I read Heidegger, to do philosophy is precisely to concern oneself with what things *mean* for human beings. This is true whether what is being studied is a hammer or a cloud or moral goodness or aesthetic judgment or the mind or a knowledge claim or the human being itself.

This understanding of the philosophical enterprise entails a kind of end run around the skepticism that has dogged philosophy since Descartes. The inaugurating move of the *Meditations*, in which Descartes throws the reliability (and thus the significance) of all of his beliefs into doubt, automatically puts him at a certain distance from the phenomena he studies. What Descartes doubts is precisely that the ordinary objects before him—the famous ball of wax in the second meditation, the fire before which he perhaps just dreams he is sitting, and so forth—exist. But why care whether things "exist" in the sense that exercised Descartes? As the average beginning philosophy student is inclined to object, whether what philosophers have come to call "the external world" exists or not has no bearing on our experience. The sort of recalcitrance evinced by beginners in philosophy is easy to write off as a sign that a student lacks a taste or even an aptitude for the subject. But from a Heideggerian point of view, what is being resisted here—and rightly so—is a turning of philosophical attention away from what matters to a distorted picture of the world, one in which objects are salient, not in their everyday contexts, but as generic metaphysical entities. This is not to suggest that the student who merely fails to be gripped by the idea of Cartesian doubt epitomizes, in his recalcitrance, the proper stance of the philosopher. On Heidegger's view, attending to the being of phenomena requires thinking deeply and seriously about exactly how to resist something like Descartes' move, lest we yield to the temptation to allow the nature of the philosophical problem we are addressing—in Descartes' case, at least on his understanding of it, the problem of chaos in the science of his day—to distort our investigations from the start.[15] A central point of *Being and Time,* as I read it, is to explore, understand, and ultimately attempt to resist this temptation.

And how does the notion of *Mitsein* fit into this picture? Heidegger does not introduce the idea of "Being-with" until section 26 of *Being and Time,* which is to say after he lays out the basic picture that I've sketched above. A major goal of section 26 is to observe that when I attend properly to the being of *things*—hammers, for instance—I will notice that I encounter them "from out of the world in which they are ready-to-hand for Others" (154).[16] It is part of what it means to be a hammer, for instance, that it is something that *people* (and not just I) use. The existence (in Heidegger's sense) of a hammer, then, *entails* the existence (in that same sense) of other people. "The world," as Heidegger puts it, "is always one that I share with Others. The world of Dasein is a *with*-world [*Mitwelt*]" (155; brackets and italics in original). Furthermore, Heidegger stresses, human beings naturally take an interest in or *care* about *(sorgen)* not just the objects in the world, those things with which, in his terms, they *concern* themselves, but also other human beings as such. We comport ourselves toward others, Heidegger claims, in the form of what he calls *solicitude* or, in German, *Fürsorge,* which means, literally, *caring-for.*

The idea of "caring for," however, can be misleading: it might seem to suggest that Heidegger is arguing that human beings naturally, ontologically, have a desire to *help* other people, to take care of them. Here, in fact, we find the source of what I'm claiming is the decidedly un-Heideggerian view that *Mitsein* is in the first instance a broadly ethical notion, one that grounds the idea that to be a human being means, fundamentally, to reside in a mutually beneficial—caring, helpful—community. And yet Heidegger takes great pains in section 26 to forestall this interpretation. Indeed, in his first pass at fleshing out the notion of *Fürsorge*, he says explicitly that human beings ordinarily comport themselves in "the *deficient* modes of solicitude" (158, my emphasis).[17] "Being for, against, or without one another," he writes, "passing one another by, not 'mattering' to one another—these are the possible ways of solicitude. And it is precisely these last-named deficient and Indifferent modes that characterize everyday, average Being-with-one-another." Even the "positive" modes of solicitude can fail to create or maintain what we might think of as fellowship or community. When solicitude actively takes the form of my attempting to spare someone else the pain of living his or her own life, "[i]t can, as it were, take away 'care' from the Other and put itself in his position in concern: it can *leap in* [*ein-springen*] for him" (emphasis in original):

> This kind of solicitude takes over for the Other that with which he is to concern himself. The Other is thus thrown out of his own position; he steps back so that afterwards, when the matter has been attended to, he can either take it over as something finished and at his disposal, or disburden himself of it completely.

When this happens, "the Other can become one who is dominated and dependent." Heidegger goes on to suggest a connection between our impulse to leap in (and thus dominate) the other and our investment in the idea of *empathy* [*Einfühlung*]. The problem with empathy is that, to put the idea in a pointedly un-Heideggerian way, we often come by it on the cheap: we act too quickly as though we understand another person as a way of avoiding the hard work of getting to know him or her, "so that a genuine 'understanding' gets suppressed, and Dasein takes refuge in substitutes" (163). Empathy with another person can easily constitute a denial of her humanity. The bonds I imagine I am establishing with her are false bonds; the community I fantasize I am forging is one in which the Other and I remain profoundly unknown to each other.

And just as I take the paradoxical risk of pushing the other away (both from herself, as it were, and from me) when I leap in "empathetically," so I indulge in a kind of epistemological violence when I construe the problem of *how* to "be-with" the other as the so-called "problem of other minds," and when I try to solve this problem through a misplaced appeal to empathy. To ask how I can know that other people have minds that are basically just like mine, that they think and experience and feel things in essentially the same way I do, is, on Heidegger's view, to deny the ontological fact of our Being-with one another. And to respond to this problem with some sort of "argument from analogy"—namely, by suggesting that I know that "other minds" like mine exist because I interpret other people's actions (their "pain-behavior," for instance) as best explained by their having experiences just like mine—is to ignore the basic ontological fact that my very perception of some phenomenon as "pain-behavior" is a function of the *Mitsein* and, specifically, of our shared concept "pain."[18] So just as Heidegger's understanding of what it means to *be* an object sidesteps the skeptical "problem of the external world," his development of the concept *Mitsein* circumvents the closely related problem of "other minds."

And yet Heidegger's "solution" to both of these skeptical problems carries its own dangers, dangers that Heidegger himself fully recognizes and indeed discusses in section 27 of *Being and Time,* that is, the section that directly follows his introduction of the concept of *Mitsein.* For if my world is through and through a world marked by the being of other people—if, specifically, the only objects and concepts I have at my disposal are those that are through and through public, then there is a massive disincentive for me to make these objects and concepts *my own.* If for Descartes the potential crisis is that I may turn out to be alone in the world, for Heidegger it is that I may *drown myself in it.* Here we find Heidegger's first use of his notorious *"das Man,"* most commonly, albeit awkwardly, rendered in English as "the 'they.'" If I attend to how I actually comport myself, I will see that far from worrying about whether other people exist, I am endlessly inclined to allow *das Man* to do the hard work for me of living my own life. Rather than make my own decisions, I do what "everyone" does. Rather than struggle with the problem of how to make our words mine, I engage in what Heidegger calls "idle talk." It is important to see that for Heidegger *das Man* is not some group of "other" people: rather, the term refers to our tendency to disburden *ourselves* by allowing the *Mitsein* to, as it were, leap in for us. As Heidegger puts it,

> In these characters of Being which we have exhibited—everyday Being-among-one-another, distantiality, averageness, leveling down, publicness, the disburdening of one's Being, and accommodation—lies that "constancy" of Dasein which is closest to us. This "constancy" pertains not to the enduring Being-present-at-hand of something, but rather to Dasein's kind of Being as Being-with. Neither the Self of one's own Dasein nor the Self of the Other has as yet found itself or lost itself as long as it is [*seiend*] in the modes we have mentioned. In these modes one's way of Being is that of inauthenticity and failure to stand by one's Self. (166)

Here, then, Heidegger indicates that one of his signature concepts, "authenticity," has to do with one's success in "standing by one's Self" and in participating in the *Mitsein* in ways in which one has the chance both to find *and* to lose oneself. Thus, far from constituting some kind of salutary primordial human fellowship, the Heideggerian *Mitsein* confronts us with the challenge of living authentically. And notice that part of what "living authentically" will have to mean is figuring out a way to relate to other people that is not "deficient" or "indifferent" or characterized by premature "empathy" or the phenomenon of "leaping-in." (In other words, Heidegger is not here espousing some sort of crude individualism.) If being human is fundamentally being-with, then creating a genuine human community, on any scale, will be massively difficult—but not impossible—work.

In its broad strokes, this picture of *Mitsein* and its implications is, I submit, what Simone de Beauvoir takes away from her reading of *Being and Time*. If we put this picture against what I claimed is her appropriation of Hegel's master-slave dialectic, we get the view—the view that I claim she is developing in *The Second Sex*—that to be a genuine human being one must strive both to "stand by one's Self" and to allow, indeed encourage, others to do so as well. On Beauvoir's view, these tasks pose a particular challenge to women. But to see why, we need to turn to her own appropriation of the concept of *Mitsein*.

BEAUVOIR'S *MITSEIN*

Beauvoir appeals to the concept of *Mitsein* in *The Second Sex* not to endorse or deny the idea that human beings are bonded to one another in some sort of fellowship or community but to acknowledge, along with Heidegger, that his way of sidestepping the so-called "problem of other minds" raises a new problem: the problem of how an individual is to find the courage to be herself, to distinguish herself, to find her voice, in a world in which she is inevitably *with*—even smothered by—others, and particularly by men. I read Beauvoir as appropriating the concept of *Mitsein* in *The Second Sex* in her quest to understand why men and women are inclined to exploit the fact of sex difference as a way of negotiating their fundamental fear of being human—of being, that is to say, endlessly tempted to let themselves be reified (for men as essentially "for-itself" and for women as essentially "in-itself") in the objectifying judgments of others.

I want to position my interpretation of Beauvoir's use of *Mitsein* with respect to the only two sustained treatments of her use of this concept that I know: one by Debra Bergoffen in her book *The Philosophy of Simone de Beauvoir*, and one by Eva Gothlin, starting in her book *Sex and Existence* and continuing through several more recent papers of hers. I wish not only to throw my own view into relief but also to show just how dependent one's interpretation of *The Second Sex* inevitably is on one's way of understanding why and how Beauvoir engages the thought of her philosophical forebears. Both Bergoffen and Gothlin interpret the notion of *Mitsein* in *The Second Sex* as intersecting somehow with Beauvoir's appropriation of Hegel's master-slave dialectic—quite rightly, in my view, of course. But because Bergoffen and Gothlin are operating with different understandings of what Hegel and Heidegger mean to Beauvoir, they vary sharply on the question of the role *Mitsein* plays in Beauvoir's thought. While Bergoffen sees Beauvoir's appropriation of the concept of *Mitsein* as in tension with her appropriation of Hegel, Gothlin sees the two appropriations as compatible—and yet ultimately separate.

On Bergoffen's view, to appreciate the force of Beauvoir's appeals to Heidegger one must see how they link up with her claims that women fail to demand a certain sort of Hegelian recognition from men. One reason for this failure, according to Bergoffen's interpretation of Beauvoir, is that women are heavily invested in a primordial bond of reciprocity that exists between woman and man, one that, as Bergoffen understands it, "expresses the common sexual desire and desire for children of both men and women" (*The Philosophy of Simone de Beauvoir*, 167). If a woman believes that she is, from the outset, bonded with men (typically represented for her in the form of her heterosexual partner), then she is likely to devote herself to its requirements—those of, for example, friendship and generosity—rather than to demand some further species of recognition from men. This might be all well and good if, as Beauvoir on Bergoffen's view claims, there really *were* a primordial *Mitsein* between the sexes. But, Bergoffen warns, there is not: "At best," Bergoffen thinks, "it's a (utopian?) hope, not something originally given" (167; parenthetical question in original). And yet, Bergoffen observes, not only Beauvoir but indeed patriarchy itself not surprisingly *endorses* the myth of a primordial *Mitsein* between men and women, precisely because so doing keeps women from demanding recognition. In effect, patriarchy forces women to exemplify the values of generosity and friendship while encouraging them not to demand these things for themselves. "According to the codes of patriarchy," Bergoffen writes, "[woman] is required to subordinate herself to the requirements of the heterosexual couple. Once required, however, the generosity of nonrecognition is mutilated" and "becomes the ground of an ethics of exploitation" (172).

Indeed, Beauvoir's apparently straight endorsement of the idea that there is a primordial *Mitsein* between women and men is troublesome not just from a feminist point of view, according to Bergoffen. For the idea of a primordial *Mitsein* belies Beauvoir's "Cartesian roots" as expressed in the view—and here I am quoting Bergoffen quoting the English translation of *The Second Sex*—"that every concrete human being is always a singular, separate individual" (Bergoffen, 174; *TSS*, xx; *LDS* I, 13).[19] To resolve this tension in her ontological commitments, Bergoffen argues, Beauvoir ultimately "puts the ethic of the bond of the *Mitsein* aside" (172) in favor of the more Hegelian idea that we begin ontologically, not with some primordial Being-with, but rather

with our differences from each other. The ethical question concerns the ways in which we negotiate these differences. For Beauvoir the key to this negotiation is the concept of reciprocity. To be moral we must cultivate the desires of reciprocal recognition. (175)

That is to say, on what Bergoffen takes to be Beauvoir's considered view, we must be willing to forego the temptations of the idea of a primordial *Mitsein* between men and women in favor of a Hegelian project of demanding recognition from one another.

According to Bergoffen's reading of the role of the concept of *Mitsein* in *The Second Sex*, Beauvoir's appeal to Heidegger is, at best, dangerous. This is because, under patriarchy at least, the idea that there is some primordial bond between men and women feeds right into the myth of the feminine: it serves to justify women's role as, in Beauvoir's words, "the inessential other." If woman is invested in the idea that there is a deep, original bond between herself and man, then, Bergoffen claims, she can rationalize her failure to risk demanding recognition from men. Why bother when the bond is already there? And of course endorsing the notion of some sort of primordial bond between the sexes allows men to justify their subordination of women and at the same time, insidiously enough, to glorify the "feminine" ideal of generosity that characterizes women's investment in *Mitsein*. "From this perspective," Bergoffen writes, "the story of *The Second Sex*, as an account of the genealogy of patriarchy, is the story of what happens when generosity and concern for awareness of the meaning of the bond is transformed from an existential insight demanded of all of us into a codified sexed position called mother and wife, and only required from some of us" (171–72). If we mistake Beauvoir's appeal to the idea of a primordial *Mitsein* as a straightforward endorsement of it, Bergoffen seems to suggest, then we risk reinforcing the insidious workings of patriarchy.

Notice that this understanding of what Beauvoir means by *Mitsein* depends on the idea that the concept is inherently value-laden, that by definition it entails some sort of commitment to the norms of, for example, harmony, friendship, and generosity. Now, Bergoffen has done groundbreaking work in showing how heavily invested Beauvoir is in these values—how they lie at the very heart of her faith in the possibility of reciprocal recognition between men and women. But I find no evidence that Beauvoir thinks of *Mitsein*, per se, as by definition characterized by these values.

Beauvoir appeals to the concept of *Mitsein* only a handful of times in *The Second Sex*, albeit almost always at crucial junctures in the book. Herewith are all the instances in which the concept appears, in the order one encounters them:[20]

1. At the end of a profound study of the diverse forms of primitive societies, Lévi-Strauss was able to conclude: "The passage from the state of Nature to the state of Culture is defined by man's ability to think biological relations under the form of systems of opposition: duality, alternation, opposition and symmetry, whether they present themselves under definite forms or fluid forms, constitute less phenomena to be explained than fundamental and immediate givens of social reality." These phenomena would not be comprehensible if *Dasein* were exclusively a *Mitsein* based on solidarity and friendship (*LDS* I, 17; my translation; compare *TSS*, xxiii, and note the fateful translation of *la réalité humaine*, the French term for Heidegger's *Dasein* as "human society" in Parshley's translation).

2. The proletariat could propose to massacre the ruling class; a fanatical Jew or Negro could dream of monopolizing the secret of the atomic bomb and making all humanity Jewish or Negro: even in her dreams woman cannot exterminate the males. The bond that unites her to her oppressors is not comparable to any other. The division of the sexes is indeed a biological given, not a moment of human history. It is in the bosom of an original *Mitsein* that their opposition becomes apparent, and she has not broken it (*LDS* I, 19; my translation; compare *TSS* xxv).

3. From woman's point of view we shall describe the world in which women must live; and we will be able to comprehend the difficulties with which they collide in the moment in which, trying to make their escape from the sphere hitherto assigned them, they aspire to participate in the human *Mitsein* (*TSS*, xxxv; TA; *LDS* I, 32).

4. Here again the case of the human species cannot be reduced to any other; it is not as individuals that human beings define themselves in the first place; men and women have never defied each other in single combat; the couple is an original *Mitsein*, and itself always appears as a permanent

or temporary element in a much larger collectivity (*TSS,* 35; TA; *LDS* I, 75).

5. Symbolism did not come down from heaven nor rise up from subterranean depths—it has been elaborated, just like language, by that human reality [*Dasein*] which is at once *Mitsein* and separation (*TSS* 47; TA; *LDS* I, 89).

In none of these instances does Beauvoir suggest that *Mitsein* has some obviously positive or normative value. She does not imply, to be more specific, that the *way* in which human beings, either as heterosexual couples or on a larger scale, are "with" one another is inherently marked in any way by generosity, friendship, reciprocity, or any other ethically laudable feature. Note that in quotation (1), for example, the phrase "based on solidarity and friendship" is restrictive and thereby denotes a particular kind of human community, one that, Beauvoir is saying, cannot plausibly be construed as being within Dasein's grasp in any pure, uncomplicated way. Indeed, the natural reading of the quotation, at least to my ear, has Beauvoir saying that we must not construe *Mitsein* as a phenomenon that is foundationally characterized by solidarity and friendship. In quotation (2), Beauvoir is clearly not suggesting that "the original *Mitsein*" that binds men and women is one of reciprocity. What she is suggesting is that since sexual reproduction requires the existence of male and female elements, women, unlike other systematically oppressed peoples, cannot even dream of eradicating their oppression by converting their oppressors into versions of themselves. One might be inclined to charge Beauvoir with heterosexism on the basis of this passage, but her observation that women and men are inevitably and intimately thrown together in this world entails, if anything, that their "original *Mitsein*" is part of the problem, not (necessarily, at least) the basis of a solution. I take it that this reading of this phrase applies equally well to quotation (4). Quotation (5) is part of a discussion of the psychoanalytic discovery of symbolism in dreams. That we tend to draw on a common stock of symbols is not some mysterious mystical phenomenon (as a Jungian might argue), Beauvoir suggests. Rather, it is a product of the simple fact of the *Mitsein*—of our sharing of the world or, if you prefer, of various worlds or what we like to call "cultures."

Quotation (3), with which I also launched this paper, tempts us more than any other, I suspect, to imagine that by *Mitsein* Beauvoir means to suggest some currently existing, fully human but at present exclusively or at least predominantly male fellowship. I do not find this reading convincing, but I will not be in a position to say why until after I look briefly at Eva Gothlin's views. My quick perusal of the other quotations was meant simply to increase the plausibility of the idea that Beauvoir conceives of our being-with others as a simple, if fateful ontological *fact:* the world of any single individual just is, inevitably and through and through, a world shared with others. It's a simple fact insofar as it says nothing, inherently, about the nature of our mutual state. And it's a fateful fact insofar it creates at least as many philosophical problems as it solves: if the *Mitsein* means that I no longer must find a way beyond the nightmarish Cartesian possibility that I am fundamentally alone, it also means that I must fight for my own identity—and indeed, fight for the courage to have the *desire* to have an identity—in a world in which the path of least resistance endlessly tempts me just to melt into the crowd. For Heidegger, if this limb I'm going out on can bear just a little more weight, *the* challenge to the human being, whose world is inevitably a world of human beings, is to negotiate a path to authenticity not only *through* the "bond," in Bergoffen's argot, but also *against* it (as when Nietzsche argues in *The Birth of Tragedy* that culture both constricts us, in some instances even to death, and at the same time serves as the medium through which we must develop our humanity).

My claim that Beauvoir's appropriation of Heidegger's notion of *Mitsein* is not necessarily one of generosity, harmony, cooperation, and friendship jibes with Gothlin's interpretation of the term, a term Gothlin regards as "central to the philosophy of Simone de Beauvoir" (*Sex and Existence*, 220). Although, as Gothlin observes, Beauvoir does not use the term *Mitsein* before *The Second Sex*, from her earliest philosophical essays she espouses a picture of the human being as fundamentally, ontologically dependent on and depended on by other human beings; "*Mitsein*," then, according to Gothlin, names this interdependence.[21] Unlike Bergoffen, Gothlin sees no inherent conflict between the Heideggerian and Hegelian strands of *The Second Sex*. According to Gothlin's Beauvoir, the apparent tension between the idea of *Mitsein* as interdependence and Hegel's insistence on the inevitability of conflict among human beings is to be resolved by paying heed to the essential *historicity* of Beauvoir's account of *Mitsein* (a historicity that itself is to be understood, Gothlin notes, as an homage to Hegel and his vision of the historical unfolding of the human spirit, or *Geist*).

On Gothlin's view, if I understand it correctly, in *The Second Sex* Beauvoir in effect appeals to three distinctive types of *Mitsein*, corresponding to three stages in human history. The first is an "original" *Mitsein* among human beings, and in particular among men and women. Of this first type or moment of *Mitsein*, Gothlin writes,

> For Beauvoir, the human being, both in its infancy and in the infancy of humanity, is *Mitsein*. The human being does not originally experience himself or herself as separate, but as part of the All, in symbiosis with the mother, and as part of a collective, respectively. (*Sex and Existence,* 221)

In a second stage of human history, this original *Mitsein*, characterized by what Gothlin calls "symbiosis," degenerates in the wake of conflicts produced by men's—male human beings'—demands for Hegelian recognition from one another (*Sex and Existence,* 222). And yet, Gothlin argues, Beauvoir identifies a second kind of *Mitsein* persisting even throughout such conflicts and functioning as a sort of cultural glue, one producing what Gothlin calls "common features and symbols in any given epoch among people living under similar social conditions" (221). Because the idea of *Mitsein* as cultural glue is compatible with the idea of intra-cultural conflict, Gothlin argues, Beauvoir's superimposition of Hegel and Heidegger, although yielding a "somewhat ambiguous picture" (221), nevertheless works. Heidegger's notion of *Mitsein* helps Beauvoir to analyze the shared social underpinnings of culture, while Hegel's conceptualization of social history as produced through conflict and struggle allows us to understand how these cultures evolve and, in particular, how women's oppression is to be transcended ("Simone de Beauvoir's Philosophy of History," 50).

The hope that Beauvoir harbors for this transcendence suggests to Gothlin that there is a third conception of *Mitsein* at work in *The Second Sex*, namely, the consciously created solidarity that follows in the wake of the resolution of various master-slave conflicts as human beings come to bestow reciprocal recognition upon one another. Although Gothlin doesn't quite put the point this way, I think one could sum up her understanding of the crucial function of *Mitsein* in *The Second Sex* as follows: it gives Beauvoir an ontological basis for imagining that women's demands for recognition from men might ultimately issue in a sort of reciprocity between the sexes characterized by, in Bergoffen's idiom, generosity, the gift, and the bond. Unlike the Sartre of *Being and Nothingness*, whose Cartesian understanding of the ontological grounds of subjectivity is radically atomistic and who thus regards any sort of robust reciprocity of recognition as metaphysically impossible, Beauvoir's Heideggerian understanding of the human being as *primordially* and *socially* Being-with gives her the conceptual tools to reject Sartre's picture and to encourage us women to dare to demand what Gothlin calls "a consciously created *Mitsein*" (222).

This brings us back to quotation (3) above, in which Beauvoir announces that in *The Second Sex* she will explore what happens when women, "trying to make their escape from the sphere hitherto assigned them, ... aspire to participate in the human *Mitsein*." Gothlin's analysis gives us the means to understand Beauvoir here as suggesting, not that women (in certain circumstances may) aspire to join some sort of *preexisting* human (read: male) fellowship, but that they can come to aspire consciously to *create* such a fellowship—as though there is no genuinely human *Mitsein* apart from women's aspirations to participate in it. I think that this way of reading the quotation brings us a step closer to what Beauvoir had in mind in her appropriation of the notion of *Mitsein*. To see why I think we're not quite there yet, however, I need to spend a few moments sketching the broad outlines of my own understanding of what is going on philosophically in *The Second Sex*.[22]

My interpretation begins with the claim that in *The Second Sex* Beauvoir is attempting to understand why both men and women are so heavily invested in the fact of sex difference and why, in particular, this investment tempts men to play the role of Absolute Subject and women that of Inessential Other. Beauvoir's discovery, I argue, is that in their different ways both men and women are endeavoring to avoid something fundamental about what it is to be a human being, namely, that one is always both a subject (or, in the Hegelian-Sartrean terminology, "for-itself") and an object (or "in-itself")—and she clearly does retain at least this Cartesian distinction in *The Second Sex*. Even in her pre–*Second Sex* writings, Beauvoir, following Hegel, calls this condition of being simultaneously both subject and object *ambiguity*. But it is not until she starts thinking about ambiguity in the context of her inquiry into the nature of sex difference (and specifically, of what it is or means to be a woman) that she begins to develop a detailed, original, convincing picture of exactly what this ambiguity is like and why it is so difficult for us to bear it.

Beauvoir's picture deviates markedly from both Hegel's and Sartre's understanding of what horrifies us about our unstable status as subjects and objects. For both Hegel and Sartre, we come to experience this instability under the objectifying pressure of another person's judgment—of the "Look," in Sartre's parlance. Hegel famously claims that the natural response to this pressure is to try to get the Looker to recognize my fundamental humanity and not to freeze me as essentially whatever (mere) thing his judgment entails I am. Sartre stresses the idea, at best downplayed in Hegel, that, far from avoiding petrifaction, people often invite it (and thereby consign themselves to a species of thinghood or slavery) in the bad faith that they might thereby succeed in abrogating responsibility for their humanity.

Beauvoir's twofold discovery in *The Second Sex* is that these two responses to the phenomenon of the Look tend to split along the lines of sex and that both of them express a desire for petrifaction. Men, she tries to show, harbor the paradoxical wish to be objectified in the eyes of women as relentlessly existentially free—that is, as objects that are *essentially* non-objects. And women, she claims, are happy to pretend to reify men in this way, as long as it means that they can fantasize that playing this role absolves them of the need to confront and embrace their own fundamental existential freedom.[23] But what exactly is so threatening about this freedom? Beauvoir's answer to this question is complicated, and it would take me too far afield to explore it (let alone the question of exactly what existential freedom *is*) in any depth here. But I submit that at least a piece of the answer is that coming to terms with one's fundamental freedom requires acceptance of the fact that one's relationship to the world is not fixed: that nothing guarantees your place—your significance—in the world. This, for Beauvoir, is the truth in the Cartesian picture.[24] And *The Second Sex* is an exhaustive account of the ways we take advantage of sex difference to avoid reckoning with this truth (and, of course, of the ways people in power systematically deny others the opportunity to do this reckoning).

Beauvoir, on my reading of *The Second Sex,* believes that overcoming our present condition will require coming to terms with our ambiguity. The task is to accept oneself and others as simultaneously both subjects and objects. Notoriously, Sartre thought this task impossible. Hegel, in *The Phenomenology of Spirit,* was not so pessimistic. But he thought the only way to reconcile our dual nature would be for individuals to identify themselves fully with their cultures. For Beauvoir, this sort of identification, one in which cultural criticism becomes obsolete, is both unrealistic and undesirable. It is unrealistic because the sort of struggle for mastery that Hegel so memorably describes in the master-slave dialectic is on Beauvoir's view perennially essential to what it is to be human: under cover of attempting to master others, we are constantly struggle to master our own ambiguity.

Where Beauvoir diverges from Sartre is on the question of whether this struggle is destined to be conducted in bad faith and in metaphysical isolation from others (i.e., under the Sartrean condition that only one person at a time in any given encounter can be a subject). On Beauvoir's view, we make progress when the struggle comes to take the internal form of finding the courage to offer up our subjective selves to the reifying gaze of others. The hallmark of subjectivity for Beauvoir is the willingness to be the object of another person's judgment, which entails the willingness for continual expressivity, continual exposure. The willingness to judge the world and be judged by it also entails both a rejection of Hegel's synthesis between the individual and his or her society and a fundamental commitment to an ongoing practice of cultural criticism. (Needless to say, I think *The Second Sex* enacts this commitment at least as well as it argues for it.) But committing ourselves to this productive way of coming to terms with our ambiguity is incompatible with our investment in the current social meanings of sex difference.

It is the concept of the *Mitsein* that allows Beauvoir to make sense of the depth of this investment. *Mitsein* means for Beauvoir not that human beings are primordially bonded together in some salutary way or even that they are interdependent—socially, psychologically, or biologically. Rather, my being-with others is foundationally important insofar as it endlessly provides me with the means, the cultural resources, to hide my ambiguity from myself. But at the same time, as Gothlin rightly stresses, the *Mitsein* is also the fount of our opportunities, not least as men and women, for genuinely reciprocal recognition. My being-with others, our sharing of a humanly meaningful world, leaves open the possibility that I may invite them to judge me freely, not as I wish to be reified, but as they genuinely—in their own assumed freedom—are inclined to experience me. What the other's free judgment can dramatize to me is the extent to which my struggle for recognition is in essence a struggle with myself: I struggle to avoid exploiting our being-with one another to get another person to provide me a false, fixed picture of myself. And it is in thereby finding the courage to let myself and the other be that I aspire to participate in—and not just to subject myself to—the human *Mitsein*.

Notes

A version of this paper appeared in *Continental Philosophy Review* 34, no. 3 (July 2001). I am grateful to Peg Simons both for inviting me to give the conference talk at the annual meeting of the Society for Phenomenology and Existential Philosophy in October 2000 that led to both papers and for soliciting this version of the material for the present volume. Thanks also to those in attendance at a talk I gave on Beauvoir and Heidegger at the New School University in April 2001, especially Alice Crary and Jay Bernstein, and at the "Engaging with Simone de Beauvoir Conference" at Oxford in July 2001. I am especially thankful to Eva Gothlin for her friendship and her inspiring work, on which, as will become obvious, I am deeply dependent.

1. Simone de Beauvoir, *The Second Sex*, translated by H. M. Parshley (New York: Vintage, 1989), xxxv. The relevant passage reads: *"nous pourrons comprendre à quelles difficultés elles* [women] *se heurtent au moment où, essayant de s'évader de la sphère qui leur a été jusqu'à présent assignée, elles prétendent participer au* mitsein *humain"* (*Le Deuxième Sexe* [Paris: Gallimard, 1949], I:32). Parshley translates: "we shall be able to envisage the difficulties in their way as, endeavoring to make their escape from the sphere hitherto assigned them, they aspire to full membership in the human race." The translation of "mitsein *humain*" as "human race" of course preempts the question of why and how Beauvoir employs the Heideggerian neologism *Mitsein* in this climactic final passage of the introduction to *The Second Sex*. (Future references to *The Second Sex* will be cited as follows: *TSS* [pp.]; *LDS* [vol. #, pp.]. I will use "TA" to indicate that I have amended the English translation.)

2. The locus classicus of papers on the inadequacies of the English translation of *The Second Sex* is Margaret A. Simons's "The Silencing of Simone de Beauvoir: Guess What's Missing from *The Second Sex*," *Women's Studies International Forum* 6, no. 5 (1983): 559–64. The paper is reprinted in Simons's book *Beauvoir and* The Second Sex:

Feminism, Race, and the Origins of Existentialism (Lanham, Md.: Rowman & Littlefield, 1999), 61–71. See also Toril Moi's important "While We Wait: The English Translation of *The Second Sex*," *Signs* 27, no. 4 (Summer 2002): 1005–36.

3. Even a careful reader of the English translation of *The Second Sex* might be surprised to find the word *Dasein* on this list. Evidently unbeknownst to Parshley, the translator, the French phrase for the German *Dasein* (Heidegger's signature—and difficult—term of art for what it means to be a human being) is *"la réalité humaine."* Of course, the translation "human reality" would have been bad enough, given its unfamiliarity to Anglophone readers, but Parshley, disastrously, chooses the phrase "human nature." Beauvoir speaks to this problem in a 1985 interview with Margaret Simons (reprinted in *Beauvoir and* The Second Sex, 94): "[Y]ou tell me that he [Parshley] speaks of human nature whereas I have never believed—nor Sartre either, and on this point I am his disciple—we never believed in human nature. So it's a serious mistake to speak of 'human nature' instead of 'human reality,' which is a Heideggerian term. I was infused with Heidegger's philosophy, and when I speak about human reality, that is, about man's presence in the world, I'm not speaking about human nature, it's completely different."

4. Of course, whatever cachet Heidegger had in France in 1949 was complicated by vexing questions about the nature and significance of his collaboration with the Nazis. Mindfulness of this fact helps deflate the temptation to assume that Beauvoir's use of Heideggerian concepts is merely gratuitous.

5. Notable revisionist readings of *The Second Sex* as a work of philosophy are to be found in the following works: Sonia Kruks, *Situation and Human Existence* (London: Unwin Hyman, 1990); Margaret A. Simons, ed., *Feminist Interpretations of Simone de Beauvoir* (University Park, Pa.: Penn State Press, 1995); Eva Lundgren-Gothlin, *Sex and Existence: Simone de Beauvoir's* The Second Sex (Hanover, N.H.: Wesleyan University Press/University Press of New England, 1996); Karen Vintges, *Philosophy as Passion: The Thinking of Simone de Beauvoir* (Bloomington: Indiana University Press, 1996); Debra Bergoffen, *The Philosophy of Simone de Beauvoir: Gendered Phenomenologies, Erotic Generosities* (Albany: State University of New York Press, 1997); Toril Moi, *What Is a Woman? and Other Essays* (New York: Oxford, 1999); Simons, *Beauvoir and* The Second Sex; Kristana Arp, *The Bonds of Freedom: Simone de Beauvoir's Existentialist Ethics* (Chicago: Open Court, 2001); and my *Simone de Beauvoir, Philosophy, and Feminism* (New York: Columbia University Press, 2001).

6. The general lack of interest in exploring the connection is sometimes explicit and sometimes implicit. The Finnish philosopher Sara Heinämaa, who has done first-rate work on Beauvoir and Husserl, for example, vehemently denies that Heidegger's philosophy plays any significant role in *The Second Sex*. Heinämaa's view, voiced in panel discussions at a 50th anniversary celebration of the publication of *The Second Sex* in Paris in January of 1999 and at the Eastern Division meetings of the American Philosophical Association in December of 2000, is that since Husserl and (his former student) Heidegger were heavily critical of one another's views in the wake of Heidegger's publication of *Being and Time*, one cannot plausibly maintain that Beauvoir appropriates the views of both thinkers. A central goal of this essay and of my book *Simone de Beauvoir, Philosophy, and Feminism* is to challenge the conception of appropriation implicit in Heinämaa's view.

Other of Beauvoir's philosophically astute readers have accepted that Heidegger's philosophy influenced Beauvoir but have evidently found the connection not worth exploring at any length. For instance, in her watershed book on Beauvoir and ethics, *Philosophy as Passion*, Karen Vintges unhesitatingly acknowledges Heidegger's strong influence on *The Second Sex* (see, e.g., 34, 42, 142–43, and 146–47) but stops short of exploring details. See note 7 below for a crucial exception to the rule that feminist philosophical readings of Beauvoir tend to ignore Heidegger's influence on her thought.

7. In "Reading Simone de Beauvoir with Martin Heidegger" (delivered at the Eastern Division meetings of the American Philosophical Association in December 2000; published in French as *"Lire Simone de Beauvoir à la lumière de Heidegger"* in *Les Temps Modernes* 619 [juin–juillet 2000]: 53–75; and in English in *The Cambridge Companion to Simone de Beauvoir,* edited by Claudia Card [Cambridge: Cambridge University Press, 2003]), Eva Gothlin hypothesizes that the reluctance of readers to take Beauvoir's appropriation of Heidegger's thought seriously can be traced to two factors: first, Heidegger's notorious flirtation with Nazism and the ensuing postwar debates among French intellectuals about how to read his philosophy, with or against his politics; and, second, the French publication in 1947 of parts of Heidegger's scathingly anti-Sartrean "Letter on Humanism." I regard my own speculation on this front as complementing Gothlin's. For several years now Gothlin has been for the most part shouting into the wind, arguing—absolutely correctly, on my view—that one cannot make the best sense of Simone de Beauvoir's philosophical achievements, in *The Second Sex* and elsewhere, apart from a willingness to take seriously the way Beauvoir appropriates certain key concepts in Heidegger's *Being and Time.* "Reading Simone de Beauvoir with Martin Heidegger" goes far beyond her previous attempts to drive this point home (for these attempts, see note 21). Those who are still loathe to accept her view now face the daunting task of reckoning with the mountain of evidence that she so cogently interprets to support it.

8. Probably the most sustained attempt, at least in English, to work up such an understanding of *Mitsein* is to be found in Frederick A. Olafson's *Heidegger and the Ground of Ethics: A Study of Mitsein* (New York: Cambridge University Press, 1998). This reading of *Mitsein* rests on a straightforward interpretation (which I contest in some detail below) of Heidegger's explicit claim that the human being—or *Dasein*, in his idiom—by its nature comports itself in its Being-with-others (its *Mitsein*) in the mode of "care" [*Sorge*] and specifically in the mode of "solicitude" [*Fürsorge*]. The claim is proffered by Heidegger in section 26 of *Being and Time,* pp. 153–63, of the English translation by John Macquarrie and Edward Robinson (New York: Harper and Row, 1962).

9. Toril Moi, whose command of the secondary literature on Beauvoir is unparalleled, reports that "the great majority of American feminists criticize Beauvoir for being male-identified in some way or other, and for failing to appreciate the virtues of women" (*Simone de Beauvoir: The Making of an Intellectual Woman* [Cambridge: Blackwell, 1994], 182). One finds the "masculinism" charge expressed explicitly or implicitly in the writings of, for example, Stevie Smith (see "The Devil's Doorway," *The Spectator,* no. 6543 [November 20, 1953]: 602–603); Mary Evans (see *Simone de Beauvoir: A Feminist Mandarin* [New York: Tavistock Publications, 1985], 56–57); and Jean Grimshaw (see *Philosophy and Feminist Thinking* [Minneapolis: University of Minnesota Press, 1986], 45–46).

10. The page numbers here refer to the 1966 version of *Being and Nothingness*, translated by Hazel E. Barnes (New York: Pocket Books).

11. The question of exactly who the master and slave are for Hegel (archetypes? historical figures? everymen?) is beyond the scope of this paper. What matters for my purposes here is that Beauvoir appropriates the master-slave dialectic in an effort to understand the everyday dynamics between human beings, and especially between men and women.

12. Beauvoir doesn't just flatly assert either this claim or the one about women that follows. But to provide her argument for the idea that there is a gender gap here would be to take us too far afield. I provide a sketch of this argument and explore in detail her appropriations of Hegel's and Sartre's views in *Simone de Beauvoir, Philosophy, and Feminism*, chapters 3–7.

13. See Cian Séan Dorr, "The Simplicity of Everything" (Ph.D. diss., Princeton University, 2002), 74; on the Web at www.pitt.edu/~csd6/SimplicityOfEverything. pdf/.

14. In this exposition of the hammer example, I am taking my cues from David Cerbone's excellent essay "Composition and Constitution: Heidegger's Hammer," *Philosophical Topics* 27, no. 2 (Fall 1999).

15. I am not suggesting that we take Descartes' understanding of his motivations at face value. Sometimes—frequently, most likely—philosophers have at best a fuzzy or self-serving story to tell about why they are doing what they are doing. Thus, one can contend, as for example Susan Bordo does in her critique of Cartesianism, that what actually motivated Descartes and his ilk was a desire to push Mother Nature away in response to anxiety that she was trying to push *them* away herself. My point still stands. (See Bordo, "The Cartesian Masculinization of Thought," *Signs: Journal of Women in Culture and Society* 11, no. 3 [1986]: 439–56. As it happens, I'm not convinced by Bordo's story. I explain why in chapter 2 of *Simone de Beauvoir.*)

16. "Ready-to-hand" is a central term of art for Heidegger. It signifies the "for-us" nature of the things in the world (like hammers) with which we interact and is to be contrasted with the "present-at-hand" nature of such things, their properties as physical or abstract entities, which comes to the fore only when we conceptualize or study them apart from the roles they play in our lives, as when they break down—or when we philosophize about them (in, of course, a non-Heideggerian way).

17. All quotations are from *Being and Time*, 158.

18. Here is a place where I see lines of affinity between Heidegger's views in *Being and Time* and those of Wittgenstein in *Philosophical Investigations,* although of course this is not the place to work out the exact nature of any such connections.

19. It seems to me crucial that here we have another poor Parshleyan translation on our hands. The French reads as follows: *"tout être humain concret est toujours singulièrement situé."* What has dropped out in the English version is the idea of being singularly *situated*—where "situation," it is easy to show, is a central technical term in *The Second Sex* (and in Beauvoir's earlier works and Sartre's *Being and Nothingness,* for that matter). So Beauvoir is *not* saying that people are (metaphysically) separate individuals; she's saying that each person's "situation" is different. One needn't have an account of "situation" in order to see that Beauvoir is not at this juncture expressing her "Cartesian roots," to use Bergoffen's phrase.

20. Eva Lundgren-Gothlin says in *Sex & Existence: Simone de Beauvoir's 'The Sec-*

ond Sex', translated from the Swedish by Linda Schenck (Hanover, N.H.: Wesleyan University Press/University Press of New England, 1996), 220, that she counts seven uses of the word in *The Second Sex.* I can find only five. I leave it to the reader to assess whether my interpretation of Beauvoir's use of *"Mitsein"* illuminates these passages.

21. See Gothlin, "Simone de Beauvoir's Existential Phenomenology and Philosophy of History in *Le Deuxième Sexe,"* in *The Existential Phenomenology of Simone de Beauvoir,* ed. Wendy O'Brien and Lester E. Embree (Dordrecht: Kluwer, 2001). See also Gothlin's analysis of "interdependence" in her "Gender and Ethics in the Philosophy of Simone de Beauvoir," *NORA: Nordic Journal for Women's Studies* 3, no. 1 (1995). Gothlin also convincingly connects Beauvoir's interest in the activity of "disclosure" with Heidegger's emphasis in *Being and Time* on "disclosedness." See her "Simone de Beauvoir's Ethics and Its Relation to Current Moral Philosophy," *Simone de Beauvoir Studies* 14 (1998). In "Reading Simone de Beauvoir with Martin Heidegger" (see above, n. 7), Gothlin implies that the notion of interdependence *(interdépendance)* plays the role of *Mitsein* in Beauvoir's book *The Ethics of Ambiguity.*

22. I fill in the details and provide support for the interpretation I'm about to summarize in *Simone de Beauvoir, Philosophy, and Feminism.*

23. In *The Second Sex* Beauvoir has much to say about the temptations of petrifaction and why they tend to cleave into a masculine and a feminine version. Exploring this material is of course beyond the bounds of the present essay.

24. In appealing to the idea of the truth "in" the Cartesian picture, I mean to be following Stanley Cavell, who at many junctures in his writing speaks of the truth "in" skepticism. Cavell is not suggesting that skepticism *is* true. Rather, the idea is that there is a truth about our relationship to the world—in Cavell's idiom, that it is not, or not fundamentally, one of *knowledge*—that lies at the heart of expressions of skepticism. (For stimulating discussions of the relevant stretch of Cavell's thought, see Sanford Sheih's "The Truth of Skepticism," *Reading Cavell,* ed. Shieh and Alice Crary [New York: Routledge, 2005] and Edward Minar, "Wittgenstein, Cavell, and Other Minds Skepticism," *Wittgenstein and Scepticism,* ed. Denis McManus [New York: Routledge, 2004].)

MARRIAGE, AUTONOMY, AND THE

FEMININE PROTEST

Debra B. Bergoffen

5

MARRIAGE, AUTONOMY, AND THE FEMININE PROTEST

MARRIAGE, AUTONOMY, AND THE FEMININE PROTEST

To date, most feminist discussions of marriage have been either critical or reactive. Having declared that it is immoral to treat married women as property and unjust to position the wife as subject to the husband, feminists have either rejected the institution of marriage as exploitive or argued that they as individuals have found ways to make marriage work. The effect of this strategy has been to cede the territory of positive marriage discourse to those who speak of family values in nostalgic and patriarchal terms. According to this discourse, the meaning of marriage lies in the natural and/or divine order that prescribes both the necessity of marriage and the structure of the marriage relationship. None of this is helpful to/for feminists, for the laws of God and nature are generally read as justifying the subordination of women and as apologies for patriarchy.

It is not enough for feminists who value marriage to declare that marriage can escape its patriarchal trappings. To reclaim marriage for feminists, we need to do more. We need to make the case that patriarchal marriage is a perversion of the meaning of marriage and that this perversion is of concern to feminists. To make this case, we need to attend to the fact that as an erotic and ethical relationship that is also established as a political institution, marriage points to the relationship among the erotic, the ethical, and the political. Given these considerations, the question to be asked is this: What is the state being asked to recognize when it legitimates the erotic relationship? In asking this question, I am pursuing the hypothesis that there is a direct relationship between a state's ability to pursue justice and its understanding of marriage such that, when a state sanctions marriage traditions that betray the meaning of marriage, it forecloses the possibility of justice.

I do not think the prevalent misunderstandings of marriage are innocent. Neither do I think they reflect a conspiracy of men against women, for it is not only men who take up these misunderstandings, and it is not only women who protest them. As neither innocent nor personal, these misunderstanding are, however, structural and material. They are the marks of a patriarchal system that erases the ethical meanings of the erotic and ignores the political implications of these meanings. Simone de Beauvoir's *The Second Sex* (1952) exposes the relationship between patriarchal marriage arrangements and the exploitation of women. It also shows that women are not entirely duped by, or complicitous with, patriarchal marriage ideologies. In Beauvoir's words, "woman may fail to lay claim to the status of subject because she lacks definite resources, because she feels the necessary bond that ties her to man regardless of reciprocity, and because she is often very pleased with her role as the *Other*" (1952, xxiv–xxv). Beauvoir does not directly develop the implications of this commitment of women to the bond; but if this phrase is read within the context of *Pyrrhus et Cinéas* (1944), *The Ethics of Ambiguity* (1948), and "Must We Burn Sade?" (1966) to take it as the sound of her muted voice, these words point to a certain protest on the part of women regarding the erasure of the ethical significance of intimate relationships (Bergoffen 1997, 164–65).

Sigmund Freud (1961, 50–51) and G. W. F. Hegel (1955, 466–82; 1967, 114–15) also acknowledge this feminine protest. In their view, however, the antagonism between the married woman and the state speaks to a problem with women rather than to a deficiency of the state. The social contract tradition takes a different approach (see Pateman 1988). Distinguishing the private from the public spheres, it isolates women from the state as it allows the state to regulate the rights of married men and women. Applying a unique logic that identifies marriage as both natural and political, social contract discourse manages to insulate the state from the challenge of the feminine protest. Hegel, Freud, and the social contract thinkers are part of a long and tangled conversation concerning women, marriage, and politics. In joining this conversation as an heir of Beauvoir, I ask whether it has anything helpful to say to feminists.

Beauvoir was no fan of marriage. Neither her personal choices nor her writings give us reason to believe that she considered the institution of marriage as she knew it to be conducive to the life of an independent, liberated woman. Beauvoir did not, however, consider the question of marriage closed. Seeing it as a living institution, she saw it as subject to change and transformation. Consider her analysis of marriage in *The Second Sex*. Beauvoir begins by noting, "Marriage is the destiny traditionally offered to women by society" (1952, 425). The key term here is *destiny;* for at the heart of Beauvoir's critique of marriage is the fact that for most women, marriage is not a choice but a destiny. Furthermore, because it is a woman's but not a man's destiny, marriage, framed as a contractual relationship, is not a contract between equals and not, therefore, a reciprocal relationship. It is a contract where men become women's guardians, where men appropriate women's reproductive and productive labor, and where women are duty-bound to be sexually available to their husbands. Insisting that individuals are not to blame for the failure of marriage, but that the institution itself is perverted, Beauvoir identifies the concept of duty as key to the perversity of marriage. She writes, "To hold and proclaim that a man and a woman, who may not even have chosen each other, *are in duty bound* to satisfy each other in every way throughout their lives is a monstrosity that necessarily gives rise to hypocrisy, lying, hostility and unhappiness" (1952, 479). True to her existentialist commitment to the concept of transcendence, however, Beauvoir insists that marriage is not a static institution; it is in transition: "Economic evolution in woman's situation is in process of upsetting [*bouleveger*] the institution of marriage: it is becoming a union freely entered into upon by the consent of two independent persons; the obligations of the two contracting parties are personal and reciprocal. . . . Woman is no longer limited to the reproductive function which has lost in part its character as natural servitude and has come to be regarded as a function to be voluntarily assumed" (1952, 425).

As women achieve economic parity, they will no longer be obliged to marry. The relationship between marriage and duty will have to be severed. Perhaps. There is still the matter of the state. Marriage is never merely a personal matter. It is also a social and political affair. As traditionally conceived, the aim of marriage is "to make the economic and sexual union of men and women serve the interests of society" (Beauvoir 1952, 434). It is possible, then, that the economic equality that frees women from the duty to marry will incite the state to impose marriage as a duty on men and women so that its interests may continue to be served. As an institution in transition, marriage, according to Beauvoir, may become a contract freely entered into by both individuals, or it may become a union mandated by the state (1952, 425–26). There is also a third possibility. It would recognize that "the marriage ceremony displays its universal and abstract significance: a man and a woman are united in accordance with symbolic ritual in full view of all; but in the secrecy of the marriage bed they are concrete and single individuals alone together, and all eyes are averted from their embraces" (1952, 440). This third possibility would draw on this ambiguity of marriage as a political and an intimate relationship to identify marriage as an institution that recalled the state to its duty to recognize the ethical ground of its political practices.

Between Beauvoir's critique of patriarchal marriage and her view of marriage as an institution in transition is her statement that "modern marriage can be understood only in light of the past it tends to perpetuate in part" (1952, 426). Working from this statement, the question becomes: Is there anything in the institution of marriage worth perpetuating? I believe that there is. It concerns the value of the erotic bond. Yet the question returns: Is marriage the best way to preserve this value?

When it comes to assessing the relationship between marriage and the erotic, Beauvoir's discussion becomes tortured. She finds that traditional marriage cannot create the best conditions for awakening female eroticism, but she notes that Americans are working to integrate marriage and sexuality (1952, 439). She accuses marriage of killing the erotic in its effort to regulate it, but she also finds that marriage can be the site of genuine sexual intimacy (1952, 444). Amidst these conflicting assessments, Beauvoir notes that though marriage is supposed to give ethical standing to a woman's erotic life, it actually suppresses it (1952, 436). This breach between the *ought* and the *is* identifies both the failure and promise of marriage. A feminist defense of marriage would call upon marriage to bridge the breach. It would demand that marriage fulfill its promise to give ethical standing to the couple's (not just the woman's) erotic life as it respects the secrets of the bedroom (that is, without prejudice to the desires articulated in or by the couple).

Attending to the complexity of *The Second Sex*'s analysis of marriage, I do not think Beauvoir's critique of patriarchal marriage ought to be taken as a critique of marriage per se. It certainly ought not be mistaken for a critique of the couple or of heterosexual erotic life. Given the importance Beauvoir ascribes to the erotic, and given the ethical possibilities she invests in the (not necessarily heterosexual) couple, I am lead to rethink the meaning of marriage (Beauvoir 1952, 480; Bergoffen 1997, 196). This thinking takes me back to Beauvoir's *The Ethics of Ambiguity* (1948).

For some time now, I have been reading *The Ethics of Ambiguity*'s description of our twofold intentionality as key to Beauvoir's analysis of the ambiguity of the human condition (Bergoffen 1997, 76–82). Lately, I have come to see this description as a way to mark the difference between the ethical and the political modes of existence and as a way to understand the relationship between these distinct existential modalities. Furthermore, following Beauvoir's injunction to philosophize in the concrete, I have come to see marriage as the place where the esoteric issues of intentionality and the abstract questions of ethics and politics are lived in the concrete particular.

We have long known that marriage is the place where women's bodies are on the line. The bodies of battered women confront us with dramatic examples of the ways in which marriage legitimates the abuse of women. Changing laws regarding domestic violence and marital rape, however, alert us to changing concepts regarding a husband's rights over his wife. I see these changes, as well as the reactionary discourses of the Promise Keepers and the Million Man March, as alerting us to the fact that marriage is the place where the desires of the erotic body and the demands of the body politic intersect, and as alerting us to the fact that we will not have a politics of justice unless and until we attend to the ethical meanings and political implications of erotic desire.

We have often heard it said that a state should be judged according to the way it treats its children, its poor, or its elderly. The point of this essay is to propose that we judge a state by the ways in which it institutionalizes marriage. I propose that a state that perverts the erotic ethical meanings of marriage, that is, a state that sees marriage either as an exclusively political institution (fascism) or as an institution that is irrelevant to politics (classical democracies) cannot be just, for such states refuse to recognize their debt to the ethical and refuse to be informed by their relationship to the ethical.[1]

It is often helpful to approach complex issues through small clues. In this case, the clue comes from Beauvoir's discussion of marriage in *La Longue marche* (1969). In writing about China, Beauvoir argues that political freedom is impossible so long as marriage and erotic desire are severed. A politics of liberation is tied, Beauvoir tells us, to the abolition of the rule of the father. So long as the children are married according to the father's desire rather than their own, so long as one's legitimate/legal erotic life is severed from one's desire, politics has no ethical ground from which to pursue justice (1969, 124). Beauvoir did not pursue her insight into the relationship between the politics of marriage and the possibilities of justice. She assumed that the marriage issue in China was settled. Everyone knew that the Chinese communists were opposed to family arranged marriages. Beauvoir assumed that this was an attack on patriarchy and a recognition of the relationship between validating erotic desire and political justice. Had she been able to read Jung Chang's *Wild Swans* (1991), she would have had second thoughts. In identifying the communists with the liberated couple, Beauvoir was as deceived as Jung Chang's mother's friend who saw running away to join the communists as the only way to escape a family-arranged marriage and to marry her beloved (Chang 1991, 124). These lovers presumably learned what Jung's parents learned: the party assumed the role of the patriarch. Marriage and permission to talk about love required the party's consent (1991, 127, 137). Given Beauvoir's critique of the first emperor Song's Edict of 966 and 967, her assessment of the Chinese Republic might have been less glowing had she attended to the party's marriage regulation laws (1991, 152).

Today the right of the heterosexual couple to marry in accordance with its desire has been established in some, but not most, parts of the world. Those societies that legitimate heterosexual desire, however, only recognize the desires of those couples they define as legitimate. Structurally, then, the rule of authority continues to trump the voice of desire. Marriage's past continues to pervert its ethical and political meaning.

That neither the father nor the state has the right to legislate the intimate erotic of marriage becomes clear if we read Beauvoir's somewhat puzzling reference to the relationship between marriages grounded in the desire of the couple and the possibility of political justice as more than passing and perhaps questionable observations regarding Chinese history, and if we attend to the unique ways in which Beauvoir develops and deploys the meanings of intentionality, ambiguity, and the erotic. For whether or not her remarks speak accurately of the Chinese situation, they point to crucial strains of Beauvoir's thinking and to ways of exploring the ethical and the political meanings of marriage.

INTENTIONALITY AS A TWOFOLD DESIRE

Working with Edmund Husserl's concept of intentionality, Beauvoir determines that the bywords of phenomenology, consciousness is always consciousness of . . . , describe a twofold encounter with reality. As an intending consciousness of . . . , we reach out to the real in a mood of joyful disclosure. As human, however, we are unable to remain at or sustain this original intentionality. We necessarily and inevitably move to a subsequent intentional moment of judgment. Now we are a consciousness of . . . that reaches out to the real to take it up as world and make it our own. Not content to discover meanings, we now create meanings and imprint them on the originally disclosed phenomena (Beauvoir 1948, 12–13; Bergoffen 1997, 75–113). Discovering beauty, for example, we determine that the world ought to be beautiful. We formulate aesthetic judgments and create aesthetic standards. We hire architects to create pleasing as well as functional structures; we applaud designers who transform clothes from body coverings to fashion statements; we establish practices that produce bodies that conform to our ideals. As engaged in these projects, we envision ourselves as autonomous. That is, pursuing the desires of the second moment of intentionality, we identify ourselves as authors of the meanings of the real and authorize ourselves to create a meaningful world. Left to itself, this experience of creative mastery degenerates into a justification of domination. Bounded by the experience of the first intentional moment, however, this experience of authority accepts its limits; for the experience of the first intentional moment reveals me to myself as in relationship with, rather than as the master of, the real. Maintaining the fluidity of these experiences of intentionality, I situate myself neither as the passive conduit of the meaning of reality, nor as the autonomous master of a self-created world, but as the ambiguous being of the in-between.

With this unique description of intentionality, Beauvoir transforms consciousness from an epistemological activity to a site of contesting moods and desires. She establishes us as ambiguous, neither pure receivers of meaning nor absolute creators of meaning. Our twofoldedness puts us in two distinct relationships to the other and the world. The original relationship, the mode of disclosure and mood of wonder, situates us in the ethical, gifting stance of letting be. The secondary relationship, the mode of judgment and mood of decision, situates us in the political judgmental stance of engagement.[2] As a twofold intentionality, we are called upon to be both ethical and political; we are called upon to understand the difference between these ways of being and to recognize the legitimacy and limits of each of these ways of being. Marriage embodies this twofoldedness of our being. As an erotic relationship, marriage is the ethical site of the gifting couple. It embodies the ethical intentionality of letting be. As a promissory relationship, marriage is the political site of judgmental engagement. It embodies the decision to preserve a particular way of being. As both erotic and promissory, marriage materializes the fluidity, complexity, and contestations of our twofold intentionality.

THE ERROR OF AUTONOMY

Reading the meaning of marriage through Beauvoir's analysis of intentionality puts us at odds with the traditional democratic understanding of marriage; for this understanding is based on the social contract determination that the subject is to be understood as autonomous and that marriage is to be understood either as a relationship that transforms two individuals into a distinct autonomous moral being or as a relationship between two autonomous persons. Either way, the ambiguity of the subject is lost. With this loss we lose the meaning of marriage.

According to the social contract tradition, it is as autonomous individuals that we accept the authority of the state, and it is as autonomous persons that we establish our rights vis-à-vis the state. From this perspective, political justice is tied to recognizing and respecting human autonomy, autonomy being understood as denoting personal freedom, individual sovereignty, and subjective independence/self-sufficiency.

In appealing to the ideal of autonomy, the social contract tradition taps into a certain truth of our existence and a certain political truth. It also mistakes the part for the whole. The political and existential truth of the social contract tradition is this: as situated in the second intentional moment, we experience ourselves as autonomous, authorized to create the world in our own image. Experiencing ourselves as autonomous, we formulate judgments and take up political projects. The social contract tradition, however, sees autonomy as self-grounding. Appealing to the fiction of the state of nature, it ignores the realities of human social life and individual development and is blind to the meanings of intentionality.

The social contract tradition that grounds classical democratic theory determines that the criteria of autonomy captures the meaning of our humanity. Beauvoir's phenomenology challenges this determination. For if we follow the implications of Beauvoir's description of intentionality, the meanings and criteria of autonomy speak only to one dimension of our being. It may well be that these criteria capture the political dimensions of our being, but once they are taken for a complete account of the subject, they distort the meaning of our being as human beings. Moreover, insofar as this distortion severs the political dimensions of subjectivity (the desires of the second intentional moment) from the context of the ambiguous subject (the site of the contesting desires of two moments of intentionality), it risks becoming the ground of a politics of mastery and control rather than of justice. Understanding ourselves as autonomous beings engaged in the project of creating the world, we will not understand our obligation to keep the receptive spaces of the first moment of intentionality open. If the concept of autonomy determines our concept of ourselves, we can neither understand nor privilege the ways in which we are relational rather than independent beings. We will be hard-pressed to understand the erotic of marriage as anything other than a marginal, emotional irrationality that threatens the integrity of the political subject and the stability of the social order. We will certainly not be receptive to the idea that the erotic event is the mark of an ethical relationship that challenges the justice of a politics of autonomy.

Following Beauvoir's description of intentionality, we discover that we are ambiguous. As an original opening to otherness, as an ethical/erotic intentionality, we are the desire that gives the other the space to be an other. As a subsequent creativity, as a political intentionality, we are the desire to intercede in the spaces of the world. Given the ways in which these intentionalities contest each other, it is tempting to see them as opposed to each other. It is tempting to see one as the betrayal of the other, to privilege one over the other. Beauvoir's logic of ambiguity refuses these temptations. For though she gives a certain priority and privilege to the first moment of intentionality (the ethical), she insists on the inevitability of the second, the political intentional moment, and argues for its importance. Given Beauvoir's phenomenology, these contesting desires of intentionality establish us as ambiguous, and it is in recognition of our ambiguity that we are directed to keep the tensions of consciousness in play.

Keeping these tensions in play, however, we are directed to remember that the desires and projects of the political subject must be understood as rooted in prior intentional desires. As political, the subject is also called upon to be ethical, and it is in the first, not the second, moment of intentionality that the criteria of ethics are found; for in the ethical relationship, I address the other in the mood of the disclosing intentional moment. I acknowledge and respond to the otherness without moving either to take it up for myself or to possess it.

Translated into principles of intersubjectivity, the mood of our original opening to the world speaks the language of generosity and the gift. With this language, it establishes the criteria of the ethical relationship.

In reading Beauvoir's phenomenology as a call to set ethical limits to the political, I find her account of intentionality leading to more radical conclusions than the social contract tradition that grounds democratic thought. Social contract theory distinguishes between the meaning of autonomy as applied to myself and to others. As applied to me, the idea of autonomy authorizes me to create, remake, and impose my will upon others and the world. When applied to others, however, the idea of autonomy limits my authority; for in recognizing you as also autonomous, I am barred from establishing myself as the author who has the right to reduce you to a character in my script. Thus, the politics of autonomy acknowledges the desire to be God of the second intentional moment but constrains it by the law of mutual recognition. A phenomenology that distinguishes between the ethical and the political and that situates the ethical as the ground of the political reminds us, however, that the law of mutual recognition, insofar as it is a criteria of political intentionality, does not speak to the full complexity of our subjective/intersubjective condition. It reminds us that the desires of autonomy are constrained both from within and from without. The law of recognition constrains it from without. The ethical intentionalities of generosity constrain it from within.

As politics is the domain of the judging and creative subject, ethics is the sphere of the spontaneous and receptive subject. Here freedom does not refer to the right to make judgments, but to the pre-reflective choice to abstain from judgment. Here the activity of consciousness refers to a certain generous passivity—a way of creating an opening for the unfolding of the other and the otherness of the world. Here I do not look to enlist the other as my ally, but I receive the other as the stranger who calls me to my desire.

As a political subject, I appeal to the other to support me in my projects and to echo my judgments. As an ethical subject, I speak to the other as an elusive freedom that can be touched but not spoken for. The working body, the body activated by teleologies and projects, instantiates the creative energies of the second moment of intentionality. The erotic body, the aimless, curious, explorative body, is the concrete expression of the life of the first intentional moment; for it is as an erotic, desiring being that I am open to the touch of the other and experience the joy of the meeting without purpose. Here the body exists as flesh, and the subject exists as the freedom that circulates and intersects without enclosing or wounding. As the rallying cry of the French Revolution established fraternity as the standard of/for the political relationship, Beauvoir's phenomenology identifies the caress as the paradigm of the moral order.

Bringing Beauvoir's remarks about the history of Chinese marriage to the implications of her discussion of intentionality, we discover that in distinguishing marriages of love from marriages of alliance, and in indicating that a politics of justice must recognize the claims of the erotic, Beauvoir recalls us to Jean-Paul Sartre's discussions of the caress in *Being and Noth-*

ingness (Sartre 1966) and to her discussions of the erotic in *The Second Sex*. These discussions take up the idea of embodied consciousness to direct our attention to the fact that it is as embodied that we experience the intersubjective bond and that it is as embodied that we are vulnerable to each other. These discussions also teach us that the erotic and pragmatic bodies live this vulnerability differently. As Sartre and Beauvoir describe it, the erotic body lives its vulnerability as the risks of facticity and contingency. It reveals itself to the other as vulnerable to the other's touch. It establishes itself as desiring the other. It takes up the risks of its vulnerability for the sake of its desire and responds to the other's desire by receiving it in its contingent vulnerability. As erotic, the body takes up the risks of violation for the sake of the gift. The erotic body marks us as ethical; for it is as ethical that we accept our desire for each other as the sign of a bond with/to the other that exceeds the laws of reciprocity and recognition.

The ethical-erotic cannot be confined to any institutional arrangements. This fact has led many to see marriage as a betrayal of the erotic event. This judgment is too quick. The fact that marriage has often betrayed the ethical-erotic does not mean that it *must* betray it. Marriage is a promise—an impossible promise insofar as it promises to sustain what cannot be sustained, the erotic-ethical event—whose effect is to recognize and acknowledge our sustained desire for the other.

In following Beauvoir's description of intentionality to marriage and in understanding marriage through her twofold account of consciousness, we follow the direction, if not the letter, of Beauvoir's thought. However abstract her discussion of intentionality may seem, Beauvoir never intended it as a description of a transcendental ego. As an existentialist, Beauvoir always understood the intentionalities of consciousness as the intentionalities of a concrete, embodied, situated person. As the author of *The Second Sex*, she insisted that as concrete, embodied, and situated, we are also always and necessarily sexed and gendered. Thus, we are led to marriage. For once we move this discussion of intentionality from the abstract to the concrete, we discover that marriage lies on the cusp of the ethical and the political. It is the site where the contesting intentionalities of the ambiguous subject are materialized and lived.

Experienced from the perspective of the desiring couple, marriage speaks of the ethical-erotic event marked by the openings of the flesh and the generosities of the gift. Articulated as a public promise, however, marriage expresses a judgment. It takes up the political project of stabilizing the erotic, of preserving the place of/for the erotic-ethical event. Entering into the institution of marriage, the couple accepts the authority of the state. In accepting this authority, however, the couple reminds the state that its authority over the subject is never absolute; for as a political subject, the married person is also an ethical subject, or it is as an ethical subject that the married person becomes a political subject. None of this is meant to imply that unmarried people are less ethical persons or less competent citizens than married people. The point of this focus on marriage is to say that it articulates what is true for all of us—we are ambiguous, not autonomous—we are ethical before we are political; it is only insofar as we recognize ourselves as ethical that we can become political subjects competent to pursue justice. Marriage institutionalizes this recognition. The mistake of arguing that because the married person instantiates the ethical ground of the political, only married persons recognize the ethical ground of the political, or of claiming that in recognizing its obligation to the married subject the state is freed from recognizing its obligation to the unmarried subject ought to be clear. As a paradigm of the relationship between the ethical and the political, marriage does not exhaust the possibilities of this relationship. It is as a paradigm, however, that marriage deserves our attention.

As promise, marriage is a political institution. It is the couple's project and is sanctioned by the state. As event, marriage is ethical. As both event and project, marriage holds the tensions of the two moments of intentionality together. It is the visible mark of the contesting desires of consciousness, the institutional sign of the ambiguity of our condition. Marriage contests the social contract ideal of autonomy. It recalls the politics of the project to the ethic of generosity, and in this recall it curbs the autonomous subject's tendencies to forget its ethical responsibilities to let the other be.

In following Beauvoir's remarks on Chinese marriage back to her descriptions of intentionality, we discover that her observations prod us to reconsider the relationship between the recognition accorded erotic desire and the possibilities of political justice. Her remarks move us to examine the ways in which the idea of an ambiguous subject challenges a politics grounded in the idea of an autonomous subject. They suggest that the inconsistency of insisting that marriage is a public institution that exists in the private domain is more than a matter of a category confusion, for in insisting that as regulated by the state marriage exists outside the political domain, the state seems on the one hand to recognize the ethical meanings of marriage but on the other to negate this recognition. In calling marriage a natural relationship, the state evades its political implications.

Much work has been done on the disaster this view of marriage has been for women. Taking this work into account, I return to the question of autonomy. As I see it, if we succeed in discrediting the concept of women's natural subordination and establish that women, like men, are autonomous, we will still be working with a flawed account of humanity. Appealing to this mistaken view of the subject, we will not succeed in understanding the patriarchal perversion of marriage, will not acknowledge the feminine protest, and will not understand why understanding the meaning of marriage is essential to the feminist project of a politics of justice.

ROUSSEAU'S AMBIGUITY

Ironically, Jean Jacques Rousseau is helpful here. Though he mimics other social contract thinkers in his defense of the idea of autonomy and in his vision of marriage as an institution that transforms the heterosexual couple into a moral entity where the husband is elected to rule his wife, the tensions within his writings reveal certain fissures in this concept of the autonomous subject and in this image of marriage. Alerted to these fissures, we discover that Rousseau is an unexpected ally; for like feminists, he draws our attention to the feminine protest.

One sign of these tensions is the chronology of *Emile* (Rousseau 1955). As an extended account of the education of the ideal man and an abbreviated account of the education of the ideal woman, *Emile* claims to instruct us in the art of producing the autonomous person. This person is said to be free from the corruptions of society and fit for the responsibilities of moral and political life. Read closely (perversely?), however, *Emile* reveals the impossibility of the ideal of autonomy and discloses the problems with a concept of marriage that charges it with transforming the erotic experience of sexual difference into a moral experience of sexual unity. Moreover, read within the context of Rousseau's other writings, *Emile*, identified by Rousseau as his most important work, underscores the problem of accounting for the transition from natural to social life and suggests that it is a mistake to abstract political questions from questions of education, marriage, and the family.

An abbreviated version of the social contract is part of Emile's education in/for citizenship. For the most part, *Emile* presents citizenship as requiring autonomy and marriage as supporting it (for men)—but only for the most part. Parts of *Emile* undermine the ideal of autonomy. This reading focuses on these other parts, not in order to argue that they reveal the real Rousseau, but to show the ways in which *Emile* may be read as destabilizing the patriarchal legacies of marriage.

As an infant and a boy, Emile is situated in a world designed to foster his sense of autonomy. He is never positioned to rely on others. He is taught to master nature. He is trained to be self-sufficient. He thus experiences himself as free, competent, and independent. Given the social contract account of the nature of the man who is fit to consent to become a political person, this education ought to make Emile eligible to become a citizen. Oddly enough, it does not; for reading *Emile*, we discover that this preadolescent education, though necessary for the citizen, is not a sufficient condition for citizenship. Emile must become a husband before he can become a member of the body politic (Rousseau 1955, 384–553). He must, through the experience of his passion, discover his need of/for the other and must, through the decision to marry, acknowledge the endurance and legitimacy of this need.

In other times (ours?) and other hands (mine?) an author/reader might discern the ways in which Emile's experience of passion alienates him from his education for autonomy and might question the legitimacy of this education and the ideal that guides it. In Rousseau's hands, the alienating experience of passion becomes the basis for a theory of marriage where autonomy, exiled as independence, returns as the right to rule. Having been raised to value autonomy, the husband camouflages his need of his wife by imagining her as dependent, in need of him, and by establishing himself as her teacher, tutor, master. To become a member of the body politic, then, a man must give up the idea that he can live independently of others but need not accept the implications of interdependence. Now defined as the one who rules himself and/or as the one who is not ruled by another, the autonomous man is identified as the husband who, as the head of the moral person created by marriage, has the right to rule his wife (the body of this new person) and legislate for the couple. As husband schooled in the art of ruling, he may become the citizen who accepts the authority of the state insofar as its laws reflect the general will, the law to which he has given consent.

According to Rousseau, there is no such thing as an autonomous woman. A girl's education is said to reflect her natural bond to/with others. The girl is taught to experience this bond as a sign of her dependency/ weakness. Brought up from the very beginning to experience her need of others as a deficiency, Sophy's ability to stir Emile's passions introduces her to a strange sensation of power. For the first time in her life, she finds that someone else needs her, that someone else is willing to submit to her desire. The tutor teaches Sophy to use this power discretely (deceitfully?) and never to mistake it for a sign of autonomy, the right to rule herself or another.

Reading Rousseau's descriptions of the education of the passions through Beauvoir's description of intentionality, we see the ways in which the ideologies of sexual difference transform the ambiguities of intentionality into fixed heterosexual positions that establish men as privileged insofar as they are identified as instantiating the desires of political intentionality. We also see how the erotic disturbs this fixing and privileging. Furthermore, we discover that this disturbance has no effect so long as marriage is seen as a way to regulate rather than recognize the erotic and so long as the focus of marriage discourse is the child rather than the couple.

Rousseau's discussion of marriage may be read as both an acknowledgment of the ways in which the erotic disturbs the social contract view of the subject and as a protection of the autonomous subject from this disturbance. Moving to control the troubling effects of desire, Rousseau pursues two strategies. First and most familiar, the tutor teaches Sophy to regulate Emile's access to her body. The erotic must not be allowed to become an experience of strange freedom. Sophy must teach Emile to keep his passions in check. Insisting on her modesty, she will ensure that Emile rediscovers his autonomy. Second and also familiar, men and women are said to become each others' husbands and wives in order to produce and educate their children. The purpose of the marriage bond is to create another bond, the bond between a father and his child (son); for it is by virtue of the marriage relationship that a man can be sure of his paternity. Given this assurance, the husband recognizes himself as a father and accepts the obligation of educating the child (son). He takes up what Rousseau calls the most important responsibility of his life, he becomes his child's (son's) tutor. As a tutor, the husband's need of the mother is suspended. As a father, the husband is autonomous. Through this twofold strategy, Rousseau distorts the moral meanings of marriage. He closes the erotic off from its generosities and transforms the erotic body into a productive one. Identified as a means to the end of the child rather than as an end in itself, marriage cannot call us to the risks of our vulnerability and cannot recall the politics of the project to the ethics of the erotic.

Although written in the eighteenth century, Rousseau's account of marriage remains current. The mantras of the Promise Keepers and the Million Man March echo Rousseau's account of the marital order. Opponents of gay marriage also take their cue from Rousseau, for they argue that legitimating the gay couple would destroy the social fabric by violating the meaning of marriage—that meaning being the procreation and education of children. Forgetting for the moment that current technologies make it possible for gay couples to fulfill this so-called purpose of marriage, this argument and the passion with which marriage is identified as the exclusive right of heterosexual couples shows us how far we are from understanding marriage in the way Beauvoir's description of intentionality directs us to understand it. It shows us that though we no longer accept the father's right to override the desire of the couple, we do not accept the legitimacy of the couple's desire per se. Inverting the priorities of consciousness, we subordinate the ethical to the political—we demand that the couple's desire legitimate itself by serving the purpose of producing and assuming responsibility for children. Instead of seeing the caress as the paradigm of the ethical event, we position it as a foreplay and identify it as a means to an end. In continuing to follow the letter of Rousseau's politics of marriage, current discourses on marriage (both those that support this natural law account of marriage and those that reject the legitimacy of marriage because it insists on the subordination of women to men) ignore the question raised by *Emile:* Why marriage before citizenship?

On Rousseau's analysis of human nature, it is our natural sympathy for others that makes us available for and amenable to social life. According to Rousseau, however, it is through friendship, not marriage, that this natural sympathy is expressed and cultivated. It is not that this sympathy is foreign to marriage. Once the passions have cooled, according to Rousseau, marriage becomes friendship. In its origin, however, marriage is erotic. It is not a matter of mutual sympathy but a question of intimacy. In positing marriage rather than friendship as the prerequisite for citizenship, Rousseau is indicating that something more than sympathy for others makes us fit for political life.

It is possible to see this something else as control of the passions, and certainly, given the general tone of social contract discourse, this seems to be the right answer to the question, Why marriage before citizenship?[3] Taking our direction from Beauvoir, however, we are pointed to another reading of this prerequisite. Reading Rousseau through Beauvoir, we read Rousseau's attention to the relationship between marriage and citizenship as an affirmation of the relationship between the ethical and the political and as an acknowledgment of the ethical, political implications of the erotic.

Friendship does not threaten our status as autonomous beings. As your friend, I remain independent. My passion for you, however, undermines my autonomy. If friendship is designated as the basis for politics, then politics is the business of autonomous subjects who choose to associate with each other for utilitarian or pleasurable purposes. If the erotic is the basis of politics, however, politics is the work of relational subjects living out their need of, and vulnerability to, each other. In recognizing marriage as grounded in the desire of the couple and in situating marriage at the origin of the political, Rousseau indicates that it is in understanding ourselves as vulnerable to each other rather than as independent of each other that we become reliable political subjects.

In opening up these ideas, *Emile* does not argue for them. Committed to the autonomous subject, Rousseau produces other arguments. They read like attempts to shore up the Ptolemaic vision of the universe. These arguments, however, stand or fall together. In rejecting those arguments that justify the subordination of women to men (all this talk of marriage as the basis for citizenship only applies to men, for women, married or single, are never competent, according to Rousseau, to be citizens), we must also reject the arguments for autonomy. It is as wrong to argue that marriage requires us to recognize each other as autonomous equals as it is to argue that it requires us to recognize the rule of the husband. The married couple's passion speaks of its desire for the difference of the other and of its need to give this desire its due.

Rousseau's trouble with marriage, including the ways he camouflages the trouble, reveals the lie of the ideal of the autonomous subject. As troubling for Rousseau's politics of autonomy, *Emile*'s discourse on marriage is also troubling for a feminist defense of marriage that argues for the equal autonomy of husbands and wives. For if we read *Emile*'s account of the relationship between marriage and politics through Beauvoir's accounts of intentionality, the erotic, and the couple, we find the feminine protest lodged in women's commitment to the bond challenging the ideal of the autonomous subject and any theory of marriage, politics, or justice that relies on it.

In liberating marriage from its patriarchal history, we transform the feminine protest into a feminist critique and ethical demand. Within patriarchy, women (as woman) were obliged to defend the value of the bond. Hence the feminine protest. Moving beyond patriarchy, women, no longer captivated by the myth of woman, will be freed from their obligation to the bond. A feminist critique that understands that it is not the value of the bond that is immoral but the obligation to value it that is exploitive, will also understand that in a post-patriarchal society where no one is obliged to subordinate themselves to an other for the sake of the bond, the ethical meanings of the bond will prevail. Getting from here (a patriarchy in transition) to there (a post-patriarchal society) will require women and men to take up the protest (once identified as feminine) of/for the bond.

The feminist critique that takes up this protest would not argue against Rousseau's account of woman to argue for women's autonomy. Instead, it would argue that neither women nor men are autonomous and that it is in recognizing the lie of autonomy that we become fit for citizenship. Beginning in this way, this feminist critique would ask what the body politic would be like if it required its citizens to recognize themselves as interdependent rather than autonomous. Exploring the implications of the politics of the bond, this critique would take up Beauvoir's remarks about

Chinese marriage to explore the ways in which intimate relationships (not an education in autonomy) prepare us for political life.

We might wish to retain the social contract idea of the promise as the ground of legitimate politics. Instead of seeing this promise as a contract autonomous men make, however, we would see the political promise as the effect of a prior promise, the promise of the couple. This promise to love, not to rule, is ethical. It expresses our experience of responsiveness to the other and articulates our desire to take up the responsibility of preserving this opening to the other. In taking the promise of love to the promise of marriage, the couple indicates that it too depends on others. In taking up the vows of marriage, the couple cannot and does not ask the state to preserve its love or to sustain its passion. It does, however, ask the state to acknowledge its interest in the couple and to properly identify this interest. It asks that the state not violate the meaning of the couple by reducing the promise of marriage to a promise about property or children. In making its intimate promise of love the public promise of marriage, the couple asks the state to make a promise to it. That promise is to engage in a politics that recognizes its debt to the ethical by remembering that justice always has an interest in preserving the opening of/for the erotic event.

Notes

1. Eva Lundgren-Gothlin notes that *The Second Sex* ends by quoting Karl Marx's *Economic and Political Manuscripts of 1844*, where "the relation between the sexes is seen as a measure of the humanity of human beings or of the extent to which the human has really become human" (1995, 9).

2. There are many ways of delineating the ethical and political domains and of mapping their intersections. In being guided by Beauvoir's description of intentionality to identify the ethical as the stance that responds to the other's freedom with the gift of generosity and to identify the political as the stance that responds to the other's freedom with appeals for justice, I am following the tradition of Martin Buber, Jacques Lacan, and Emmanuel Lévinas rather than the tradition that aligns the ethical with the judgments of autonomous subjects. This distinction is worked out in greater detail in my "Between the Ethical and the Political: The Difference of Ambiguity" (2001).

3. Nicole Ferman (1997, 93, 119, 177) takes this position when she argues that Rousseau insists on marriage before citizenship because the man who becomes a husband gives evidence of his ability to keep a promise and demonstrates his capacity to govern others and to be governed by self-willed laws. She sees Rousseau as concerned with the education of the passions because he finds the domesticated passions essential

to public life but wild passion as a threat to public order. Women, as wives and mothers, are charged with domesticating the passions and are therefore crucial to the stability of the state. On this view, the function of marriage is to regulate the couple's desire. Allan Bloom, in his introduction to his translation of Rousseau's *Emile* (1979), identifies the sexual contract as the basis of all other contracts. He sees Emile's passion for his wife as creating a concern for his unborn child, and it is this concern that activates his interest in justice and civil society. Hence the dictate: marriage before citizenship.

References

Beauvoir, Simone de. 1944. *Pyrrhus et Cinéas.* Paris: Gallimard.

———. 1948. *The ethics of ambiguity.* Trans. Bernard Frechtman. New York: Philosophical Library.

———. 1952. *The second sex.* Trans. H. M. Parshley. New York: Vintage Books.

———. 1966. Must we burn Sade? In *The marquis de Sade.* Trans. Annette Michelson. New York: Grove Press.

———. 1969. *La Longue marche.* Paris: Gallimard.

Bergoffen, Debra. 1997. *The philosophy of Simone de Beauvoir: Gendered phenomenologies, erotic generosities.* New York: State University of New York Press.

———. 2001. Between the ethical and the political: The difference of ambiguity. In *The existential phenomenology of Simone de Beauvoir,* ed. Wendy O'Brien and Lester Embree, 18–204. Boston: Kluwer Academic Publishers.

Bloom, Allan. 1979. Introduction to *Emile,* by Jean Jacques Rousseau. Trans. Allan Bloom. New York: Basic Books.

Chang, Jung. 1991. *Wild swans: Three daughters of China.* New York: Doubleday.

Ferman, Nicole. 1997. *Domesticating passions: Rousseau, woman and nation.* Hanover, N.H.: Wesleyan Press.

Freud, Sigmund. 1961. *Civilization and its discontents.* Trans. James Strachey. New York: W. W. Norton.

Hegel, G. W. F. 1955. *The phenomenology of mind.* Trans. J. B. Baillie. London: Allen & Unwin.

———. 1967. *Philosophy of right.* Trans. T. M. Knox. London: Oxford University Press.

Lundgren-Gothlin, Eva. 1995. Gender and ethics in the philosophy of Simone de Beauvoir. *Nora* 1: 1–21.

Pateman, Carole. 1988. *The sexual contract.* Stanford, Calif.: Stanford University Press.

Rousseau, Jean Jacques. 1955. *Emile.* Trans. Barbara Foxely. London: Everyman.

———. 1979. *Emile.* Trans. Allan Bloom. New York: Basic Books.

Sartre, Jean-Paul. 1966. *Being and nothingness.* Trans. Hazel Barnes. New York: Washington Square Press.

TRANSCENDENCE AND IMMANENCE IN THE ETHICS OF SIMONE DE BEAUVOIR

Andrea Veltman

6

Perhaps it is permissible to dream of a future when men
will know no other use of their freedom than [the] free
unfurling of itself; constructive activity would be
possible for all; each would be able to aim positively
through his own projects at his own future. But today
the fact is that there are men who can justify their life
only by a negative action.

—*The Ethics of Ambiguity*, 112

In the last few decades, critiques of *The Second Sex* raised by feminist philosophers have contested its thesis that transcendence distinguishes the human being, its denigration of maternity as uncreative labor, and its general failure to acknowledge any specifically female values based on women's traditional work. Simone de Beauvoir's use of the Hegelian dichotomy between transcendence and immanence has been a primary target in feminist critiques of *The Second Sex* since the 1970s, when feminist theorists celebrating women's difference began criticizing Beauvoir for developing a vision of the liberated woman as one who surpasses feminine immanence to

achieve masculine transcendence.[1] These feminist critiques have either assumed or asserted that Beauvoir's dichotomy between transcendence and
immanence is a piece of Sartrean metaphysics, arguing that the masculinist
elements of Sartre's philosophical framework render it inadequate for analyzing the female condition.

Although recent revisionist scholarship on Simone de Beauvoir has
since supplanted the assumption that the transcendence/immanence dichotomy is primarily Sartrean with an interpretation of the dichotomy as
Hegelian and Marxist,[2] some feminist philosophers and Beauvoir scholars
continue to view the dichotomy as outmoded, primarily metaphysical, and
above all, "male-identified." Eva Lundgren-Gothlin, for instance, argues
that the dichotomy is Hegelian and Marxist rather than Sartrean but ultimately concedes the basic force of the feminist critique: the major difficulty of the dichotomy, she argues, is its implication that "motherhood and
domestic labor are regarded as immanence, i.e., as non-creative and non-
productive, as not being projects, and thus as not creating value."[3] In trying
to separate more pertinent analyses in *The Second Sex* from its core conceptual framework, Michèle Le Doeuff also characterizes the concept of transcendence as "a trifle obsolete":

> Along with . . . highly valuable analyses of the feminine condition, one also
> finds in *The Second Sex* a whole conceptual apparatus which is now a trifle ob-
> solete. What is one to make of this, for instance: "Every individual preoccu-
> pied with justifying his existence experiences this existence as an indefinite
> need for self-transcendence. Now what marks the specificity of women's situ-
> ation is that, while being, like every human being, an autonomous freedom,
> she discovers and chooses herself in a world where men force her to assume
> herself as the Other: they claim to fix her as an object and to vow her to im-
> manence, since her transcendence is itself to be perpetually transcended by
> another, essential and sovereign consciousness." Indeed! Is it really necessary
> to have recourse to such concepts as these in order to reveal the nature of
> women's oppression? Supposing one were unwilling to concede any sense to
> these categories?[4]

Whereas Le Doeuff and others ask whether the categories of existentialist metaphysics serve any use in feminist analyses of female oppression,
Kristana Arp also characterizes the dichotomy between transcendence and
immanence as primarily metaphysical. In *The Bonds of Freedom*, Arp repre-

sents the transcendence immanence dichotomy as a direct corollary of the distinction between subjectivity and facticity and argues that the metaphysical nature of the dichotomy creates irresolvable difficulties for Beauvoir's account of oppression, in which the oppressed are said to "fall back into immanence."[5]

The concepts of transcendence and immanence in *The Second Sex* are indeed loose and multifaceted, but I would like to argue that they are neither masculinist nor classist nor are they outmoded remnants of Sartrean metaphysics. As early as *Pyrrhus et Cinéas*, transcendence refers less to the movements of an intentional conscious subjectivity and more to constructive activities that situate and engage the individual with other human freedoms. Immanence, on the other hand, refers neither to facticity nor to Sartre's *en-soi* but to the negative labor necessary to maintain human life or perpetuate the status quo. In the full development of the dichotomy in *The Second Sex*, transcendence encompasses activities that enable self-expression, create an enduring artifact, or in some other fashion contribute positively to the constructive endeavors of the human race. Labors of immanence required for the sheer perpetuation of existence, on the other hand, are characteristically futile—unable to provide a foundational justification for existence.

Reinterpreted as a distinction between constructive work and maintenance labor, Beauvoir's distinction between transcendence and immanence bears significant similarity to Karl Marx's distinction between productive and unproductive labor. However, Beauvoir's concept of transcendence is more multifaceted than Marx's concept of productive work, and Beauvoir's critique of labor exploitation is directed primarily at the private realm rather than at labor specializations in the public realm. Moreover, Beauvoir's sense of transcendence as constructive activity emerges in *Pyrrhus et Cinéas* in her discussion of Pascal, Gide, Epicurus, and other writers from Western literature who suggest that human unhappiness arises from active engagement with the world. This sense of transcendence as constructive activity takes on an ethical dimension in *The Ethics of Ambiguity*, where it informs Beauvoir's existentialist account of oppression and gains its greatest prominence in analyses of female oppression in *The Second Sex*.

TRANSCENDENCE IN *PYRRHUS ET CINÉAS*

Beauvoir's early ethical writings, particularly *Pyrrhus et Cinéas*, use the concept of transcendence in part as Sartre uses the concept in *Being and Nothingness*, in which transcendence is equated with the movement of the for-itself and contrasted with facticity. In *Pyrrhus et Cinéas* transcendence refers occasionally to the "perpetual surpassing" of intentional consciousness and, occasionally, to the process whereby one makes oneself at every moment through some project.[6] Transcendence is the spontaneous directness of consciousness at something, a reaching outward beyond oneself toward some end, or a "[throwing oneself] toward the future" (*PC* 141). In this sense of transcendence, all human beings continually transcend themselves, for every look, act, or thought of an intentional consciousness is an act of transcendence (*PC* 121).

The obvious undertones of the Sartrean for-itself in this early characterization of transcendence has led even revisionist Beauvoir scholarship to concede a Sartrean influence on *Pyrrhus et Cinéas* in particular. Eva Lundgren-Gothlin, for example, writes that while *The Second Sex* develops a Hegelian rather than Sartrean sense of transcendence, "in *Pyrrhus et Cinéas* Beauvoir mainly uses the concept of transcendence as Sartre defines it in *Being and Nothingness:* transcendence is tied to the actions of the intentional consciousness."[7] Although Lundgren-Gothlin and other scholars emphatically reject the view that *Pyrrhus et Cinéas* taken as a whole merely parrots or defends the Sartre's views, they acknowledge a predominant Sartrean mark upon the concepts of freedom and transcendence in this work in particular.[8]

I would like to suggest that in addition to the obvious Sartrean uses of transcendence in *Pyrrhus et Cinéas*, this work also introduces the specifically Beauvoirean notion that transcendence is constructive activity, rather than simply any movement of an intentional consciousness. This sense of transcendence as constructive or creative work gains greater prominence in *The Second Sex* but emerges here in the course of Beauvoir's response to the suggestion scattered throughout Western literature that human unhappiness arises from active engagement with the world.[9] Pascal, for instance, writes in his *Pensées* that "all the unhappiness of men arises from a single fact, that they cannot stay quietly in their own chamber."[10] Beauvoir finds this idea repeated in the French essayist Gide and prefigured in the writings of Aristippus, Horace, and the Epicureans generally:

> It is the moral of Aristippus, that of Horace's *Carpe diem*, and Gide's *Nourritures [Fruits of the Earth]*. Let us turn away from the world, from undertakings and conquests; let us devise no more projects; let us remain at home, at rest at the heart of our enjoyment. (*PC* 118)

Contrasting repose with movement and transcendence, Beauvoir suggests against Pascal and others that it is *disengagement* from the world through repose and passivity that cannot provide fulfillment for human beings, for human transcendence cannot be successfully realized in states of rest (*PC* 120–25). The nature of transcendence is active movement, perpetual surpassing, or going beyond the given; and transcendence is thus truly achieved, not in the enjoyment of relaxation, but in some endeavor that moves an individual beyond the present status quo toward an open future. One achieves transcendence when he "studies science, writes poetry, or builds motors" (*PC* 140) but not when he sits idly by devising no project or relaxing in passive enjoyment.

The contrast between passivity and activity present in *Pyrrhus et Cinéas*, which becomes taken up into the dichotomy between transcendence and immanence in *The Second Sex*, is here drawn from a host of French, German, Latin, and Greek writings. Beauvoir identifies and contests the implicit endorsements of passivity in figures such as Aristippus, Horace, Epicurus, Gide, and Pascal and develops the association between transcendence and activity with reference to Hegel, Valéry, Arland, and Chardonne, rather than with reference to Sartre (*PC* 118–23). Beauvoir's sense of transcendence as constructive activity does borrow from the Heideggerian and Sartrean notion of project, but the distinction developed in *Pyrrhus et Cinéas* between constructive action and the passive enjoyment of life is absent in the Heideggerian notion of project and the Sartrean sense of transcendence. Sartre's metaphysical conception of transcendence as the movement of the for-itself, indeed, does not permit a distinction between the constructive activity of transcendence and the passivity of rest, for intentional movements of the for-itself occur even in relaxation and withdrawal from the world.

Beauvoir's association of transcendence with constructive activity, on the other hand, enables her to respond to the suggestion made by Pyrrhus at the outset of the treatise that when finished with his world conquests, he shall enjoy the paradise of rest. Since restful paradise—conceived as an existence bereft of constructive endeavors—promises only eternal tedium, Pyrrhus "lacks imagination" in suggesting in the first place that he shall rest when finished. Associating transcendence with active pursuits in the world once again, Beauvoir writes:

> Paradise is rest; it is transcendence abolished, a state of things that is given and does not have to be surpassed. But then, what shall we do [in restful paradise]? In order for the air there to be breathable, it must leave room for actions and desires. . . . The beauty of the promised land is that it promised new promises. Immobile paradises promise us nothing but eternal ennui. . . . Once returned home, [Pyrrhus] will hunt, he will legislate, he will go to war again. If he tries to stay truly at rest, he will only yawn. (*PC* 122)

Pyrrhus et Cinéas thus uses "transcendence" to refer not only to the upsurge of the for-itself or only to the projection of the self into the world through any conscious activity, but also to an active mode of existence filled with accomplishments and a continual surpassing of given states of affairs. One salient difficulty with the simultaneous presence of these concepts of transcendence in this work, however, is the clear incommensurability of the former Sartrean senses of transcendence with the latter sense of transcendence as constructive activity. Where this latter sense excludes passivity and repose from "transcendence," the metaphysical and Sartrean sense of transcendence includes any movement of intentional consciousness, even those that occur in moments of passivity. "Transcendence" cannot consistently refer to any subjective movement of consciousness and yet to the considerably more circumscribed set of human actions that accomplish, produce, or push back the boundaries of the present.

Some of the literature discussing Beauvoir's use of transcendence has granted that the concepts of transcendence and immanence are "contradictory and illusive,"[11] and in the respect that these incongruent concepts of transcendence occur simultaneously in *Pyrrhus et Cinéas* and in other treatises, this assessment appears warranted. However, the presence of contradictory concepts of transcendence in *Pyrrhus et Cinéas* also reflects the very development of the concept of transcendence in this work away from the Sartrean definition of transcendence as intentional consciousness toward the less metaphysical definition of transcendence as constructive activity. The eventual maturation of the concept of transcendence in *The Second Sex*, in which transcendence designates an active, creative mode of existence, would indicate that Beauvoir ultimately found the less metaphysical and more Hegelian senses of transcendence to be more fruitful. *Pyrrhus et Cinéas*, at any rate, works to extend a Sartrean sense of transcendence to a sense of transcendence that is more illuminating for questions concerning the human need to act in the world.

TRANSCENDENCE AND IMMANENCE IN
THE SECOND SEX

Although Beauvoir's earlier ethical treatises incorporate a Hegelian and Sartrean concept of transcendence, associating transcendence with activity, progression, and the surpassing movement of consciousness, it is not until *The Second Sex* that Beauvoir appropriates the Hegelian concept of immanence as a counterpart to transcendence. Once paired with immanence in *The Second Sex*, transcendence refers to constructive work and, more generally, to an active mode of existence in which one attempts to surpass the present, burst out onto the future, and remain free from biological fate. Immanence, by contrast, designates the round of futile and largely uncreative chores necessary to sustain life as well as a mode of existence marked by passivity, ease, and submission to biological fate.

The concepts of transcendence and immanence in *The Second Sex* are multifaceted and simultaneously descriptive and normative, but the metaphysical meanings of transcendence largely drop out in *The Second Sex*, and transcendence and immanence become delineated primarily in terms of a typology of activities or active and passive modes of existing. The account of oppression developed in *The Ethics of Ambiguity* using the distinction between maintenance and progression becomes imported in full into *The Second Sex*, together with the thesis that an authentically lived existence requires that one establish reason for being for oneself through transcendent activities. Activities of transcendence include precisely those activities of progress, creation, and discovery that are opposed to the maintenance of life in *The Ethics of Ambiguity*, while the mechanical chores that minister to the life process are here activities of immanence.[12]

The Introduction to *The Second Sex* does contain two salient descriptions of transcendence in terms of Sartrean metaphysics,[13] but the length of *The Second Sex* delineates transcendence and immanence primarily as a typology of activities (see especially xxvii, 65–69, 186–87, 226, 313–14, 451–52, 470–74, 477–80, 505, 551, 634, and 675). Transcendence and immanence are contrasted not only in terms of their relation to time—transcendence expands present horizons into the future, whereas immanence perpetuates the present—but also in terms of what transcendence and immanence accomplish. Achieved "in work and action" (*SS* 183), transcendence engages the individual in the world and situates her among other freedoms by laying a foundation for a new future, creating an enduring artifact, enabling individual self-expression, transforming the world, or in some other fashion contributing positively to the constructive endeavors of the human race. Transcendent activities—precisely the same as those distinguished from maintenance labor in *The Ethics of Ambiguity*—enable us to surpass the present "toward the totality of the universe and the infinity of the future" (*SS* 471).[14]

Immanence, on the other hand, produces nothing durable through which we move beyond ourselves but merely (1) perpetuates life or (2) maintains the status quo. Activities of immanence include not only the everyday labors that sustain and repair the body and mind, like cooking, cleaning, and, presumably, television watching, but also bureaucratic paper pushing and biological functions such as giving birth. Beauvoir occasionally characterizes immanence as repetitive and uncreative (*SS* 65–69, 474–478), although immanence is not demarcated from transcendence in terms of its repetitiveness or uncreativity, for activities of immanence can involve creativity or self-expression in like manner as activities of transcendence can involve repetition. Activities of immanence are characteristically futile—immanence consumes time and labor but accomplishes nothing—and the combination of necessity and futility involved in maintenance labor, in turn, makes some forms of immanence necessarily repetitive. The labor required to cook, clean, wash, or rake leaves, for instance, is necessary for the maintenance of life but is eventually negated and brought to nothing once taken up into the endless cycle of life itself (*SS* 474–78).

Furthermore, since activities of immanence merely sustain life and achieve nothing more than its continuation, they cannot themselves serve as the justifying ground for living. *The Second Sex* employs a contrast between life and existence that mirrors the point made in *The Ethics of Ambiguity* concerning the inability of maintenance activities to lend meaning to human existence. "Life," Beauvoir writes here, "does not carry within itself its reasons for being, reasons that are more important than the life itself" (*SS* 68). Reason for living must be established through some activity that reaches beyond the maintenance of life itself toward the future; otherwise one labors to maintain life in the absence of an initial reason for laboring to maintain life. Putting the matter in terms of the reproduction of species-life as a whole, Beauvoir writes:

> Here we have the key to the whole mystery. On the biological level a species in maintained only by creating itself anew; but this creation results only in repeating the same Life in more individuals.... In the animal, the freedom and variety of male activities are vain because no project is involved.... Whereas in serving the species, the human male also remodels the face of the earth, he creates new instruments, he invents, he shapes the future. (*SS* 68)

Transcending the repetition of biological life, man has historically represented transcendence, given his participation in the activities that set up the world over and against nature: he remodels the earth, creates new values, takes risks, fights, progresses, conquers—in short, he accomplishes what transcends the maintenance of life itself. Woman, on the other hand, has originally represented immanence, the repetition of life, given her bondage to the natural functions of childbirth and childrearing (*SS* 65–69).

The Second Sex delineates the dichotomy between transcendence and immanence as a distinction in types of activity—and entangles the dichotomy with gender—not only in characterizing the historically divided masculine and feminine spheres but also in prescribing the conditions for women's emancipation from the role of the Other. Noting that the Hegelian dialectic between master and slave applies more appropriately to the historical relationship between man and woman, Beauvoir argues that maternity has served to confine women to the status of the Hegelian slave, "'the dependent consciousness for whom the essential reality is the animal type of life'" (*SS* 68, quoting Hegel). Playing the ontological role of the Hegelian other becomes borne out in concrete practice in performing the labor that repeats the life of the species. Writing of nomadic women particularly handicapped by "the bondage of reproduction," Beauvoir characterizes immanence as biological function rather than intentional action:

> The woman who gave birth, therefore, did not know the pride of creation; she felt herself the plaything of obscure forces. . . . Giving birth and suckling are not *activities,* they are natural functions; no project is involved; and that is why woman found in them no reason for a lofty affirmation of her existence—she submitted passively to her biologic fate. The domestic labors that fell to her lot because they were reconcilable with the cares of maternity imprisoned her in repetition and immanence; they were repeated from day to day in an identical form, which was perpetuated almost without change from century to century. (*SS* 66–67; emphasis in original)

Biological functions such as giving birth and suckling infants are by definition not transcendent activities, for these functions require only that women be passive instruments of the forces of nature, not that women create something in the manner that a craftsman makes an object.

The derogation of maternity and traditionally feminine labor contained in the normative distinction between transcendent work and immanent labor brings us to the feminist critique of Beauvoir as a male-biased thinker who is unable to appreciate or adequately acknowledge the existence of specifically feminine vales. Feminist theoretical evaluation of *The Second Sex* has singled out the dichotomy between transcendence and immanence as a special culprit in the "masculinist" values underpinning the work, for it is the transcendence/immanence dichotomy that glorifies traditionally male activities and that denigrates maternity and traditionally feminine labors as unproductive labor. The resulting implication is indeed that existential self-realization requires that women transcend what has been specifically feminine and, as Susan Heckman writes, "become like men . . . if they are to attain freedom."[15] Not only has some recent revisionist literature on Beauvoir voiced support for this view, but the now-classic feminist critiques of the transcendence/immanence dichotomy have also argued principally that the dichotomy renders Beauvoir unable to acknowledge any gender-specific values. For instance, Charlene Seigfried writes that Beauvoir jumps too far into "denigrating childbearing itself. . . . The upshot is that any values that might have their source in maternity are denigrated and consequently Beauvoir has trouble saying what specifically feminine values women create."[16] Margaret Simons also writes that Beauvoir fails to appreciate both the values that arise from the experience of mothering and the limitations of an ethic defined by the pursuit of transcendence.[17]

The reinterpretation of transcendence and immanence given above suggests two points to be added to a Beauvoirean defense of the transcendence/immanence dichotomy. Of note first is that the classic feminist critiques of the dichotomy have misrepresented the dichotomy as a piece of Sartrean metaphysics when, in fact, transcendence is associated with Sartrean ontology only briefly in the Introduction to *The Second Sex*. In critiquing the transcendence/immanence dichotomy from a feminist point of view, Seigfried, for instance, attempts to explicate the dichotomy while referring to the use of transcendence that appears sporadically in Beauvoir's early ethical treatises:

> Transcendence refers to nothing less than the central thesis of Sartrean existentialism. . . . The free subject, in ordering his life, makes of himself something. . . . While the object is always some definite thing, the subject is nothing insofar as the subject, freed from all constraints, unconditionally chooses to choose and thus continuously creates and re-creates his self.[18]

Associating transcendence with free subjectivity and immanence with facticity, Seigfried proceeds to argue that the transcendence/immanence dichotomy glorifies male transcendence as a human value while undermining the construction or acknowledgement of specifically female values based in women's experience as child-bearers. Similarly, in her critique of the transcendence/immanence dichotomy as masculinist, Genevieve Lloyd argues that Beauvoir's indebtedness to the concepts of "Sartrean immanence" and "Sartrean transcendence" "left its [male] mark on the very concepts of 'transcendence' and 'immanence.' "[19]

Although "transcendence" carries metaphysical connotations in Beauvoir's early ethical treatises, transcendence does not refer simply to free subjectivity à la Sartre once it is paired with immanence in *The Second Sex*. As a distinction between creative work and unfulfilling forms of maintenance labor, the transcendence/immanence dichotomy in fact stands at odds with a Sartrean notion of transcendence as an intentional consciousness. The primary problems with construing the transcendence/immanence dichotomy as Sartrean are therefore not only that Sartre does not employ the notion of immanence but also that Sartre's concept of transcendence stands opposed to facticity rather than to unproductive maintenance labor. In *The Second Sex* transcendence becomes simultaneously Sartrean, Marxist, and Hegelian and designates not consciousness itself but the realization of the self through creative or constructive work.

Moreover, criticisms of *The Second Sex* as antithetical to feminine values tend to overstate Beauvoir's denigration of maternity and do not acknowledge that the transcendence/immanence dichotomy itself holds potential to critique continuing inequities in the institutions of motherhood and marriage.[20] Although Beauvoir indeed does not admire feminine values, and although transcendence indeed distinguishes the human being, Beauvoir's view of motherhood is not unremittingly bleak. Her negative characterization of giving birth as an uncreative function has been distinguished in the revisionist literature from her more positive portrayal of motherhood itself in the chapter on motherhood in *The Second Sex*.[21] In her later discussion of motherhood in *The Second Sex*, Beauvoir notes that motherhood can be an enrichment for existence and can enable women to develop the value of generosity, although her larger point is that motherhood alone cannot serve as a reason for being (*SS* 511, 522–27).

Critiquing the institution of motherhood rather than the experience of mothering, Beauvoir herself claims, not that mothering per se is an activity of immanence, but that the occupations consequent upon motherhood tend to mire women in immanence. Writing on the situation of women in antiquity, for instance, Beauvoir characterizes the domestic labors associated with raising children as activities of immanence, rather than motherhood itself as immanence:

> *The domestic labors* that fell to her lot because they were reconcilable with the cares of maternity *imprisoned her in repetition and immanence;* they were repeated from day to day in an identical form, which was perpetuated without change from century to century; they produced nothing new. (*SS* 63; emphasis added)

The principal obstacle that motherhood presents to the free pursuit of transcendence is not the care of children itself (for childrearing can enable women to create relatively durable human beings) but it is the tendency of motherhood to relegate women to activities of immanence in the private realm.[22] The gendered inequalities in parenting workloads that inundate mothers with activities of immanence, of course, remain an obstacle to the achievement of a balance between work and family even at the turn of the twenty-first century.

In light of the continuing tendency of motherhood to mire women in activities of immanence, a Beauvoirean feminism clearly has the advantage of drawing attention to gendered inequities in divisions of labor in parenting at a time when equitable divisions of labor cannot be taken for granted. By subordinating a positive revaluation of maternal values and reproductive labor to an assessment of everyday domestic work as drudgery, Beauvoir furthermore avoids re-inscribing patriarchal divisions of domestic labor, more so than do forms of difference feminism that attempt to assert the dignity of women by celebrating feminine values.

Furthermore, Beauvoir's distinction between transcendent work and immanent labor also lends positive support to a feminist critique of gender inequities in marriage and divisions of domestic labor.[23] An ethics directed by the pursuit of transcendent work has as an advantage over other ethical theories as a means of judging qualitatively inequitable divisions of domestic work. An ethics structured around the distinction between transcendence and immanence not only captures the basic character of housework as unfulfilling labor but also establishes a need to participate in work that lends meaning to human existence. A Kantian ethics, by comparison, can establish a moral wrong in qualitatively inequitable divisions of domestic labor if such divisions of labor treat women merely as means, but it is a normative distinction between transcendent work and immanent labor that underpins a moral obligation to share less fulfilling forms of domestic maintenance labor. Since the transcendence/immanence dichotomy functions as a normative framework for critiquing inequitable divisions of domestic work, this dichotomy is, in fact, an important component in arguing for the continuing relevance of *The Second Sex.*

Lastly, we should note that although domestic work—with the possible exception of parenting—largely comprises activities of immanence, work that enables transcendences does not correspond to work performed in the public realm.[24] Late in *The Second Sex* Beauvoir notes that the majority of blue-collar and middle-class jobs do not allow for genuinely creative or productive work but themselves tend to require mostly activities of immanence (*SS* 624–25).[25] Additionally, some of the most prestigious professional jobs do not necessarily enable self-expression through creative work: doctors, for example, function primarily to maintain life and perform what are activities of immanence in Beauvoirean terms. Rather, work in the public realm enables transcendence only in some instances (and to varying degrees in different occupations); most genuinely transcendent activity remains the province of a few writers, artists, scientists, and academics.

Since the majority of blue-collar and middle-class jobs do not enable transcendence, it may appear that Beauvoir's analysis of work in terms of transcendence and immanence is a bourgeois prejudice, an analysis of meaningful work drawn from the perspective of the upper-middle class. In a notable critique of *The Second Sex* as inattentive to class and racial inequalities, Elizabeth Spelman maintains that, although Beauvoir expresses some insight into race and class privilege, her glorification of the ideal of transcendence leads her to neglect the significance of race and class inequities.[26] Beauvoir does indeed occasionally contrast "man" as citizen and producer with "woman" as "shut up in the home," as Spelman notes, and there is therefore a certain problematic classist conflation of "women" with white middle-class housewives in *The Second Sex*.[27]

I would like to argue, however, that a critique of the dichotomy between transcendence and immanence as itself classist is wrongheaded for at least two reasons. Firstly, given that middle-class and even upper-middle-class jobs do not necessarily enable transcendence, the dichotomy between transcendence and immanence does not reflect the values of the middle or upper classes. Rather, the distinction reflects the values of French artists and intellectuals, who are not necessarily part of the middle and upper classes. The distinction also reflects a philosophical tradition present since Plato of valuing the permanent and the durable over the impermanent and the ephemeral. Insofar as Beauvoir's distinction between transcendence and immanence accords a higher value to artistic and intellectual work, Beauvoir shares company with the broader tradition of ethical and political philosophers from Plato to Mill who distinguish intellectual or artistic endeavors as largely constitutive of human flourishing. Of course, Beauvoir's distinction between transcendent work and maintenance labor does not reduce to the distinctions made by Plato or Mill, for the transcendence achieved in creative work is not simply an intellectual pleasure. But if the classic philosophical hierarchies between the pleasures of the mind and the mundane pleasures of the body are tenable, so is the existentialist/Marxist claim that participation in constructive activity is partly constitutive of a meaningful existence.

Secondly, to assert that Beauvoir's distinction is classist for the reason that few people participate fully in transcendent work misconstrues the methodological relationship between ethical analyses and existing social arrangements. It is not a shortcoming of an ethics of transcendence that transcendent work is not available to all people, nor is it a shortcoming that not all people choose such work when it is available. Consider that one would not object to a eudaimonistic ethics in which happiness, relations with others, or intellectual pleasure are posited as objectively good for human beings on the grounds that not all people have these goods or desire them. Such an objection rests on the assumption that ethical theory should be built up in accordance with the dictates of existing social arrangements and socially manufacturable desires, and this objection reduces philosophical ethics to a contrived justification of individuals' life choices. Rather, in the event of a discrepancy between what some individuals pursue and what enables human flourishing or individual self-realization, an ethical analysis of human flourishing serves precisely to provide ground for advocating change. Thus, an ethics of intellectual pleasure provides ground for telling the ignoramus to cultivate his mind, for intelligence is a good for human beings; an Aristotelian ethics tells the hermit to cultivate friendships, for friendships are good for human beings; and so forth. Conversely, if oppressive social structures prevent individuals from obtaining or desiring what enables human flourishing or self-realization, then an ethical analysis of the human good provides ground for changing social arrangements so that the good for human beings becomes within the reach of more people.

The transcendence/immanence dichotomy is itself normative and therefore provides ground for evaluating inequitable divisions of transcendent activity as oppressive or exploitative. The fact that some individuals lack opportunities to participate in transcendent endeavors is not a reason to reject an ethics structured around the dichotomy between transcendence and immanence, but on the contrary, it is a reason to advocate that existing social orders change so that more people confront real opportunities to participate in transcendent activities. An ethics that posits transcendent activity as constitutive of self-realization is therefore not "exclusionary" or "elitist" because some do not participate in transcendent activity; rather, an ethics of transcendence serves precisely to provide a normative foundation for practical social change.

NOTES

1. Feminist critics of the transcendence/immanence dichotomy include Charlene Haddock Seigfried, "Gender Specific Values," *The Philosophical Forum* XV (Summer 1984); Jean Leighton, *Simone de Beauvoir on Women* (Rutherford, N.J.: Fairleigh-Dickinson University Press, 1975); Genevieve Lloyd, *The Man of Reason: "Male" and "Female" in Western Philosophy* (Minneapolis: University of Minnesota Press, 1993); Nancy Hartsock, *Money, Sex, and Power: Toward a Feminist Historical Materialism* (Boston: Northeastern University Press, 1985); and Alison Jaggar and William McBride, "'Reproduction' as Male Ideology," in *Hypatia Reborn: Essays in Feminist Philosophy*, ed. A. al-Hibri and M. Simons (Bloomington: Indiana University Press, 1990).

2. Most notably, Eva Lundgren-Gothlin, *Sex and Existence: Simone de Beauvoir's The Second Sex*, translated from the Swedish by L. Schenck (London: Athlone Press, 1996), chapters 3–8.

3. Eva Lundgren-Gothlin, *Sex and Existence*, 239.

4. Michèle Le Doeuff, "Operative Philosophy: Simone de Beauvoir and Existentialism," in *Critical Essays on Simone de Beauvoir*, ed. Elaine Marks (Boston: Hall & Co., 1987), 144–45, citing Le Doeuff's own translation of p. lix of the Introduction to *Le Deuxième Sexe*.

5. Kristana Arp, *The Bonds of Freedom: Simone de Beauvoir's Existentialist Ethics* (LaSalle: Open Court, 2001), 139–44. Since Arp sees transcendence as associated primarily with consciousness and immanence as associated with "the material side of existence," she considers it problematic and even nonsensical that Beauvoir characterizes the oppressed as reduced to immanence.

6. Beauvoir, *Pyrrhus et Cinéas* (Paris: Gallimard, 1944); hereafter *PC*. An English translation of *Pyrrhus et Cinéas* is published by University of Illinois Press in Simone de Beauvoir, *Philosophical Writings*, ed. M. Simons, M. Timmerman, and M. B. Mader (2004).

7. Lundgren-Gothlin, *Sex and Existence*, 231. Nancy Bauer also finds Beauvoir's position on freedom and transcendence in *Pyrrhus et Cinéas* to resemble that of Sartre: "The idea that all human beings are forced by the fact of their unimpeachable metaphysical liberty to [do one thing or another], the idea that Beauvoir has been at pains to elaborate and defend for almost all of *Pyrrhus et Cinéas*, is pure Sartre" (Bauer, *Simone de Beauvoir, Philosophy, and Feminism* [New York: Columbia University Press, 2001], 145). Sonia Kruks also characterizes transcendence in *Pyrrhus et Cinéas* in Sartrean terms: "Transcendence," she writes, "is the upsurge of the for-itself in the world, but it

becomes concrete, it particularizes itself in the specific projects of individuals" (Kruks, "Beauvoir: The Weight of Situation," in *Simone de Beauvoir: A Critical Reader*, ed. E. Fallaize [New York: Routledge, 1998], 51).

8. Bauer's main point concerning *Pyrrhus et Cinéas* is that this early work reflects a Hegelian influence in its understanding of the self; Kruks argues that although *Pyrrhus et Cinéas* employs Sartrean notions of freedom and transcendence, Beauvoir develops a more reasonable account of situation and oppression than Sartre develops (Bauer, *Simone de Beauvoir*, 137–58; Kruks, "The Weight of Situation," 47–55).

9. See especially the section of *Pyrrhus et Cinéas* titled "The Instant," 118–25.

10. Pascal, *Pensées*, translated by A.J. Krailsheimer (London: Penguin [1966] 1995), citation taken from Pensee #136, p. 37.

11. Lundgren-Gothlin, *Sex and Existence*, 230.

12. Notably, Eva Lundgren-Gothlin has argued that Beauvoir's concepts of transcendence and immanence in *The Second Sex* are influenced more by Hegel and Marx than by Sartre. Indeed, *Being and Nothingness* does not employ the concept of immanence but contrasts transcendence with such concepts as facticity, the in-itself, and objectivity. There is one relevant usage of "immanence" in Sartre's discussion of being-in-itself, in which Sartre says that he does not want to refer to being-in-itself as "immanence" (*BN* lxv). On the other hand, Lundgren-Gothlin notes, a Hegelian influence on the concepts of transcendence and immanence is particularly clear in Beauvoir's anthropological description of the historical development of human society, in which the pure repetition of life in its generality is transcended for the singularity of existence in the public realm. In a 1985 interview with Lundgren-Gothlin, Beauvoir reported that she herself did not attend the seminars on Hegel given by Alexandre Kojève in the 1930s, which related the works of Hegel and Marx to phenomenology and existentialism, but that she read Hegel's *Phenomenology of Spirit* and Kojève's *Introduction to the Reading of Hegel* during the war years. See Lundgren-Gothlin, *Sex and Existence*, chapters 4 and 7, especially pp. 57–59 and n. 16, p. 273.

13. Both Sartrean characterizations of transcendence occur on p. lix. Consider especially the passage in which Beauvoir links transcendence and immanence with the concept of the *en-soi*: "Every time transcendence falls back into immanence, stagnation, there is a degradation of existence into the '*en-soi*'—the brutish life of subjection to given conditions—and of liberty into constraint and contingence" (*The Second Sex*, trans. and ed. H.M. Parshley [New York: Knopf, 1952 (1993 reprint)]), lix; hereafter *SS*.

14. Consider especially pp. 78–83 in *The Ethics of Ambiguity*, trans. Bernard Frechtman (New York: Citadel Press, 1948).

15. Susan Hekman, "Reconstituting the Subject: Feminism, Modernism, and Postmodernism," *Hypatia* 6 (1991): 44–63.

16. Seigfried, "Gender Specific Values," 433.

17. Simons, *Beauvoir and* The Second Sex, 76–79. Although Simons is sympathetic with the criticisms of Beauvoir that have been given from the perspective of maternal ethicists, she does take back her earlier critique of *The Second Sex* as masculinist (see esp. 83–84). For a feminist evaluation of the transcendence/immanence dichotomy as masculinist, see also Lundgren-Gothlin's discussion of the dichotomy in *Sex and Existence*.

18. Seigfried, "Gender Specific Values," 426.

19. Lloyd, *The Man of Reason,* esp. 100–101. Lloyd argues that transcendence is necessarily a transcendence of what is feminine, so that the transcendence requires excluding and surpassing of feminine immanence. The transcendence/immanence dichotomy is itself masculinist, she argues, insofar as "it is only from a male perspective that the feminine can be seen as what must be transcended" (101).

20. Critics who have taken Beauvoir's critique of maternity at face value include Mary O'Brien, *The Politics of Reproduction* (Boston: Routledge and Kegan Paul, 1981); Seigfried, "Gender Specific Values"; Leighton, *Simone de Beauvoir on Women;* and Jaggar and McBride, "Reproduction as Male Ideology."

21. See Margaret Simons, *Beauvoir and* The Second Sex, 73–91, or Linda Zerilli, "A Process without a Subject: Simone de Beauvoir and Julia Kristeva on Maternity," *Signs* 18 (1992): 111–35. Zerilli reinterprets Beauvoir's discussions of the maternal body, whereas Simons notes that Beauvoir's characterization of motherhood is considerably less negative later in *The Second Sex.*

22. Making the same contrast between the institution of motherhood and motherhood itself, Beauvoir remarks in a 1982 interview with Alice Schwarzer that "there can be modes of existence where motherhood does not mean slavery. But these days it still comes down to the same thing. . . . Given that one can hardly tell women that washing up saucepans is their divine mission, they are told that bringing up children is their divine mission. But the way things are in this world, bringing up children has a great deal in common with washing up saucepans. In this way, women are thrust back into the role of a relative being, a second-class person" (Schwarzer, *After* The Second Sex: *Conversations with Simone de Beauvoir* [New York: Pantheon, 1984], 114). In her 1976 interview with Schwarzer, Beauvoir similarly comments: "I do not reject motherhood. . . . I'm against the circumstances under which mothers have to have their children" (76).

23. For an elaboration of the argument that the transcendence/immanence dualism provides a normative framework for critiquing continuing gender inequities in the home, see Andrea Veltman, "The Sisyphean Torture of Housework: Simone de Beauvoir and Inequitable Divisions of Domestic Work in Marriage" in *Hypatia* 19, no. 3 (Summer 2004).

24. Susan James similarly writes on the lack of strict overlap between transcendence and immanence and the public and private realms: "The [public] male world . . . reveals itself, in Hegelian vein, not simply as a realm of transcendent subjects, but as one where men, like women, can be rendered immanent. . . . The crucial difference between [the public and private realms] is not that the public realm contains uniformly transcendent men, while the private one contains both transcendent men and immanent women. Rather, transcendence and immanence are to be found in each" (James, "Complicity and Slavery in *The Second Sex,*" in *The Cambridge Companion to Simone de Beauvoir,* ed. Claudia Card [Cambridge: Cambridge University Press, 2004], 150–51).

25. When asked in a 1972 Paris interview with Alice Schwarzer about the conditions of independence, Beauvoir similarly commented on the inability of some waged occupations to provide an outlet for the exercise of freedom: "Work today does have a liberating side, but it is also alienating. . . . Work is not a panacea, but all the same, it is the first condition of independence" (Schwarzer, *After* The Second Sex, 42).

26. Elizabeth Spelman, "Simone de Beauvoir and Women: Just Who Does She Think 'We' Is?" in *Inessential Woman: Problems of Exclusion in Feminist Thought* (Boston: Beacon Press, 1988), 57–79. Spelman maintains, however, that *The Second Sex* contains the conceptual resources to build an adequate account of race and class oppression, although she thinks that Beauvoir herself does not fully develop these resources.

27. Criticisms of the transcendence/immanence dichotomy as classist have come from the general direction of third-wave feminists and have also been voiced at conferences such as the Midwest Society for Women in Philosophy.

BEAUVOIR AND SARTRE ON

APPEAL, DESIRE, AND AMBIGUITY

Eva Gothlin

7

Simone de Beauvoir is often read as a writer whose contribution to philosophy is to have applied the existentialism of Jean-Paul Sartre to the woman's question. During the last ten years this misconception has come increasingly under attack.[1] As I have argued in my book *Sex and Existence, Simone de Beauvoir's "The Second Sex"* (Lundgren-Gothlin 1991, 1996), this is a gross misconception that hides an original and interesting philosopher who should be part of our philosophical canon. Beauvoir developed her own existential phenomenology inspired by Martin Heidegger, Edmund Husserl, and Jean-Paul Sartre, and combined it with a philosophy of history inspired by G. W. F. Hegel, Alexandre Kojeve, and the young Karl Marx. This means that Beauvoir has a different concept of freedom, situation, and autonomy than the early Sartre—she does not accept the idea of an absolute freedom or a self-transparent *cogito*. She was in many respects closer to Maurice Merleau-Ponty than to Sartre (Kruks 1990; Heinämaa 1996).

In this paper, I focus on some important notions in Beauvoir's philosophy: ambiguity *(ambiguïté)*, which I see as central not only in the philosophical essay which bears that name, *The Ethics of Ambiguity* (*Pour une morale de l'ambiguïté*, 1946–47), but also in *The Second Sex* (*Le Deuxième sexe*, 1949); and appeal *(appel)*, a concept denoting intersubjectivity, which is important in Beauvoir's earlier essays. Both of these notions, appeal and ambiguity, are transposed in *The Second Sex* to characterize the female body and desire while continuing to bear ethical connotations. This points to a conception of femininity that runs contrary to the dominant view of femininity in *The Second Sex*. One aim of this paper is to disclose the complexity of Beauvoir's image of feminine desire.

In *The Ethics of Ambiguity* Beauvoir declares the human condition to be ambiguous. According to Beauvoir, we are both separate and connected to each other, a unique subject and an object for others, consciousness and body, free and unfree. On a deeper, ontological level, this notion of the human condition as ambiguous rests upon a re-reading of Sartre and Heidegger. I have elsewhere argued that Beauvoir's concept of ambiguity is founded upon two Heideggerian concepts, *Erschlossenheit* (disclosedness) and *Mitsein* (Being-with), which indicate that her ethics is less dependent on Sartre than has previously been assumed (Gothlin 2001).

One fundamental aspect of the ambiguity of the human condition— and this aspect deals with interhuman relationships—is the fact that human beings are simultaneously separate and interdependent. In *The Ethics of Ambiguity* Beauvoir underlines that "each one depends upon others," and this is referred to as human "interdependence" *(interdépendance)*.[2] For Beauvoir, the other is not a hindrance to my freedom, but a condition for my freedom to be realized. "The me-others relationship is as indissoluble as the subject-object relationship," Beauvoir says in *The Ethics of Ambiguity*. This leads to the conclusion that "to will oneself free is also to will others free" (1947, 102; 1948, 72ff.). Authenticity in interhuman relationships is to see others as free and creative, not as things or objects to own. In *The Second Sex* this notion of interdependence is also conceptualized as *Mitsein*, which points to its Heideggerian origin.

Ambiguity, which is thus an important notion in *The Ethics of Ambiguity*, appears less often as a term in *The Second Sex*. But ambiguity as a concept is still of importance in *The Second Sex*, and one of its interesting aspects is that it is related to the female body and desire.

Beauvoir does not view the body as something dominated by and subordinated to consciousness. She maintains, in *The Second Sex*, that the body "is a situation," and the human being "a historical idea." The biological nature of humans, therefore, is never experienced apart from a second social nature. Body, as well as body-consciousness, is always historically mediated

(Lundgren-Gothlin 1996, 92–97). Beauvoir emphasizes differences between the sexes, but also acknowledges that the meaning of these differences is always dependent on a historical situation and the interpretation given them. This should be borne in mind, considering the description of the differences between the sexes outlined below.

A characteristic of woman, Beauvoir writes in *The Second Sex,* is that she has a special relationship to the species. When she menstruates or when she is pregnant she is, and experiences herself as, alienated, because the species has then taken hold of her: "Woman, like man, *is* her body; but her body is something other than herself" (Beauvoir 1981, 61; 1949, I:66). Woman thus is and is not her body. Her relationship to it is ambiguous; she does not fully coincide with it. The man, on the other hand, always *"is"* his body" (Beauvoir 1981, 58; 1949, I:62). This ambiguity is also reflected in the fact that when an egg has been fertilized, woman is "at once herself and other than herself" (Beauvoir 1981, 54; 1949, I:58). It is also difficult to discern when the fetus/child is autonomous. Is it at conception, at birth, at weaning, or much later? The woman creates a bond, a relation to her child, after delivery, which further complicates this picture, Beauvoir says (1949, I:58).

If we relate this to the concept of ambiguity from her earlier essay, this means that in *The Second Sex* Beauvoir pictures woman as embodying more explicitly than man the ambiguity of the human condition, being separate as well as interdependent, body as well as consciousness. As we shall see, the same also applies to the notion of feminine desire (*"le désir feminine,"* sometimes *"le désir femelle"*).

In an argument with Sigmund Freud, Beauvoir maintains that feminine desire has not been sufficiently analyzed. As Elisabeth Roudinesco has pointed out in her *L'Histoire de la psychanalyse en France,* Beauvoir was a pioneer in introducing to France the debate over female sexuality, which engaged Helen Deutsch and Karen Horney among others during the 1920s and 1930s (Roudinesco 1986, 516ff.). In *The Second Sex* Beauvoir criticizes Freud for not having analyzed and described the feminine libido *(la libido féminine)* independently from the male libido *(la libido mâle)* (1981, 81; 1949, I:91). It is not clear if she argues for a specific feminine libido, but she maintains that "the psychoanalysts have never studied it [the feminine libido] directly, but only in taking the male libido as their point of departure" (1981, 81; 1949, I:91).

So Beauvoir maintains that feminine desire or sexuality has not been analyzed independently, as something that might differ from male desire or sexuality. She uses the notion of libido mostly in relation to her discussion of Freud and, as it seems, synonymously with the notion of desire.[3] The latter is frequent throughout *The Second Sex*. One can then conclude that Beauvoir is interested in analyzing phenomenologically the specific forms that feminine desire might take in her time and society, independently of the question of whether these forms apply to all women at all times.

In *The Second Sex* Beauvoir presupposes an original and common desire in children of both sexes, a desire characterized as an "aggressive eroticism" *(l'érotisme agressif)*, which involves a desire to grab, hug, and caress something that is smooth, creamy, and elastic (1981, 397; 1949, II:136). This desire is connected to the child's primary relationship to the mother's body, which is an object of desire for both male and female children (Beauvoir 1949, II:13).

In the male, this "aggressive eroticism" remains dominant, and the man can continuously satisfy his desire in relation to the woman, whose body has the desired characteristics. Most women on the other hand, according to Beauvoir, supplement this "aggressive eroticism," which is played out in lesbian relationships and in relation to their children, with a "passive eroticism" *(l'érotisme passif)*.[4] This means that "woman likes to be embraced, caressed, and especially after puberty she wants to be flesh in a man's arms" (Beauvoir 1981, 398).[5] This desire is not, as is the man's, connected to a will to grab and hold, and incarnated in a single organ. It is instead spread out in the body and not forwarded by will-connected activity. The woman is activated body and soul, but she makes herself also in some sense into an object.[6] She is simultaneously subject and object.

Feminine desire is thus ambiguous in that it can take the form of two types of sexuality, but also in the fact that the specific feminine desire is seen as contradictory if the male norm is applied: the idea of a "passive libido" seems to Beauvoir like a contradiction: "The notion of a 'passive libido' is baffling, since the libido has been defined, on the basis of the male, as a drive, an energy; but one would do no better to hold the opinion that a light could be at once yellow and blue—what is needed is the intuition of green" (1981, 81; 1949, I:91). It is important to note, however, that Beauvoir maintains that she is not referring to passivity in the traditional sense: "To *make* oneself an object, to *make* oneself passive, is a very different thing from *being* a passive object" (1981, 400; 1949, II:139).

Because male desire is concentrated in one organ, a greater instrumentality is encouraged. In his desire, a man is and remains a subject that directs himself toward an object, with the female as the object of desire.

> Man is, sexually, *subject,* and therefore men are normally separated from each other by the desire that drives them towards an object different from themselves. But woman is the absolute *object* of desire. . . . (Beauvoir 1981, 366; 1949, II:96ff.)

A woman, whose body in its entirety develops into an erotic zone, since these zones are so many, does not have such an instrumental relationship to the other (Beauvoir 1949, II:70). Her desire is not singularly represented in an organ, and woman feels ambivalence in relation to the man and his body. His body is not such a privileged object of desire. Beauvoir refers to "the fundamental ambivalence of the attraction exerted on the female by the male" (1981, 81; 1949, I:91). The woman is both attracted to and rejects the man. Feminine desire is, according to Beauvoir, an "appeal" *(appel):*

> We should regard as an original fact this sort of appeal, at one and the same time urgency and apprehension, which is female desire: it is the indissoluble synthesis of attraction and repulsion that characterizes it. (Beauvoir 1981, 81, translation modified; 1949, I:91)

That feminine desire is characterized as an "appeal" means that it is associated to a "calling out" to the other (see also Beauvoir 1949, II:137ff.).

Whether this is a description of feminine desire in a patriarchal society or a general one is hard to discern. One could point to the previously mentioned concept of situation that implies a rejection of ahistorical differences between the sexes, and in line with this to Foucault's and Butler's critique of all desire as culturally constructed. Furthermore, whether or not this is a problematic description of female sexuality is beyond the scope of this paper.[7] The analysis given here is intended to point to a greater complexity in Beauvoir's image of feminine sexuality than has generally been acknowledged.[8]

Instead, I focus on the interesting fact that the descriptions of feminine desire as well as of female embodiment correspond with Beauvoir's own definition of the human condition as ambiguous, a definition that differs from Sartre's view, in *Being and Nothingness*, of human beings as autonomous, separate subjects with instrumental and conflictual relationships to each other. Beauvoir does not repeat Sartre's dualistic image of the consciousness-body relationship but instead replaces it with a notion of a fundamental ambiguity.

One could argue that Beauvoir describes man and his relationship to the other in desire more in line with Sartre's view in *Being and Nothingness*—that is, man as a subject in front of whom the other and things appear as objects—and that she describes woman and her relationship to the other according to her own view in *The Ethics of Ambiguity*—that is, human beings as at once separate and interdependent. This means that woman, who is pictured as a more complicated and ambiguous being, represents to a greater extent Beauvoir's conception of human nature.

According to Beauvoir, there are differences between the sexuality of men and women, but she nevertheless assumes that intersubjectivity in heterosexual love is possible. Both masculine and feminine desire can degenerate into a will to dominate, to violence and sadism, or to passivity, subordination, and masochism. This degeneration is for Beauvoir inauthentic. In *The Second Sex* she sees conflict between human beings as fundamental but also as possible to transcend in a reciprocal recognition. Sartre, on the other hand, argues in *Being and Nothingness* that interhuman relationships are inherently conflictual and that love is inevitably sadistic/masochistic (Lundgren-Gothlin 1996, 149, 217ff.).

In *Notebooks for an Ethics (Cahiers pour une morale)*, Sartre's posthumously published manuscript on ethics written in 1947–48, Sartre connects intersubjectivity with authenticity. The only relationship where intersubjectivity seems to be excluded—that is, if sexual desire is to be maintained—is the relationship between the sexes:

> No love without that sadistic-masochistic dialectic of subjugation of freedoms that I have described. No love without deeper recognition and reciprocal comprehension of freedoms (a missing dimension in B[eing and] N[othingness]). However, to attempt to bring about a love that would surpass the sadistic-masochistic stage of desire and of enchantment would be to make love disappear, that is the sexual as type of disclosure of the human. (Sartre 1992, 414ff., translation slightly modified; 1983, 430)

The image of desire as sadistic/masochistic is thus maintained in *Notebooks for an Ethics*, even though Sartre also maintains that love is impossible without reciprocity and recognition. That he continues to connect desire with sadomasochism might be explained by the fact that Sartre sees desire as connected to violence: violence in the sense of a conflict between being a subject and object in the sexual relation, but also violence in the sense of the body "conquering" the consciousness in desire. In desire it "is consciousness that turns itself into a body but it is also the invasion of consciousness by the body" (1992, 180; 1983, 189). For Sartre, the tendency of the body in sexual desire to take over is threatening; it is compared to what happens in torture: "in both cases consciousness *surrenders* to the body" (1992, 180; 1983, 189). That the relationship between the sexes in *Notebooks for an Ethics* is treated as an example of inauthenticity further indicates that Sartre sees love and desire as dominated by conflict rather than by reciprocal recognition.[9]

Beauvoir, on the other hand, connects love with intersubjectivity and argues that this does not kill desire: "To recognize in woman a human being is not to impoverish man's experience: this would lose none of its diversity, its richness, or its intensity if it were to occur between two subjectivities [*dans son intersubjectivité*]. . . . It is simply to ask that behavior, sentiment, passion be founded upon the truth" (Beauvoir 1981, 291; 1949, I:393). She maintains that authentic love is founded on reciprocal recognition, friendship, generosity, and understanding. It requires that man refrain from trying to dominate woman and refrain from the violence that Sartre saw as connected to desire. The union of the sexes in love and desire, when it is grounded in a "reciprocal recognition," is also declared to represent intersubjectivity in an especially emblematic way because the ambiguity of the human condition is here bodily enacted. For Beauvoir, desire and the sexual union is not a sadomasochistic dialectic, but it is more of a merging with the other, where autonomy is simultaneously enacted and dissolved:

> Under a concrete and carnal form there is mutual recognition of self and of the other in the keenest awareness of the other and of the self. Some women say that they feel the masculine sex organ in them as part of their own bodies; some men feel that they *are* the women they penetrate. These are evidently inexact expressions, for the dimension of the *other* still exists; but the fact is that alterity has no longer a hostile implication, and indeed this sense of the union of separate bodies is what gives its moving character to the sexual act;

and it is the more overwhelming as the two beings, who together in passion deny and assert their boundaries, are alike (equals) and yet different. (Beauvoir 1981, 422, translation modified; 1949, II:167)

The sexual union of separate bodies resembles thus a psychoanalytic drama of symbiosis and separation being lived through. In desire, at least in feminine desire, which seems here to be projected as a norm, you are both subject and object, with the limits separating you and me both there and erased. The previously mentioned ambiguity—the human reality as characterized by freedom and interdependence—is mirrored also in the description of feminine desire and of the authentic sexual encounter. Note that Beauvoir does not envision desire as a conflict between consciousness and body as Sartre does in *Notebooks for an Ethics*. The authentic sexual union is recognition between consciousnesses, but it is enacted in "a concrete and carnal form." Desire is not seen as a threat to consciousness; according to Beauvoir, in desire you can have "the keenest awareness of the other and of the self."

In *The Second Sex*, feminine desire is characterized as an appeal. Interestingly, "appeal" is a term that appears in Beauvoir's earlier essays, but it is not associated with feminine sexuality. Beauvoir says in *The Ethics of Ambiguity*, "Thus, we see that no existence can be validly fulfilled if it is limited to itself. It appeals to the existence of others" (1948, 67; 1947, 95). In *Pyrrhus et Cinéas*, published in 1944, the concept of appeal is related to communication, to the directing of oneself to and speaking to the other, and to the opening up of possibilities for communication: "If this relation to the other is to be established, two conditions must be fulfilled. To begin with, it must be permitted for me to appeal. I therefore fight against those who want to silence my voice, prevent me from expressing myself, prevent me from being. . . . Then I must have in front of me, men [humans] who are free *for me*, who can answer my appeal."[10] The condition for the appeal is being able to make your voice heard, that is, that there is no silencing.

The term for feminine desire, *appeal*, had previously been associated with a will to communication and to intersubjectivity in Beauvoir's earlier philosophy. A metaphorical connection therefore lies between intersubjectivity and femininity because feminine desire is named an "appeal to" the other, and comprises the ambiguity of the human condition. This means that feminine desire is not conceptualized in an altogether negative manner in *The Second Sex*.

Interestingly, in *Notebooks for an Ethics*, which was written after *Pyrrhus et Cinéas* and *The Ethics of Ambiguity*, appeal is a concept that represents intersubjectivity and recognition. But for Sartre, this concept seems to deal mainly with the relationship between men. The relationship to woman in desire and sexuality is, as we have seen, partly placed outside the sphere of intersubjectivity. When the appeal appears in Sartre's philosophy as an ethical concept, it is thus simultaneously disconnected from the feminine and the corporeal.

Sartre maintains that "the appeal is first of all concrete, not abstract, recognition of the other," which presupposes that one "understands" the other (Sartre 1992, 283; 1983, 294). This, in turn, sets limits to it: "Differences of class, of nationality, of condition form limits to the appeal in its nature" (Sartre 1992, 285; 1983, 296). From this, Sartre concludes that: "an authentic appeal therefore has to be conscious of being a surpassing of every inequality of condition toward a human world where any appeal of anyone to anyone will always be possible" (1992, 285; 1983, 296ff.). Differences between the sexes are not explicitly mentioned as something that sets "limits" to the appeal, which is perhaps not surprising considering that the inequality between the sexes is not analyzed in Sartre's philosophy. Perhaps the relationship to woman, at least in sexuality, is for Sartre unconsciously of such a different character that it is placed in a separate sphere.

In *The Second Sex*, Beauvoir has analyzed how the inequality between the sexes has hindered reciprocal recognition and intersubjectivity. But possible differences between the sexes, and between masculine and feminine desire, are not seen as a hindrance in themselves to reciprocal recognition. Equality does not require sameness. Even when men and women are "mutually recognizing each other as subject, each will yet remain for the other an *other*" (Beauvoir 1981, 740; 1949, II:576). "Thus it is quite true that woman is other than man, and this alterity is directly felt in desire, the embrace, love; but the real relation is one of reciprocity; as such it gives rise to authentic drama" (1981, 283; 1949:I, 383ff.).

In *Notebooks for an Ethics*, Sartre uses the term *appeal* to designate the authentic meeting between humans, just as Beauvoir did in *Pyrrhus et Cinéas*. Beauvoir, on the other hand, uses *appeal* in *The Second Sex* to describe feminine desire. The term *appeal* does appear in Sartre's early philosophy, in *Being and Nothingness,* but it is associated with the feminine and the obscene. He says, "The obscenity of the feminine sex is that of everything which 'gapes open.' It is an *appeal to being* as all holes are. In herself woman appeals to a strange flesh which is to transform her into a fullness of being by penetration and dissolution. Conversely woman senses her condition as an appeal precisely because she is 'in the form of a hole'" (1956, 613f.; 1943, 706).

Originally then, for Sartre, the appeal is something obscene and corporeal, something feminine; whereas originally, for Beauvoir, it is something ethical, not specifically connected to the feminine, but instead to communication in general. While Beauvoir in *The Second Sex* and Sartre in *Being and Nothingness* characterize feminine desire and to a lesser extent woman herself as an appeal, Sartre in *Notebooks for an Ethics* exemplifies the ethical and the authentic relationship between humans as an appeal. On the other hand, this appeal is no longer associated with the feminine or the corporeal as it is when mentioned in *Being and Nothingness.* Instead, the relationship to the feminine and to woman in desire and sexuality is something that is partly placed outside the sphere of reciprocal recognition.

In *The Second Sex,* appeal, originally an ethical concept, has come to signify feminine desire, while "reciprocal recognition" *(recognition réciproque)* is more frequently used to denote intersubjectivity. On the other hand, we have seen that there is a metaphorical connection to ethics in that the appeal is a "calling out to the other," and in that authentic love and desire are connected to intersubjectivity. Sexuality, femininity, and body are thus not placed outside the sphere of ethics, as is common in the philosophical tradition, but in the center of it; and ambiguity and appeal, which originally are ethical concepts, are, in *The Second Sex,* associated with the feminine.[11]

Sartre's use of the concept of appeal in *Notebooks for an Ethics* as connected to communication and ethics, like Beauvoir's in *Pyrrhus et Cinéas,* might suggest Beauvoir's philosophical influence upon Sartre. Or Beauvoir's connection of the concept of appeal in *The Second Sex* to femininity might suggest Sartre's philosophical influence on her. An important distinction, though, is that while intersubjectivity for Sartre, conceptualized as appeal, seems to be problematic in relation to love and desire, the relationship between men and women is for Beauvoir the emblematic intersubjective relation.

Sartre tends to place the erotic relationship between the sexes in a special sphere, a sphere in which the reciprocal recognition does not fully apply. This is in line with traditional gender ideology, where such a relationship is placed outside the sphere of justice and rights (Pateman 1988). When Beauvoir refers to the relationship between the sexes in love and sexuality as the emblematic intersubjective relationship, she implicitly criticizes this traditional gender ideology and its division into the private and the public.

Beauvoir describes the feminine desire and the female embodiment as ambiguous, something that corresponds to her picture of the human reality as ambiguous. In the authentic sexual relation, the ambiguity of the human reality is concretely lived, being both subject and object, separate and interdependent. Woman is closer to this experience, according to Beauvoir's description, since feminine desire is an appeal to the other, not an instrumental subject-object relation. Beauvoir does not echo Sartre's more dualistic view of the body-consciousness relation. For him, desire is in some ways threatening because the body then tends to overwhelm the consciousness. For her, the authentic sexual relation is a concrete and carnal form of reciprocal recognition between two conscious beings.

I add that the concept of ambiguity, so central in Beauvoir's philosophy, is also important to Luce Irigaray, who in her *This Sex Which Is Not One (Ce sexe qui n'en est pas un)* and *An Ethics of Sexual Difference (Éthique de la différence sexuelle)* analyzes differences between the sexes in relation to the body and sexuality. Irigaray suggests elements that the morphology of the female body could contain, something which according to her could initiate a change in the symbolic order and affect a different symbolization of the feminine.

In this connection, Irigaray describes feminine desire and the female sex as impossible to reduce to oneness, to something unambiguous: Woman "*is neither one nor two,*" and her desire is *plurielle* (multiple, manifold) (Irigaray 1991, 26ff.; my translation). Irigaray further maintains that the female body does not have such clear limits as the male body. The man can enter it in coitus, and the child leaves it in being born. The female sex is a "threshold" *(seuil),* she says in *An Ethics of Sexual Difference:* "The threshold of the *lips*, which are strangers to dichotomy and oppositions" (Irigaray 1993, 18; 1989, 24). The female sex is thus one and two, both inside and outside—it is ambiguous.

Though there are important differences between the philosophies of Beauvoir and Irigaray, it is interesting to note that both connect ambiguity in different ways, implicitly or explicitly, with the female body and desire. For both of them, ambiguity, connected to women, is something positive. This tentative description of femininity—which in neither of their philosophies should be read as an advocacy of essentialism—also contains an image of a different relationship to the other, thereby indicating a connection between ethics and the feminine body or desire.

Notes

I would like to thank Toril Moi, Margaret A. Simons, and Mats Svensson for valuable comments to this paper.

1. See Simons (1986), Le Doeuff (1989), Kruks (1990), Fullbrook and Fullbrook (1993), Vintges (1996), and Bergoffen (1997).

2. Beauvoir (1948, 82; 1947, 116). On Beauvoir's concept of interdependence and its philosophical roots, see Lundgren-Gothlin (1995).

3. Like Beauvoir, Lacan generally prefers to speak in terms of *désir*, and when the term *libido* appears, it is in relation to a discussion of Freud.

4. Beauvoir (1981, 399; 1949, II:138). Or on "passive sexuality" *(sexualité passive);* see Beauvoir (1981, 398; 1949, II:137).

5. In the original French text, woman is given a more active role in "making herself flesh": *"la femme aime être étreinte, caressée et singulièrement depuis la puberté elle souhaite se faire chair entre les bras d'un homme"* (1949, II:137).

6. Beauvoir (1949, II:90, 137–39). "For the young girl, erotic transcendence consists in becoming prey in order to gain her ends. She becomes an object, and she sees herself as object; she discovers this new aspect of her being with surprise: it seems to her that she has been doubled; instead of coinciding exactly with herself, she now begins to exist *outside*" (1981, 361; 1949, II:90).

7. Passages such as the following do not give a positive image of female sexuality: "The sexual life of the little girl, on the contrary, has always been secret; when her eroticism changes and invades all her flesh, its mystery becomes agonizing: she suffers from the disturbances as from a shameful illness; it is not active: it is a state from which, even in imagination, she cannot find relief by any decision of her own. She does not dream of taking, shaping, violating: her part is to await, to want, she feels dependent; she scents danger in her alienated flesh" (1981, 345; 1949, II:73).

8. See, e.g., Toril Moi's interpretation in *Simone de Beauvoir, The Making of an Intellectual Woman* (1994), chapter 16, where she argues that Beauvoir glorifies male sexuality and depreciates female sexuality. This is more in line with my earlier interpre-

tation, where I focus only on the problematic aspects of Beauvoir's description of feminine desire and sexuality (Lundgren-Gothlin 1996, 202–10). I have thus modified my earlier interpretation. Note that Moi's interpretation of Beauvoir's concept of ambiguity differs from mine in that she sees this ambiguity as a result of woman's situation in a patriarchal society. For further references to the discussion about Beauvoir's view of sexuality, see Lundgren-Gothlin (1996, 149, 217ff.).

9. See the section on *la prière* (Sartre 1983, 245ff.) and the section on *la violence* (Sartre 1983, 187–90).

10. 113, my translation. I find it interesting that Beauvoir relates her concept of appeal to metaphors relating to the voice rather than to sight. As far as I know, the only other scholar that has written about the appeal is Debra Bergoffen. She writes about the appeal in *Pyrrhus et Cinéas* only, and does not analyze it in relation to gender or to Sartre's concept of appeal (Bergoffen 1997, 50–54).

11. In *The Second Sex*, one passage describes the female sexual desire as an appeal in negative terms, as in *Being and Nothingness:* "Feminine sex desire is the soft throbbing of a mollusc. Whereas man is impetuous, woman is only impatient . . . man dives upon his prey like the eagle and the hawk; woman lies in wait like the carnivorous plant, the bog, in which insects and children are swallowed up. She is suction, leech-like, humus, she is pitch and glue, a passive *appeal,* insinuating and slimy: thus, at least, she vaguely feels herself to be" (Beauvoir 1981, 407, translation modified; 1949, II:148; my italics).

References

Beauvoir, Simone de. 1944. *Pyrrhus et Cinéas.* Paris: Gallimard. (Translated as "Pyrrhus and Cineas.")

———. 1947. *Pour une morale de l'ambiguïté.* Paris: Gallimard. (Translated as *The ethics of ambiguity.*)

———. 1948. *The ethics of ambiguity.* New Jersey: Citadel Press.

———. 1949. *Le deuxième sexe.* 2 vols. Paris: Gallimard. (Translated as *The second sex.*)

———. 1981 (1953). *The second sex.* New York: Penguin Books.

———. 2004. "Pyrrhus and Cineas." In Simone de Beauvoir, *Philosophical writings,* ed. M. Simons, M. Timmermann, and M. B. Mader (Urbana: University of Illinois Press), 89–149.

Bergoffen, Debra. 1997. *The philosophy of Simone de Beauvoir.* New York: State University of New York Press.

Fullbrook, Kate, and Edward Fullbrook. 1993. *Simone de Beauvoir and Jean-Paul Sartre: The remaking of a twentieth-century legend.* London: Harvester Wheatsheaf.

Gothlin, Eva. 2001. Simone de Beauvoir's existential phenomenology and philosophy of history in 'Le Deuxième Sexe.' In *The existential phenomenology of Simone de Beauvoir,* ed. Wendy O'Brien and Lester Embree, 41–51. Dordrecht: Kluwer.

Heinämaa, Sara. 1996. Woman—nature, product, style? Rethinking the foundations of feminist philosophy of science. In *Feminism, Science, and the Philosophy of Science,* ed. L. H. Nelson and J. Nelson. Dordrecht: Kluwer.

Irigaray, Luce. 1989 (1984). *Éthique de la différence sexuelle.* Paris: Les Éditions de Minuit. (Translated as *An ethics of sexual difference.*)

———. 1991 (1977). *Ce sexe qui n'en est pas un.* Paris: Les Éditions de Minuit. (Translated as *This sex which is not one.*)

———. 1993. *An ethics of sexual difference.* London: Athlone Press.

Kruks, Sonia. 1990. *Situation and human existence, freedom, subjectivity and society.* London: Unwin Hyman.

Le Doeuff, Michèle. 1989. *L'étude et le rouet: Des femmes, de la philosophie, etc.* Paris: Seuil.

Lundgren-Gothlin, Eva. 1995. Gender and ethics in the philosophy of Simone de Beauvoir. *Nordic Journal of Women Studies* 3 (1).

———. 1996 (1991). *Sex and existence: Simone de Beauvoir's* The Second Sex. London: Athlone; New England: Wesleyan University Press. Originally published in Swedish as *Kön och existens, studier i Simonxe de Beauvoir's 'Le Deuxième Sexe.'* Göteborg: Daidalos, 1991.

Moi, Toril. 1994. *Simone de Beauvoir: The making of an intellectual woman.* Cambridge, Oxford: Blackwell.

Pateman, Carole. 1988. *The sexual contract.* Cambridge: Polity Press.

Roudinesco, Elisabeth. 1986. *Histoire de la psychanalyse en France 2, 1925–1948.* Paris: Fayard.

Sartre, Jean-Paul. 1943. *L'être et le néant, essai d'ontologie phénoménologique.* Paris: Gallimard. (Translated as *Being and nothingness.*)

———. 1956. *Being and nothingness: An essay on phenomenological ontology.* New York: Philosophical Library.

———. 1983. *Cahiers pour une morale.* Paris: Gallimard. (Translated as *Notebooks for an ethics.*)

———. 1992. *Notebooks for an ethics.* Chicago: University of Chicago Press.

Simons, Margaret A. 1986. Beauvoir and Sartre: The philosophical relationship. In *Simone de Beauvoir: Witness to a century,* Yale French Studies, no. 72, ed. Hélène Vivienne Wenzel.

Vintges, Karen. 1996. *Philosophy as passion: The thinking of Simone de Beauvoir.* Bloomington: Indiana University Press.

RECIPROCITY AND FRIENDSHIP IN

BEAUVOIR'S THOUGHT

Julie K. Ward

8

"The real relation is one of reciprocity"

—Beauvoir, *The Second Sex*

In an early passage from *The Prime of Life* (1962; *La Force de l'âge*, 1960), Simone de Beauvoir describes her life in 1929 when she was finally living independently in Paris after succeeding in the university *agrégation* exam. At this time, her close relationship with Jean-Paul Sartre began. At the outset, they seem to have spent some time exchanging ideas about the nature and terms of their relationship, prizing honesty and complete openness with each other, even making a pact that neither should conceal anything from the other. To this rule they added the provision, formulated by Sartre, that though they shared a "necessary" love, it would be good for each to experience "contingent" love affairs.[1] But nonetheless they agreed that it would be reasonable to devote themselves entirely to the relationship for a certain period of time. On all points, Beauvoir seems to have supported Sartre's views, remarking confidently, "We were two of a kind, and our relationship would endure as long as we did" (1960, 27). Despite the assurance of these words, one incident during the same period stands out, suggesting real differences in their conceptions of relation to the other and ideas about reciprocity.

As Beauvoir recalls the episode, she was strolling with Sartre through a garden near the Louvre one fall afternoon. Stopping to rest momentarily on a bench, they found a small cat that had become trapped near the bench:

> There was a kind of balustrade which served as a backrest a little way out from the wall, and in the cagelike space, a cat was miaowing. How had it slipped in there? It was too big to get out. Evening was coming on; a woman came up to the bench, a paper bag in her hand, and produced some scraps of meat. These she fed to the cat, stroking it tenderly the while. It was at this moment that Sartre said: "Let's sign a two-year lease." (Beauvoir 1960, 27)

This account is arresting on a number of points, first, perhaps, because it is placed in the middle of her recounting the beginning of their relationship. In such a context, the episode about the trapped cat is strangely anomalous. But then subtle differences appear in their reactions to the cat and their ways of being in relation to the woman who feeds the cat and, by extension, to one another. I would like to enlarge upon these differences and to use the passage as a parallel to what emerges in other parts of Beauvoir's work concerning the "problem of the other." From a philosophical perspective, the narrative provides a figurative entrance into the issue of relation to others and the possibility of true reciprocity.

In the above passage, Sartre's presence dominates the end of the scene, whereas Beauvoir's presence is merely implicit. She seems to be nowhere, her subjectivity absent from the passage, while Sartre breaks the descriptive scene with his decisive utterance. In effect, his statement closes her narrative about the trapped cat without his having made mention of the cat. Sartre seems to have "appropriated" the narrative scene, even as Beauvoir's own recollection structures the event. In this respect, the passage suggests or implies a displacement of Beauvoir's subjectivity as Sartre pronounces not an interrogative but a virtual command, to which she later acquiesces. While Beauvoir's presence is not individuated in verbal expression as is Sartre's, she is not absent from the passage.

In fact, Beauvoir is present in what at first appears as her absence, through her awareness of and sympathetic response to the woman feeding the cat. As she recalls the event, she found the trapped, meowing cat and did not know how to rescue it. Then she relates that a woman approached the cat with some scraps and fed it, "stroking it tenderly," thus revealing Beauvoir's awareness focused beyond herself and Sartre and upon the woman ministering to the animal. In that instant Beauvoir manifests herself as the other who perceives the response of another to need; and in so doing, she participates in that same response to the other. In this respect, she presents a mode of being to others that stands in contrast to the self-absorbed presence of Sartre, who appears to remain unaffected by this event even though he is with her and she is caught up by the scene.

Beauvoir's recollection of the trapped cat is thus suggestive on two points. First, although she thinks that she and Sartre are "two of a kind,"[2] she does not show Sartre sharing or trying to share her experience; rather, she shares his in the respect that she acquiesces to participate in his beliefs and his projects. This tendency is exemplified within the episode: when Beauvoir observes the exchange between the cat and the woman, Sartre intercedes with his desire to "sign a two-year lease." As Beauvoir's memoir explains, Sartre's phrase meant that they would share each other's attention exclusively for two years while they lived in Paris, after which they would plan to live apart for two or three years, and then rejoin. Beauvoir accedes to Sartre's plan, though she expresses some reservation about the idea of a planned separation. Nonetheless, on the whole, she neither objects to Sartre's act of sovereignty nor tries to make him accept her on her own terms. On the contrary, she seems to support his ideas about love and his conditions for their relationship with great alacrity.

Yet that Beauvoir sometimes subordinates her desires to Sartre's is not so much the focal concern as is as the way the passage represents an attitude, or a way of being with the other, that is evident in his interaction with her. At the same time, the episode gives us a glimpse of another kind of relation, one that falls outside the one Beauvoir states she shares with Sartre. This is the relation of sympathetic awareness that Beauvoir observes between the trapped cat and the woman, an exchange that excludes Sartre insofar as Beauvoir depicts him as unaware of and unmoved by the situation. By her recollection, she responded emotionally to the plight of the cat, just as the woman with the food had. This fact reveals her identification with the unnamed woman, here representing the person who can perceive need and act accordingly; and in this respect, she reveals her difference from

Sartre. Her awareness is of the specific relation that transpires between the trapped cat and the woman who responds to it. Here Beauvoir's gaze is turned toward the cat itself, finding itself in an impossible cage, unable to escape, which then experiences the welcome ministrations of a woman who appears to feed it. To all this, Sartre remains a silent bystander.

Though the incident forms but a small episode in Beauvoir's memoirs, it looks backward, in one sense, to her personal development, and more significantly, forward, to her later philosophical treatment of being with others and reciprocity. The trapped cat and the female response stand as a kind of psychological motif for a recurring problem in lived experience. On this level, the incident suggests a metaphorical parallel for Beauvoir's own situation when, because of some constraining experience, she finds herself "trapped" and in need. Certainly, prior to that fall in 1929, such an experience came to her after her closest childhood friend, Zaza, died, and perhaps also after the separation from her first love, Jacques. These events, together with the constraints she felt from living with her family, help explain both her elation at living by herself in Paris for the first time and her rush into the relationship with Sartre. For it was at this point that Sartre fully entered her life and seems to have taken it over: as she describes it, he gave her the same certainty as belief in God.[3] But a further meaning is suggested: while she writes in *La Force de l'âge* (1960, 27–28) that she welcomed Sartre's presence, finding in his companionship complete security, freedom, and happiness, the cat episode indicates, perhaps in inchoate form, something to the contrary. For it is not Sartre but an anonymous woman who sees the need and rescues the cat; therefore, the unexpressed thought is that Sartre, whom she spares no superlatives in describing, is in some sense a bystander who does not know how to respond to need. Whether the trapped cat is a metaphor for Beauvoir herself or whether she simply participates, by extension, in the response of the woman to the cat remains undetermined; what matters is that the figure who does respond is not Sartre but another woman.

Considering the incident at a philosophical level, the story may be read as an allusion to Beauvoir's longstanding aim for a relationship of mutual equality—one that allows for true reciprocity and mutual subjectivity. Beauvoir refers to the need for such a relationship to the other throughout her works: it forms a constant theme in her early 1927 diary; in *She Came to Stay* (1954; *L'Invitée*, 1943), the protagonist, Françoise, is continually seeking some kind of recognition from the younger woman, Xavière;[4] and, as was mentioned, in *Prime of Life* (1962), Beauvoir claims to have found reciprocity with Sartre. Yet all of these texts indicate that she finds recognition and reciprocity difficult, perhaps unattainable, and the few moments of real reciprocity she relates are with her sister, Hélène, or with her friend, Zaza.[5] Beauvoir's recollection of her relationship with Zaza gives us the flavor of the sought-for relation: "To achieve basic understanding with someone is a very rare privilege in any circumstance; for me it took on a literally infinite value. At the back of my memory there glowed, with unparalleled sweetness, all those long hours that Zaza and I had spent hidden in Monsieur Mabille's study, talking" (1962, 27).

Although one of Beauvoir's central aims is to reach a "basic understanding" with the other, her attempts are almost always unproductive of their end. She aims at relations of mutual reciprocity, but she more often ends up like the trapped cat, unable to get out, without someone to feed her. This problem takes a deeply psychological turn in some later chapters of *The Second Sex* (1989; *Le Deuxième sexe*, 1949), where Beauvoir is exploring female development within a Freudian theoretical framework. Therein the reason for the difficulty, especially for women, in attaining reciprocal relationships concerns their psychological development from infancy. Women, more than men, she finds, have the road to reciprocity blocked, in part because of the social significance of being "castrated." Here, although she does not explicitly do so, she has the theoretical material necessary to suggest that the obstacle to female reciprocity can be overcome through the projection of one's ego onto a female other, a friend who mirrors her self.

While themes of the other, recognition, and reciprocity figure prominently both in Beauvoir's early diary and in her novel, *She Came to Stay* (1954), the canonical philosophical analyses of these problems are formulated in *The Second Sex* (1989). That the early works provide the psychological corollaries to the philosophical discussion is evident even in the 1927 diary, where Beauvoir acknowledges the conflict of self and other: "I must clear up my philosophical ideas . . . deepen the problems which have confronted me. The theme is almost always the opposition of oneself and the other that I have felt from the beginning of my life" (Beauvoir 1927, 95; Simons 1999b, 4).[6] From the outset of the diary, Beauvoir describes herself as "waiting impatiently for the day when there will be no longer *the other* nor *me*, but only and definitively *us*" (Beauvoir 1927, 7; Simons 1999b, 14). But the young Beauvoir does not achieve this union, and she vacillates between two poles in her thinking. She swings either toward masochism—accepting the position of an inferior to a superior subject by fusing herself with that other—or isolation—demonstrating her autonomy and independence by withdrawing herself to a safe position away from others.[7] Over and over again, the 1927 diary recounts how she is drawn to her cousin, Jacques, and later to Barbier, a fellow student, by a need to be dominated. She describes the attraction to Barbier thus: "What attracts me is his manner of domination, of being strong, and such that one could walk simply in the light that his eyes reflect" (Beauvoir 1927, 38; Simons 1999b, 13). As Simons (1999b) has suggested, the need to be powerfully domi-nated by the other constitutes the need for the other as absolute, as God—a need that, though it promises fulfillment, actually poses a danger in its loss of self.

Yet the 1927 diary records, as well, an equal uncertainty about the value of domination and a sense of self-sufficiency: "Others can no longer be anything definitive and complete; the great renunciation that I had dreamed of is impossible. They are not anything but themselves, as I am but myself, and above all, I have no need of them" (Beauvoir 1927, 18–19; Simons 1999b, 15). In such fashion, Beauvoir expresses her need of in-dependence, mentioning Merleau-Ponty's comment about her: "He tells me that I am an individualist: I feel especially that no one can do anything for me, that I can only count on myself, that I have only myself" (Beauvoir 1927, 138). Yet, though she constantly insists on her capacity to rely on herself ("I count on myself; I know that I can count on myself"), Beauvoir also quietly remarks, "but I would like not to have to count on myself" (Beauvoir 1927, 57; Simons 1999b, 16). Near the close of the diary, Beau-voir once again ponders the value of autonomy over relationship, exclaim-ing on the one hand, "I refuse to submit to any servitude," and yet she con-tinues, "But, at base, I do not know . . . perhaps I could sacrifice everything for him, and it would not be a sacrifice" (Beauvoir 1927, 90; Simons 1999b, 6).[8] Thus, in the space of the early diary, the dilemma of how to attain a stable relation between oneself and the other remains unresolved as Beauvoir shifts from one side of the opposition to the other, from the pole of isolated self-sufficiency to that of undifferentiated fusion with other.[9]

Although the early diary reveals Beauvoir's thinking of the other in terms of a relation of domination and complete fusion, it also presents another mode of being with others. This second kind appears in the interrelation between Beauvoir and her friend, Zaza, or between Beauvoir and her younger sister, Hélène. Typical of her attachment to Zaza is Beauvoir's exclamation: "the beauty of the night, of life, everything that I want to write about Zaza. Joy! Joy! Immense friendship of my heart, which will not end" (1927, 159). In a similar vein, Beauvoir describes the "joy of refuge" in the "real tenderness" of her sister's eyes. Throughout the early diary, Beauvoir's descriptions of her feelings and interactions with her female friend and her sister point to a kind of relation in which Beauvoir experiences what she will later describe in her philosophical works as a mutual recognition of subjects. It is also noticeable that these accounts stand in complete contrast to the descriptions she develops in the diary concerning male lovers' domination of the self. Among female friends, Beauvoir feels recognized and, importantly, preserved; whereas with her male love-objects, she experiences a loss of self. So the early diary not only shows that Beauvoir possesses a positive notion of being seen by the other but also that the model of this positive relation to another is evident in some of Beauvoir's female friendships.[10] For Beauvoir, it is precisely with Zaza and Hélène that being with the other is a comfort, not a conflict, and provides continuity, not disruption, to being a subject.

Nor does *She Came to Stay* (1954) controvert this idea of female friendship with the destruction of one woman by another.[11] For what one finds in the novel is not the attainment of positive recognition and reciprocity but their failure, as the ending of the story represents. Thus, Françoise's violent action of killing Xavière in the final scene gives us the literary parallel to Beauvoir's rejection of the domination mode of relation.[12] Sovereignty over another annihilates the freedom of the other, and thus is disallowed. It must be noted, too, that *She Came to Stay* (1954) traces a more complex sketch of the problem than that of Beauvoir's early diary in which a simple opposition between masochism and isolation appears. In the novel, Beauvoir includes narcissism as another line of force—as a force parallel to that of masochistic fusion evident in the early diary. In *She Came to Stay*, Beauvoir sees both tendencies as constituting limits of positive being seen by the other, something that the early diary does not acknowledge. And it is precisely these two problems, narcissism and masochism, that figure prominently in her later philosophical account of the other.

In *The Second Sex* (1989), Beauvoir refines and develops the two modes of being with the other. The "domination model" of relation, the psychological attitude that involves an asymmetrical, oppositional mode of being between subject and other, is traceable in the metaphysical correlate claimed in the Introduction to *The Second Sex* (1989): "[Following Hegel] we find in consciousness itself a fundamental hostility toward every other consciousness; the subject can be posed only in being opposed—he sets himself up as the essential, as opposed to the other, the inessential, the object" (xxix).[13] At present, no state of reciprocity obtains between men and women: woman comes to be separated from her self as a subject through the masculine representation of her as "the other, the inessential, the object." Consequently, woman's ontological situation is one of alienation because she, as a transcendent being, stands as an equal partner with man but does not enjoy equality and reciprocity with him. Current society, with its many institutions privileging men, presents obstacles to the normalization of gender relations and to the attainment of reciprocity between men and women.

Yet this does not mean that Beauvoir rules out reciprocal recognition between the sexes as unattainable because of some eternal, ahistorical conflict; she uses the oppositional structure of consciousness to explain the origin of oppression.[14] As I see it, Beauvoir employs the Hegelian opposition of consciousness as a corrective to Claude Lévi-Strauss's interpretation of biological differences between the sexes as "the fundamental . . . data of social reality," claiming that to pose sexual difference as oppositional presupposes a prior opposition (Beauvoir 1989, xxviii–xxix). As well, Beauvoir argues against Friedrich Engels by claiming that historical materialism is inadequate to account for women's oppression, again invoking "the imperialism of human consciousness, seeking always to exercise its sovereignty in objective fashion" (1989, 58). But though the origin of sexual difference begins with the antagonism between consciousnesses, sexual conflict is not an inescapable, noncontingent fact.[15]

Evidence of an alternative conception of relation to others appears in Beauvoir's treatment of literary writers. Thus, she approvingly discusses the work of Stendhal (Marie-Henri Beyle) and his characterization of women: only he is capable of the recognition of woman as she is, an actual subject, and not merely an object for man. She claims that Stendhal's treatment of women is distinct in that it illustrates the very thing that is lacking in Hegel's conception of woman: "Woman truly is in Stendhal what Hegel was for a moment tempted to make of her: that other consciousness which in reciprocal recognition gives to the other subject the same truth that she receives from him" (Beauvoir 1989, 247). What Stendhal appreciates in women and rejects in his female characters, she finds, is that woman is a "subject in her own right" and not "pure alterity" (1989, 247). Beauvoir marks here an alternative to the fundamental opposition of consciousnesses posited first.

The alternative model is characterized as one of equality and respect, involving a state of "fellowship based on solidarity and friendliness" (Beauvoir 1989, xxix). That two consciousnesses are able to attain the state of mutual recognition instead of being locked in a fundamental conflict is evident in her acknowledgment that the Hegelian master-slave relation may be overcome. So, she claims:

> It is possible to rise above this conflict [that of the master-slave] if each individual freely recognizes the other, each regarding himself and the other simultaneously as object and as subject in a reciprocal manner. But friendship and generosity, which alone permit this recognition of free beings, are not facile virtues; they are assuredly humanity's highest achievement. (1989, 140)

Here Beauvoir characterizes reciprocity as a mode in which subjects recognize each other equally both as object and as subject, implying that the fundamental opposition of the other as object is overcome by a parallel recognition of other as subject.[16] A further reference to this mode of relation is offered in the final chapter of *The Second Sex*, where Beauvoir uses Karl Marx's notion that "the direct, natural, necessary relation of human creatures is the relation of man to woman" to illuminate her notion of mutual reciprocity: "To emancipate woman is to refuse to confine her to the relations she bears to man, not to deny them to her; let her have her independent existence, and she will continue for him also: mutually recognizing each other as subject, each will yet remain for the other an other" (1989, 731). But two facts for Beauvoir would appear to block the attainment of reciprocal recognition. First, reciprocity is not possible without a prior equality between subjects, what Beauvoir terms "friendship and generosity," which she claims are "not facile virtues." Second, women are further disadvantaged in that they have not yet engaged in the demand for recognition, as have men.[17] Women are disadvantaged because of their peculiar history, by the difficulties that masculine society poses for them in recognizing themselves as subjects; we see thus the persistent alterity of woman to man through myth, mores, and philosophy of Western culture. From Aristotle to Aquinas, and on to Hegel and contemporary thinkers, Beauvoir thinks, the category of woman stands to man as a fundamental other.[18] For this reason, then, the sought-for relation of mutual recognition of women is not to be identified with the bond that women presently experience in relation to men, in which they are regarded as the "inessential other."[19]

But, it may be objected, given the difficulties, both the entrenched institutions and individual obstacles, the goal of reciprocity is perhaps practically unattainable; therefore, why aim at it? For Beauvoir, the crucial gain is that reciprocity allows for a resolution to the dialectical opposition of consciousnesses. More importantly, only mutual recognition of subjects allows the kind of freedom proper to our humanity. Still, the goal of reciprocity is, as she has always noted, hard-won, and it cannot be substituted by a flawed universality in which subjects desire sovereignty for themselves individually, an inadequate position that Xavière typifies in *She Came to Stay* (1954); Xavière professes friendship, but merely desires sovereignty over Françoise. The failure of reciprocity, its falling short and becoming mere egoism, is thus a constant theme in Beauvoir's fictional works as well.

One arrives, then, at the question of how a genuine sort of mutual recognition between subjects may arise. This problem becomes especially acute for women in relation to other women, given their tendency to accept nonrecognition and the fact that they have not engaged with men in a struggle for mutual recognition. At first glance, *The Second Sex* (1989) provides no account of how real universality for women comes about, focusing instead on the various problems within the Hegelian opposition, such as why a dominant subject refuses to seek reciprocity with a subordinate. One obvious reason for the reluctance is that a reciprocity of subjects would threaten the dominant subject's sovereignty. It is by thus posing woman as absolute other that man finds "a means of escaping that implacable dialectic which has its source in the reciprocity that exists between free beings" (Beauvoir 1989, 141). Yet there is some indication of a resolution to the problem in the later chapters of *The Second Sex*, where Beauvoir gives a psychological explanation for girls' and women's failure to move toward reciprocity.

Beauvoir gives a Freudian psychological account of female development in which the girl's perception of what it means to lack a penis leads to significant differences in her mentality. In contrast to the boy, who, with his penis is able to project his fears onto something external and thus cope, the little girl is more concerned with her "insides," and so is "more opaque to her own eyes" (Beauvoir 1989, 278). Though Beauvoir parts with Freud on the reality of "penis envy" for the girl, she notes that "the absence of the organ will certainly play an important role in her destiny" (1989, 278). The crucial contrast in their development comes to this: while the penis serves as an alter ego for the little boy in that he projects himself into an object that is also himself, the little girl cannot do this, she "cannot incarnate herself in any part of herself" (1989, 278), and so is given a doll to serve as her alter ego. The problem for the girl, according to Beauvoir, is that the doll is at once foreign to her, a "passive object," and yet it represents the whole body (1989, 278), causing the girl to take her whole person as "an inert given object" (1989, 279). The import of this simple difference looms large: "While the boy seeks himself in the penis as an autonomous subject, the little girl coddles her doll and dresses her up as she dreams of being coddled and dressed up herself; inversely, she thinks of herself as a marvelous doll" (1989, 279). Whereas the little boy can attain a position of subjectivity through his ego identification with his penis, Beauvoir argues that the girl does not do so. She finds that the girl's resultant attitude is instead narcissism and a loss of true subjectivity.[20]

On Beauvoir's account, the little girl seeks to find her subjectivity in making herself an object for others. To illustrate this childhood narcissism,

Beauvoir quotes an author who describes dressing up in laces and flowers at five years old to dance in the drawing room, "I was a great dancer . . . and the whole family was there to look at me" (1989, 279). For Beauvoir, the girl's difficulty resides in this opposition between her possible autonomous subjectivity and the actual mediated subject position, this "being-the-other" (1989, 280) where she makes herself object for others. The danger that Beauvoir finds in a subjectivity that is wholly being for others involves its tendency toward inauthenticity and an avoidance of choice. This mode of being she terms "narcissism," finding it undesirable on the grounds that it obviates responsibility for one's own choices and limits one's autonomy. That she perceives it as narcissism thus suggests that it is not selflessness or altruism as such to which she objects, but its tendency as a feminine attitude to be expressed in ways harmful to the self, and so to tend towards masochism.

Beauvoir's account in *The Second Sex* of the female's relation to and being for others transcends both her early diary and *She Came to Stay*, neither of which is able to explain adequately masochism, domination, or the need to be seen by others, that is, "to be reflected in the eyes of others" as she puts it in the early diary. There she finds that egoistic isolation is no answer, nor is masochistic fusion with the other; to these she adds narcissism as a third limit. This last represents a danger to the girl's self-knowledge, for Beauvoir seems to think that the psychological reasons that conduce to the girl "being-the-other" to others also conduce to her "being-the-other" to herself. As I interpret Beauvoir's point, the girl identifies wholly with the others' conception of herself as other; figuratively, she knows herself as the doll that is other than herself. If this is correct, then "being for others" exclusively supports both slavishness and a kind of self-deception.

But if the previous accounts are correct, if female development must culminate either in narcissism or in masochism, there is no possibility for women to attain reciprocal relations, or indeed, to become subjects at all. So the question arises whether Beauvoir offers any solution from the psychological analysis of the female situation caught between narcissism and masochism. I suggest that she has the material for the solution in her discussion of female-female relations but does not make the answer explicit.[21]

In Beauvoir's chapter on the lesbian, various passages approach the issue of female homosexuality without bias as she discusses the advantages of female-female relations. In a particularly striking passage, she claims that the woman more easily sees herself as a subject in relation to another female than to a male: "Between women, love is contemplative; caresses are intended less to gain possession of the other than gradually to re-create the self through her; separateness is abolished, there is no struggle, no victory, no defeat; in exact reciprocity each is at once subject and object, sovereign and slave; duality becomes mutuality" (1989, 416). The language in this passage is so strikingly similar to that used in previous descriptions of mutual recognition that one is led to think that Beauvoir is suggesting the means by which women attain recognition, which seems problematical because such means exclude labor and production. But the contrast between heterosexual and homosexual love Beauvoir draws is pointed: between men and women, "love is an act; each torn from self becomes other," whereas between women, "separateness is abolished in exact reciprocity, each is at once subject and object . . . duality becomes mutuality" (1989, 416). In seeking sexual relations with a man, a woman is willing to be changed into a passive object: she seeks to find herself "under the aspect of a thing," hoping "to find herself in her otherness, her alterity" (1989, 416). This search, Beauvoir implies, is misdirected: in heterosexual relations, a woman knows her body through the male touch only "for herself—as she herself perceives it, not as it is to others" (1989, 416), whereas between women sex allows for reciprocal self-knowing. But are we to take this as recommendation for women tout court? The scope of the proposal remains unclear: Beauvoir specifically mentions that the narcissistic woman will recognize herself inadequately through sexual relations with men. Thus, she implies that for women of this attitude, lesbian relations will lead precisely to reciprocity, rather than to mere alterity.

However, her line of reasoning is not forthright in this passage, for instead of claiming lesbianism as the solution to female narcissism, she pulls back, noting that narcissism does not always lead to homosexuality (1989, 417). Surely this remark is beside the point: if narcissism is a typical feminine attitude, and if sexual relations with men only reiterate the alterity of the narcissist, while relations with women provide reciprocal recognition for them, then lesbianism should be seen as a resolution to the problem of female alterity. I find this conclusion to be what Beauvoir moves toward, although she does not argue it explicitly. That this is her conclusion is evident from additional passages in *The Second Sex* (1989), for example, where she contrasts the nature of heterosexual and homosexual intimacy. Between men and women, women are always playing a part to men, in part because they are dependent upon them. Thus, for the heterosexual woman, "[n]ever in the presence of husband or lover can she feel wholly herself; but with her woman friend she need not be on parade: they are too much of a kind not to show themselves frankly as they are. This similarity engenders complete intimacy" (1989, 420).

The eroticism between women differs also from that between women and men: Beauvoir finds sexual love between women to be less violent, more even, and more continuous. Lesbian lovers are "not carried away in frenetic ecstasies, but they never sink back into hostile indifference," whereas when heterosexual lovers separate, "they again become strangers; the male body again becomes repulsive to the woman" (Beauvoir 1989, 420). So, in spite of the lack of explicit argument on Beauvoir's part about homosexual love holding promise for female reciprocity, the further passages in *The Second Sex* suggest a resolution to the problem of recognition, at least in regard to the narcissist. In contrast to male-female relationships, female-female friendships and lesbian attachments are more beneficial because of their tendency to allow for more reciprocity among women than do female-male relations. Given what Beauvoir thinks to be general female liabilities toward narcissism and masochism, the scope of her proposal may be wider than it first appears.

In summary, while Beauvoir claims that she found in Sartre the basis for mutual recognition and reciprocity, it seems she owes her conception of the relation, at least as experienced, to her young female friend, Zaza, and to Hélène, her sister. The initial road to reciprocity for women is endangered by narcissism and masochism, and blocked by their absolute otherness to men. Yet if Beauvoir's analysis of the lesbian is correct, the difficulties of such attitudes may be overcome by the woman's projection of her ego onto a female friend, an other who mirrors her own self in mutual recognition. Thus, woman's subjectivity is not blocked or negated, but is preserved in the loving gaze of her female friend, her other self. The irony is that while Beauvoir praises Sartre as being the one with the philosophical mind, it is Beauvoir's philosophical system that solves the problem of the fundamental conflict between subjects by allowing for their mutual recognition.

NOTES

I would like to thank Peg Simons, friend, Beauvoir scholar, and editor of this volume, for her support; and two anonymous referees for their comments and objections to this paper, which have improved it.

1. In *La Force de l'âge,* Beauvoir says Sartre held that "entre nous, m'explicait-il en utilisant un vocabulaire qui lui était cher, il s'agit d'un amour nécessaire: il convient que nous connaissions aussi des amours contingentes" (1960, 26–27). So Sartre seems either to have formulated the terms or been the one who imposed them on their relationship.

2. Beauvoir remarks, "Nous étions d'une même espèce . . ." (1960, 27; 1962, 24), and she makes a similar remark elsewhere, "the identical sign on both our brows" (1962, 26) to describe what she perceives to be the similarity of character she shares with Sartre.

3. Beauvoir claims, "My trust in him was so complete that he supplied me with the sort of absolute unfailing security that I had once had from my parents, or from God. . . . All my most remote and deep-felt longings were now fulfilled; there was nothing left for me to wish" (1962, 27).

4. In one passage, Françoise takes Xavière home in a taxi: "Xavière collapsed on the seat and Françoise slipped her arm around her; as she closed her hand over Xavière's small, limp hand, she felt flooded with joy. Whether she wanted or not, Xavière was bound to her by a bond stronger than hatred or love; Françoise was not her prey along with the rest, she was the very substance of her life and all the moments of passion, of pleasure, of desire could not have existed without this firm web that supported them" (Beauvoir 1954, 250–51). Although this interpretation is not uncontroversial, I suggest that Françoise seeks recognition from Xavière, but her gesture comes to nothing as Xavière turns away from her, and Françoise is "ashamed of that futile gesture of tenderness" as she climbs the stairs to her room alone (1954, 252).

5. In claiming this, I acknowledge the apparent counter-evidence about her feelings for Sartre in her memoir, *Prime of Life* (1962), and have touched on this problem in what has preceded.

6. References to Beauvoir's 1927 diary arise from the French text of the MS that was included in an early version of Margaret Simons' paper "From Murder to Morality: The Development of Beauvoir's Ethics" (Simons 1997). The published version of this paper (without the French text) appeared in 1999, and is cited as "Simons 1999b."

7. In this, I agree with Simons (1999b).

8. In the line "peut-être que je lui sacrificerai tout, tout et que çe ne sera pas un sacrifice," Simons contends the reference to "lui" is to Jacques (Simons 1997, 14).

9. As Simons points out: "When the anguish of isolation becomes too acute and the need for the other becomes extreme, the self is abandoned as one tries to merge with the other, seeking to be dominated. When the attempt at fusion is frustrated . . . by differences between self and other, the only alternative is an egoistic individualism that verges on solipsism and the cycle repeats itself" (1999b, 13–14).

10. Simons (1999b) is right to find Beauvoir's account of being seen by the other as wholly distinct from that of Sartre, but she overlooks the point that the positive accounts of inter-relation, the ones that do not involve complete fusion and domination, are always with other women.

11. The book's opening quotation from Hegel, "Each consciousness seeks the death of the other," leaves no doubt that *She Came to Stay* (1954) should be taken as rejecting a literary depiction of the Hegelian conflict.

12. Simons (1999b, 2) argues that Xavière's murder represents Beauvoir's rejection of both ethical egoism and selfless devotion as adequate moral standpoints.

13. While it is true that the Hegelian account of the opposition of consciousness refers to a fundamental aspect of human consciousness, Beauvoir employs it as a starting point of her discussion about why women fail to dispute male sovereignty and become the other (1989, xxx).

14. In this reading, I am following the excellent discussion of Beauvoir's use of Hegel and Alexandre Kojève in Eva Lundgren-Gothlin (1996).

15. It should be noted that this reading is not uncontroversial; see, for example, Simons (1995).

16. This mode of relation to the other is either equated with friendship or seen in its analogue, the couple constituting "a primordial *Mitsein*" (Beauvoir 1989, xxxi). Lundgren-Gothlin points out that Sartre does not pose this mode of relation, "reciprocal recognition," as a solution to the dialectical conflict (1996, 70–71).

17. Debra Bergoffen (1997, 166–76), and Lundgren-Gothlin (1996, 70–76) agree on the point that women presently existing lack the same history as men in encountering the other and in demanding recognition, partly because of their separation from production.

18. In a similar vein, Beauvoir faults Emmanuel Lévinas for marking the feminine as the absolute contrary, a notion that "deliberately takes the man's point of view, disregarding the reciprocity of subject and object. When he writes that woman is mystery, he implies that she is mystery for man. Thus, his description, which is intended to be objective, is in fact an assertion of masculine privilege" (1989, xxvii).

19. Bergoffen argues that as the inessential other, women value the bond with their patriarchal relations more than their own recognition, embodying instead the gift of "generosity," the acceptance of nonrecognition (1997, 163).

20. The alternative psychological attitudes that Beauvoir's text suggests are: (1) domination (male variant): I am seen by the other who is not like me, and I am threatened; I seek to dominate the other in order to protect myself (fear of castration); (2) narcissism (female): I am seen by the other who is not like me (the male), I seek to be dominated by the other to recover myself.

21. On the issue of lesbian relations in Beauvoir's own life as well as her thought, see Simons (1992; 1999a, 115–48).

References

Beauvoir, Simone de. 1927. 4d Cahier. Holograph manuscript. Paris: Bibliothèque Nationale. Transcription by Barbara Klaw, Sylvie Le Bon de Beauvoir, and Margaret Simons. English translation in Simons (1999b), and French text in Simons (1997); translations here are my own.

———. 1943. *L'Invitée.* Paris: Gallimard.

———. 1949. *Le deuxième sexe.* 2 vols. Paris: Gallimard.

———. 1954. *She came to stay.* Trans. R. Moyse and R. Senhouse. Cleveland, Ohio: World Publishing.

———. 1960. *La force de l'âge.* Paris: Gallimard.

———. 1962. *The prime of life.* Trans. P. Green. Cleveland, Ohio: World Publishing.

———. 1989. *The second sex.* Trans. H. M. Parshley. New York: Vintage.

Bergoffen, Debra B. 1997. *The philosophy of Simone de Beauvoir: Gendered phenomenologies, erotic generosities.* Albany: State University of New York Press.

Lundgren-Gothlin, Eva. 1996. *Sex and existence: Simone de Beauvoir's* The Second Sex. Trans. Linda Schenk. Hanover, N.H.: Wesleyan University Press.

Simons, Margaret A. 1992. "Lesbian connections: Simone de Beauvoir and feminism." *Signs: Journal of Women in Culture and Society* 18, no. 1: 136–61.

———. 1995. *The Second Sex:* From Marxism to radical feminism. In *Feminist interpretations of Simone de Beauvoir,* ed. Margaret A. Simons. University Park: Penn State Press.

———. 1997. "From murder to morality: The development of Beauvoir's ethics." Paper presented at Simone de Beauvoir Circle, meeting with the American Philosophical Association, Pacific Division, Berkeley, California.

———. 1999a. *Beauvoir and "The Second Sex": Feminism, race, and the origins of existentialism.* Lanham, Md.: Rowman and Littlefield.

———. 1999b. "From murder to morality: The development of Beauvoir's ethics." *International Studies in Philosophy* 31, no. 2: 1–20.

SEXUALITY SITUATED: BEAUVOIR ON "FRIGIDITY"

Suzanne Laba Cataldi

9

The term *frigidity* covers a wide range of meaning—including lacking in ardor or warmth, a marked aversion or abnormal indifference to sexuality, and a physical inability to attain orgasm. The word is, or was, usually applied to women.

This essay examines Simone de Beauvoir's understanding of frigidity in women by situating it, as she does, in the context of women's oppression. I relate scenes from her novels to her views of female eroticism and frigidity in *The Second Sex* (1989). In doing this, I hope to show how Beauvoir alters the sense of frigidity. Rather than viewing it as an instance of female passivity or an organic incapacity, she constructs it as a symbolic use that women may make of their bodies.

Symbolic expressions of frigidity often signal unjust power relations in Beauvoirean literature. They represent an active, voluntary rejection of dominance in heterosexual relationships. As such and as I argue, exhibitions of frigidity need not be interpreted, as they sometimes are, as demonstrations of bad faith. If instead we view frigidity as a means or method of resistance, or as a harm that women suffer in a culturally oppressive or sexist environment, we will be more apt to notice the agency behind the passivity and the assumptions implicit in labeling a woman "frigid."

In Beauvoir's existential view, women's eroticism "reflects the complexity of the feminine situation" (Beauvoir 1989, 372). Female sexuality "not only involves the whole nervous system but also depends on the whole experience and situation of the individual" (1989, 373). In *The Second Sex* her catalog of reasons for frigidity are situational rather than physiological—for example, (inbred) shame of bodily appearance (309); resentment of male power and privilege (393); the "humiliation" of lying beneath a man (728); hygienic procedures (387) or the planned use of contraceptives (388); fear of pregnancy (388); "too sudden or too many changes in position, any call for consciously directed activities" (379); moral inhibitions (391); repugnance at the idea of treating, or having one's body treated, as a thing (387). Situationally, for Beauvoir, the man's attitude is "of great importance" (392). Female eroticism may be repulsed by male "crudeness" and "coarseness"; or by maladroit (382), detached (393), or mechanical (397) lovemaking; or it may be incapacitated by roughness and force (377): that is, the "brutality of the man or the abruptness of the event" (389).

The body for Beauvoir is not merely or simply biological; it is also the instrument of our grasp and our means of communication with the world (1989, 34). Transcendently subjective and immanently objective, embodiment is ambiguous. Understood existentially, bodies as they are lived or experienced generate meanings and make "statements" about their situations—meanings and statements that are themselves ambiguous. Sexually speaking, as expression or speech, frigid bodies intentionally and ambiguously point beyond themselves; they are meaningful as gestures. A gesture of frigidity can be interpreted as a symbolic outburst (1989, 609) or a "reaction of refusal" (393). It may be construed as a form of protest or an expression of frustration—an attitude that women are always prepared to take (608). Resentment over patriarchal injustices and constraints is the most common source of frigidity in women, according to Beauvoir. A woman may resort to it to deliberately insult (466) or to punish "the male for all the wrongs she feels she has endured" (393). She may deny herself pleasure as a form of self-punishment (400). She may use her body as a weapon or a refuge, for or against herself—as an instrument of revenge or a means for eluding, disarming, and infuriating males (608–609).

According to Beauvoir, the (heterosexual) erotic drama may be lived out in amity or enmity. The "battle of the sexes" need not be: "In those combats where they think they confront one another, it is really against the self that each one struggles, projecting into the partner that part of the self which is repudiated" (1989, 728). Moral eroticism involves for Beauvoir the assumption of ambiguity, the striking of a delicate and precarious balance on the part of partners who regard each other as equally ambiguous in their being-for-each-other, who grasp "existence in one's self and in the other as both subjectivity and passivity" and "merge in this ambiguous unity" (1966, 21–22). To respond erotically (in Beauvoir's sense of the word) a woman must be able "to reconcile her metamorphosis into a carnal object with her claim to her subjectivity" (1989, 392–93). "She wants to remain subject while she is made object . . . she retains her subjectivity only through union with her partner; giving and receiving must be combined for both. If the man confines himself to taking without giving or if he bestows pleasure without receiving, the woman feels that she is being maneuvered, used" (1989, 397). The "normal and happy flowering" or full development of female eroticism requires that a woman find "in the male both desire and respect" (1989, 401). If a man "really seeks domination much more than fusion and reciprocity," if he does not renounce the illegitimate, privileged position of absolute or sole subject (1989, 397), then his sexual advances may evoke in women, instead of sexual interest, "reactions of refusal."

Reactions of refusing repulsive sexual advances are elaborated in Beauvoir's fiction and are contrasted with normal or respectful erotic response. We see this in her novel *The Mandarins* (1956), for example, where the protagonist Anne describes her experiences of sex before her lover stops loving her:

> The man whom I had chosen and who had chosen me was going to lie down at my side. . . . I felt no constraint; he couldn't hurt me by looking at me, for he didn't judge me, didn't compare me. . . . His desire transformed me. I who for so long a time had been without taste, without form, again possessed breasts, a belly, a sex, flesh. (341)
>
> He gave me his heart. With his hands, his lips, his sex, with his whole body. (548)

and after he stops loving her:

> Suddenly, he was lying on top of me, entering me, and he took me without a word, without a kiss. It all happened so fast that I remained dumfounded. . . . Not for an instant had he given me his presence; he had treated me as a plea-

> sure machine. Even if he didn't love me any more, he shouldn't have done that. . . . Sleeping together cold like that, it's . . . it's horrible! (547–48)

In the latter, loveless exchange, Anne's body is dumbstruck; it cannot speak its pleasure because of the abruptness of the event and the way that they are sleeping together. Notice that the coldness is not attributed to Anne, but to her situation.

The experience of "sleeping together cold" is prefigured in the novel when Anne has sex with a relative stranger. Again, the *experience itself* is not so hot: "A man," she discovers, "isn't a Turkish bath" (1956, 83). His "foreplay" consists of rushing her to bed, imposing his fantasies on her, and becoming angry when he learns that she is not using birth control. Not surprisingly, Anne relates,

> When he went into me, it had almost no effect upon me. . . . "Tell me what you feel?" he said. "Tell me." I remained mute. Inside me, I sensed a presence without really feeling it, as you sense a dentist's steel tool against a swollen gum. "Do you like it? I want you to like it." His voice sounded vexed, demanded an accounting. "You don't? That's all right—the night is long." . . . I unclenched my teeth and with great effort ripped words from my mouth.
> "Don't worry so much about me. Just let me. . . ."
> "You're not really cold," he said angrily. "You're resisting with your head. But I'll force you . . ."
> "No," I said. "No . . ."
> It would have been too difficult to explain my feeling. There was a look of hate in his eyes. . . .
> "You don't want to!" he was saying. "You don't want to! Stubborn mule!" He struck me lightly on the chin; I was too weary to escape into anger. I began to tremble. A beating fist, thousands of fists. . . . "Violence is everywhere," I thought. I trembled and tears began running down my cheeks.
> He crushed me ardently against him and once more went into me. "I want it to happen together," he said. "All right? When you're ready, say 'now.'" (1956, 82–83)

Of course Anne doesn't want to, and it is true that she is "not really cold." Although sexually unresponsive in this particular situation, Anne is not abnormally averse to sexuality, and neither is her body organically lacking in its sexual ability. The situation is just that nothing in this man's behavior erotically appeals to her. Nothing serves as a basis for sexual feeling or functioning on her part because nothing but dominance serves as a basis for his. In other words, no ambiguous unity is here. Her partner's attempts to control her pleasure only constrain her sexuality; his dominance only crushes her desire. She cannot respond erotically to his "mechanical" insistence on synchronicity, and neither can she respond erotically to his "drilling" her with questions or with his "steel tool." "If the male organ . . . seems not to be desirous flesh but a tool skillfully used, woman will feel . . . repulsion" (Beauvoir 1989, 392).

In this situation, Anne's normal desires for a reciprocal, ambiguous union with someone who both desires and respects her are frustrated. She is simply and understandably too repulsed by the male's attitude, dominance, and brutality to respond to him in any genuinely erotic way. As if to underscore this point, Beauvoir has Anne escape her situation by faking an orgasm, willing to sigh and moan in order "to be done with it." This charade on Anne's part mirrors her situation—exposes it to the reader as one that is not truly or genuinely erotic but only a parody or perversion of eroticism, in Beauvoir's view. Given situations like these and Beauvoir's understanding of eroticism, her provocative remark that "the whole desire of women called frigid tends toward the normal" (1989, 392) is revealing[1] and can lead to questions such as who is calling, and why might someone be calling a woman "frigid"?

It is interesting to note that Anne acknowledges some responsibility in this sexual situation, admitting that "it was my fault too. I had slept with him out of curiosity, out of defiance, out of weariness, to prove to myself God only knows what" (Beauvoir 1956, 86). In other words, she shouldn't have. Anne's sharing part of the blame for the way this sexual encounter turned out is consistent both with Beauvoir's recognition of woman's complicity in her oppression and with the bourgeois sexual morality Anne espouses, a morality based on respect and reciprocity and symbolized in the text by her white kid gloves (1956, 80).

Nadine, Anne's daughter in the novel, rejects her mother's sexual morality. It amazes Anne that "Nadine could give herself so easily to total strangers" and claims to be "as indifferent about getting into bed as sitting down at table" (1956, 80). The text suggests that Nadine does not derive much physical pleasure out of her sexual activity (1956, 104); and we know from Beauvoir's memoirs that she did conceive of this character as actually frigid, seeing her frigidity unpleasantly revealed in "a sexual coarseness" characteristic of many younger women whom Beauvoir knew (1965, 265).

In her study of sexuality in Beauvoir's *The Mandarins,* Barbara Klaw has pointed out that, according to Beauvoir, "woman often likes sex only when she is freely choosing sexual intimacy or her own pleasure," and that Nadine is frigid because she is not affirming her sexual subjectivity in either of these ways. "She wants only to trick men into spending time with her" (Klaw 1995, 204–205). Nadine casually (and ironically) sleeps with men as a way of "breaking the ice" in the hopes that they will like and want to be with her (Beauvoir 1956, 63). In response perhaps to a question posed by her mother earlier in the novel—"Why should a woman who's free to do as she pleases sleep with everyone on earth?" (1956, 80)—Nadine retorts "How do you expect me to have relationships with guys if I don't fuck? . . . if I want to go out with them, I have to sleep with them; I have no choice" (1956, 373).[2]

Despite her disavowals of choice and her sexually aggressive behavior, Nadine seems to Beauvoir "more to be pitied as a victim than to be blamed" (1965, 265–66). Nadine's frigidity is to be understood in the context of her circumstances, a male-dominated society that "has taught women to exchange their bodies as material goods in return for fleeting attention" (Klaw 1995, 205). Beauvoir implies, through Nadine, that this situation is deplorable and that Nadine, who does "sleep with everyone on earth" is not really free to do as she pleases. Her frigidity is an example of how society destroys healthy women (Klaw 1995, 200), and thus is related to her oppression.

Another instance from Beauvoir's fiction of a woman who may be called frigid can be found in *She Came to Stay* (1954). While *The Mandarins* (1956) would seem to imply that frigidity and bad faith are unrelated to each other (by suggesting that Nadine's behavior is more coerced than free), a recent interpretation of certain passages in *She Came to Stay* invites us to explore the relation between these two phenomena in more depth.

Generally speaking in existential literature, *bad faith* means a self-deceptive flight from the burden or anguish of liberty, that is, treating oneself as thing. In *The Second Sex* (1989), Beauvoir charges people with bad faith when they relinquish their own (651–55) or deny another's (191) transcendent subjectivity. She also uses the expression "bad faith" to refer to a self-deceptive lie (571).

In their study of Beauvoir and Jean-Paul Sartre, Kate and Edward Fullbrook focus attention on the contrasting behaviors of two young women characters in parallel passages of *She Came to Stay*. They do this in support of their argument that this novel anticipates and "articulates a philosophical system that in its basic structure differs almost not at all from the one found in *Being and Nothingness*" (Fullbrook and Fullbrook 1994, 101). A key aspect of this basic structure is the concept of bad faith. To be sure, the similarities between the passages they cite and Sartre's famous example of a woman who in bad faith is seemingly indifferent to the sexual intentions of her companion are striking.

Sartre's example is of a woman who is out for the first time with a man and refusing to apprehend his desire as a desire which is "addressed to her body as object":

> But then suppose he takes her hand. This act of her companion risks changing the situation by calling for an immediate decision. To leave the hand there is to consent in herself to flirt, to engage herself. To withdraw it is to break the troubled and unstable harmony which gives the hour its charm. The aim is to postpone the moment of decision as long as possible. We know what happens next; the young woman leaves her hand there, but she does not notice that she is leaving it. She does not notice because it happens by chance that she is at this moment all intellect . . . and during this time the divorce of the body from the soul is accomplished; the hand rests inert between the warm hands of her companion—neither consenting nor resisting—a thing. (Sartre 1956, 55–56)

In Beauvoir's example:

> [A] young woman with green and blue feathers in her hair was looking uncertainly at a man's huge hand that had just pounced on hers.
> "This is a great meeting-place for young couples," said Pierre.
> Once more a long silence ensued. Xavière had raised her arm to her lips and was gently blowing the fine down on her skin. . . . (Fullbrook and Fullbrook 1994, 99)

A few minutes later:

> The woman with the green and blue feathers was saying in a flat voice: "I only rushed through it, but for a small town it's very picturesque." She had decided to leave her bare arm on the table and as it lay there, forgotten, ignored, the man's hand was stroking a piece of flesh that no longer belonged to anyone.
> "It's extraordinary, the impression it makes on you to touch your eyelashes," said Xavière. "You touch yourself without touching yourself. It's as if

you touched yourself from some way away." (Fullbrook and Fullbrook 1994, 99)

Despite the manifest similarities between Beauvoir's and Sartre's examples, the Fullbrooks' interpretation of the woman with the feathers is somewhat misleading. While it may appear to be true that her response to what they describe as the "flirtatious" male "is to dissociate the two sides of her human reality, which is that she is simultaneously subject and object," I do not believe that the woman's behavior is vividly illustrative of the concept of bad faith,[3] as they contend (Fullbrook and Fullbrook 1994, 100). For even as they attempt to substantiate their case for Beauvoir's influence on Sartre, they still make the mistake of reading Sartre back into Beauvoir by relying exclusively on Sartre's interpretation of the strikingly similar and frequently cited passage found in *Being and Nothingness* (Sartre 1956, 55–56). The Fullbrooks do not allow that Beauvoir might have written these passages to illustrate something other, or something more, than the concept that became known, through Sartre's unattributed use of her example, as bad faith. Framed in the context of Beauvoir's *own* thought—on female frigidity, male impetuosity, and the equivocal nature of touch and of virginal desire in young women—these passages lend themselves to a different interpretation.

In *The Second Sex* (1989), Beauvoir describes man's approach to sexuality as impetuous: "[M]an dives upon his prey like the eagle and the hawk" (386). According to her, this precipitousness not only sets up in women "resistance to the subjugating intentions of the male, but also a conflict with herself" (Beauvoir 1989, 386). She may feel, simultaneously, attracted and repulsed.

The man in Beauvoir's example is obviously impetuous, and the woman is just as obviously wearing feathers, like some kind of prey. I agree with the Fullbrooks that she is in a quandary. However, I disagree with their claim that, in deciding "to leave her bare arm on the table . . . forgotten, ignored" (Beauvoir 1954, 61), as the text states, the woman with the feathers "decides to experience her arm as a mere thing impersonally related to her consciousness" (Fullbrook and Fullbrook 1994, 100)—a *very* Sartrean take on the situation. In suggesting that the woman's decision to experience her arm "as an inert piece of flesh" is made in bad faith, the Fullbrooks suggest, in one fell swoop, that she is entirely responsible for this experience of her self (rather than one into which she is pressured) and that she bears some kind of fault. No responsibility or bad faith is assigned to the man in the example, perhaps because the Fullbrooks ignore, in their commentary, a key aspect of the situation: that it is initially *he* who treats her arm "as a mere thing" by treating it as something to pounce upon; and that he does so without her consent and continues stroking it without any evident desire on her part. One might say, following Beauvoir, that in setting himself up as the "sole essential" subject in the situation, *he* is the one in bad faith (1989, 191).

And so, perhaps, neither is it, as the Fullbrooks, following Sartre, say, that she is engaged in a self-deception—that she dissociates her "self" from her body because "although she does not welcome the man's desire, she also, perhaps, does not wish to shatter her impression that he 'desires' her conversation" (1994, 100). I should think that his pouncing hand would have shattered that impression already, and she doesn't seem very interested or excited about conversing with him (Beauvoir describes her voice as flat). However, it may instead be that her bodily dissociation is a form of protest against *her companion's* bad faith treatment of *her* as a thing. To "cold shoulder" or try to disarm him in this manner may be her way of resisting his subjugating intentions, an attempt to establish some distance between them (notice how her conversation has drifted to some other, more distant spot). It may be a reaction of refusal, a means of rejecting advances that are experienced not as erotic but only as expressive of male dominance. She may resent being pounced upon. Perhaps she considers this gesture coarse or crude. She may find it, or him, repulsive or frightening. Perhaps she feels overwhelmed or overpowered by his "huge" hand. Dominance is threatening; and it is perfectly normal to "freeze" or stay still when one is afraid. Beauvoir's phenomenology certainly allows for just these sorts of contingencies, circumstances that may cause a woman to dissociate from her body and strategically "detach" from some undesirable element in her situation.

One problem with imposing Sartre's analysis of bad faith on Beauvoir's example is that it tends to exclude these and other scenarios. In the use that Sartre makes of her example—the hand of a woman resting inertly and thing-like between (as Sartre puts it) "the warm hands of her companion" (Sartre 1956, 97) (suggesting, through innuendo, that the woman herself is "cold")—the woman's bad faith consists in her being "profoundly aware of" and yet refusing to apprehend the desire she inspires in the male "for what it is"—that is, directed to her body as object. But as I've shown for Beauvoir, it is precisely this sort of apprehension, that is, of oneself as objectified in a way that excludes one's subjectivity, that may initiate, in women, reactions of refusal—reactions that Beauvoir would consider normal but that may be *mis*characterized as a sexual coldness or frigidity. Sartre's example does not indicate the woman's apprehension of herself as a desiring subject or the nature of her own desires. In the Sartrean scenario, the woman who is profoundly aware of the male's desire is ignorant of her own. "She does not quite know what she wants," Sartre says (1956, 97). (Why? Because she doesn't want him or what he wants?)[4]

The woman with the feathers in Beauvoir's example may also not know what she wants; this is not necessarily because she is ignorant of her own desires but because she may be experiencing them as conflicting. Given the youth of Beauvoir's characters and the way she explicitly contrasts them, she may have meant by their example to say nothing at all about bad faith (at least on the woman's part), but something about how, in the course of heterosexual initiation, a woman may feel "divided against herself." Consider what Beauvoir later says about the conflicts of virginal desire in *The Second Sex:*

> The virgin does not know exactly what she wants. The aggressive eroticism of childhood still survives in her; her first impulses were prehensile, and she still wants to embrace, possess. She wants her coveted prey to be endowed with the qualities which, through taste, odor, touch, have appeared to her as values. For sexuality is not an isolated domain, it continues the dreams and joys of early sensuality; children and adolescents of both sexes like the smooth, creamy, satiny, mellow, elastic. . . . She has no liking for rough fabrics, gravel, rockwork . . . ; what she, like her brothers, first caressed and cherished was her mother's flesh. In her narcissism, in her homosexual experiences, whether diffuse or definite, she acts as subject and seeks possession of a feminine body. When she confronts the male, she feels in her hands . . . the desire to caress a prey actively. But crude man, with his hard muscles, his rough and often hairy skin, . . . his coarse features, does not appear to her as desirable; he even seems repulsive. . . .
>
> Thus she is divided against herself; she longs for a strong embrace that will make of her a quivering thing, but roughness and force are also disagreeable deterrents that offend her. Her feeling is located both in her skin and in

her hand, and the requirements of one are in part opposed to those of the other. (Beauvoir 1989, 376–78)

As discussed in this passage, the equivocal nature of touch may help to explain a woman's passivity or presumed frigidity as a bodily ambivalence or conflict in feeling, a type of inhibited intentionality. We may reasonably suppose that the woman with the feathers is tied up in this conflict.

Beauvoir may have intended in her example for the woman's feathers to contrast with the fine down of Xavière's skin.[5] The woman with the feathers is not so attached to her "feathers." They are not natural to her. They are tacked on or pinned to her body (as the male hand is); and their colors are depicted as clashing in a visual representation of the tactile conflict she is experiencing in her hand—a hand which, like the feathers, is simply lying there—"a piece of flesh that no longer belonged to anyone" (Beauvoir 1954, 61). Still we may suppose, because after all she is sporting them, that she enjoys "feminine" things, things that are feathery soft. Xavière certainly does; she is clearly (autoerotically, narcissistically) enjoying herself—engrossed in the extraordinary sensations of touching her own eyelashes and gently blowing on the fine down, the innermost covering, of her own skin. Xavière is not so separated from herself,[6] not separated from active bodily intention or the "joys of early sensuality." To quote again from *The Second Sex*, "In her narcissism . . . she acts as subject and seeks possession of a feminine body" (1989, 377). Indeed she does, and as she does, she forms within herself a type of ambiguous unity that is, for Beauvoir, characteristic of erotic experiences generally. Xavière's eroticism is unimpaired, uninterrupted. She is more joined, more assured, more in touch with her self. Her virginal desire is more "intact."

The delicate sensitivity of Xavière's gestures, her obvious enjoyment of her own soft touch, vividly contrast with the "crude" pouncing of the man's hand and the way that it leaves the other woman unaffected, "cold." It is not the case as Sartre would have it, in "his" example of bad faith, that "she realizes herself as *not being* her own body"—accomplishing "a divorce of the body from the soul" (Sartre 1956, 98) and eclipsing into the transcendent nothingness of some disembodied consciousness that she strives in vain to "be." Because the body is not for Beauvoir simply or solely objective, because it has transcendent or lived dimensions,[7] the opposition in her fictional situation may be considerably more fleshed out than that. It may be that the *transcendent* aspects of her *body*—the active intentions of her embodied subjectivity—are detained, or inhibited, because the passive requirements in her skin (how she likes to be touched/what she likes to be touched by) are opposed, through the tactless male gesture, to the requirements in her hand (her own desire to actively caress a "prey"). Her desire is immobilized by this conflict in her feeling; and that is why, I suspect, the young woman with the feathers isn't "quivering" at all! She is not necessarily frigid.

Frigidity is known in contemporary psychiatric discourse as Inhibited or Hypoactive Sexual Desire Disorder and has been included, along with related sexual dysfunctions (for example, Female Sexual Arousal Disorder and Inhibited Female Orgasm Disorder) in the *Diagnostic and Statistical Manual of Mental Disorders* since 1980. While a deficiency or absence of sexual desire may be a recognizable and valid concern, there are dangers in viewing problems with sexual desires on the model of a disease or mental illness. Beauvoir's existential approach can be credited for avoiding such dangers.

For example, Janice Irvine's analysis of Inhibited Sexual Desire also points out that sexual desire is not simply reducible to a biological urge, and that the "content of medical diagnoses are shaped by social, economic and political factors" (Irvine 1995, 326). Professional reliance in the disease model on organic, neurochemical explanations of the phenomenon tends to ignore this. Based on the assumption that sexual desire resides in the body (as an object and not as it is lived as part of a situation), the medical diagnosis "ensures that proposed solutions to the problem will be individual and not structural or cultural" (328).

Although a preponderance of brain-centered sexual theories may be responsible for its categorization as a mental illness, the diagnosis of Inhibited Sexual Desire in the medical literature is nevertheless frequently related—as symbolic expressions of frigidity are in Beauvoir's texts—"to fear, anger and marital problems; some studies suggest that power struggles and lack of respect are major dynamics for ISD in women" (Irvine 1995, 329).[8] Apart from the obvious difficulty of determining a normal amount of sexual desire for everyone, Irvine also points out that because the concept of desire discrepancy is inevitably relational in character, depending on who they are with, "individuals can easily shift diagnoses" and that "an angry and dissatisfied partner is often the impetus for someone to seek professional treatment" for inhibited sexual desire (323). While a medical diagnosis may appear to confer legitimacy and neutrality on a set of difficulties, as does a disease in a discourse of sickness, Inhibited Sexual Desire is a negative social judgment, with a "taint of stigma and deviance" that is potentially coercive in its application and effects (329–30).

Despite its inadequacies as a medical diagnosis, however, Irvine believes that the construction of Inhibited Sexual Desire can still draw on "feminist assertions of the importance of pleasure and desire for women." The diagnosis can serve, for example, "as a cultural protest by women, a demand for satisfaction in sex and a refusal to settle for less" (1995, 332). Beauvoir's existential analysis and literary depictions of frigidity serve these feminist purposes as well. By situating sexuality in the historical context of women's oppression and relating sexual desire to transcendent, subjective aspects of embodiment, she contributes to the literature on this topic perspectives on female eroticism often lacking in the clinical constructs and biomedical models.

Notes

1. Beauvoir's remark summarizes a finding of W. Stekel's in *Frigidity in Women* (1943). In developing her ideas, Beauvoir cites a number of case histories from Stekel's study, relating concrete instances of oppressive treatment to Stekel's discussions of how men's attitudes and behaviors contribute to the problem of women's frigidity.

2. As Klaw points out, the English translation ("if I don't go to bed with them") considerably weakens the impact and vulgarity of Nadine's remark (1995, 204).

3. Also see Debra Bergoffen (1992, 221–27).

4. See Beauvoir's remarks on reactions to *The Second Sex:* "Most men took as a personal insult the information I retailed about frigidity in women; they wanted to imagine that they could dispense pleasure whenever and to whomever they pleased; to doubt such powers on their part was to castrate them" (1965, 190).

5. Beauvoir also may have intended to compare these two characters. It may be argued, for example, that in not desiring Pierre and resisting any physical relationship between them, Xavière is in the same position as the woman with the feathers.

6. At least she is not in this passage. In a later scene, however, we find Xavière deliberately burning herself with a cigarette, and then with "rounded, coquettish" lips,

"gently blowing on the burnt skin which covered her wound" before burning herself again (Beauvoir 1954, 283–84).

7. In this respect and as I discuss elsewhere (Cataldi 2001), Beauvoir's view of embodiment is much closer to Merleau-Ponty's than to Sartre's.

8. Also see the recently published (and publicized) study on "Sexual Dysfunction in the United States" (Laumann, Paik, and Rosen 1999). *Newsweek*'s account of this study (Leland 1999), entitled "Bad News in the Bedroom," is also interesting.

Using the DSM-IV classification, the study finds sexual dysfunction to be more prevalent for women (43%) than men (31%). An outcome that appears "more extensive and possibly more severe for women than men" is the high association of sexual dysfunction with "unsatisfying personal experiences and relationships" (Laumann, Paik, and Rosen 1999, 542).

Another finding of this study is that sexual problems are most common among young women and older men. It attributes the problems young women experience to stress generated by the "instability" of being single (high partner turnover rate, spells of inactivity) coupled with inexperience. Curiously, while the authors note that young men "are not similarly affected" (1999, 542) with sexual problems, they don't explain why. Because young men are also inexperienced and single, one would expect them to be affected. In any event, some of Beauvoir's insights on young women's sexuality may be pertinent here.

REFERENCES

Beauvoir, Simone de. 1954. *She came to stay.* Cleveland, Ohio: World Publishing.

———. 1956. *The mandarins.* Trans. Leonard M. Friedman. New York: Norton.

———. 1965. *Force of circumstance.* Vol. 1. Trans. Richard Howard. New York: Harper Row.

———. 1966. Must we burn Sade? In *The marquis de Sade,* trans. Annette Michelson. New York: Grove Press.

———. 1989. *The second sex.* Trans. H. M. Parshley. New York: Vintage.

Bergoffen, Debra. 1992. The look as bad faith. *Philosophy Today* 36 (3): 221–27.

———. 1997. *The philosophy of Simone de Beauvoir: Gendered phenomenologies, erotic generosities.* New York: State University of New York Press.

Cataldi, Suzanne. 2001. The body as a basis for being: Simone de Beauvoir and Maurice Merleau-Ponty. In *The existential phenomenology of Simone de Beauvoir.* Dordrecht: Kluwer Academic Publishing.

Fullbrook, Kate, and Edward Fullbrook. 1994. *Simone de Beauvoir and Jean-Paul Sartre: The remaking of a twentieth-century legend.* New York: Basic Books.

Irvine, Janice. 1995. Regulated passions: The invention of inhibited sexual desire and sexual addiction. In *Deviant bodies,* ed. Jennifer Terry and Jacqueline Urla. Bloomington: Indiana University Press.

Klaw, Barbara. 1995. Sexuality in *Les mandarins.* In *Feminist Interpretations of Simone de Beauvoir,* ed. Margaret Simons. University Park: Pennsylvania State University Press.

Laumann, Edward O., Anthony Paik, and Raymond C. Rosen. 1999. "Sexual dysfunction in the United States—prevalence and predictors." *Journal of the American Medical Association* 281 (6): 537–44.

Leland, John. 1999. Bad news in the bedroom. *Newsweek,* 22 February, 47.

Sartre, Jean-Paul. 1956. *Being and nothingness.* Trans. Hazel Barnes. New York: Washington Square Press.

Stekel, W. 1943. *Frigidity in women.* New York: Liveright Publishing Corporation.

BEAUVOIR'S PARRHESIASTIC CONTRACTS: FRANK-SPEAKING AND THE PHILOSOPHICAL-POLITICAL COUPLE

10

Laura Hengehold

How does one avoid losing one's soul—or create a soul in the first place? Does one have to get free of others, or seek them out in some community of speech or feeling? Paramount importance would be placed on the choice of a partner from whom to escape, to help one escape, or with whom to join forces—the wrong city, the wrong movement, the wrong couple or family might prevent one from ever forming a relationship to oneself that could be consistently active and trustworthy.

In some of his late lectures, Foucault referred to the kind of interpersonal relationship capable of putting someone in relation to the truth—creating and strengthening his or her soul—as a "parrhesiastic contract,"[1] a mutual commitment between two or more people to speak frankly and to risk hearing the truth from one another.[2] A citizen who risks his or her political capital to speak frankly about the city's weaknesses, the prince who allows a court counselor to challenge his self-deception, or individuals seeking therapeutic guidance can be said to care for their souls. But in caring for themselves, they also illuminate the relationships of power giving rise to those souls and the particular scene of truth that they reveal. Because "truth" does not exist outside such relationships and their real effects on the bodies who confess or profess, *parrhesiastes* also care for the city in which these lines of force hold sway.

Beauvoir's novels and philosophical essays offer rich descriptions of women striving to create and preserve their souls amid shifting historical circumstances. She also reproaches women who fail to engage in this labor or who assume that the self is a "given" requiring only narcissistic expression rather than active creation. Much of Foucault's later work was absorbed in the task of understanding how power relations could produce a field of truthfulness and subjects who relate to themselves and to political institutions or conflicts in terms of truth (just as he was preoccupied with understanding the power relations making a field of *visibility* possible in an earlier phase of his research). According to Foucault, sexuality served as an "imaginary" object around which souls might be created, elaborated, and constrained for the sake of truth (Foucault 1978, 155). But Beauvoir's work is not concerned with the true nature of this imaginary object. Rather, she examines the relations of *sexual attraction* within which many women try to grasp the truth about the historically specific opportunities and constraints that characterize their society—including those imposed in the name of sexuality.[3] These intimate, but truth-disclosive power relations have been described by Michèle le Doeuff as an "erotico-theoretical" transference limiting the outlet for women's intellectual energies while supporting the far greater prestige of male thinkers' truth-telling (1989, 104–107).

Beauvoir recognizes that many women mistake truth concerning or disclosed by the men they love for the truth about the society that envelops them, just as Foucault criticizes sexual liberationists who mistake the truth about their own desire for the truth of the power relations that make their desires an issue. But relations of sexual and emotional power also seem to be important elements of women's "parrhesiastic" practice; Beauvoir and her most interesting fictional characters seek relationships in which their intellectual ambitions and moral integrity can be challenged and sustained. Her goal, I hope to show, is to undo the "transference" without giving up either eroticism or theory, and to integrate risk, labor, and disappointment into the practice of truth-telling.

In "The Subject and Power" (1983) Foucault defined power as "a mode of action upon the actions of others" without touching their person directly. Such power is multiplicative rather than repressive because it leaves the one subjected room to vary and invent upon the instructions received from outside, saving the directing agent energy and increasing the flexibility of the resulting ensemble. Within such relations, the "soul" or "self" emerges as a style of acting on one's *own* actions and increasing their efficiency or improvisational force with respect to outside expectations. In his lecture series from 1984, Foucault reported his surprise upon discovering that Roman aristocrats' moral practice of exchanging frank speech with one another and with their counselors—a practice concerned with the general health of the patient's body and soul—originated in *parrhēsia*, a political practice by which individuals offered their public "diagnosis" of the Athenian city-state's health.[4] Often such speech had a purely rhetorical character and situated the speaker only with respect to a flux of opinions and interests. Marcel Detienne (1996) and Paul Veyne (1988) have explored the emergence of "truth" as a stable, though elusive, referent of oral and written discourse between soldiers and citizens in Homeric and classical Greece. But Socrates deliberately employed this style of discourse to *test* or *sift* false from true self-representations, whether in dialogue with the city as a whole or with individual citizens (Foucault 2001b, 20–23, 97). Socrates' practice later lost its public dimension in the Hellenistic world, when the philosopher's therapeutic testing of his prince's integrity and ability to govern became indistinguishable from a commitment to recognize and eliminate character defects through criticism in a personal relationship (102–104).

The "parrhesiastic contract" is a situation of risk in many senses. The one who seeks the truth risks losing face; the one who tells the truth risks revenge if his or her comments prove distasteful—above all, the relationship may misfire if the person chosen as a *parrhesiastes* is blinded by self-love or inconstancy. Social and economic factors also influence choice of a truth-teller: Foucault quotes Galen as recommending that one consult a *parrhesiastes* who is wealthy and unlikely to gain anything by flattering his client. But he notes that the poverty and relative vulnerability of Diogenes the Cynic rendered his challenge to Alexander's understanding of royal entitlement all the more credible, since it could hardly have advanced him materially (Foucault 2001b, 126–33; 141–42). *Parrhesia* should be a kind of "anti-flattery," enabling the other to "constitute a relation to himself that is autonomous, independent, full and satisfying," rather than leaving him or her dependent on the speaker, "as is the case in flattery" (Foucault 2001a, 362). Though Foucault is less explicit on this score, sexual considerations are also relevant: a woman is less likely to participate in the kinds of power relations making truth possible, including arrangements ensuring her economic or social independence. But Plato avers that a beloved boy may offer access to the truth, albeit by disadvantaging him as a potential equal within the city's relations of masculine power (Foucault 1990, 204–207).

Where do Beauvoir and her characters fall in this taxonomy of truth-tellers and parrhesiastic couples? In her memoirs, Beauvoir explicitly praises her relationship with Jean-Paul Sartre as testing and maintaining her own capacity for truthfulness, above and beyond intrinsic emotional, social, and sexual satisfactions. In the fall of 1929 the two writers made what we might consider a modern "parrhesiastic contract"; they swore never to lie to one another and to distinguish this permanent love-in-truth from secondary loves they anticipated as being chiefly sexual in nature. As Beauvoir wrote in *The Prime of Life*, "Not only would we never lie to one another, but neither of us would conceal anything from the other" (1992, 24–25). At first, she admits, she relied too heavily upon Sartre to reflect the truth about herself, creating a soul that had rather more to do with his point of view than with her own. Nor was the truth constructed through their exchange of correspondence always complete, challenging, or straightforward. But as she discovered new techniques for disclosing and mediating relationships with reference to the truth—primarily by writing, secondarily through activism—she never detached these techniques from the sign of the original interpersonal relationship that marked their uniqueness (1992, 26). By contrast to the confessional relationships described by Foucault, in which the soul is inscribed in a field of bureaucratic power by the truth regarding its own sexuality, Beauvoir and her characters hoped to use intimate and desiring relationships to build souls capable of recognizing and affirming truths about economic and political power despite the threat of isolation or retribution.

Beauvoir's student diaries indicate an early concern for the role Others, and especially lovers, play in preparing the self to assess and confront reality with minimal self-deception. "There is this subject of 'love' which is so fascinating and of which I've traced the broad lines," she wrote in 1927;

"it would be necessary to start from there . . . and then as an easier but related problem friendship—its dangers, the nature of the education that it brings, in brief how souls can act one upon the other [*comment les âmes peuvent interagir les unes sur les autres*]" (Simons 1999, 216). Her earliest novels explore the ways in which women's "bad faith" *(mauvaise foi)* regarding their own needs or aggressive impulses prevents them from being reliable touchstones against whom friends or daughters can test themselves and achieve their own relation to the truth. For example, in *Quand Prime le Spirituel* [1937, unpublished until 1979], a young teacher, Chantal, diverts herself from loneliness by encouraging students and friends to engage in romantic adventures, while evaluating the tragic family conflicts these adventures provoke from a purely aesthetic standpoint. Marguerite, one of several philosophy students on the fringe of Chantal's circle, attempts to flee the superficial "spirituality" of Chantal's aesthetic rebellion and of the pious families in her social class by choosing an errant brother-in-law as her internal critic and guide through the Parisian *demi-monde*. When Denis reveals himself as wholly lacking the discipline to be a criminal, much less a poet, Marguerite is devastated, but she recognizes her own bad faith in willfully supporting his false self-image for her own ends (Beauvoir 1979, 246–48).

Françoise, the main character of *L'Invitée* [1943], murders to "save" her soul because for so long she has denied the genuine *alterity* of her partner Pierre, on whom she relies for confirmation of her own judgments, and of her younger friend Xavière, whom she initially hopes to mentor and to liberate from a restrictive family, but who turns out, given Pierre's support, to have her own ideas of freedom (Beauvoir 1975). As Margaret Simons has suggested, these characters cannot motivate one another to act on their own actions because they refuse to assume an external standpoint on each other (2003, 116–17). Françoise feels less and less "real" in proportion to her frantic efforts to dissimulate resentment of Xavière and fear of abandonment by Pierre beneath a sociable mask. When Xavière challenges Françoise's motives for secrecy regarding a second mutual lover, Françoise is unable to bear the ambiguity of the loyalties, hatreds, and intimacies involved and can only maintain (or perhaps create) her independence by literally suffocating her onetime friend. These novels present others as real or perceived obstacles to the individual's disclosure of a socially mediated but individually strengthening truth. By striking contrast to Beauvoir's later fiction, political events are only distantly illuminated by the characters' epistemological and emotional conflicts.

In *Being and Nothingness* (1943), Sartre also characterized the Other as a formal structure both making possible the intersubjective validity of truth and *undermining* the emotional conviction that gives value to one's intentional objects (1956, 143–46, 362–64). Despite the catastrophic conclusion of *L'Invitée* and several stories in *Quand Prime le Spirituel*, Beauvoir's subsequent philosophy and novels sought to explain such failures as contingent and to articulate relationships in which individuals would be *motivated* to seek truth and renounce hypocrisy.[5] *Pyrrhus et Cinéas* (1944) and *The Ethics of Ambiguity* (1947) argue that the object whose truth is disclosed by the individual subject loses significance in the *absence* of others who can adopt, critique, and respond to one's perspective on events (see Beauvoir 1947 and 1994, respectively).

Like all values discussed in *The Ethics of Ambiguity*, truth and honesty must accommodate and reflect the freedom of others who also establish values. For Beauvoir, like Sartre, a truth that might exist apart from or encompass all individual perspectives ceases to be truth *for* anyone and sinks into the blindness of ignorance or the obvious. Thus, neither in his necessary being nor in his supposed omniscience could God be a model for truth. But where Sartre views emotion as a form of flight from the lucidity of consciousness, Beauvoir gives it a significant role in human relationships capable of disclosing and sustaining the value of truth.[6] Emotions have long been regarded as *data* indicating whether a subject is active or acted upon in a power relationship.[7] Not by expressing an inner truth called "sexuality," but by arousing powerful emotions of joy, anxiety, vulnerability, and audaciousness, can intimate relationships inspire men and women to seek the truth about themselves and the world or to rest in self-deception.

The Ethics of Ambiguity even offers a provisional criterion for judging sexual or emotional partnerships with respect to the establishment and affirmation of truth. The liberatory value of truthful disclosure, Beauvoir states, requires us to "create a situation of such a kind that the truth might be bearable [*supportable*] and that, through losing his illusions, the deluded individual might again find about him reasons for hoping" (1994, 143).[8] This comment expands upon remarks found earlier in *Pyrrhus et Cinéas:*

"In order that men be able to give me a place in the world, it is first necessary that I make rise around me a world where men will have their place" (1947, 353–54). Far from damning one's parrhesiastic integrity, happiness and emotional responsiveness are preconditions for the moral value of truthfulness. Beauvoirean individuals may even have a responsibility to cultivate emotional (including sexual) relationships in which truth becomes possible.

Les Mandarins (1954) and *Les Belles Images* (1966) offer examples of women (and some men) attempting to create and sustain such relationships. In *Les Mandarins,* psychoanalyst Anne Dubreuilh's search for the truth regarding herself and her political circumstances is paralleled by that of a male character, the journalist and novelist Henri Perron. Henri is torn between the choice of art or politics as a medium for truth. But his faith in the possibility of recognizing and speaking the truth has been damaged by repeated acts of deception in his failing love relationship with Anne's friend Paule, who refuses to recognize his indifference or pursue a creative career of her own. Anne is horrified by Paule's psychological deterioration—expressed in symptoms ranging from abject denial to violent jealousy and mental illness. But Anne also has difficulty empathizing with the obsessive sexual activity through which her own daughter has been trying to overcome grief for a lover killed by the Gestapo. Anne's concern about the lack of passion in her marriage to Robert Dubreuilh, a politically engaged author, coincides with fear regarding the future of French politics and the postwar balance of power between the United States, Europe, and the Soviet Union.

> No, the future isn't assured, neither the near nor the distant. I looked at Robert. Was it really his truth reflected in all those eyes? People also watched from elsewhere—from America, from Russia, from the depths of the centuries. Whom do they see? Perhaps only an old dreamer, whose dream means little. And that might be the way he'll see himself tomorrow; he'll think that what he did served no purpose, or worse, that it served only to confuse people. If only I could decide: there is no truth! But there will be one. Our life is there, heavy as a rock, and it has another side which we don't know: it's frightening. (Beauvoir 1956, 223, translation altered)

Both Anne and Henri (for whom Robert serves as mentor, critic, and friend) wonder whether Robert remains sufficiently perceptive regarding

France's historical situation and, given his political utilitarianism, sufficiently sincere in the personal realm to be an adequate *parrhesiastes*. Terrified by the war's social transformation and by changes in Robert's own self-conception as an intellectual, Anne needs to explore and assess the world apart from her husband, engaging with new places, colleagues, and lovers in order to speak frankly in her own professional role as psychoanalyst. Henri must trust himself to make independent decisions regarding his literary values and the eventual political affiliation of his newspaper, despite admiration for Robert, given that these choices may shape French perceptions of the Soviet Union's prison camps.

Our life is there, heavy as a rock, *Les Mandarins* implies—and we have a moral obligation to overcome fear of its imperviousness. A love affair in the United States leads Anne to better understand her daughter, Nadine, for their shared disorientation has international and intergenerational dimensions. The desire to resist indifference, however, strengthens Anne's desire for the truth and her reluctance to push responsibility for its emotionally charged ambiguities onto others. "Our love isn't a story I can pull out of the context of my life in order to tell it to myself," Anne reflects in trying to understand Lewis's role in her imagined future: "It exists outside of myself." But this does not free her from its emotional effects or the moral obligations they imply: "That rejection was still another sham [*feinte*]; the truth is I was in no way master of my heart [*ne disposais de mon coeur*]" (Beauvoir 1956, 530). Despite passion for Lewis, Anne insists on returning to her husband and to her career. This is an ambiguous victory, for Anne is motivated as much by intuition concerning Lewis's growing indifference and by her attachment to the past with Robert as by enthusiasm for her own professional goals. As Lewis comments cryptically after admitting to a lie during one of Anne's crises of anxiety regarding emotional miscommunication: "Whether you lie to yourself or whether you don't, the truth is never said" (1956, 471, translation altered).

In her memoirs, however, Beauvoir suggested that she identified with Henri as much as with Anne (1965, 264, 268). Henri wonders if he is entitled to the ambiguity of his own truth in the political sphere but hopes to tear himself loose from specific struggles and to pursue a literary genre that will resist easy appropriation by any one party. "What truth do I want to express?" Henri asks himself in confronting the blank page. "*My* truth. But what does that really mean?" . . . "It's frightening, plunging into empty space with nothing to clutch at. Maybe I have nothing more to say" (1956, 132). Henri is unable to tell Paule he no longer loves her, but this reticence actually aggravates, rather than softening, the violence of her disappointment. Fear of Paule's potential for suicide is uppermost in his mind when the mother of his new lover, Josette, informs him that a former Gestapo informer threatens to publicly humiliate Josette unless Henri lies in court and discredits the testimony of two Jewish women who have identified him as the agent who sent them to Dachau. As he struggles to recognize the depth of the Occupation's everyday treachery and violence, he decides to protect Josette, whose crime was to have loved an insignificant German officer at a time when her mother would rather have prostituted her to wealthy supporters of her own prestigious *maison de couture*. As Eleanor Holveck has argued (2002, chap. 7), Henri risks the anger of political comrades to represent his own complicity in the victimization of women, even though this gesture also harms the women who have testified against Josette's blackmailer. In the courtroom, rightly or wrongly, Henri attempts to tell a kind of truth in fiction: whether or not he lied, some part of the truth would never be said.

Les Belles Images (1966) addresses women's mystification and epistemological instability in a very different social milieu and moment of French history. In this novel, an advertising artist named Laurence is roused from middle-class contentment and optimism by her daughter Catherine's untimely discovery of social injustice. Laurence's first instinct is to promise her daughter a "beautiful image" of a future without poverty or suffering, in keeping with the technocratic beliefs of her husband and her social circle. But when Laurence's divorced mother, Dominique, sinks into self-destructive rage at a lover's betrayal, she reflects that even a just society cannot entirely prevent emotional pain and disappointment. Like the reader of *The Ethics of Ambiguity*, Laurence faces the task of making the truth "bearable" for her daughter while preserving her freedom in a world where communication has ceased to aim at the freedom of others, but aims only at their management.[9]

After a dispute with her husband regarding the relative importance of a bicyclist's life (which she saved by wrecking the family car), Laurence's skepticism regarding his moral judgment devolves into radical disorientation with respect to all the relationships she had assumed would anchor her, ethically and politically. Like Henri, she immerses herself in news reports but never feels that social and historical knowledge provides her with an adequate context for developing convictions that must, themselves, *give* a context to the individual facts about which she reads. When her father, an austere anti-modernist whose values she often referenced as a test of her own, decides to reconcile with Dominique, Laurence is overcome with rage and fear for her child's moral and psychological well-being. The distance between the truth, heavy as a rock, and the web of images through which her family members act on themselves and one another is breached in a hysterical fit that seems arbitrary because no one has explicitly denied Laurence's self, only failed to care for it. But her daughter, she insists, "won't be mutilated . . . bringing up a child is not making her into a pretty picture" (Beauvoir 1968, 220, translation altered). Laurence, like Anne, is saved from despairing isolation by the hope that there are *others* for whose sake the truth will someday be desirable, especially their daughters. "Either one founders in apathy [*indifférence*], or the earth becomes repeopled," Anne reflects after her definitive break with Lewis. "I didn't founder. Since my heart continues to beat, it will have to beat for something, for someone" (1956, 610).

Even when women choose men to be their primary interlocutors, they also sustain a variety of relationships with other women. Sometimes these friendships serve parrhesiastic functions, as when the narrator of *L'Âge de Discretion* accepts her friend and former student Martine's assessment of her scholarship or overcomes uncertainties about aging by referring to her mother-in-law Manette's fiery political convictions (Beauvoir 1967). Disclosing truth and having one's truth tested by and for the sake of a female gaze may be uniquely empowering for women. The fact that lesbians are financially and socially independent of men gives them a sense for their own capacities and for reality's resistance to their projects seldom achieved by women who live vicariously through male success (1957, 421–22). But often Beauvoir's female characters substitute emotions of aggression, anxiety, and jealousy for the erotic tension of heterosexual disclosure.

In her discussion of lesbianism as choice and situation in *The Second Sex* (1949), Beauvoir notes that women's physical similarities and the absence of biologically justified positions of dominance in women's friend-

ships make self-discovery and equality more likely than in heterosexual relationships (1957, 416–20). But just as heterosexual women adopt rigid attitudes and poses in order to attract and hold men's attention, the burdens
of social disapproval may also encourage lesbians to adopt unnecessarily
stereotypical roles or to follow the male pattern of demanding narcissistic
reinforcement from their lovers' gaze as well (1957, 423). Indeed, Beauvoir's own attitude toward her sexual encounters with women has been
criticized as manipulative, satisfying curiosity or fear of solitude rather
than the generosity she later insisted should accompany eroticism. Until
very late in her life she omitted all reference to these liaisons from published memoirs and interviews. Yet Beauvoir intended her works to reach a
largely female readership, presented unusually frank and sympathetic de-
fenses of female sexuality in her novels and *The Second Sex*, and eventually
became a prominent supporter of the French women's liberation movement. As an adolescent she was passionately attached to her friend Zaza
(Elisabeth La Coin) and rejected her younger sister for the sake of their
conversations, whose spirit she claimed to have rediscovered with Sartre
(Beauvoir 1992, 27). The choice of students as female lovers reinforces the
impression that something like an "erotico-theoretical transference," involving emotion and physicality but irreducible to either, made these relationships attractive to either Beauvoir or her lovers. Finally, like her characters Anne and Laurence, she invested emotional energy in an (adopted)
daughter, Sylvie le Bon, toward the end of her life.

Did Beauvoir have trouble regarding women as parrhesiastic interlocutors for the better part of her life due to a weaker homosexual interest?
Did she fear abandonment in female friendships after the death of Zaza?
Or rather, was her sexual interest unstable because the culture in which she
loved and wrote could only conceive of truth as the product of power relationships involving men and could not allow her relationships with women
to convey the "reality" or *gravitas* of heterosexual loves?[10] Perhaps the elements for an emotionally compelling disclosure were present in these relationships but organized through relations of power that neither she and the
women to whom she was attracted, nor the rest of her heterosexual world
could recognize as "truth"—whether she lied or spoke frankly about her experiences.[11] In this case, one could hear Beauvoir's own voice toward
women in the words of Lewis Brogan as well as those of Henri Perron.

In her theoretical texts, Beauvoir develops both an ontological and a sociopolitical explanation for the parrhesiastic promise of sexual relationships, as well as for their dangers and disappointments. *The Second Sex* draws on the Hegelian image of consciousnesses in confrontation with each other to explain the importance of emotional tension, mutual vulnerability, and the opportunity for independent work in women's quest for truth concerning themselves and their time (Beauvoir 1957, xvii). In the section of *Phenomenology of Spirit* entitled "Lordship and Bondage," these consciousnesses seek truth about themselves and the forces that compose them through a game of mortal risk (Hegel 1977, 111–19). Insofar as each consciousness understands itself purely in terms of the other's biological life or abstract recognition, it learns nothing about itself. This understanding only comes to fruition when the relationship between consciousnesses is rephrased in terms of the object on which one *labors* in order to demonstrate his or her recognition of the Other. Why? Because labor, unlike violence, establishes a *power relationship*—that is, in Foucault's terms, an ability to act on the actions of others. Without servitude, Hegel believes, the truth of self-consciousness can neither be disclosed nor tested; the individual does not learn to act on his or her own actions. The relations of power connecting lord and bondsman are elements of Hegel's general attempt to articulate a field of truth in relation to each individually situated consciousness's capacity for self-deception, abstract self-understanding, and ignorance.

According to Sartre, consciousness can *only* exist in relations of servitude or mastery with respect to Others.[12] In life, the lover seeks to become an essential element "in-itself" of the beloved's project; in bed, he or she seeks to lose his or her conscious individuality, if only temporarily, in the ambiguous experience of the flesh. Although lovers and comrades may be joint witnesses to public events or be the collective object of a public gaze, this mutuality always comes at the cost of objectifying or being objectified by the Other for whom they form a couple. "The essence of the relations between consciousnesses is not the *Mitsein*; it is conflict" (Sartre 1956, 555). By contrast, Beauvoir declares in *The Second Sex* that women are unable to regard themselves in collective opposition to males taken as a whole because the sexes are joined in a fundamental *Mitsein*. "The division of the sexes is a biological fact, not an event in human history," she writes. "Their opposition is drawn [*se dessinée*] at the heart of an original *Mitsein* and woman has not broken it" (Beauvoir 1957, xix, translation altered).

How should we understand this *Mitsein,* which prevents women from asserting themselves as a class on the basis of their more-or-less common situation? Is it a biological fact, like the anatomical distinction between sexes? Is it the canvas on which a historical interpretation of sexual differ-ence is drawn by biologists, which women have accepted as a horizon of their political existence? The basic trait of woman is to be "the Other in a totality of which the two components are necessary to one another" (1957, xx), but Beauvoir clearly believes that specific communal or conflictual manifestations of this *Mitsein* are contingent and need not, for example, identify women any more than men with "Otherness" in general. Unlike the power relationships that concern Hegel; that is, those that produce truth and relate individuals to truth as *conscious subjects,* the power relation-ships constituting Beauvoir's sexual *Mitsein* are outside of consciousness and condition its disclosive properties—although they are well within the realm of life and labor, nonconscious relations of power through which self-consciousness is developed.[13] Rather than being a form of conscious solidarity, sexual *Mitsein* is both a *situation* shared by men and women through which the biology of each sex comes to take on a meaning, and an *indeterminacy* haunting the historical practice and meaning of sexual dif-ference that leaves opportunities for innovation and future change.[14]

The historically contingent opposition between women and men in erotic life and labor helps us understand why the emotions involved in sex-ual relationships promise to improve women's access to the truth but so often fail to deliver on that promise. On the one hand, they subject women to *male* discourses of truth that deny women's capacity to disclose the world as subjects (Beauvoir 1957, xxii–xxvi). On the other hand, they allow men to persist in self-serving illusions about their moral and social worth *as sexual males* rather than as creative and self-aware individuals ontologi-cally comparable to women. In terms of Hegel's dialectic, sexist power re-lations deprive the (male) master from drawing any real self-understanding from his experience of being loved and recognized by women because they identify the capacities for immanence and transcendence possessed by every ambiguous consciousness with the specific biological qualities of fe-male and male human beings respectively. But they also prevent the (female) bondsperson from achieving self-understanding through mediating *labor* on any object other than the master's personality, a task she supports more or less enthusiastically.

Neither consciousness is abolished in a battle to the death, but neither consciousness engages in the risk and work that Hegel requires for eventual access to truth about oneself, humanity in general, and the social relations mediating individual and collective registers. Male and female founder and are lost in a realm comparable to pre-Socratic *opinion*, prejudice, or ignorance:

> This, then, is the reason why woman has a double and deceptive visage: she is all that man desires and all that he does not attain. . . . She is All, that is, on the plane of the inessential; she is all the Other. And, as the other, she is other than herself, other than what is expected of her. Being all, she is never quite *this* which she should be; she is everlasting deception, the very deception of that existence which is never successfully attained nor fully reconciled with the totality of existents. (Beauvoir 1957, 197–98)

Insofar as lovers regard their beloved as a God who *knows* or *is* truth rather than a *parrhesiastes* who *tests* their truthfulness, they cannot see themselves as active participants in the process of mutual self-creation, they risk themselves less and suffer from ignorance or jealousy. For women like Paule and Monique (narrator of "La Femme Rompue," in Beauvoir 1967), the male personality is not only a master but the privileged object of labor. Lacking opportunities for independent work on the world and on themselves, they are unstable *parrhesiastes* who neither know themselves well enough to *test* their partners' relation to the truth nor are able to survive and create new relationships in their absence. Neither of these women believes, for neither has been taught to believe, that men *need* them to have an independent relationship to the truth. But Beauvoir's independent women are almost as distraught as those who made love their life project when partners with whom they believed themselves to share a "parrhesiastic contract" stray sexually, abandon previous ideals, or disqualify themselves as interlocutors. Like Laurence, the main characters of *L'Invitée* (1943) and the novella *L'Âge de Discretion* (1967) temporarily lose faith in the value of their own professional or intellectual work when they lose faith in the intellectual or moral rigor of men with whom they chose to share their lives.

Le Doeuff suggests that disappointment with particular male teachers or interlocutors is what drives men to philosophize independently (1989, 107).[15] Of course, as she and other scholars have recently discussed, the truth sought by Beauvoir and her characters is not always "philosophically" phrased; it arises through a deeper act of disclosure that is a "way of being" rather than a way of thinking, much less a particular system of thought— and concerns a state of affairs whose possibilities are *one's own*.[16] The risk of disappointment, like the risk of domination, is implicit in any human's struggle to attain a relation to the truth in community with others.[17] Just as Heidegger claimed to renounce philosophy for the "task of thinking," moreover, it is not inconceivable that Beauvoir's disclaimer about her own philosophical activity represented an active effort to resist the kinds of power relations vested in the "philosophical" soul and to engage with real and imaginary publics who were seldom considered addressees or participants in philosophical eros—including most women. Coupling can only be a suitable context for truth given forces that exist beyond the qualities or acts of an immediate partner, and one test for the viability of a parrhesiastic relationship might be whether it permits critical reflection and action upon political and economic conditions shaping the couple.

For example, *The Second Sex* indicates that women's emotional and moral satisfaction in sexual partnerships (like men's) depends enormously on the economic and legal or political conditions under which lovers desire, confront, and comfort one another. Beauvoir's condition "that the truth might be bearable" inaugurates a new kind of parrhesiastic contract within and regarding sexual relationships, one involving generosity as well as risk (1957, 692, 724–28). One must first create a world—that is, a balance of forces and material conditions—in which a soul can be formed, a sturdy and reliable practice of truthful disclosure. If men and women are to be capable of hearing and telling the truth to one another, they will need to have equal access to meaningful work, protection from violence and poverty, and respect as individuals rather than on the basis of their performance in familial and sexual roles. In order to maximize their assurance that others are truthful, they need to subscribe to political movements and institutions that aim at the freedom of others and grant others freedom to criticize their own political institutions. Such an ethic is not exercised outside of power but is the way of organizing and limiting the asymmetry of power relations that Beauvoir believed were most likely to promote individual welfare and emotional satisfaction.

In the ancient parrhesiastic relationships studied by Foucault, family status or sexual relationships were unlikely elements of an individual's effort to construct, test, and strengthen a soul in relation to the guidance of others. A *parrhesiastes* might challenge his interlocutor's misuse of pleasure, and sexual excesses might indicate his essential self-deception or ignorance, but this ignorance would not have been interpreted as blindness to the significance of *sexuality* as a principle. Nor was the parrhesiastic contract suffused with sexual desire. The *"relation* of the self to truth or to some rational principles" (Foucault 2001b, 165) *revealed* through personal relationships occupied a different analytic level than the truth regarding sexual or parrhesiastic relationships themselves. Sexuality only become a principle one was obliged to apprehend truthfully when sexual relationships became suffused with a capacity to orient individuals toward a nonsexual truth, as in Plato's *Phaedrus* or *Symposium. Ars erotica*—knowledge regarding power relations that produce bodily pleasure—made room for *scientia sexualis*—a variant on the power relations that produce truth in the form of principles, including, in this case, the principle of "sexuality."

The early activists of second wave feminism assumed that women could only establish truth about the world to the extent that they escaped the mystifications imposed by the couple and the family, structures of power enabling men to tell the truth while leaving women in *doxa* or opinion concerning their own interests and pleasures. On the one hand, feminists attempted to read the power relations of oppressive classist and racist Western societies as a whole writ small in sexual couples. On the other hand, women attempted to construct relationships of truth for and among themselves using conceptual elements and social practices that had little to do with men or with women's relationships to men. Experimenting with new forms of sexual interaction and with nonsexual forms of friendship promised an alternative to hierarchical forms of sexual power, if not all forms of power, and relieved women of the moral obligation to risk themselves in heterosexual contexts that seemed to require personal and political self-deception.

Beauvoir's most successful and enduring effort to create and preserve a soul capable of truth arose through *written* contact with women who were mostly strangers. At first, her texts were received by the (male) reading public as contributions, welcome or unwelcome, to the body of knowledge Foucault refers to as *scientia sexualis*.[18] In other words, they were interpreted as conveying more-or-less true and potentially scandalous knowledge *about* women's sexuality (according to the rules for games of truth among men) rather than as female experiments in creating new forms of truth and new practices of truth-telling around sexual topics and relationships. But this is exactly the kind of challenge women around the world read in their pages—an incitement to create new discourses and methodologies and to speculate about their ontological presuppositions.[19] As a result of these new "games of truth," many feminists perceived a conflict between Beauvoir's willingness to persist in heterosexual fascination and disappointment, and her success in inaugurating a woman-to-woman discourse on the nature of reality and social power. Feminists from different cultures and generations continue to disagree about the truth-disclosive properties of various erotic and political experiments, the extent to which certain bodies and forces facilitate or frustrate women's ability to know and act on their historical surroundings.

As has been shown, Beauvoir never believed that women could be *agents* or transcendent *subjects* of truth rather than recipients or immanent *objects* of truth in the absence of erotic and emotional risk, any more than they could desire or survive these risks if denied the ability to work on the world and themselves *apart* from individual partners. Although Beauvoir would not have used the language of power relations to describe this situation, I think we can also safely say that she would not have considered relationships to be capable of truthful disclosure *apart* from sustaining networks of power.[20] She might well have said, however, that creating or saving a soul means using one's capacity for passion to sustain relationships in which reality is both visible and alterable, rather than to reinforce one's ignorance, deceive others, or obscure their ability to disclose a world in which the exercise of freedom is meaningful.

Foucault's reflections on gay culture and forms of friendship suggest that it is not sexuality per se that clouds our ability to disclose truths but the limited variety of social practices, forms of friendship, and structures of community in which sexuality plays an important role (e.g., Foucault

1988b, 301–302). The truth revealed in any parrhesiastic contract includes, explicitly or implicitly, the emotional and political conditions for altering and varying the power relations making disclosure possible. These practices are distinguished from Le Doeuff's "erotico-theoretical transference" neither by their lack of eroticism nor by their inability to provoke theory, but insofar as they enable individuals to remember that truth and freedom are values transcending individual couples. Such values organize forces that can be detached from and recomposed with new lovers and communities.

Given Beauvoir's analysis, women should be careful when choosing interlocutors with whom to test themselves—whether men, other women, movements, or nations. As Paul Veyne suggests, "It is difficult . . . not to begin to believe a little in the foreign dogmas against which one has formed an offensive or defensive confederacy. . . . The moment an individual wishes to convince and be recognized, he must respect different ideas, if they are forces, and must partake of them a little" (1988, 56). Only the above-mentioned sociopolitical conditions can ensure that a lover, community, or public is a desirable interlocutor who has no need to support his/her narcissism with debilitating challenges.

When Beauvoir asserts that the meaning of an individual's freedom comes from the horizon set by the freedom of all others, she implies that his or her ability to disclose truth implies the existence of one or more publics capable of "making up their own minds," emotionally responsive but resisting seduction in ways that make the achievement of love more real and indicative of reality's contours. Thus, labor and eroticism are important nonconscious elements of the power relations linking lovers, thinkers, and their publics. Labor, by which one acts on oneself and negotiates with others, requires reality to present a "coefficient of adversity" irreducible to conscious interpretation. Eroticism and emotion allow consciousness to enjoy, assess, and alter its dependency on the resistance or generosity of bodies. One will never be able to tell the truth about everyone and everything: God is not among the set of possible parrhesiastic partners. However, each scene and level of disclosure is implicated in others, and the ability to form new loves and publics may be evidence that one's soul is not yet lost.[21]

NOTES

1. From *parrhēsia*, a Greek word meaning "boldness, or freedom of speech." See Foucault 2001b, p. 11.

2. For discussions of truth in the care of the self, see "The Concern for Truth" (Foucault 1988a); "Truth, Power, Self" (in Martin et al. 1988), and *The Care of the Self* (Foucault 1988c). For specific discussions of *parrhesia*, see *L'Hermeneutique du Sujet: Cours au Collège de France 1981–1982* (Foucault 2001a), and *Fearless Speech* (Foucault 2001b).

3. A number of recent books have approached Beauvoir's aesthetics of existence and autobiographical practice as twentieth-century models for "care of the self." Vintges identifies Beauvoir's philosophical contribution with a particular style of "existential practice" that included rituals distinguishing "work" from pleasure or social life and that protected her opportunities to grow and change as an individual (1996, especially chaps. 6–7). Tidd (1999) and Fraser (1999) use Foucault's analysis of the institutional function of "authorship" and "sexuality" to understand Beauvoir's relation to the public and the ways in which the understanding of selfhood as *identity* obscured the significance of bisexuality and mourning in her "care of the self."

4. Unpublished manuscript; personal communication from James Bernauer.

5. According to Sartre, the value of "truth" or "truthfulness" is implicit in the intentional nature of human consciousness. But one must *choose* this value to orient one's acts of intentional disclosure. An unfinished essay from the 1940s entitled "Truth and Existence" defines truth as the individual's apprehension of intentional objects that have already been "worked over" and interpreted by others (1992, 6). Both *Being and Nothingness* and "Truth and Existence" agree with Beauvoir that valuing the truth about oneself and one's world is morally foundational and requires humans to fight against bad faith or self-deception. But neither clearly acknowledges the fact that truth is both an argumentative and a perceptual medium of relationships with other speakers and that the phenomenon we most often seek to apprehend truthfully is not ourselves but the web of intersubjective power.

6. See *The Emotions: Outline of a Theory* (Sartre 1948). Arp (2001) and Vintges (1996) discuss Beauvoir's objections to a philosophical and moral perspective emerging from emotional *indifference* in her discussions of the Marquis de Sade and Camus' *l'Étranger*, respectively.

7. For a classic formulation of this distinction, which is important throughout the history of modern philosophy, see Descartes 1985, 335–36. Perceptions felt in the soul but having their causes "outside" of the soul are referred to as "passions," while volitions of the soul and acts of imagination or thought that rely on no external beings for their effectiveness are called "actions," despite the fact that we can only become aware of them as "passions" with a special emotional valence.

8. See also Beauvoir's discussion of sincerity and truth in sexual relationships from *The Prime of Life* (1992, 26).

9. As Fallaize notes, both *Les Belles Images* and *Les Mandarins* are critical of therapeutic strategies that deaden the emotional capacities of suffering women: here, "pain and suffering are identified as the truth—not only the truth of the individual's suffering but also . . . as a moral and political truth" (1988, 132). This is in keeping with Beau-

voir's emphasis on the emotional conditions for disclosure of being in *The Ethics of Ambiguity* (see above).

10. Card (1990) characterizes Beauvoir's attitude toward lesbianism in *The Second Sex* as fundamentally heterosexual because she emphasizes the element of existential "choice" expressed by a woman's desire for other women while suggesting that the "woman in love" is ordinarily hetero. By contrast, Ferguson (1990) and Simons (1992) situate Beauvoir on a "lesbian continuum" à la Adrienne Rich. Ferguson points out that the experience of lesbianism as a "choice" rather than a "weakness" rests in part on access to empowering political and social networks; according to Simons, fear of endangering Sylvie Le Bon's career led her to downplay the erotic aspect of their relationship in all public statements.

11. See Klaw 1995, 202–203. Bair (1990, 511–13) discusses the difficulty—and potential injustice—of efforts to classify Beauvoir's relationship with Sylvie le Bon according to any taxonomy of lesbian or other female friendships.

12. Note that this conflict-ridden portrait of human relationships is tempered to a certain extent in Sartre's later political philosophy, which addresses phenomena of positive solidarity and group identification or commitment (see Anderson 1993). The possibility of such positive and mutually liberatory relations between consciousnesses is also, perhaps to a greater extent even than in his political writings, broached in discussions of the historical and moral ties between writers and their audiences in *What Is Literature?* (Sartre 1988).

13. See Bauer (2001) and Lundgren-Gothlin (1996) for alternate explanations of Beauvoir's claim that male-female relations do not mirror the situation of master and slave in Hegel's *Phenomenology*.

14. Beauvoir follows Merleau-Ponty in defining the human body as a *situation* rather than an *object*. Thus, the female body is neither determining nor determined; it is a means for the development and expression of human freedom. Beauvoir remedies Merleau-Ponty's lack of attention to the gendered nature of bodily situation in *The Second Sex* (the generic human is presumed to be male); but from the fact that "femininity" is a specific situation we can also infer that "masculinity" is a situation defined, empowered, and limited by reference to women. See Ward (1995, 231–33) for a discussion of Beauvoir's views on embodiment.

15. Beauvoir's struggle with an admired female teacher's efforts to tempt her back into the Catholic faith, as described in the student diaries, may provide the model for such a disappointment (Simons 1999, 211–12).

16. Beauvoir's refusal to identify herself as a "philosopher" rather than a "novelist" despite repeated exploration of philosophical themes in novels and essays (including essays on the philosophical status of literature) is explored by Vintges (1996), Bergoffen (1997), Holveck (2002), and Bauer (2001). See also "Littérature et Metaphysique" (Beauvoir 1986).

17. Sade, according to Beauvoir (2001), is the exemplary case of a man who refuses to engage in the risk and emotional labor that might enable his fictions to enter into truth-telling relations of power with lovers or readers. Although *The Ethics of Ambiguity* acknowledged that liberators might be required to treat opponents violently (as means rather than ends) due to the difficulty of persuading or reeducating them quickly and efficiently, she contends that Sade resorts to cruelty in order to escape ambiguity, emotional entanglement, or fleshliness. Beauvoir insists that Sade's isolation is not an

ontological given, but is *affirmed* and *reinforced* by the dominating attitude with which he experiences his own eroticism and that of others.

18. *The Second Sex* was originally translated into English for sale as a sort of thinking woman's "sex manual" (Bair 1991, 432). Many thanks to Anna Alexander for pointing out this irony.

19. Standpoint epistemology, Irigaray's phenomenology of sexual difference, and MacKinnon's demystification of gender as power are only a few of the best-known philosophical elaborations of the experience described by consciousness-raising—theories whose truth makes more sense as an effect of the power generated among women than as "representations" of reality apart from relations of power.

20. Arp (2001, 120–23) discusses the implicit recognition of power relations in Beauvoir's *Ethics of Ambiguity*.

21. I owe the inspiration for this essay to presentations by Karen Vintges and Alexander Miranda at the Society for Phenomenology and Existential Philosophy conference, October 2001. Many thanks to Margaret Simons for her criticisms and suggestions.

References

Anderson, Thomas C. 1993. *Sartre's two ethics: From authenticity to integral humanity.* Chicago: Open Court.

Arp, Kristana. 2001. *The bonds of freedom: Simone de Beauvoir's existentialist ethics.* Chicago: Open Court.

Bair, Deirdre. 1990. *Simone de Beauvoir: A biography.* New York: Simon and Schuster.

Bauer, Nancy. 2001. *Simone de Beauvoir, philosophy and feminism.* New York: Columbia University Press.

Beauvoir, Simone de. 1975 [1943]. *She came to stay [L'Invitée].* Trans. Yvonne Moyse and Roger Senhouse. Glasgow: Fontana Books.

———. 1947 [1944]. *Pyrrhus et Cinéas.* In *Pour une morale de l'ambiguïté.* Paris: Gallimard.

———. 1994 [1947]. *The ethics of ambiguity.* Trans. Bernard Frechtman. New York: Citadel.

———. 1986 [1948]. Littérature et métaphysique. In *L'Existentialisme et la sagesse des nations.* Geneva: Éditions Nagel.

———. 1957 [1949]. *The second sex.* Trans. H. M. Parshley. New York: Alfred A. Knopf.

———. 1953 [1951–52]. The Marquis de Sade [Faut-il Brûler Sade?] Trans. Annette Michelson with selections from his writings chosen and translated by Paul Dinnage. New York: Grove Press.

———. 1991 [1954]. *The mandarins.* Trans. Leonard Friedman. New York: W.W. Norton.

———. 1992 [1960]. *The prime of life [Force de l'Âge].* Trans. Peter Green. New York: Paragon House.

———. 1965. *Force of circumstance [La Force des choses].* Trans. Richard Howard. New York: Putnam.

———. 1968 [1966]. *Les Belles images.* Trans. Patrick O'Brian. London: Collins.

———. 1967. *L'Âge de discretion. Monologue. La Femme rompue.* Paris: Gallimard.

———. 1979. *Quand prime le spirituel.* Paris: Gallimard.

Bergoffen, Debra B. 1997. *The philosophy of Simone de Beauvoir: Gendered phenomenologies, erotic generosities.* Albany: State University of New York Press.

Card, Claudia. 1990. Lesbian attitudes and *The Second Sex.* In *Hypatia reborn: Essays in feminist philosophy,* ed. Azizah Al-Hibri and Margaret A. Simons, 290–99. Bloomington: Indiana University Press.

Descartes, René. 1985. The passions of the soul. In *The philosophical writing of Descartes,* Vol. 1, ed. John Cottingham, Robert Stoothoff, and Dugald Murdoch. Cambridge: Cambridge University Press.

Detienne, Marcel. 1996. *The masters of truth in archaic Greece.* Trans. Janet Lloyd. New York: Zone Books.

Fallaize, Elizabeth. 1988. *The novels of Simone de Beauvoir.* London: Routledge.

Ferguson, Ann. 1990. Lesbian identity: Beauvoir and history. In *Hypatia reborn: Essays in feminist philosophy,* ed. Azizah Al-Hibri and Margaret A. Simons, 280–89. Bloomington: Indiana University Press.

Foucault, Michel. 1978. *The history of sexuality.* Vol. I: *An introduction.* Trans. Robert Hurley. New York: Vintage Books.

———. 1983. The subject and power. Afterword to *Michel Foucault: Beyond structuralism and hermeneutics,* 2nd edition, ed. Hubert L. Dreyfus and Paul Rabinow, 208–26. Chicago: University of Chicago Press.

———. 1988a. The concern for truth. In *Politics, philosophy, culture: Interviews and other writings, 1977–1984,* ed. Lawrence Kritzman. New York: Routledge.

———. 1988b. Sexual choice, sexual act: Foucault and homosexuality. In *Politics, philosophy, culture: Interviews and other writings, 1977–1984,* ed. Lawrence D. Kritzman. New York: Routledge.

———. 1988c. *The care of the self (History of sexuality,* Vol. 3). Trans. Robert Hurley. New York: Vintage.

———. 1990. *The use of pleasure (History of sexuality,* Vol. 2). New York: Vintage.

———. 2001a. *L'Herméneutique du sujet: Cours au Collège de France, 1981–1982.* Paris: Gallimard/Seuil.

———. 2001b. *Fearless speech.* Ed. Joseph Pearson. Los Angeles: Semiotext(e).

Fraser, Mariam. 1999. *Identity without selfhood: Simone de Beauvoir and bisexuality.* Cambridge: Cambridge University Press.

Hegel, G. W. F. 1977. *Phenomenology of spirit.* Trans. A. V. Miller. Oxford: Oxford University Press.

Holveck, Eleanore. 2002. *Simone de Beauvoir's philosophy of lived experience: Literature and metaphysics.* Lanham, Md.: Rowman and Littlefield.

Klaw, Barbara. 1995. Sexuality in Beauvoir's *Les Mandarins.* In *Feminist interpretations of Simone de Beauvoir,* ed. Margaret A. Simons, 193–22. University Park: Penn State University Press.

Le Doeuff, Michèle. 1989. Long hair, short ideas. In *The philosophical imaginary.* Trans. Colin Gordon. London: Athlone Press.

Lundgren-Gothlin, Eva. 1996. *Sex and existence: Simone de Beauvoir's* The Second Sex. Trans. Linda Schenck. Hanover, N.H.: Wesleyan University Press.

Martin, Luther H., Huck Gutman, and Patrick H. Hutton. 1988. *Technologies of the self: A seminar with Michel Foucault.* Amherst: University of Massachusetts Press.

Sartre, Jean-Paul. 1948. *The emotions: Outline of a theory.* Trans. Bernard Frechtman. New York: Philosophical Library.

———. 1956. *Being and nothingness: A phenomenological essay on ontology.* Trans. Hazel E. Barnes. New York: Washington Square Press.

———. 1988. *"What is literature?" And other essays.* Ed. with introduction by Steven Ungar. Cambridge, Mass.: Harvard University Press.

———. 1992. *Truth and existence.* Trans. Adrian Van den Hoven. Ed. with Introduction by Ronald Aronson. Chicago: University of Chicago Press.

Simons, Margaret. 1992. Lesbian connections: Simone de Beauvoir and feminism, *Signs* 18:1, 136–61.

———. 1999. Beauvoir's early philosophy: The 1927 diary. In *Beauvoir and The Second Sex: Feminism, race, and the origins of existentialism,* 185–243. Lanham, Md.: Rowman and Littlefield.

———. 2003. Bergson's influence on Beauvoir's philosophical methodology. In *The Cambridge Companion to Simone de Beauvoir,* ed. Claudia Card, 107–28. Cambridge: Cambridge University Press.

Tidd, Ursula. 1999. *Simone de Beauvoir, gender and testimony.* Cambridge: Cambridge University Press.

Veyne, Paul. 1988. *Did the Greeks believe in their myths? An essay on the constitutive imagination.* Trans. Paula Wissing. Chicago: University of Chicago Press.

Vintges, Karen. 1996. *Philosophy as passion: The thinking of Simone de Beauvoir.* Trans. Anne Lavelle. Bloomington: Indiana University Press.

Ward, Julie. 1995. Beauvoir's two senses of "body" in *The Second Sex.* In *Feminist interpretations of Simone de Beauvoir,* ed. Margaret Simons, 223–42. University Park: Penn State University Press.

BEAUVOIR'S IDEA OF AMBIGUITY

Stacy Keltner

11

In *The Ethics of Ambiguity*[1] Beauvoir provides a diagnosis of the sociopolitical problematic of late modernity through an articulation of the historical, philosophical, and political significance of the appearance of *ambiguity*. Ambiguity refers to our social and temporal being in conditions of late modernity and contains three essential moments: the existent's experience of itself in the world; its fundamental ethical relation to others; and the temporal unity of existence between past, present, and future. For Beauvoir, the significance of ambiguity is marked by the insight it provides into the sociopolitical problematic of late modernity; the mechanisms of traditional and modern discourses; and the ethical, political, and historical relevance of the appearance of existentialism and its provision of an orienting movement of situated ethical and political action.

Ambiguity signals the tension between seemingly opposing experiences of the self as both a free subject and an object for others. "Man asserts himself as a pure internality against which no external power can take hold, and he also experiences himself as a thing crushed by the dark weight of other things," Beauvoir claims (*EA* 7; *PM* 9). The human being is both "a sovereign and unique subject" and *at the same time* "an object for others . . . nothing more than an individual in the collectivity on which he depends" (*EA* 7; *PM* 10). For Beauvoir, existence is a phenomenon that can be reduced neither to a pure "I" that stands over and against a material, social world nor to the inert being of material things. Ambiguity escapes the traditional determinations of existence via definitions of the existent either as pure freedom, transcendence, interiority or as pure object, immanence, exteriority. Beauvoir's description of ambiguity draws on the tension between transcendence and facticity.[2] The thought is that one's facticity is lived in such a way that the self also accomplishes an escape from its facticity. The self can neither be reduced to its facticity nor be identified with a radical break from it. Subjectivity, in other words, is not substantive but a temporal and situated process or movement. Beauvoir favors Heidegger's description of human existence as a *project;* that is, as a projection toward the future that simultaneously establishes a unity with the past and the present.[3]

Nevertheless, beyond the description of ambiguity, Beauvoir seeks to diagnose the conditions of its emergence and significance. The historical relevance of its appearance *as* ambiguity is a central concern of *The Ethics of Ambiguity.* If ambiguity is not diagnosed by traditional or modern discourses, what is the condition of its emergence and what is its historical significance? Why has it become a concern? And, what, exactly, is Beauvoir's account of the problematic of late modernity that has resulted in the appearance of ambiguity such that traditional and modern discourses no longer function to conceal it? In short, why does ambiguity appear *as such* and *for us?*

Beauvoir claims that there is something about late modern society that makes the evasion of ambiguity more difficult than in the past: "Men of today seem to feel more acutely than ever the paradox of their condition" (*EA* 9; *PM* 11–12). For Beauvoir, ambiguity appears in conditions where experiences exceed the articulations of existence provided by religious, modern secular, and philosophical discourses. The conditions of the emergence and significance of ambiguity divested of any philosophical elaboration to encompass it lie precisely in the "grandeur" ambiguity has taken on in late modernity (*EA* 9; *PM* 12). For Beauvoir, we no longer "succeed in fleeing it," but rather live it in the absence of any articulation to adequately understand ourselves, the world, and the possibility of meaningful action.

Never before in history, Beauvoir suggests, has the paradox been *lived* with such forcefulness. She claims that humanity recognizes itself as the ultimate end *at the same time* that it treats itself as purely a means; humanity's "mastery of the world" is most widespread *at the same time* that it finds itself "crushed by uncontrollable forces"; humanity has mastered the atomic bomb *at the same time* that this mastery is for its own destruction; it has the "incomparable taste" of its own life *at the same time* that it has the feeling of an utter insignificance. The historical appearance of ambiguity is in direct relation to a technological prowess that has resulted in the dramatization of these two poles of existence. "Perhaps in no other age have [human beings] manifested their grandeur more brilliantly, and in no other age has this grandeur been so horribly flouted. . . . [A]t every moment, at every opportunity, the truth comes to light, the truth of life and death, of my solitude and my bond with the world, of my freedom and my servitude, of the insignificance and the sovereign importance of each man and all men" (*EA* 9; *PM* 12). Beauvoir thus diagnoses late modernity as a technological-industrial destruction of the forms of thought that have traditionally functioned to provide meaning and coherence to existence. These forms of thought are no longer equipped to handle the ambiguity that conditions our sociocultural existence—thereby resulting in the emergence of ambiguity as such in the historical loss of those discourses to account for modern experience.

The historical disclosure of ambiguity reveals certain mechanisms at work in those discourses that once gave form and sense, albeit inaccurately, to existence. Ambiguity has functioned as the condition of possibility of the historical discourses of philosophy, religion, and politics. The experience of ambiguity has led philosophers to create discourses that, perhaps unknowingly, evade and conceal this very experience. For Beauvoir, discourses of philosophy, religion, and politics have functioned to conceal our fundamental condition of ambiguity by instituting mechanisms designed to obliterate ambiguity either through a philosophy of the subject that takes the subject as an atom or through a philosophy that obliterates the subject in an organic unity. Both are implicated in a denial of the very experiences that condition our existence. Traditionally, philosophy and the discourses it has underwritten have concealed ambiguity through an either/or logic in which the philosopher is determined to reduce the human condition to mind, matter, or a single substance that merges the two: "It has been a matter of eliminating the ambiguity by making oneself pure inwardness or pure externality, by escaping from the sensible world or by being engulfed in it, by yielding to eternity or enclosing oneself in the pure moment. Hegel, with more ingenuity, tried to reject none of the aspects of man's condition and to reconcile them all" (*EA* 8; *PM* 10).

Beauvoir thus charges the Western philosophical tradition with an evasive logic. Grounded in a primordial ambiguity, the either/or logic of Western rationality flees ambiguity through an articulation of reality that denies its existential base. Beauvoir challenges this tradition to think the ambiguity of its ground. This requires that we think the simultaneity of what appears to be mutually exclusive according to an either/or logic. In other words, thinking is challenged to think simultaneity or a thinking of a both/and logic. However, Beauvoir warns against the both/and thinking of Hegelian dialectics. Dialectical logic's reconciliation of opposing terms fails to maintain the tension or separation between those terms. For Beauvoir, separation is a condition of genuine connection.[4] Existentialism proposes a thought of separation and connection that exceeds both traditional and dialectical logic.

Given Beauvoir's characterization of the appearance of ambiguity in late modernity, her claim that existentialism is "a philosophy of ambiguity" (*EA* 9; *PM* 13) suggests that, for her, existentialism arises as a diagnosis and description of the appearance of ambiguity, which carries with it, in light of the failure of the historical discourses that have attempted its mastery, the feeling of absurdity and of despair. Existentialism provides insight into that which has exceeded the framework of ambiguity's traditional determinations and thereby has brought into question those discourses that have lost the capacity to provide sense to modern experience. Thus, if existentialism thematizes experiences of absurdity and despair, it is precisely the outcome of the loss of the forms and meanings traditionally attached to existence. However, this does not necessitate the conclusion that existentialism cannot offer any positive articulation of meaning and orientation in social and historical existence. For Beauvoir, the essential problematic that must be addressed is the possibility of an ethics that does not result in the exclusion of ambiguity, but one that rather "assumes" or "realizes" ambiguity (*EA* 9, 13, 156; *PM* 12–13, 18, 226).

Existentialism, as a philosophy directly concerned with ambiguity, provides insight into the mechanisms of traditional discourses that seek the dissolution of ambiguity. This permits it both to measure the legitimacy of those discourses and to positively reconstruct an elaboration of social and historical existence that provides sense to action. However, existentialism has been charged precisely with lacking the means to do so. Beauvoir summarizes the critique of existentialism thus: "[E]xistentialism is a philosophy of the absurd and of despair. It encloses man in a sterile anguish, in an empty subjectivity. It is incapable of furnishing him with any principle for making choices" (*EA* 10; *PM* 13). Or, again: "[T]here are many who charge existentialism with offering no objective content to the moral act" (*EA* 16; *PM* 23). If the critics of existentialism are right, then it would seem that there is a complete lack of resources for understanding and articulating ambiguity, since the traditional elaborations have failed.

The ambiguity diagnosed by Beauvoir thus has implications for how the social bond is to be thematized. Beauvoir is critical of any conception of the existent that establishes a non-ambiguous interpretation. The existent must be understood not only in its connection with the world but also as fundamentally connected to others. Beauvoir seeks an articulation of separation and connection that does not obliterate ambiguity in traditional or dialectical logic. The two dominant modes of evasion are *atomistic individualism* and *communitarianism*. Atomistic individualism, governed by traditional logic, results in a social theory and concept of reason that understands relations to others in the framework of its interpretation of external relations among things. Against the relations of externality of individualism, Beauvoir insists that the existent is, existentially, bound up with others. Against the internal fusion of communitarianism, governed by dialectical logic, Beauvoir insists that the existent is, existentially, separate.

As early as 1944 in *Pyrrhus et Cinéas*, Beauvoir claims to be steering a path between individualism and communitarianism. Taking the "garden of Candide" as exemplary of existence, Beauvoir claims: "The garden of Candide can neither be reduced to an atom nor confounded with the universe."[5] In *The Ethics of Ambiguity*, Beauvoir draws on Sartre's concept of the *detotalized totality* from his, then unpublished, *Notebooks for an Ethics* to designate the task of articulating separation and connection in a way that does not deny ambiguity. For Beauvoir, the "detotalized totality" indicates that "separation does not exclude relation, nor vice-versa" (*EA* 122; *PM* 176). Sociality is thus to be articulated neither as mere totality (that is, communitarianism) nor as a collection of untotalized atoms (that is, individualism).

Contra the trend of critique against existentialism as solipsistic, Beauvoir insists that the ethics that existentialism proposes is the only ethics that can account for a philosophy of existence that insists simultaneously on the social bond as equally primordial to the separation of the existent. "An ethics of ambiguity will be one which will refuse to deny *a priori* that separate existents can, *at the same time,* be bound to each other" (*EA* 18; *PM* 24, emphasis mine). Beauvoir seeks an account of the ambiguous phenomenon not just of subjectivity as an active existing between transcendence and immanence, but also of the ambiguity of the "indissoluble" "me-others" relation (*EA* 72; *PM* 104) through an account of separation and connection.

In contrast to those discourses that exercise an exclusion of ambiguity for the sake of constituting an unambiguous interpretation of the self and the social world, Beauvoir proposes that existentialism, as a philosophy of ambiguity, is the *only* discourse capable of articulating ambiguity in a way that avoids its exclusion: "Existentialism proposes no evasion" (*EA* 159; *PM* 229). Moreover, she claims it is the only discourse that can outline an ethics: "The existentialist doctrine permits the elaboration of an ethics, but it even appears to us as the only philosophy in which an ethics has its place" (*EA* 34; *PM* 48). Religion, philosophy, and political discourses have failed precisely because their giving of form and sense was a denial that could not handle the fluid borders of the self and its experience. Beauvoir insists that ambiguity appears within a situation that other discourses lack the means to negotiate. In other words, social and historical experience exceeds the form and meaning of modern and traditional discourses. Existentialism arises, historically, to diagnose what is revealed and remains, for Beauvoir, *the* resource for articulating an ethics adequate to social and historical existence.

Beauvoir does not seek to impose a form onto ambiguity, but asks whether ambiguity might have its own ethical orientation. At the heart of *The Ethics of Ambiguity* is a desire to understand the practical implications for the philosophy of ambiguity. "It is in the authentic conditions of our life that we must draw our strength to live and our reason for acting" (*EA* 9; *PM* 13, translation modified), and not, she might have said, in an abstract and ideal elaboration of objective values that flee these conditions. The task of *The Ethics of Ambiguity* is to develop certain precepts for action that do not evade ambiguity by formulating criteria that are fixed in their meaning. Beauvoir seeks an articulation of ambiguity in an ethical direction, which means in a direction that provides sense to action, but a sense that "is never fixed" and "must be constantly won" (*EA* 129; *PM* 186). This means she will not propose a set of values. Rather, ethics for Beauvoir will be figured according to the historical situation, thereby offering a method or formative movement to be filled out with an historical content.

Beauvoir's ethical and political project seeks to depart from the ethical and political theories of the Western philosophical tradition. As early as 1945, in "Moral Idealism and Political Realism," Beauvoir criticized Kantian ethics for being abstract and claimed, furthermore, that abstract ethics is, historically, losing its validity:

> We must admit that, despite all the verbal assertions through which it is perpetuated, ethics, as conceived by most moralists, is in the process of being discredited. The traditional, classical ethics by which society claims to live nowadays is a more or less adulterated legacy of Kantian ethics. It enjoins men to submit their behavior to universal, timeless imperatives, to model their actions on great idols inscribed in an intelligible heaven—Justice, Law, and Truth—and by positing its principles as absolutes, it considers itself as being itself its own end.[6]

Beauvoir insists that *today* ethics must be concrete. This means that ethics must not formulate principles that are abstract and universal; rather, meaningful action must arise from the sociohistorical situation. Against the universal, abstract subject that is a source of values according to the tradition of Kant, Hegel, and Fichte, Beauvoir insists that for existentialism, it is "the plurality of concrete particular men projecting themselves toward their ends on the basis of situations whose particularity is as radical and as irreducible as subjectivity itself" (*EA* 17; *PM* 24). In other words, Beauvoir insists that the concrete, historical situation orients the production of values and reasons for acting. However, "existentialist ethics does not propose recipes," rather it establishes a "method" for action (*EA* 134; *PM* 194). In "Moral Idealism and Political Realism," Beauvoir claims: "Ethics is not an ensemble of constituted values and principles; it is the constituting movement through which values and principles are posited."[7] Moreover, these values and principles, under existentialist ethics, will be historical. The problem of existentialist ethics is to figure the orientation of this formative movement within ethical sociality.

In *The Ethics of Ambiguity* Beauvoir claims that the other is an escape: "It is only as something strange, forbidden, as something free, that the other is revealed as other. And to love him authentically is to love him in his otherness and in that freedom by which he escapes" (*EA* 67; *PM* 96). Moreover, Beauvoir characterizes the other not only as an escape but as an "interference" that frustrates and orients my projects (*EA* 71; *PM* 101). For Beauvoir, I am *solicited* by the other (*EA* 137; *PM* 142). The central ethical claim of *The Ethics of Ambiguity* is that the condition of possibility of my freedom lies in the freedom of all. To will myself free, I must will the freedom of all the others. This claim, at first glance, sounds fundamentally egoistic since it appears that the freedom of others is subordinate to my own. Though Beauvoir seeks to elaborate an understanding of social being that exceeds a conception of the subject indebted to individualism and to elaborate an ethics that accounts for more than my own self-interest, the structure of this ethical willing seems essentially tied to exactly what Beauvoir seeks to challenge. I will the freedom of others because it is requisite for my own freedom.

However, the initial formulation of ethical sociality is not that I *must* will the freedom of others for my own freedom, but that to will my own freedom *is* simultaneously to will the freedom of others. The implication is that my freedom is dependent upon that of others. For Beauvoir, the other reveals to me a difference and a freedom. Beauvoir's claim is a claim about a priority in the philosophy of action. It is not that I will the freedom of others *for the sake of* my own freedom, but that the other's freedom is equiprimordial. In other words, the freedom of the other that appears as an escape, reveals to me my own freedom. Thus, separation arises in relation to others. "Only the freedom of others keeps each one of us from hardening in the absurdity of facticity" (*EA* 71; *PM* 102)—an absurdity since then human existence would be indistinguishable from the being of objects. The other opens and sustains my freedom insofar as I am only free through others. Beauvoir claims that the other imposes a limit on action and gives it a content (*EA* 60; *PM* 90).

The ethical claim that to will myself free, I *must* will the freedom of all, appears as the concrete ethical formulation of the movement of the project. The existential concept of separation is one that discloses the sense in which the other's "appearance" solicits me to will the freedom of the other in revealing to me my own, separated freedom—thereby situating "my" freedom as a dependence on the other that precedes self-interest.[8] Beauvoir defines freedom, not as license, but as a departure or transcendence *from* the thingliness of existence. Only a being that is free can liberate me in my recognition of her/his freedom. Otherness, for Beauvoir, is initially experienced as the liberation of the self from the kind of being that governs the existence of things before existence becomes dominated by the turning of otherness into thingliness.

Though Beauvoir insists that ethical decision requires the willing of the freedom of all, she recognizes the limitation of action insofar as I cannot will the freedom of all at the same time, for "the Other is multiple" (*EA* 144; *PM* 207–208). The problem of ethical decision, says Beauvoir, requires that politics precede ethics. The condition of possibility of realizing an ethics that promotes freedom requires that we calculate politically and historically. Ethics requires political calculation due to the unavoidable historicity of the decision. In negotiating concrete action, a question arises concerning how one is to calculate. And, this, Beauvoir claims, is a question that is "political before being moral" (*EA* 89; *PM* 128).

This brings Beauvoir to a reflection on history, a concept that Beauvoir does not fully address until *The Second Sex.*[9] Beauvoir draws on the concept of history to establish the orientation of the philosophy of action. Action requires a prioritization of the past that serves as the historically necessitated, situated criterion of ethical decision. However, for Beauvoir, modern conceptions of history that might provide a direction for action are implicated in the same ethics of evasion as the traditional philosophical, religious, and political discourses she has criticized—an implication that must be accounted for if we are to further grasp the possibility of figuring a method for action. Beauvoir claims that the criteria for meaningful ethical action must be political before being moral. Thus, concrete action must be preceded by orienting, calculative judgments that are directed toward a future that remains open. Moreover, such orienting judgments cannot calculate via a rationality that is ahistorical.

In order to determine a method of calculation that does not lapse into the universal criteria of analytical reason, Beauvoir turns to a reflection on history. Indeed, if Beauvoir's "Idéalisme moral et réalisme politique" attests to the fact that politics requires a justification of its goals, then the conclusion to the problem of ethical action in *The Ethics of Ambiguity* insists that its goals must be grounded in a historical reflection on the force of the past within the present. Moreover, for Beauvoir, this force appears as an appeal—not in the sense of a request, but in the sense of a 'demand for' or 'claim upon.' In short, the binding between present and past appears as an appeal that makes us responsible (*EA* 95; *PM* 137). Thus, for Beauvoir, the analysis of social binding in *concrete,* existential ethics must pass into an analysis of historical binding as the measure of concrete action. Indeed, Beauvoir claims that a conception of the past must be negotiated if the other, in its multiplicity, is not to be denied: "To abandon the past to the night of facticity is a way of depopulating the world" (*EA* 92; *PM* 134). To represent history as dead and gone, as disconnected from the present, evades the ambiguity of the relation to the past. For Beauvoir, without a historical reflection that can represent the past, the orienting criterion of the situation remains lost.

For Beauvoir, the project represents a way of negotiating both an understanding of ethical and political decisions as aiming at the future and the concrete criterion of such action—a criterion, moreover, that proceeds from the past but is contained in the historical situation. Indeed, Beauvoir defines the past as an appeal that is, furthermore, sustained within the contemporary structuration of relations to others. In a discussion of oppression, Beauvoir claims, "One does not love the past in its living truth if he insists on preserving its hardened and mummified forms. The past is an appeal; it is an appeal toward the future which sometimes can save it only by destroying it" (*EA* 95; *PM* 137). For Beauvoir, the claim of mastery over the representation of the other's future and the other's past is essentially brought into question by an appeal that reveals the social and historical content of historical temporality. Thus, one might say that Beauvoir's thinking at this time centers on the problem of historical reflection in politics. Beauvoir further represents the past as a dialogue with the present: "We know that if the past concerns us, it does so not as a brute fact, but insofar as it has human signification" (*EA* 93; *PM* 135). However, Beauvoir sharply distinguishes her understanding of history based on the past as an appeal toward the future from other concepts of history. For Beauvoir, the past is a signification that is revealed as solicitation.

For Beauvoir, history is not a simple concept. It is above all a standpoint, one that claims epistemic priority over all other modes of knowing. Beauvoir's critique of history refers, not to the "concept" of history, but, in line with phenomenological method, to the *standpoint* of history, suggesting that the concept of history has a certain social and historical location. To adopt the attitude of history is to assume a purely contemplative relationship to the world. Separating itself from the world under the auspices of detached contemplation, the subject takes itself as a contained individual existing both apart from and above history, thereby giving history the status of an object over against which the subject stands. Beauvoir opposes this to an understanding of history that is concretely *lived*. She writes: "One who adopts [the aesthetic attitude] claims to have no other relation with the world than that of detached contemplation; outside of time and far from men, he faces history, which he thinks he does not belong to, like a pure beholding; this impersonal version equalizes all situations; it *apprehends them only in the indifference of their difference;* it excludes any preference" (*EA* 75; *PM* 108, emphasis mine). For Beauvoir, detached contemplation is an attempt to avoid the ambiguity of existence. Having shown that evasion is not escape, Beauvoir suggests that since detached contemplation is impossible, then so is the standpoint of history.

Beauvoir makes this allegedly detached contemplation intelligible by grounding it in the concrete project and takes as her example the French situation during the German occupation. Upon the Germans' arrival in Paris in 1940, says Beauvoir, many said: "Let's take the point of view of history" (*EA* 76; *PM* 109–10). Aloofness and impartiality was a way of escaping the concrete situation through a concept of history as dead and gone— an understanding attributable only to a concept that presupposes the possibility of an epistemic position differentiated from history and thereby capable of achieving indifference. Using the standpoint of history, the aesthetic attitude denies that it is part of history, that it is socially and historically located *in situation*. But for Beauvoir, aloofness is a historical act. Despite the desire to treat the present impartially, as if it were a moment of the past that we could contemplate, the present is the moment of choice, decision, and action lived through a project. To occupy the standpoint of history, meant as a position of impartiality, is to make a decision. There is no purely contemplative project because one always projects toward the future in situation: "To put oneself 'outside' is still a way of living the inescapable fact that one is inside" (*EA* 76; *PM* 110). If, in other words, the standpoint of history is indifference, it is an indifference that is non-indifferent.

For Beauvoir, the act of representing a history from which one is detached is an act that does not escape. To pretend indifference is a situated method for coping with a situation that actually makes a difference, that is, has meaning in situation. Beauvoir implicates Hegel in this abstraction. She claims that his concept of history is "an abstract evasion" of ambiguity (*EA* 122; *PM* 176) insofar as it relies on a judgment of history that is passed from a position supposedly outside of history. Against Hegelian idealism, Beauvoir insists that the orientation in history must be understood as a real appeal that issues from others—past, present, and future. Moreover, against the inherent determinism of Marx's dialectical materialism, Beauvoir argues that existentialism insists that the sense of the situation can only be grasped in and through projection (*EA* 20; *PM* 27). Beauvoir claims that the project marks the essential difference between dialectical materialism and existential ontology. Thus, Beauvoir sets her ethics against a Marxist ethic.

Beauvoir suggests that the significance of the project is discovered in relation to history. The project provides an articulation of history that avoids a static determination of the future *and* a static, masterful relationship to the past. Rather, the project provides the possibility of concretely articulating the sense of the historical situation. This sense involves a privileged relationship to the past as a force inhabiting the present that, in turn, provides the concrete method for political judgments and decisions. The proper and concrete *sens* of ethical action is only established via historical reflection and is only realizable through concrete action. How this calculation is to proceed is explained through a reflection on the status of the past. For Beauvoir, the past is a force that charges the present with a responsibility—indeed, shapes the present as a responsibility. Moreover, in order for action to be ethical, it must first recognize and respond to this unbidden presence.

Beauvoir's ethics provides an articulation of the formal structures of existence as tending in an ethical direction, a claim that fundamentally challenges the claims that existential social theory is incapable of providing an ethics or a politics by theorizing an ethical and political method that arises from the concrete. Indeed, Beauvoir orients existential phenomenology toward a concept of history commensurate with her account of ambiguity precisely for a positive articulation of concrete ethical and political philosophy.

NOTES

1. *The Ethics of Ambiguity,* trans. Bernard Frechtman (New York: Carol Publishing Group, 1996); French: *Pour une morale de l'ambigüité* (Paris: Editions Gallimard, 1948); henceforth abbreviated *EA* and *PM* respectively.

2. The tension between transcendence and facticity is a common point of analysis among Beauvoir, Sartre, Merleau-Ponty, Jaspers, Husserl, and Heidegger.

3. Beauvoir's notion of the project differs from Heidegger's in two major ways. First, she counters Heidegger's privileging of the future by emphasizing the weight of the past. Second, in *Pyrrhus et Cinéas,* she criticizes Heidegger's privileging of death as the futural limit of human existence. She argues that the future is radically open, that the project can surpass death, and that it is the project that makes death meaningful. See especially the section entitled "La Situation" (Paris: Editions Gallimard, 1944).

4. This reading of Hegel revolves around two different problems. First, Beauvoir seems to be expressing concern over the notion of reconciliation insofar as it connotes an overcoming of contradiction. Beauvoir wants, instead, to maintain that existence is a tension that is irreconcilable, even if it has been concealed by differing determinations. This critique seems to express sympathy toward Kierkegaardian *synthesis,* especially given her claim that Kierkegaard was the first philosopher of ambiguity. Second, she is perhaps implicitly referring to Heidegger's critique of Hegelian idealism as steeped in subject/object thinking. See *Being and Time* (New York: Harper and Row, 1962); German: *Sein und Zeit* (Tübingen: Neomarius Verlag, 1926), ¶82.

5. *Pyrrhus et Cinéas,* 60.

6. Simone de Beauvoir, "Moral Idealism and Political Realism," in *Philosophical Writings,* ed. M. Simons, M. Timmermann, and M. B. Mader (Urbana: University of Illinois Press, 2004), 177.

7. Ibid., 188.

8. One might say that the "must" of the concrete ethical claim is one that concerns living "authentically" but in a way that radically departs from Heideggerian authenticity.

9. It is beyond the limits of this essay to adequately address Beauvoir's developed concept of history in *The Second Sex.* Rather, I seek here to establish the groundwork for a further interrogation into the question of history and its relationship to sexual difference in the later text. I would suggest that in that text Beauvoir rethinks sexual difference as the destabilization of dialectics. For a novel construal of the concept of history in *The Second Sex,* see Eva Lundgren-Gothlin's *Sex and Existence,* trans. Linda Schenck (Hanover, N.H.: Wesleyan University Press, 1996).

SIMONE DE BEAUVOIR: A FEMINIST THINKER FOR THE TWENTY-FIRST CENTURY

Karen Vintges

12

Contemporary feminist theorists often assume that Beauvoir's thinking is rationalistic, male-biased, and Eurocentric. At the Fiftieth Anniversary of *The Second Sex* conference in Paris in 1999, the main opinions were that Beauvoir's work should be valued only for historical reasons and that her ideas were really outdated. In contrast to this apparent dismissal, I want to show that Beauvoir's philosophy encompasses important insights for contemporary and future feminism. However, these insights are not immediately obvious. I will argue that if we look closely at her work, it becomes apparent that Beauvoir's supposed rationalistic approach is only a cliché and that in fact she wants both men and women to become sensitive selves. I will also argue that Beauvoir's concept of the self is relevant and powerful in light of the postmodern critique of the essential, unitary self and the multiculturalist critique of the autonomous self. I will begin with a discussion of some of the topical themes of Beauvoir's thinking, which are relevant, in my opinion, for many current philosophical debates. Next I will outline my interpretation of Beauvoir in relation to contemporary feminism, especially in relation to its logic of equality and difference and to its themes of identity and diversity. My conclusion is that Beauvoir's thinking gives us important clues as to how to solve some of the apparent dilemmas of contemporary feminism, and how to conceive of a feminism for the twenty-first century.[1]

BECOMING SENSITIVE SELVES

The Second Sex (1984 [1949]), Beauvoir's study of the situation of women, provoked much dispute and discussion at the start of the second feminist wave of the late 1960s and early 1970s. Exploring the historic situation of women, Beauvoir concluded that women have been prevented from taking active control of their lives. Woman has been the Other throughout culture; man has been the Self, the subject. Woman has been subjected to man, who, partly with woman's consent, has made her into the negative of himself: "passivity confronting activity, diversity that destroys unity, matter as opposed to form, disorder against order" (Beauvoir 1984, 112). For the first time in history, so Beauvoir wrote in 1949, through the availability of contraceptives and the access to paid work, women have the chance to develop into a Self as well. *The Second Sex* is a passionate appeal to women to take this chance.

Twenty years after the book's appearance, it was "discovered" by the new feminist movement. This movement focused on the liberation of female sexuality and on socioeconomic autonomy for women. Its most influential works were by Betty Friedan, Kate Millett, and Shulamith Firestone, all of whom admitted—in the case of Millett and Friedan only many years later—that Beauvoir's works started them "on the road" (Dijkstra 1980, 293). However, within a few years the new women's movement became radicalized with respect to the theme of female sexuality and began to stress the *difference* between men and women, between masculinity and femininity. Instead of becoming *equal* to men, women were to develop their own values, which would amount to a complete cultural revolution. Although part of the movement still embraced Beauvoir, other factions now criticized her intensely: *The Second Sex* was condemned as a male view of women and was superseded by the new, "real" feminism.

Psychoanalytical theory became important as a source of knowledge about female sexuality and became an inspiration for the articulation of a feminine form of thinking and writing. Feminist theoreticians such as Luce Irigaray and Julia Kristeva, and French writers such as Hélène

Cixous, sought to develop an *écriture féminine,* arguing that femininity lies outside the dominant subject form in Western society. Because it has been excluded from culture, the feminine would be culture-critical above all, and its articulation was seen as a revolutionary project. These French feminists all mentioned Beauvoir in one way or another as an extremely important figure for their own lives, but they explicitly criticized her so-called male philosophical point of view.[2]

Beauvoir's *The Second Sex* was considered a mere application of Sartrean existentialism; however, Beauvoir did not simply copy Sartre's ideas.[3] The philosophy of *The Second Sex* does not fit the purely ontological type of philosophy that Sartre practiced in *Being and Nothingness* (1943), nor does it fit his Cartesian concept of the self.[4] Beauvoir situated her own work at a specific moment in history, the moment when the emancipated woman was about to come into existence. She dealt with contemporary reality, criticizing the past and stating, as mentioned earlier, that through the availability of contraceptives and the access to paid work, women would, on a large scale, have the chance to develop into a Self as well. Instead of pure ontology, Beauvoir's study can be characterized as "critical interrogation of the present"—to borrow a phrase of the philosopher Michel Foucault, who argues that philosophy should not be timeless reasoning but a "critique of what we are," or "the historical analysis of the limits imposed on us and an experiment with the possibility of going beyond them" (Foucault 1997a).

The Second Sex is also a "critique of what we are." Beauvoir describes the Self-Other relationship of men and women in history and does not point to the necessity for women to become the Self that men have been (see Vintges 1995, 1996). On the contrary, she argues that *both men and women have to change* so as to overcome their enmity. She states that both sexes "live out in their several fashions the strange ambiguity of existence made body . . . projecting into the partner that part of the self which is repudiated. . . . If, however, both should assume the ambiguity . . . they would see each other as equals and would live out their erotic drama in amity" (Beauvoir 1984, 737). To fully understand Beauvoir's argument, we have to read *The Second Sex* in the light of her earlier work on ethics, specifically *The Ethics of Ambiguity* (1948 [1947]).

In *The Ethics of Ambiguity*, Beauvoir advocates living as a unity of body and consciousness. Her philosophical framework in this respect is the phenomenological perspective that approaches humans as situated and incarnated beings, or "living bodies."[5] She shares this approach, which has been influenced by Edmund Husserl and Martin Heidegger, with Maurice Merleau-Ponty and Emmanuel Lévinas. But she adds to this the view that our status as pure consciousness is also an element of our human condition, one that separates us from others and from ourselves. The human condition is "ambiguous": we are both empty consciousness and incarnated beings. Beauvoir succeeds in theoretically reconciling the two sides of our ambiguous condition by stating that we continually have to transform separatedness into commitment by a "moral conversion," thus rising to the level of incarnated, situated beings and thus overcoming the separation between ourselves and others. The ambiguous elements of our human condition are not merely set alongside each other but are placed in a specific hierarchical order. We should strive for an existence as an ethical, incarnated self; such an existence appears as *a higher phase* above pure consciousness.

Whereas the early Sartre strongly advocates lucid, pure conscious existence and conceives of emotion as self-deceit, Beauvoir right from the start develops her own existentialist philosophy in which our bodily existence, emotions, and connectedness to others are critical. In contrast to Sartre, she sees emotion as the positive experience through which we have contact with the world and with our fellow human beings. Not to experience emotion represents an inability. It is through emotion that we become a "psycho-physiological unity," an incarnated and contingent human being living with others (see especially Beauvoir 1953).

In the introduction to *The Second Sex*, Beauvoir states that every description implies an ethical background and that hers is the perspective of existentialist ethics (1984, 28). Her argument in *The Second Sex* that the enmity between men and women can be overcome clearly builds on her own ethics of ambiguity. She argued that both sexes should *assume their ambiguity* and stop using the other sex to hide from themselves their ambiguous condition, "projecting into the partner that part of the self which is repudiated." Men have to accept their contingent bodily existence; women should reject whenever possible the position of Other (Vintges 1996, 145).

Mutual recognition is possible, according to Beauvoir, "if each individual freely recognizes the other, each regarding himself and the other simultaneously as object and as subject in a reciprocal manner" (1984, 172).

Nancy Bauer brilliantly argues that in *The Second Sex* Beauvoir appropriated Hegel's master-slave dialectic in an original way. Whereas "Hegelian reciprocity demands that beings mutually recognize one another as subjects," Beauvoir believes "that a person must acknowledge himself and the other as *objects* as well as subjects in order for reciprocal recognition to be achieved" (Bauer 2001, 186). Both men and women should not only accept each other and themselves as subjects, but they should accept as well their objective, that is, bodily, dimension. Beauvoir's appeal to women in *The Second Sex* to grasp their chances at developing into a self cannot be considered a plea for women to become pure Cartesian, rational selves. She wanted women to become selves, but in contrast to Sartre, it is the situated, sensitive self she is after, for women *and* men.

POSTMODERN AND MULTICULTURALIST CRITIQUES

Thus far we have concentrated on Beauvoir's argument for the sensitive self rather than the rational self. But why a self? Why should a person become a self? I now concentrate on this question and deal with Beauvoir's ideas on the necessity of *creating* a self or an identity.

Identity is much criticized in postmodern feminist thinking. Identity is seen as restrictive on the individual as well as the collective level: on the individual level since it excludes other ways of living, on the collective level since it excludes other people. Identity is therefore seen as something that should be deconstructed rather than constructed. For Beauvoir, however, the theme of identity is crucial, and I will demonstrate how we can still benefit from her ideas. First, we need to take a brief look at contemporary debates on this issue.

We have seen that since the 1970s the two main approaches of contemporary feminism have emphasized either equality or difference. From the 1980s two other points of view have developed in this controversy. Contemporary postmodern thinkers such as Jacques Derrida and Michel Foucault have attacked the supposed unity of the subject and have formulated the need for an escape from the restrictions of the fixed, unitary self.

Identity is seen as the *ordre intérieur* of the dominant social order. Other ways of living and other forms of subjectivity have to be developed that no longer imprison us in a restrictive identity. Feminist theoreticians such as Judith Butler and Rosi Braidotti elaborate on this view with respect to the feminine subject. If we assume that a unitary subject is already a product of domination, then we can no longer speak in terms of woman as an essential feminine subject that has to be liberated. We should no longer assume the identity of woman either on the personal or on the collective level. Instead, we should unravel and deconstruct fixed meanings of womanhood so that an open space is created to permit the shaping of new ways of thinking and living. Postmodern feminism, with its suspicion of any essential subject "woman," expresses the political mood of the feminist movement today. Differences between women have come to dominate the agenda of the women's movement, and universal similarities between women are no longer taken for granted.

Diversity became the key issue also because of a fourth important—and often related—point of view that developed since the 1980s, when third world women started to criticize feminists for imposing Western values such as "autonomy" and "individual freedom" on other cultures. Multiculturalists and communitarians criticize Western philosophy's privileging of autonomy as *the* normative criterion for progress and modernity: the concept of the autonomous individual presupposes an atomistic, disengaged, and disembedded—Western—subject. Feminism is seen as presupposing this subject as well. Third world women argue that feminism should be far more attentive to differences between (groups of) women instead of imposing its Western normative framework on them (Mohanty 1991, Mahmood 2005).

I will now try to demonstrate why Beauvoir's concept of the self prefigures and anticipates the postmodern and multiculturalist critique on the essential, autonomous self. For this I again turn to her thinking on ethics.

THE ETHICAL-SPIRITUAL WAY OF LIFE

Seeing our human condition as ambiguous, Beauvoir, in opposition to abstract moral theory, introduced a so-called ethics of ambiguity. Our ambiguous condition, especially our element of separatedness, is the reason why universal positive moral laws cannot exist, for in the end, we can never speak for another person. However, the concrete existence of the situated human being can certainly be the locus of an ethical dimension. Beauvoir did share Sartre's aversion to moral theory insofar as she agreed with him that positive maxims or general rules are empty ideas. But unlike Sartre, she kept a lifelong interest in ethics. In *The Ethics of Ambiguity,* ethics comes forward as an attitude of "willing oneself free," which comes down to constantly freely shaping oneself into a specific subject in the world by taking responsibility for specific values. She adds that by willing ourselves free we commit ourselves to freedom as such and therefore to the freedom of everyone: "To will oneself free is also to will others free. This will is not an abstract formula. It points out to each person concrete action to be achieved" (Beauvoir 1948, 73). People can lack every chance to shape themselves as ethical subjects. We therefore have to intervene into power relations that impede them to do so, and thus politics immediately comes into the picture.

Beauvoir later criticized her own attempt to formulate some methodical moral rules at the end of *The Ethics of Ambiguity,* declaring that this attempt suffers from "abstract schematism," but she never criticized or abandoned the core of her argument. To shape ourselves into an ethical subject in the world has always been her crucial theme. For elaboration of this theme, we turn to her literary work and autobiography, where we find the continuation of her thinking on ethics. Because she wanted to do away with abstract schematism as much as possible, she chose the genre of philosophical literature to express her ideas on ethics. This is immediately apparent in her novel *The Mandarins* (1956 [1954]). Not only are ethical-political decisions the central theme in the novel, but a specific type of positive ethics emerges for which Beauvoir introduces a separate term, *art de vivre.*

The writer Henri plays an important role in *The Mandarins.* One of the young people in his circle, Lambert, for whom he has an exemplary function, urges him to write novels that can provide a leitmotiv for personal actions:

> "First of all, we need an ethics, an art of living," Lambert says. "You have a sense of what is real. You ought to teach us how to live for the moment." [Henri protests:] "Formulating an ethics, an art of living, doesn't exactly enter

into my plans." His eyes shining, Lambert looked up at Henri. "Oh, I stated that badly. I wasn't thinking of a theoretical treatise. But there are things that you consider important, there are values you believe in." (Beauvoir 1954, 180, 182; my translation)

Beauvoir here introduces the concept of *art de vivre*, which is art of living, as an equivalent to ethics.[6] The concept of art of living compactly expresses that political and ethical decisions come about in a continual *creative* process without the application of absolute moral rules. But it also articulates the fact that ethics and politics take on the form of a whole *way of life*. Throughout *The Mandarins* Beauvoir suggests that such an ethical life-project, or ethos, takes constant exercise, such as dialogue with oneself and writing practices. Her autobiographical work should be seen in the framework of her art of living concept of ethics. The five volumes of autobiography as well as her diaries and letters are writing practices through which she takes stock of her daily life and stylizes her daily behavior. They are the means to shape herself as the ethical subject that she wanted to be. In her autobiography, Beauvoir was not after an essential, unitary self as effect of introspection or self-realization, but after a coherent identity as an effect of *a practical philosophical self-creation*.

In this respect, Beauvoir's approach can be said to belong to the tradition of "philosophy as a way of life," which the classicist Pierre Hadot articulated in a book that bears this title. According to Hadot, the ancient Greeks thought of philosophy as "spiritual exercises" or *askesis*. Exercises such as writing, meditation, dialogue with oneself, and examination of conscience, and exercises of the imagination and of the styling of daily behavior were about transforming not only one's mind but also one's entire *mode of being*. Hadot speaks in terms of "spiritual" exercises, since they engage not only the mind but the body, heart, and soul as well; in sum, they "engage the totality of the spirit" (Hadot 1995, 127). However, for Beauvoir it is not so much *philosophy* as a way of life, but *ethics* as a way of life, that is at stake. In line with Hadot's concepts, we can qualify the "art of living" type of ethics that she has put forward as the "ethical-spiritual way of life" that involves not only one's thought but one's whole *way of life*.[7]

Through her ethics Beauvoir anticipates the postmodern critique of identity. She—like Sartre—was thoroughly familiar with surrealism and other "modernist" movements from which postmodernism inherited its suspicion of the essential self.[8] Sartre had already attacked the humanist concept of an essential, unitary self, arguing that consciousness is without a self since it is absolutely free. Beauvoir incorporated Sartre's attack on the humanist concept of the essential self but contextualized man's absolute freedom. If she wants us to win a self, this is not an essence to be found through introspection, nor is it the Sartrean concept of pure, empty consciousness. At stake for her is the ethical-spiritual self: the person that assumes his or her responsibility for a specific set of moral values by shaping his whole way of life through ethical-spiritual exercises. Beauvoir thus—*avant la lettre*—reconciles postmodernism's aversion to the essential subject with a moral and political perspective. The self for her is not an essence that has to express itself, but an effect of practicing ethical spiritual exercises. If she wants us to provide ourselves with a coherent identity, this does not imply a finalized or closed identity; it remains open to the future. Although based on the past, this openness is limited (Beauvoir 1988, 10). Her "art of living," or "ethical-spiritual" ethics not only anticipates the postmodern critique on identity, but anticipates the multiculturalist critique of individual autonomy as *the* normative criterion for feminism as well. We have seen before that she argued for the sensitive self that is closely related to one's fellow human beings. Her emphasis on ethics as art of living, or as a whole *way of life,* once more underlines that her concept of the self is not the Western, Cartesian, pre-given self that is externally related to its body and to the world, but a sensitive self embedded in context: a unity of head, heart, and soul.

A FEMINIST THINKER FOR THE TWENTY-FIRST CENTURY

Beauvoir's concepts offer important clues to put the four main approaches of contemporary feminism into perspective and to outline some contours of a feminism of the future. First, *The Second Sex* enables us to perceive the linkages between equality and difference, and it thereby clarifies how the two work together in contemporary feminism. Equality between men and women—that is, equality in not being oppressed—and the emerging of new identities for women go hand in hand. In *The Second Sex* no ready-made models for a common new identity for women exist, only the prediction that cultural differences between men and women will emerge with the disappearance of women's oppression:

> There will always be certain differences between man and woman; her eroticism, and therefore her sexual world, have a special form of their own, and therefore can not fail to engender a sensuality, a sensitivity of a special nature. This means that her relations to her own body, to that of the male, to the child, will never be identical with those the male bears to his own body, to that of the female, and to the child; those who make much of "equality in difference" could not with good grace refuse to grant me the possible existence of differences in equality. (1984, 740)

According to Beauvoir, although there will always be "certain differences" between men and women since their sexual worlds have special forms, these differences are not a set of fixed characteristics. She concludes: "New relations of flesh and sentiment of which we have no conception will arise between the sexes; already, indeed, there have appeared between men and women friendships, rivalries, complicities, comradeships—chaste or sensual—which past centuries could not have conceived" (740). For Beauvoir, sexual difference is never a matter of pre-given identities but involves a continuous work of invention: "Rather than grimly hanging onto what is dying, or repudiating it, would it not be better to try to help invent the future?" (Beauvoir 1950).

We can conclude that equality and difference are interwoven in her philosophy in a way that perfectly captures their continuing dialectic in contemporary feminism. The two seemingly contradictory principles can be combined quite well when both issues are seen as part of a larger project that aims at access to ethical-spiritual self-creation for all women.[9] Beauvoir's own life and work amount to the creation of an art of living that could inspire other women to imagine what life as an active and creative woman could be like. She thus practiced and presented the very idea that *The Second Sex* develops—that women should create new ways of experiencing life as a woman. And she explicitly invited other women to share these.

Feminists who thought *The Second Sex* merely implies the necessity for women to become identical to men severely criticized it. Closer scrutiny of the text discloses, first of all, that the text demands equality between men and women—in the end wanting them both to become sensitive selves;

and second, that its aim is to enable women to invent new ways of experiencing life as a woman on the individual and collective level. Both are feminist projects that will take us far into the twenty-first century. However, to more fully outline the contours of a future feminism, we have to take into account the themes of postmodernism and multiculturalism and the way Beauvoir anticipated these.

By considering the entire corpus of Beauvoir's philosophy, one finds that the postmodern and multiculturalist aversion to the essential, autonomous self are integral to her thought. Through her concept of ethics—that we coined as ethical-spiritual self-creation—Beauvoir's concept of the self proved not to be the rational, essential self of Western philosophy, but a sensitive and embedded self. Postmodern feminism, with its emphasis on differences between women instead of their common identity, left today's feminism without agency: if woman no longer exists, how can feminism exist? Many feminists have withdrawn from action since they no longer see any point in organizing as women. From Beauvoir's thinking, we can distill a clue to solve this apparent dilemma. We have seen that to her politics is not a matter of doctrines or Truths, but it takes on the form of an ethos, or the ethical spiritual way of life. In line with this approach, a collective political movement like feminism emerges (or can emerge) as a shared ethos, or a shared ethical-spiritual way of life, without Truth. Such a feminism resists all essentialist and fundamentalist attempts to postulate the universal Truth about woman and all normativity with regard to women and femininity that is based on scientific, religious, or metaphysical "knowledge" of what woman is (her nature, her desire, her destiny). It presents itself as a (shared) ethos that explicitly articulates gender by wanting to side with "women," demanding access for them to a life of ethical-spiritual self-creation.

This finally brings us to the multiculturalist critique of feminism: in what way, exactly, does feminism side with women? Doesn't it impose a Western normative framework? In my view, the concept of ethical-spiritual self-creation does not suffer from a Western bias. Within all cultures and religions we find practices of ethical-spiritual self-creation through "spiritual exercises," for men and women.[10] From this perspective, a global feminism can be articulated as a feminism that wants to endorse and enlarge women's ethical spiritual self-creation throughout cultures. Such a feminism takes the form of a cross-cultural coalition. It does not work from blueprints, but from inside out and bottom up, always contextually "working on limits."[11]

Beauvoir's thinking already contains some crucial elements for such a global feminism. *The Second Sex* focused on women's *oppression,* and moreover on the Western world, dealing with non-Western women only in one footnote.[12] However, given her concept of ethics as ethical spiritual self-creation, Beauvoir's thinking cannot be reduced to the Western Enlightenment type of feminism that her self-proclaimed heirs profess it to be. Beauvoir was always critical of Western Enlightenment's "dream dreamed by reason" (Beauvoir 1948, 121). As one of the first French intellectuals who opposed the French wars in Vietnam and Algeria, she most certainly would have opposed the triumphant claim of today's Western liberalism to export "freedom" and reason to the world. She would have sided with all those that try in intercultural coalitions to fight any type of fundamentalism, including the current Western one. From 1946 onward, Beauvoir engaged in a long friendship with the black writer and activist Richard Wright, who brought her in contact, during her visits to the United States, with many other Others of Western culture (see Simons 1999). This also influenced and enlarged her thinking on ethics and politics, a thinking that already suggests the contours for a feminism of the twenty-first century, that is, a cross-cultural feminism based on a shared ethos and demanding access for all women to ethical-spiritual self-creation.

Notes

This chapter is a thoroughly revised version of my earlier article "Simone de Beauvoir: A Feminist Thinker for Our Times," *Hypatia* 14, no. 4 (Fall 1999): 133–44.

1. My treatment of Beauvoir is based on Vintges (1996).

2. See Irigaray (1990) and Kristeva (1997). Both claim that Beauvoir's life has been an example for them. Kristeva wrote *Les Samourais* (1990) in a direct reference to Beauvoir's *Les Mandarins.*

3. See also Bauer 2002, Bergoffen 1997, Heinämaa 1999, Lundgren-Gothlin 1996, Simons 1999.

4. The label "Cartesian" refers to the philosopher Descartes, famously known for his dictum "cogito ergo sum": "I think, therefore I am."

5. See also Heinämaa 1999 and Bergoffen 1997.

6. Her plea is diametrically opposed to Sartre's thinking, where his theory requires us to remain free from a reflective attitude toward ourselves, because we immediately make ourselves into a thing, an *en-soi* with fixed properties, and thus we deny our freedom (our status as pure consciousness). Sartre's anarchism in fact comes close to the "nomadism" of Deleuze and Guattari. Some of the main similarities between Sartre and postmodern thinkers are brilliantly dealt with by Aarab (2002).

7. Beauvoir's emphasis on ethics as a way of life that demands constant exercise shows a remarkable similarity with the ethics of the later Foucault. I have expanded on the relevance of his ethics for a global feminism in Vintges (2004). Some major clues are present in Beauvoir's work as well, however, as I show in this article.

8. Here the term *modernism* refers to a specific early twentieth-century art form. For tracing these "modernist" sources of postmodernism, see Taylor (1989).

9. Irigaray's work as well can be interpreted as arguing for the *invention* and *creation* of new identities for women. See Deutscher (2002).

10. See, for instance, the work of Amartya Sen and Mohammed Arkoun. See Vintges (2004).

11. I use this phrase of the later Foucault to indicate that critique and transformation do not come from any point "outside" history. Foucault radicalized the attack on humanism in that he did away with human freedom as such (see Taylor and Vintges 2004). Freedom for him is situated in vocabularies that offer tools for persons to use in creating themselves as ethical-political subjects. These practices of the self are "not something invented by the individual himself. They are models that he finds in his culture and are proposed, suggested, imposed upon him by his culture, his society, and his social group" (Foucault 1997b). For Foucault, freedom is a situated thing. Beauvoir's contextualizing of the concept of freedom suggests as well that critique is always "working on the limits," which is not to say that it cannot produce thorough transformations.

12. This note reads: "The history of woman in the East, in India, in China, has been in effect that of a long and unchanging slavery" (Beauvoir 1984, 113, n. 10). To more fully articulate and argue a global, cross-cultural feminism, *The Second Sex* should be enriched with elements of ethical spiritual self-creation of women in history throughout cultures.

References

Aarab, Mustafa. 2002. *La crise du sens et du sujet: J. P. Sartre, M. Merleau-Ponty, M. Foucault, G. Deleuze: 1930–1980: Continuité et discontinuité*. Skhirat: Éditions IKHTILAF.

Bauer, Nancy. 2002. *Simone de Beauvoir, philosophy and feminism*. New York: Columbia University Press, 2001.

Beauvoir, Simone de. 1948. *The Ethics of Ambiguity*. New York: Philosophical Library. [1947. *Pour une morale de l'ambiguité*. Paris: Gallimard].

———. 1984. *The second sex*. Harmondsworth: Penguin. [1949. *Le deuxieme sexe*. Paris: Gallimard].

———. 1950. "It's about time woman put a new face on love." *Flair* 1, no. 3: 76–77.

———. 1953. *Must we burn De Sade?* London: Nevill. [1952. *Faut-il bruler Sade?* Paris: Gallimard].

———. 1956. *The Mandarins.* Cleveland, Ohio: World. [1954. *Les mandarins.* Paris: Gallimard].

———. 1988. *All said and done.* Harmondsworth: Penguin. [1972. *Tout compte fait.* Paris: Gallimard].

Bergoffen, Debra. 1997. *The philosophy of Simone de Beauvoir.* New York: State University of New York Press.

Deutscher, Penelope. 2002. *A politics of impossible difference: The later work of Luce Irigaray.* Ithaca, N.Y.: Cornell University Press.

Dijkstra, Sandra. 1980. "Simone de Beauvoir and Betty Friedan: The politics of omission." *Feminist Studies* 6 (Summer 1980): 290–303.

Foucault, Michel. 1997a [1984]. "What is enlightenment?" In *Michel Foucault: Ethics, subjectivity and truth,* ed. P. Rabinow, 303–19. New York: New Press.

———. 1997b. "The ethics of the concern for self as a practice of freedom." In *Michel Foucault: Ethics, subjectivity and truth,* ed. P. Rabinow, 281–303. New York: New Press.

Heinämaa, Sara. 1999. "Simone de Beauvoir's phenomenology of sexual difference." *Hypatia* 14, no. 4: 114–32.

Hadot, Pierre. 1995. *Philosophy as a way of life: Spiritual exercises from Socrates to Foucault.* Edited with an introduction by Arnold I. Davidson. Oxford: Blackwell.

Irigaray, Luce. 1990. *Je, tu, nous: Pour une culture de la différence.* Paris: Éditions Grasset and Fasquelle.

Kristeva, Julia. 1990. *Les Samourais.* Paris: Fayard.

———. 1997. Interview by I. Galster. *Lendemains* 85: 98–101.

Lundgren-Gothlin, Eva. 1996. *Sex and existence.* London: Athlone.

Mahmood, Saba. 2005. *The politics of piety.* Princeton, N.J.: Princeton University Press.

Mohanty, Chandra Talpade. 1991. "Under Western eyes: Feminist scholarship and colonial discourses." In *Third world women and the politics of feminism,* ed. C. Mohanty, A. Russo, and L. Torres, 51–80. Bloomington: Indiana University Press.

Sartre, Jean-Paul. 1943. *L'être et le néant.* Paris: Gallimard. [1993. *Being and nothingness.* London: Routledge].

Simons, Margaret. 1999. *Beauvoir and the Second Sex: Feminism, race, and the origins of existentialism.* Lanham, Md.: Rowman and Littlefield.

Taylor, Charles. 1989. *Sources of the self.* Cambridge: Cambridge University Press.

Taylor, Dianna, and Karen Vintges. 2004. "Introduction: Engaging the present." In *Feminism and the final Foucault,* ed. D. Taylor and K. Vintges. Urbana and Chicago: University of Illinois Press, 1–11.

Vintges, Karen. 1996. *Philosophy as passion: The thinking of Simone de Beauvoir.* Bloomington: Indiana University Press.

———. 2004. "Endorsing practices of freedom: Feminism in a global perspective." In *Feminism and the final Foucault,* ed. D. Taylor and K. Vintges, 275–99. Urbana and Chicago: University of Illinois Press.

THE SELF-OTHER RELATION IN

BEAUVOIR'S ETHICS AND

AUTOBIOGRAPHY

13

Ursula Tidd

The ethical parameters of the Self-Other relation were a source of philosophical concern to Simone de Beauvoir from the beginning of her career. All of her literary and philosophical writing can be described as marked by a concern to map an ethical relation with the Other. The epigraph to her second fictional work, *The Blood of Others,* neatly encapsulates this concern, for it carries a quotation from Dostoyevsky's novel *The Brothers Karamazov,* proclaiming: "Each of us is responsible for everything and to every human being." Perhaps unsurprisingly, Emmanuel Levinas, who like Beauvoir was preoccupied with ethical alterity, was also fond of repeating this quotation, which provocatively exhorts us to recognize our infinite responsibility to the Other (Hand 1989, 1). In the present discussion, the aim will be to explore briefly how some of Beauvoir's ethical notions about the Self-Other relation that appear in her theoretical philosophy of the 1940s were developed in her subsequent autobiography. It also considers how her engagement with autobiography might itself be viewed as ethical.

It has long been recognized that one of the areas in which Beauvoir's philosophy differs from Sartrean philosophy of the early 1940s is in the relation between Self and Other. Beauvoir and Sartre were working broadly within the same philosophical framework at this time—drawing on

Husserlian phenomenology, Hegel, Kant, and Heidegger. However, as Sonia Kruks, Eva Lundgren-Gothlin, Kate and Edward Fullbrook, and Debra Bergoffen, among others, have outlined, there is already an emphasis on reciprocity in Beauvoir's arguments concerning Self-Other relations in *Pyrrhus and Cineas,* her first philosophical essay, published in 1944. This is not evident at this time in Sartre's account in *Being and Nothingness,* where his emphasis is rather on the conflictual aspects of Self-Other relations, conceived in a broadly ontological rather than ethical context.[1] As Lundgren-Gothlin (1996, 212–13) has argued, Sartre's point of departure in his description of "being-for-others" is the "cogito," onto which he grafts Hegel's account of the relationship between consciousnesses from the *Phenomenology of Spirit.* Yet, unlike Hegel, Sartre emphasizes an "ontological separation" between consciousnesses bound within a largely ahistorical relationship, which entails that the subject constitutes itself as the subject by conceiving itself as not the Other. For Sartre, the Other transcends me and places restrictions on my freedom, and I must therefore negate and transcend the Other by making him or her into an object. The Self-Other relation in early Sartrean philosophy is therefore, as Lundgren-Gothlin argues, characterized by a double negation: the Self negates itself as not the Other and negates the Other as object to be transcended. The Self is henceforth condemned to conflict, with no room for recognition of, and reciprocity with, the Other.

Pyrrhus and Cineas is the first theoretical text in which Beauvoir begins to outline her notion of ethical subjectivity. In this text, Beauvoir raises two related questions: What is the purpose of human existence? and What is the nature of our relationship to the world and to the Other? She describes subjectivity here using the term "transcendence," although she uses it differently from Sartre. In *Being and Nothingness,* Sartre uses this term (which is derived from Husserlian phenomenology) at times as a synonym for "the For-itself," for consciousness, and at other times to indicate a process of being. In both cases, for Sartre, it represents consciousness as *"un jaillissement"* or a "surging forth," moving toward the realization of its *own* possibilities *by means of* the Other. The Other is therefore the means through which the Self might achieve its transcendence; and conversely, the Self's transcendence is therefore prioritized at the expense of the Other's transcendence. While Sartre acknowledges in *Being and Nothingness* that we do exist in a world of Others, he describes Self-Other relations in the follow-ing (rather pessimistic) way: "While I attempt to free myself from the hold of the Other, the Other is trying to free himself from mine; while I seek to enslave the Other, the Other seeks to enslave me. . . . Conflict is the origi-nal meaning of being-for-others" (Sartre 1989, 364).

In *Pyrrhus and Cineas*, Beauvoir argues for a notion of the Other as re-ciprocally equal, as a being who is always already included as the goal of this movement of consciousness toward its own perpetual self-constitution:

> It is because my subjectivity is not inertia, withdrawal or separation but rather a movement towards the Other that the difference between myself and the Other no longer exists and I can call the Other mine; only I can forge the bond which unites me to the Other and it is forged on the basis that I am not a thing but a project of selfhood in movement towards the Other—in short, a transcendent being. (Beauvoir 1944, 245)

Beauvoir argues in *Pyrrhus and Cineas* that we are transcendent beings constantly striving to make ourselves exist in a world with other people. In terms of the Sartrean account of the structure of consciousness—that it en-tails a double negation: the Self negates itself as not the Other, and negates the Other as object to be transcended—Beauvoir accepts the first negation but not the second. In her account of consciousness, the Other cannot be a mere object of consciousness to be transcended; the Other is already incor-porated within the Self's transcendental movement.

Accordingly, in *Pyrrhus and Cineas,* she refutes solipsism, as she would two years later in her third novel, *All Men Are Mortal,* on the grounds that it entails a paralytic and futile narcissism: "A man entirely alone in the world would be paralysed by the obvious realisation of the futility of all his objectives; he probably would not be able to bear to be alive" (1944, 302). The Self-Other relation is therefore necessary and potentially reciprocal, experienced as it is within *All Men Are Mortal* in a dialectical framework of history. It is this *historical* situation of the Self-Other relation that will be important in Beauvoir's ethical engagement with autobiography. More-over, she argues in *Pyrrhus and Cineas* that we need the Other to act as wit-ness to our actions, as receiver of our testimonies. This is a crucial point in relation to her conception of auto/biography as a testimonial enterprise as I will show.

In *The Ethics of Ambiguity*, which was published in 1947, Beauvoir argues that the human condition is ambiguous, or not fixed, and therefore subject to history. In the introductory section, she distinguishes between different ways of conceptualizing the relationship between freedom and existence. Beauvoir distinguishes here between natural freedom, which is the spontaneous, contingent freedom of coming into existence, and moral freedom, which is grounded by a project and involves other people. Challenging Sartre's voluntaristic view of freedom, Beauvoir argues that there are certain groups of people, such as black slaves in the Southern American states or women in patriarchal societies, who have been obliged to live in an infantile world because they have been kept in a state of slavery and ignorance. She points out that whereas a child's situation, involving a lack of (moral) freedom, is imposed upon him or her, (Western) women choose, or at least consent to, their situation, which may involve a lack of (moral) freedom. Beauvoir argues that this situation contrasts with that of a black slave in the eighteenth century or of a Muslim woman forced to remain in a harem because neither has any means of challenging her oppression. Their position has to be judged according to their relative possibilities of action that may entail no real potential of obtaining moral freedom. Once the possibility of freedom exists, however, it is an abdication of freedom and a flight into bad faith not to seize the chance to act and realize that freedom.

Self-Other relations are described in *The Ethics of Ambiguity* as constituting, reciprocally, the facticity of my situation, or the given features of my existence in the world that I have not chosen. This signifies that, for Beauvoir, the Other assumes the same importance for me as other elements of my facticity, such as my past, the specific circumstances of my birth, and my body. I did not choose these features of my existence and cannot choose to exist without them, although I can choose *how* to live them. If we want to live authentically, we cannot use the Other or retreat to collective identity as a means to avoid the burden of individual responsibility for our existence. The existential irreducibility of the Other represents a form of given as far as each individual is concerned. Citing once more the Dostoyevskian epigraph to *The Blood of Others*, "Each of us is responsible for everything and to every human being," Beauvoir explains that my individual freedom is always enmeshed with another's freedom, so that freedom is therefore a collective responsibility: "To will oneself free is also to will others free. This will is not an abstract formula. It points out to each person concrete action to be achieved" (Beauvoir 1947, 104; 1994, 73).

In *Pyrrhus and Cineas* and in *The Ethics of Ambiguity*, Beauvoir's emphasis is therefore on the need for reciprocity, although she acknowledges that it may not always be possible. Beauvoir concedes that at times violence may be necessary against those who wish to oppress me, although recourse to violence is undesirable because it destroys equality, and equality is necessary for reciprocal relations between people.[2]

In the second section, anticipating her later autobiographical self-representation, Beauvoir considers childhood from an existential perspective. Certain features of this discussion are exemplified in the case study constituted by the first volume of her autobiography, *Memoirs of a Dutiful Daughter*. In *The Ethics of Ambiguity*, she says that the child finds him- or herself in a given world, which appears absolute. The child is happily irresponsible because parents play the role of divine beings to which she or he is subject. Yet the child's world is usually metaphysically privileged because he or she escapes the anguish of freedom as a result of the existential unimportance of his or her actions (1947, 53; 1994, 36–37). This brief, existential description of the childhood "situation" is significant, for as Margaret Simons has noted, Beauvoir's philosophical interest in childhood, evident in her philosophical writing, in her fiction, and in her autobiography, is a further feature that distinguishes her work from Sartre's prior to 1950 (Simons 1986, 173–77).

Toward the end of the second section of *The Ethics of Ambiguity*, Beauvoir again rejects the conflictual account of Self-Other relations derived from Hegel and adapted by Sartre within his largely ahistorical account of Self-Other relations in *Being and Nothingness*. Citing the epigraph from her first novel, *She Came to Stay*, "Each consciousness pursues the death of the Other" (from Hegel's *Phenomenology of Spirit*), Beauvoir argues that this negation of the Other can only be a naïve, preliminary reaction to the Other, because the Other both simultaneously takes and, more importantly, *gives* the world to me:

> At every moment others are stealing the whole world away from me. The first movement is to hate them. But this hatred is naïve, and the desire immediately struggles against itself. If I were really everything there would be nothing beside me; the world would be empty. There would be nothing to possess,

and I myself would be nothing. . . . by taking the world away from me, Others also give it to me, since a thing is given to me only by the movement that snatches it from me. To will that there be being is also to will that there be men by and for whom the world is endowed with human significations. One can reveal the world only on a basis revealed by other men. (1947, 101–102; 1994, 70–71)

While we might need others, however, our relationships with them are nonetheless problematic, and in the final part of *The Ethics of Ambiguity*, Beauvoir examines various factors relating to oppressive relationships. In her discussion of oppression, she observes that it is the mutual dependence within our relationships with Others that explains how oppression exists at all and why it is unacceptable. Oppression creates two classes of people— those who parasitically depend on the oppression of the Other and who oblige humanity to forge ahead in spite of itself, and those whose lives are a mere repetition of mechanical gestures destined to serve the aims of their oppressor (1947, 120; 1994, 83).

As Kruks (1992, 100) has noted, this analysis of oppression is quite distinct from Sartre's voluntaristic account in *Being and Nothingness*. Here, although Sartre does not deny the existence of obstacles to freedom, he argues that we choose how to interpret such obstacles because, phenomenologically, we are each responsible for the construction of our individual worlds as meaningful (or not). This leads him to the inhumane and naïvely abstract position from which he argues that those who submit under torture do so freely, and that a Jew is free to choose whether to accept his or her oppression at the hands of anti-Semitic people (Sartre 1989, 524). As Kruks observes, it is astonishing that Sartre argues the latter point in the middle of World War II (1992, 97).

Beauvoir, on the other hand, in her discussion of the mechanisms of oppression in *The Ethics of Ambiguity*, addresses how we can struggle for the freedom of others—by assisting others to reach a position where they might assume their freedom—yet acknowledging that acting for some people in certain circumstances is often to act simultaneously against others. There are privileged courses of action in struggling for freedom from oppression: for example, Beauvoir acknowledges that it is more appropriate that black people struggle for other black people, Jews for other Jews, and so on (1947, 208–209; 1994, 144). To belong to an oppressed group is to have a privileged *experience* of oppression that cannot be shared by an individual who merely wishes to express solidarity with the struggle of another oppressed individual. Ethically and phenomenologically, possessing an *experience* of oppression is crucial in this instance, although that does inevitably raise questions regarding the parameters and processes of consciously possessing or being alienated from one's experience.

In her groundbreaking study *The Second Sex*, Beauvoir develops her analysis of oppression further and explores the disastrous consequences of sexual oppression on both women and men. Here she advocates reciprocal recognition between men and women rooted in friendship, generosity, and love rather than tyranny and conflict. To achieve this, women must assert themselves as independent subjects through work and must demand recognition in their own right. As Lundgren-Gothlin has shown, although women have remained outside the Hegelian master-slave dialectic throughout history, by establishing themselves as historical subjects reciprocally existing alongside men, women and men would begin to exist authentically (Lundgren-Gothlin 1996, 72–73).

In her philosophy as in her autobiography, Beauvoir emphasizes the need for an ethical relationship between Self and Other as reciprocal intersubjectivities. Yet in order to theorize such an ethical intersubjective relationship, Beauvoir recognized that the egological terrain of her philosophical training needed to be radically questioned. Like Emmanuel Levinas, in his critique of Western philosophy as being largely preoccupied with egological ontology that reduces the Other to the Self-same, thereby disregarding how we might relate ethically to the Other *qua* Other, Beauvoir sought to explore the ethical parameters of the Self-Other dynamic.[3] However, openly rejecting Levinas's claim that absolute Otherness is manifested in the feminine, Beauvoir's most developed discussion of the Self-Other relation is in *The Second Sex* where, as we have noted, she prioritizes reciprocal recognition between two equal subjects as the way forward for ethical relationships between women and men.

However, one of the most significant difficulties with which both Beauvoir and Levinas were faced in their different ethics was how to represent the radical strangeness and unknowable phenomenon of the Other. Unlike Levinas, Beauvoir does not attribute primacy to the Other within an asymmetrical Self-Other binary; rather, she argues for reciprocal subjectivities. In this, she is constrained by the traditional suppression of the Other within the Western philosophical framework in which she is working and which, according to Levinas, entails that knowledge of the Other is rooted in analogy and a reduction to the Self-same (Levinas 1969, 43). In her comments on *Pyrrhus and Cineas* in *The Prime of Life*, Beauvoir recognizes her residual egology:

> I do not disapprove of my concern to provide existentialist ethics with a material content; the annoying thing was to be still enmeshed with individualism at the very moment I thought I had at last escaped it. An individual, I thought, only receives a human dimension by recognising the existence of others. Yet, in my essay, coexistence appears as a sort of accident that each individual should somehow surmount; he would begin by creating his project in isolation, and only then ask the community to endorse its validity. In truth, society shapes me from the day of my birth and it is within that society, and through my close relationship with it, that I decide who I am to be. (Beauvoir 1989, 627–28; 1965, 549–50, translation adapted)

In *The Ethics of Ambiguity* Beauvoir notes that the Hegelian moment of recognition between Self and Other denies individuality, for it is only the universal truth of Self that is reciprocally recognized, and the singularity of the Self is passed over (1947, 150–51; 1994, 104–105). Yet it is significant that in her early fiction and in *The Second Sex*, Beauvoir only minimally represents the "alien," authentic specificity of the Other in the real, largely collapsing women's authentic experience into the masculinist Self-same. In *She Came to Stay* and *The Blood of Others*, for example, the transcendence of the Self, as constituted by the Pierre-Françoise couple and by Jean Blomart, is prioritized over the perceived "alien" subjectivity of the Other, as constituted respectively in these texts by Xavière and Hélène, who are both ultimately annihilated once they have served their purpose of ensuring the Self's transcendence. In *The Second Sex*, however, Beauvoir's relative lack of focus on the authentic specificity of woman as Other can be explained largely by her project to provide a materialist analysis of women's situation while exposing the patriarchal mythology that promotes an essentialized notion of femininity that works to further patriarchy's political advantage. While the radical unknowability of the Other inevitably means that, following Levinas, the authentic specificity of the Other is infinitely and unpredictably excessive for the Self and is therefore as such unrepresentable, Beauvoir seems, in her philosophy and early fiction of the 1940s, to collapse any space in which radical, authentic alterity might be genuinely encountered and accommodated. In short, there seems to be no space for the Self-Other relation to occur as "a structural possibility," which would then shape subsequent experience.[4]

If we now relate Beauvoir's view of Self-Other relations to the representation of subjectivity in autobiography, a preliminary question can be raised: how might Beauvoir's ethics of reciprocal intersubjectivity be represented in her subsequent volumes of autobiography? This question encompasses several subsidiary questions, such as, How might autobiography per se function ethically? How might ethical autobiography, in its practice and reception, avoid the pitfalls of universalism and the reduction of the Other to the self-same? How does Beauvoir answer the appeal of the Other? These are complex questions to which only some preliminary answers can be proposed. However, various ways will be suggested below in which we might consider Beauvoir's autobiography to function ethically within the context of her views of the Self-Other relation.[5]

Beauvoir's four volumes of formal autobiography and memoirs, published in France between 1958 and 1972, postdate her day-to-day experience of the French Occupation, the atrocities of World War II, and her related "discovery" of history: "The spring of 1939 marked a watershed in my life. I renounced my individualistic, anti-humanist way of life. I learned the value of solidarity. . . . History took hold of me, and never let go thereafter" (1965a, 359).

This discovery of the material impact of history and of the Other in the real are crucial because they shape her ethical engagement with autobiography in several ways: she sees the task of representing her past, first, as primarily a need to engage with the otherness of collective history, and second, as an ethical imperative to bear witness for the Other. This testimonial concept of autobiography is directly related to Beauvoir's ethical view of Self-Other relations, for it requires a recognition of the Other's experience as valid in its singularity as well as its universality, and an exploitation of language as a privileged means of mediation between Self and Other.

In her contribution to the "Que peut la littérature?" debate in 1964 and her 1966 lecture given in Japan, "Mon expérience d'écrivain," Beauvoir explains her Proustian notion that literature can mediate between the singular experience of the individual and the universal human predicament:

> Language integrates us once more into the human community; an experience
> of misfortune which can be expressed no longer has the power to ensure so-
> cial exclusion and it becomes less intolerable. . . . Each human being is the
> product of all human beings and understands himself only through them; he
> understands them only through what they reveal of themselves and through
> the knowledge gained in that encounter. That is the role that literature can
> and should play: it has to make us transparent to each other in the most ob-
> scure areas which we possess. (Beauvoir 1965b, 91–92)

Autobiography can be a privileged literary genre for this ethical exchange of experience between Self and Other. The act of reading autobiography involves a readiness to be open to the experience of the Other in the
real—not merely open to experiences that are similar to mine, but also to
those that are potentially unknown to me. In her lecture "Mon expérience
d'écrivain," Beauvoir explains that autobiography, unlike fiction, deals with
the contingencies and facticity of a singular existence, yet it also involves a
recognition (of common experience) that takes place between Self and
Other: "In order for autobiography to be of interest, it must deal with experiences which concern a lot of people" (Beauvoir 1979, 450).

Testimonial autobiography, however, can be problematic for both the
narrator and the reader. Trading nostalgically in impossible fantasies of
truthful self-coincidence, writing autobiography entails the risk of conflat-
ing the Other's experience with the narrator's own, and any attempt to represent the Other's experience has to be abandoned. Instead, Beauvoir opts
for approximated representations of the Other's experience through the in-
clusion of case studies in her autobiography.[6] Furthermore, she narrates
personal and collective history as a dynamic positive-negative spatial environment into which space for the event of the Other is incorporated rather
than collapsed into the potentially solipsistic universe of the autobiographer. A sustained example of the construction of autobiographical space
for the Other is Beauvoir's account of the Algerian War in *Force of Circumstance*, in which she attempts to transcend her "situation" as a bourgeois
Frenchwoman and seeks to represent the Algerian perspective. While she
can never have the experience of being a colonized Algerian subject to
French rule, she provides a historical account that creates space for the experience of the Other, for example, Djamila Boupacha, a young Algerian
woman who had been tortured and raped by French soldiers (1968, 513–
18). Moreover, the Boupacha case and Beauvoir's involvement in the cam-

paign to bring the perpetrators to justice provides a useful illustration within her autobiography of how the Other's possibilities of freedom are restricted by her "situation."

Finally, Beauvoir perpetually negotiates the representation of personal and collective history with others. This is evident in the representation of the narrative Self as an intersubjective enterprise that is shaped in her relation to Others, particularly to privileged Others such as Zaza, Sartre, and Sylvie Le Bon, and, at the level of textual production, through the cooperation of Others who supply autobiographical material that she can incorporate. Moreover, Beauvoir's notion of reciprocal intersubjectivity informs the future existence of the text as she recognizes the crucial role of the reader as a textual recipient who has the power to imaginatively reconstruct her past in his or her future time.[7] Without this author-reader collaboration to effect the re-animation of the autobiographer's past at a time beyond the writing present, the Self's experience falls away, annihilated, into the past.

As the Other *gives* the world to me, so Beauvoir represents the autobiographical Self in the world obligated to the Other and to the Otherness of history. Although as autobiographer she might be a transcendent figure shaping the narrative, as Debra Bergoffen has argued, Beauvoir operates with a notion of transcendence as *risk* (Bergoffen 1997, 217). For the autobiographical subject lays herself open to the vicissitudes of history and is bound by a perceived obligation to bear witness. This obligation exposes her contingent responses to history, which she is then obliged to assume. For example, in *The Prime of Life,* Beauvoir explains her political indifference and ignorance during the early 1930s when she and Sartre initially underestimated the importance of the Nazis' rise to power and benefited from a 70 percent reduction on the Italian rail network, which had been introduced by Mussolini to attract foreign tourists to the Fascist Exhibition in 1933 (Beauvoir 1965a, 153–55). Many autobiographers would omit such details for fear of compromising their present-day position as left-wing intellectuals. Yet one of the reasons why Beauvoir includes them is that she has a commitment to recording the contingent details of personal and collective history—for she and Sartre were by no means the only left-wing intellectuals to underestimate the force of fascism in the 1930s. At the heart of this commitment to record is an awareness of the importance of testimony and a mindfulness of history that are themselves rooted in Beauvoir's notion of the Self's obligation to the Other.

In *The Prime of Life,* she signals to the reader of her autobiography that:

> the self has only a probable objectivity, and anyone saying "I" only grasps the outer edges of it; an outsider can get a clearer and more accurate picture. Let me repeat that this personal account is not offered in any sense as an "explanation." Indeed, one of my main reasons for undertaking it is largely my realisation that one can never know oneself, but only offer an account of oneself. (Beauvoir 1965a, 368, translation adapted)

With this in mind, perhaps the ethical dimension of Beauvoir's autobiography resides in her adoption of a testimonial stance, in the knowledge that the autobiographical subject and her Others can never be known to each Other beyond their mutual, infinite obligation.

Notes

1. Sartre's view of the conflictual nature of Self Other relations is also demonstrated in his theatre and fiction of this period, notably *No Exit* (1944) and *The Age of Reason* (1945). In these texts, the Other constitutes an obstacle to the protagonists' transcendence.

2. The dilemma of whether to use violence is demonstrated by Jean Blomart's predicament in *The Blood of Others,* in which he has to decide whether to sanction further Resistance actions, which will entail further bloodshed.

3. See, for example, Levinas's comments on the suppression of the Other by Western philosophy in *Totality and Infinity,* especially 42–48.

4. I borrow here Colin Davis's terms in which he describes the Self-Other encounter in Levinas's philosophy (see Davis 1996, 45).

5. For a more extensive discussion of Beauvoir's project of testimonial auto/biography, see my *Simone de Beauvoir, Gender and Testimony* (1999).

6. See the various biographical sketches in Beauvoir's autobiography, for example, that of "Louise Perron" in *The Prime of Life,* 167–79.

7. Beauvoir explains this author-reader collaboration in "Mon expérience d'écrivain," 453–54.

References

Beauvoir, Simone de. 1944, 1974. *Pyrrhus et Cinéas.* Paris: Gallimard.
———. 1947, 1974. *Pour une morale de l'ambiguïté.* Paris: Gallimard.

———. 1948, 1994. *The Ethics of Ambiguity*, trans. Bernard Frechtman. New York: Citadel.

———. 1960, 1989. *La Force de l'âge*. Paris: Gallimard.

———. 1965a. *The Prime of Life*, trans. Peter Green, Harmondsworth, Penguin.

———. 1965b. Contribution to *Que peut la littérature?* ed. Yves Buin. Paris: Union générale d'éditions.

———. 1979. Mon expérience d'écrivain. In *Les ecrits de Simone de Beauvoir*, ed. Claude Francis and Fernande Gontier. Paris: Gallimard.

Bergoffen, Debra. 1997. *The philosophy of Simone de Beauvoir: Gendered phenomenologies, erotic generosities*. Albany: State University of New York Press.

Davis, Colin. 1996. *Levinas: An introduction*. Cambridge: Polity Press.

Hand, Sean, ed. 1989. *The Levinas reader*. Oxford: Blackwell.

Kruks, Sonia. 1992. Gender and subjectivity: Simone de Beauvoir and contemporary feminism. *Signs* 18: 89–110.

Levinas, Emmanuel. 1961, 1969. *Totality and infinity*, trans. Alphonso Lingis. Pittsburgh: Duquesne University Press.

Lundgren-Gothlin, Eva. 1996. *Sex and existence: Simone de Beauvoir's* The Second Sex. London: Athlone.

Sartre, Jean-Paul. 1989. *Being and nothingness*. London and New York: Routledge.

Simons, Margaret. 1986. "Beauvoir and Sartre: The philosophical relationship." *Yale French Studies* 72: 165–79.

Tidd, Ursula. 1999. *Simone de Beauvoir, gender and testimony*. Cambridge: Cambridge University Press.

CHALLENGING CHOICES: AN ETHIC OF OPPRESSION

Gail Weiss

14

DESTRUCTIVE CHOICES

One summer morning in June 2001, Andrea Pia Yates, a Texan mother of five, drowned all of her children in the bathtub one by one. Severe post-partum depression, early press reports speculated, was a primary motivating factor in her actions since Mrs. Yates had been under psychiatric care and had been taking antidepressant medication for this very condition following the birth of both her fourth and fifth children. After the murders took place, Mrs. Yates's husband defended her in the press, calling her a loving mother and denying that she would willingly have harmed their children. Indeed, despite accusations from Andrea Yates's family after her March 2002 trial that her husband's controlling behavior helped to "push her over the edge," he has continued to be supportive of her (at least in the public media) from the day of their children's deaths through her trial and subsequent conviction, and in the face of the recent overturning of her conviction by the First Court of Appeals in Houston in January 2005.[1]

In Toni Morrison's novel *Beloved,* the main character, Sethe, also attempts to kill her three children, but she succeeds with only one, her baby daughter. Morrison depicts Sethe as an enigmatic but nonetheless intelligible, even sympathetic, figure. As readers of her story, we are led to believe that Sethe was a loving mother who murdered her daughter (and attempted to murder her sons) in the conviction that death is preferable to being condemned to a life of slavery. Although she is never tried or imprisoned, Sethe's actions dramatically affect herself as well as her family members, ultimately leading to the breakdown of her relationship with her surviving sons.

Andrea Yates and Sethe can be starkly contrasted in terms of race, class, historical time period, age, and personal histories, but they are bound by the horrifying nature of their respective acts.[2] Both women, it could be argued, seem to have been moved by forces beyond their control, forces that presented the murder of their children as their best or even only viable option.[3] Adopting such an interpretation, one could maintain that Sethe, experiencing her family's situation as hopeless, murdered her daughter so that her daughter would not have to experience life as a slave. Despite the Texas jury's rejection of Andrea Yates's plea of not guilty by virtue of insanity, one might nonetheless plausibly conjecture that it was a state of psychosis brought on by severe postpartum depression that led her to violently terminate her children's lives. Both cases, despite the crucial differences already noted above (and despite the fact that one example is fictitious and one is not), may be more similar than not from this perspective, because for each woman, due to her oppressive situation, the horizons that gave significance to her actions seem to have been narrowed to the particular place and time in which she found herself at the moment she acted.[4] More precisely, what each woman seems to have lacked at the moment she was acting was an awareness of the broader context for her actions, a context that might have provided her with alternative ways of construing her situation as well as possible responses to it. Indeed, it is this broader context, a context that includes strong social taboos against the murder of children, especially one's own children, that outsiders usually appeal to in judging both women's actions.

In what follows, I will argue that we can best understand the tragic deaths of these children at the hands of their mothers as failures of relation rather than as failures of choice. The oppression experienced by the mothers themselves (for Sethe, through her fugitive existence as a runaway slave, and for Andrea Yates, through the psychotic state brought on by her severe postpartum depression), make it difficult to understand their actions through a traditional rational framework that blames the individual for failing to use her rational capacities before acting. Even an existential framework is problematic, for although the latter draws our attention to the broader situation that provides the context for the individual's actions, it too emphasizes the individual's responsibility for her choices and grounds this responsibility in an ontological notion of freedom that is itself rendered problematic in both of these cases.

OPPRESSIVE CONSTRAINTS AND NARROWED HORIZONS

Considerations of context are absolutely crucial to any investigation into how a particular individual acts within a given situation, much less a traumatic situation.[5] Simone de Beauvoir, despite her own emphasis on freedom and individual choice, anticipates the complexities that arise when we attempt to make sense of different people's actions in the face of oppressive circumstances. The task of understanding the experience of oppression, she claims, is a problem "complicated in practice by the fact that today oppression has more than one aspect" (Beauvoir 1997, 89). Not only may there be more than one source of oppression, but the forms that the oppression itself may take can vary tremendously and may include both psychical and physical abuse. In what follows, I will offer a critical analysis of Beauvoir's own remarks on oppression in various texts, including *Pyrrhus et Cinéas, The Ethics of Ambiguity, America Day by Day,* and *The Second Sex.* Through an examination of Beauvoir's discussions of oppressed individuals, I will show: (1) why the experience of oppression poses a severe challenge to traditional ethical theories that presuppose the existence of a rational, autonomous moral agent; and (2) how Beauvoir sets the stage for an alternative conception of morality that, unlike her earlier existential ethics presented in *The Ethics of Ambiguity,* or Sartre's existential ethics grounded in the choices made by a single individual in response to the facticity of her situation, is not grounded in freedom.

To return to the example with which I began, those who acknowledged that Andrea Yates was most likely suffering from acute postpartum depression but who still held her accountable for her actions tended to blame her for not seeking more aggressive treatment for her mental condition.[6] But to seek such treatment presupposes that one recognizes that one is, in fact, depressed, and it is precisely this broader perspective on her situation that seemed to be unavailable to Ms. Yates at the time she was drowning her children.[7] By contrast, Sethe's violent stabbing of her children has largely been viewed by Morrison's readers as less blameworthy even if no less horrific. This is due not only to the fact that *Beloved* is a fictional narrative and that the costs of identifying with Sethe are therefore not so high, but also to a recognition that Sethe's own oppression as a slave and her desire that her children not live a life of slavery is a rational, maternal desire even if her means of achieving this desire appear to be unacceptably extreme. Moreover, since the institution of slavery cannot be rationally justified, Sethe's seemingly irrational actions can themselves be seen as being the effect of an unjust social institution, and thus she may not seem personally to blame for what she did. By contrast, in the case of Ms. Yates, a middle-class housewife with a seemingly loving and supportive spouse, a nice home, and a family, there doesn't appear to be any source of institutional oppression one can appeal to in order to make sense of her actions. Clearly, one may blame the depression itself, as her supporters have done; but here too, many people who grant that she may have been severely depressed still faulted her for not availing herself of the medical care to which she had access to help combat it.

Ultimately, regardless of how one views each woman, the enclosed space of the shed depicted by Morrison, and the equally enclosed space of the Yates' bathroom (vividly described in the media coverage of her trial), present us with images of physical containment that are unable to contain the events that occurred within. This is true not only for those of us who vicariously experience these events by reading of them but also for the women themselves. In *Beloved*, the legacy of her actions haunts Sethe for the rest of her life, a haunting that is materialized in the sudden appearance of the title character, Beloved, whom Sethe takes to be the literal (re)incarnation of her murdered daughter. And one can only presume that the trial and imprisonment of Andrea Yates, her vilification in the media, her current isolation from friends and family, and most of all, her change in status from a mother of five to not being a mother at all cannot help but transform her relationship to her actions in the bathtub that morning in June.

If one accepts that both Sethe's and Andrea Yates's actions seemed to have been radically restricted to the immediacy of the "here and now," the question becomes, how are we to understand such a reduction of one's entire lifeworld and, accordingly, of one's actions, to a particular place and time?[8] Elaine Scarry, in her award-winning book, *The Body in Pain*, provides us with poignant phenomenological descriptions of just this type of experience. Specifically, she offers the testimony of torture victims who claimed that when they were in the throes of extreme pain inflicted by their oppressor the only reality that they experienced was the pain itself. In her words, "torture consists of acts that magnify the way in which pain destroys a person's world, self, and voice." A bit later she adds,

> To acknowledge the radical subjectivity of pain is to acknowledge the simple and absolute incompatibility of pain and the world. The survival of each depends on its separation from the other. To bring them together, to bring pain into the world by objectifying it in language, is to destroy one of them: either ... the pain is objectified, articulated, brought into the world in such a way that the pain itself is diminished and destroyed; or alternatively, as in torture and parallel forms of sadism, the pain is at once objectified and falsified, articulated but made to refer to something else and in the process, the world, or some dramatized surrogate of the world, is destroyed. (Scarry 1985, 50–51)

Although Sethe and Andrea Yates were not physically tortured, and despite the differences in their respective situations, I would argue that both women suffered from severe cases of psychological oppression that were no less real in their corporeal effects. I will also argue that Simone de Beauvoir's analysis of oppression provides us with a framework for rendering these women's actions intelligible as responses to situations over which they felt they had no control. To say that their actions can be rendered intelligible does not, of course, sanction them. What it does do is restore the humanity of these alleged "monsters" by enabling us to recognize these women as moral agents operating outside the realm of choice and possibility that so many of us take for granted in our daily lives.

Starting from Sigmund Freud's insistence that the abnormal is not radically distinct from the normal case but can shed light on the latter since both form part of a single continuum of behavior, let us examine the broader contexts of significance that helped to define Sethe's and Andrea Yates' respective situations, contexts that were present but not efficacious for the women themselves. Maurice Merleau-Ponty's discussion in *Phenomenology of Perception* of Schneider, a World War I shrapnel victim, is instructive here. He argues that although Schneider's brain damage causes a reduction of his world to a very concrete horizon of significance that is limited to the here and now, rendering him incapable of formulating abstract plans that extend beyond his current situation, Schneider's existence must not be seen as incomplete or impoverished because he experiences his world as a coherent whole; that is, Schneider doesn't perceive his world as lacking in any way. The lack, if you will, is applied to Schneider's experience from the outside, by "normal" subjects who view his world and his subjectivity to be defective. According to Merleau-Ponty, for Schneider, just as for these "normal" subjects, "existence has no fortuitous attributes, no content which does not contribute towards giving it its form" (Merleau-Ponty 1962, 169).

Interestingly, both Beauvoir and Sartre also describe individuals who, like Schneider, are unable to depart from fixed ways of understanding their situation. The individuals they describe, however, are not this way because of a particular disability, as in Schneider's case, or because of a specific experience of oppression, as in the two mothers' or the torture victims' cases, but rather because they choose to ascribe a necessary meaning to their situation, one that precludes alternative interpretations and yields comfort and security in the process. In *Being and Nothingness*, Sartre claims that such an individual exists in bad faith, failing to recognize that the value he gives to his existence is self-created, not eternal. One example he gives of this is the sincere person who identifies himself with a certain essential nature and attempts to coincide with that nature at all times, a project that can be summed up in the statement: "I am who I am." If this project is realizable, Sartre maintains, "If man is who he is, bad faith is forever impossible and candor ceases to be his ideal and becomes instead his being." "But" he quickly asks, "is man what he is?" (Sartre 1966, 101).

Simone de Beauvoir provides us with an even earlier example of an individual who attempts to "be herself" at all times, namely Françoise, the main character in her 1943 novel, *L'Invitée (She Came to Stay)*.[9] While Françoise eschews any belief in a God-given nature, she exhibits the extreme arrogance of assuming that her perspective on her situation, including her relationship with her lover and intellectual partner Pierre, represents the truth of that situation for both herself and others. In the course of the novel, Françoise discovers that her self-assured attempt to avoid bad faith by seeing the world on her own terms is precisely what produces it.

For both Sartre and Beauvoir, the answer to the question of whether one can ever be who one is, is a resounding "no!" And, in *The Second Sex*, Beauvoir complicates matters further by showing that the essence women are often urged to coincide with to fulfill their so-called feminine destiny is inherently impossible to achieve because it is full of contradictions.[10] While Sartre focuses on the bad faith of the sincere individual who presumes to be able to "be who he is," Beauvoir turns our attention beyond the individual to a powerful societal bad faith that pressures women to seek to realize an impossible ideal. For Beauvoir, "a fundamental ambiguity marks the feminine being," an ambiguity that cannot be eliminated by identifying with a fixed essence. And, she adds,

> The fact is that she would be quite embarrassed to decide *what* she *is;* but this is not because the hidden truth is too vague to be discerned: it is because in this domain there is no truth. An existent *is* nothing other than what he does; the possible does not extend beyond the real, essence does not precede existence: in pure subjectivity, the human being *is not anything.* (Beauvoir 1989, 257)

In *The Ethics of Ambiguity*, Beauvoir claims that the individual who nonetheless identifies with a given essence has succumbed to "the spirit of seriousness," and like Sartre, she finds him culpable for his abdication of personal responsibility for his situation. The serious man, she tells us, "forces himself to submerge his freedom in the content which the latter accepts from society. He loses himself in the object in order to annihilate his subjectivity" (1976: 45). Beauvoir invokes Hegel, Kierkegaard, and Nietzsche as philosophers who also "railed at the deceitful stupidity of the serious man and his universe." Sartre's *Being and Nothingness*, she asserts,

> is in large part a description of the serious man and his universe. The serious man gets rid of his freedom by claiming to subordinate it to values which would be unconditioned. He imagines that the accession to these values likewise permanently confers value upon himself. Shielded with "rights," he fulfills himself as a *being* who is escaping from the stress of existence. The serious is not defined by the nature of the ends pursued. A frivolous lady of fashion can have this mentality of the serious as well as an engineer. There is

the serious from the moment that freedom denies itself to the advantage of ends which one claims are absolute. (Beauvoir 1976, 46)

As Beauvoir deftly weaves her condemnation of the serious individual into Sartre's, it is easy to forget the crucial differences between their respective positions. Not only does Beauvoir emphasize the major role that society plays in inculcating the spirit of seriousness in the individual, an acknowledgement that Sartre does not fully make until years later in the *Critique of Dialectical Reason,* but she also explicitly invokes the experience of oppression as one that can vitiate the ambiguity of existence by disallowing the individual the opportunity to give more than one meaning to her situation.[11] In both *The Ethics of Ambiguity* and *The Second Sex* in particular, Beauvoir suggests that severe oppression can lead an individual to view her possibilities in life as predetermined, and, against the Sartrean position outlined above, she claims that we must not judge such a person to be in bad faith.[12] In contrast, she tells us, to those who choose a serious existence in bad faith, artificially limiting the significance of their actions and denying their freedom to act otherwise in the process, there are also those who "live in the universe of the serious in all honesty, for example, those who are denied all instruments of escape, those who are enslaved or who are mystified" (1976, 47–48). In the passage that follows, Beauvoir informs us that "to the extent that it exists, their freedom remains available, it is not denied. They can, in their situation of ignorant and powerless individuals, know the truth of existence and raise themselves to a properly moral life" (48).

What is striking about this passage is that Beauvoir does not distinguish between the dishonest serious individual and the honest one on the basis of the former's possessing but denying his freedom and the latter's failing to possess this freedom altogether. For it would seem quite plausible to argue that the serious individual who is guilty of bad faith attempts to deny his freedom (to create value) in order to endow his values with an absolute justification that comes from without, while the severely oppressed lack freedom altogether and therefore cannot be understood as proper moral agents. However, attractive as such an explanation might be, it runs the risk, as Beauvoir seems to realize, of further dehumanizing the oppressed insofar as freedom and the concomitant capacity for a moral existence is, for both Beauvoir and Sartre, precisely what distinguishes human beings from all other types of beings. Accordingly, Beauvoir maintains not only that the severely oppressed may still have a measure of freedom, but in addition, that they can "know the truth of existence and raise themselves to a properly moral life." But what type of freedom do they possess, and what kind of moral life do they have? Beauvoir, having taken us to the precipice of a breach with an existentialist ethics grounded in freedom, goes no further. And yet, by throwing down the gauntlet, she forces us to follow through the implications of her claims.

COMPROMISED FREEDOM AND THE POSSIBILITY OF ETHICS

For both Beauvoir and Sartre, freedom is not an objective phenomenon but a subjective experience whose effects are realized through concrete action capable of transforming one's situation. Hence, it will not suffice to look at a situation from the outside in order to determine whether the agents within that situation have acted freely. However, while both Beauvoir's and Sartre's early work emphasizes that the exercise of freedom is purely an individual affair, incapable of being affected by others or by the situation itself, Beauvoir, as Sonia Kruks, Debra Bergoffen, and others have pointed out, also acknowledges very early on that both others and the situation can place real constraints on our freedom.[13] In *Pyrrhus et Cinéas*, for instance, Beauvoir claims that "my action is for others, only in fact that which they make of it." "How then," she asks, "can I know in advance the meaning of what I do?" (1944, 51, my translation).[14] As Bergoffen observes, Beauvoir's

> focus in *Pyrrhus et Cinéas* is on the ways in which we are alien to each other. Here she is interested in analyzing the implications of this alienation for the ethics of the project. She takes up a twofold task: one, to create an ethic that respects the other's strangeness; and two, to prevent the idea of the other's strangeness from sliding into the idea of our necessary estrangement (the look). (Bergoffen 1997, 50)

Beauvoir fulfills this task, Bergoffen claims, by arguing that my projects must incorporate the projects of others. Since I have to confront the alterity of the other from one moment to the next in my existence, I cannot ignore the presence of others but must act in concert with them. In Bergof-fen's words:

> Because there is no givenness, no God, no temporal continuity, no human essence to ground or guarantee the fulfillment of my vision, I cannot pursue my project without at the same time appealing to others to recognize the value of my actions and to preserve their meaning. As Beauvoir sees it, in embarking on my project I also take on the task of creating a public to whom I can appeal. This public is essential to my project. It is through the project that I am linked to/with others and it is through these others that I, as my project, am linked to the future. (1997, 52)

The case of the severely oppressed individual, however, seems to contest the positive implications of this depiction of myself and others. Is the severely oppressed individual even in a position to create a public to whom she can appeal? And, if "this public is essential to my project," the inability to create such a public means that the ethical project itself, and therefore the individual's very future, is endangered from the outset. Before developing this point further, it is important to remember, as noted previously, that oppression may take many different forms and have a variety of effects in the life of an individual and/or community. As the earlier examples of Andrea Yates and Sethe amply illustrate, even when two seemingly loving mothers undertake a similar destructive action, namely murdering their children, the oppressive forces that may have influenced that action can be quite diverse. Kruks, following Beauvoir, distinguishes between less severe cases of oppression, in which the individual may too willingly claim the mantle of victim in order to discharge herself of responsibility for changing her situation, and more severe cases, in which one can not hold the individual culpable for failing to pursue alternatives. She eloquently sums up Beauvoir's position as follows:

> Some of the oppressed are complicitous in their oppression and, in bad faith, evade the revolt that alone could open the way to freedom for them. But others simply do not have that choice. Their situation has so penetrated even their ontological freedom, so modified it, that not even the commencement of a transcendent project is possible. The very withdrawal of consciousness which, for Sartre, is the origin of transcendence and which enables freedom to choose its way of taking up its situation (for example, whether or not to give in to the torturer) has ceased to be possible. (Kruks 1990, 97)

Kruks applauds Beauvoir's recognition that the situation can actively limit one's freedom, a view that she claims is in keeping with a Marxist acknowledgment of the power of the situation to shape not merely our material reality but our very subjectivity. While it is impossible from the outside to determine how oppressed a given individual actually is, and whether or not one considers controversial figures such as Andrea Yates and Sethe to be examples of severely oppressed individuals, ample evidence for the existence of severely oppressed people is readily available throughout the world. And it is precisely the actions undertaken by these latter individuals that Beauvoir wants to do justice to by acknowledging that they are not morally culpable for failing to recognize, much less seeking to liberate themselves from, the source of their oppression. For such individuals, she maintains, the possibility of liberation must come from without. In her words:

> There are cases where the slave does not know his servitude and where it is necessary to bring the seed of his liberation to him from the outside: his submission is not enough to justify the tyranny which is imposed on him. The slave is submissive when one has succeeded in mystifying him in such a way that his situation does not seem to him to be imposed by men, but to be immediately given by nature, by the gods, by the powers against whom revolt has no meaning; thus, he does not accept his condition through a resignation of his freedom since he can not even dream of any other; and in his relationships with his friends, for example, he can live as a free and moral man within this world where his ignorance has enclosed him. (Beauvoir 1976, 85)

In this passage, Beauvoir seems to equivocate on the issue of whether or not a severely oppressed individual has freedom. She tells us that such a person cannot be said to have resigned his freedom because he does not feel that he has chosen this situation to begin with; rather, his situation appears natural, and he is not even capable of imagining any alternatives to it. Thus, not only freedom but also the power of imagination seems to be radically compromised. On the other hand, Beauvoir emphatically maintains that such a person can still live as "a free and moral man within this world where his ignorance has enclosed him." What kind of freedom and what kind of morality is this? Certainly, it does not seem to be the genuine moral freedom in which I will the disclosure of the world that Beauvoir discusses at length in *The Ethics of Ambiguity*. Neither does it seem to resemble the absolute, unconditioned freedom that Sartre champions as the exclusive birthright of the for-itself in *Being and Nothingness*. Rather than deny the plausibility of Beauvoir's claim that the severely oppressed individual can be considered as free and moral within the confines of his situation, I would argue that she is unable to do justice to her own insight precisely because it challenges the entire existential ethics that both she and Sartre are committed to, an ethics that is built on the foundation of an original, ontological freedom. And yet, despite the difficulties they introduce for her own position, Beauvoir reminds us of these challenges again and again.

In both *The Ethics of Ambiguity* and *The Second Sex*, Beauvoir not only discusses the constraints that the oppressed must contend with on a daily basis but also argues that the role of oppressor itself limits the possibilities of one who is in a situation of power over others but wishes not to oppress. For, she maintains, "a colonial administrator has no possibility of acting rightly toward the natives, nor a general towards his soldiers; the only solution is to be neither colonist nor military chief" (1989, 723). Unlike the severely oppressed individual, then, the colonist or military chief can refuse to continue on in their position. On the other hand, Beauvoir, in keeping with her more general argument in *The Second Sex* that women have historically occupied a more immanent position in society and men the more transcendent one, goes on to argue that even though the colonialist or military chief may choose a different path, his options are still limited because "a man could not prevent himself from being a man." "So," she concludes, "there he is, culpable in spite of himself and laboring under the effects of a fault he did not himself commit; and here she is, victim and shrew in spite of herself" (1989, 723). "A well-disposed man," she tells us, "will be more tortured by the situation than the woman herself: in a sense it is always better to be on the side of the vanquished" (724).

Why is this so? The simple answer, I think, is power. To have power and yet at the same time to experience oneself as powerless is more devastating than to lack a power one never had to begin with. Once again, Beauvoir seems to be departing radically from her own as well as Sartre's emphasis on the inalienable freedom of the for-itself, because here, too, the situation of both men and women within a patriarchal society is presented as *inherently* constraining. In such situations, she maintains, "it is useless to apportion blame and excuses: justice can never be done in the midst of injustice" (1989, 723).

What are the ethical implications of these claims? To argue, at this point, that we could still achieve genuine freedom by willing ourselves free, by willing ourselves to be a disclosure of the world, seems inadequate. For what is disclosed is a world that limits the very movement of freedom itself. Addressing this problem in the context of anti-black racism, Lewis Gordon, in *Existentia Africana*, introduces a distinction between "choices" and "options" in order to preserve the primacy of freedom in the face of oppressive situations that seem to preclude its being exercised. "A condition of one's freedom" he tells us,

> is that one is able to choose. Yet, choosing and having options are not identical: choices may work in accordance with options, but one may choose what is not a live option. The choice, then, turns back on the chooser and lives in the world of negation. There the choice at best determines something about the chooser, though it fails to transform the material conditions imposed on the chooser. Theories that fail to make the distinction between choice and option carry the danger of using gods as the model for human choice. For gods or for that matter, God, there is no schism between choice and option, so whatever such a being chooses *is*, absolutely, what *will be*. (Gordon 2000, 76–77)

In an oppressive situation, Gordon maintains, an individual still has choices but lacks the options necessary to enable those choices to be realized. In his words, "Where there are many options, choices can be made without imploding upon those who make them. If a set of options is considered necessary for social well-being in a society, then trouble begins when and where such options are not available to all members of the society" (2000, 86).

Useful as I find this distinction to be, I am not convinced that it succeeds in capturing what is at stake in the examples with which I began this paper. In the case of Sethe, we would have to understand her actions as stemming from a choice that reflected a lack of options. That is, we could claim that she chose to kill her children because she felt that the other option available, namely, a life of slavery, was worse than death itself and hence no option at all. And, although from the outside Morrison's readers may perceive Sethe to have had more options, the point is that *she* did not so perceive it. So we may feel compassion for her terrible choice and lament her inability to recognize that other options were available. But such an interpretation seems patronizing. While it may encourage us, as

Gordon surely intends it to do, to fight to increase the options available to the oppressed so that their choices do not become self-negating but can find fulfillment in a liberatory praxis, it also can promote a sense of superiority on the part of those who stand outside this situation because they are able to perceive options that the individual in question cannot. Beauvoir herself, I believe, would not support such a view, since her existential ethics is grounded in the individual's own lived experience and not in the perspective of others.

The shortcomings of Gordon's analysis are revealed even more strongly, I would contend, in the case of Andrea Yates. For it is difficult to maintain that she *chose* to drown her five children even if we are willing to grant that she may have perceived this to be her only option. The lucidity of consciousness so championed by Sartre and Camus as requisite for freedom seems difficult to locate in the indirect, fragmentary accounts we have received of Yates's feelings as she killed her children one after the other (and I'm not sure we can claim that this lucidity is present in Sethe's case either, despite the deliberateness of both women's actions). Once again, it is relatively easy from the outside to see other options. Unlike in Sethe's case, where most would blame the institution of slavery itself for limiting Sethe's horizons, with Andrea Yates the source of the blame is less clear. Some may blame her doctors or her husband for not recognizing the severity of her depression; many blame Yates herself for not realizing that she was in need of help. Beauvoir undoubtedly would have called our attention to the oppressive institution of motherhood that sets up maternity as the quintessential source of personal fulfillment for women. The multiple factors that potentially contributed to this tragedy, I would argue, are precisely what points to the complexity of this woman's experience, a complexity that defies a simple distinction between choices and options.

Instead of trying to salvage the primacy of choice for ethics in order to preserve the freedom and humanity of the self who chooses, as Gordon valiantly does, perhaps it is time to rethink the existentialist emphasis on choice. For once we acknowledge, with Gordon, that if we lack options our choices turn out to be self-negating, in danger of destroying the very self that chooses, then we also must ask, what kind of choice is this? With Beauvoir and Gordon, I would maintain that even the severely oppressed individual can lead a moral life, but I think that this can occur in the absence of both options and choices. Elsewhere, I have argued that such a person can manifest a simple "will to endure" in the face of what others may regard as an unlivable situation.[15] This "will to endure," however, does not seem to me to fall under the category of choice as Beauvoir and Sartre have used the term. It does not presuppose a clear, conscious awareness of one's situation. One simply "does what one must" to preserve one's existence at all cost.

At this point one may legitimately ask: If choice and freedom do not provide the foundation for the moral existence of the severely oppressed, what does? Here, I believe, we can take as our point of departure a fundamental insight from the feminist ethics of care, namely, that it is the ability to enter into relations with others that precedes choice and provides the necessary grounding for a moral life. Focusing on relations with others, rather than choices, allows us to see moral failures as failures of *relation* rather than merely failures of the individual in question (though this is not to deny that there are also personal failures for which an individual alone is primarily responsible). Moreover, rather than promoting an "us versus them" mentality, in which we can blame an individual for failing to make the right choices, or even blame a society for failing to provide that individual with more options, *we* are implicated in an ethics of relation, for we can no longer remain unchallenged in the position of transcendental observers standing in judgment on the individual and her situation. The *bodily imperatives* that issue forth from the oppressed are addressed not only to her immediate others but to *us* as well, transforming us from mere observers into active participants in the process.[16] And it is precisely insofar as we may have new perspectives to offer on her situation, that it is up to us to respond to their call.

Indeed, in the closing pages of *The Second Sex*, Beauvoir asserts that changed perspectives offer the best hope of improving the immanent situation of women. "Woman" she asserts, "is the victim of no mysterious fatality; the peculiarities that identify her as specifically a woman get their importance from the significance placed upon them. They can be surmounted, in the future, when they are regarded in new perspectives" (1989, 727). As Beauvoir well recognized, individuals face challenging choices from one moment to the next insofar as they must, in the face of an inherently ambiguous situation, commit themselves to a particular course of action, an action that always implicates others in the process. Moreover, it is in the very process of acting that we individually and collectively establish the meaning that our actions will have in defining our situation.

Inspired by Beauvoir's own preoccupation with how to do justice to the reality of oppression, I am arguing that we must begin to challenge choice itself as the distinctive quality that makes us human. To do so, we must challenge the hegemony that the discourse of freedom and choice has enjoyed not only in existentialist ethics but also in deontological and consequentialist views. This does not mean rejecting the importance of freedom and choice (or even existentialism) in the pursuit of an ethical existence, but rather, recognizing that freedom and choice are not foundations for morality but goals to strive for. The starting point for this process, I maintain, must be a reevaluation of the importance of preserving and enriching our relations with others, a possibility that does not presuppose a self-aware, autonomous consciousness, but no more and no less than our own *intercorporeality*. To say that human existence is intercorporeal is to say that it is always embodied, and this embodiment itself consists of the innumerable ongoing relations that link my own body inextricably to other bodies.

The intercorporeality that marks Beauvoir's existence is poignantly invoked in her visceral reaction to the oppressive Jim Crow laws operative in the South when she paid her first visit to the United States in 1947:

> And throughout the day the great tragedy of the South pursues us like an obsession. Even the traveler confined to a bus and waiting rooms cannot escape it. From the time we entered Texas, everywhere we go there's the smell of hatred in the air—the arrogant hatred of whites, the silent hatred of blacks. (Beauvoir 1999, 233)

Beauvoir inhales and exhales the smell of hatred, her body registering the difference between the "arrogant hatred of whites, the silent hatred of blacks." Through this process, and through the unearned privilege she receives as a white woman, she comes to feel complicit with the racism that is all around her. Unable to maintain the isolated stance of "foreigner," Beauvoir assumes the failure of American democracy as her own failure to overcome the physical, social, and institutional boundaries that separate the black oppressed from their white oppressors. Even after she and her white female companion "N." help a pregnant black woman who has fainted repeatedly while sitting in the crowded rear seat of their segregated Greyhound bus, Beauvoir experiences the strength of the barriers that divide them: "She thanks us, but she seems worried and goes away quickly without accepting further aid: she feels guilty in the eyes of the whites, and she's afraid. This is only a small incident, but it helps me understand why, when we're traveling through the overcrowded black districts, the placid Greyhound gets such hostile looks" (Beauvoir 1999, 233).

Through Beauvoir's eyes, we see how even the Greyhound bus becomes complicit in the perpetuation of oppression. The vehicle's own massive presence is a tangible daily reminder of the intractability of racism, and, for the overheated bodies pressed into the bench at the rear, all the while facing the whites in front sitting comfortably in rows of two, oppression is materialized from all sides at once. While it is the very intercorporeality of our experience that enables oppression to be intensified, I would also argue that it is this same intercorporeality that provides the grounds for its eradication. For in the face of challenging choices, and even in the face of situations in which freedom does not seem to be present and the very notion of choice appears to be meaningless, what defines the humanity and moral status of those who are oppressed is their concrete relations with others.

The failures of relationship experienced by Sethe and Andrea Yates respectively are not reducible to their relations with any one individual or even a set of individuals. Rather, both cases poignantly reveal that our relations to others always unfold within a broader context that includes our relations with the institutions that define the very terms of social existence (e.g., motherhood, slavery, the medical establishment, etc.). When our relations with others are irretrievably damaged, as was the case for both Sethe and Andrea Yates, we must always look not only within but also outside the relationships to the larger social situation in which those relationships are embedded to assess why, where, and how they have broken down. Cases of extreme oppression are rarely attributable to a specific relationship alone, but require, for their eradication, a transformation in the very conditions that render a situation intelligible (or unintelligible) as such.

Through the new relationship Sethe builds with Beloved as her long lost daughter, she is able to begin to work through the horrific demons of her past, though Beloved's own phantasmatic status raises questions about how successful this relationship itself will be in opening up a new future.[17] In the case of Andrea Yates, who, in contrast to Sethe, moves from the (relative) freedom of white bourgeois motherhood into solitary confinement for twenty-three hours a day within a small cell in a state penitentiary, the legal institution that has overturned the validity of her first trial holds out more hope for a positive change in her situation than any relationships she may have managed to form and/or restore in the one hour a day allotted to her as a maximum security prisoner. Both cases reveal not only the multiple ways in which individuals can suffer severe oppression but also the irrelevance of ethical systems based on bedrock notions of freedom and choice in the face of severe oppression.

If we recognize, along with care theorists, that choice and freedom are themselves grounded on our capacity to sustain loving relationships with others, we will also recognize that the work that has to be done to repair the fabric of those relationships is itself moral labor. Beauvoir's work is instructive here, for she teaches us that the freedom and choices of the self have no meaning without reference to the freedom and choices of others. If even one person lacks the conditions necessary to will their freedom, it impoverishes us all.

Notes

1. As a guest on CBS's *The Early Show* shortly after the trial, Russell Yates stated that his wife should not have been taken off antipsychotic drugs in the period preceding the killings. "She was never diagnosed, she was never treated, and they didn't protect our family," he said (quoted in "Jurors: Yates' drowning of her children seemed premeditated," CourtTV.com, March 18, 2002). In June 2002, a headline in the *Houston Chronicle* announced, "A Year Ago, Russell Yates Tragically Lost 5 Children; He's Still Fighting for his Wife." The article affirms Yates's love and concern for his wife: "Andrea is a woman who needs compassion, who needs to be held and comforted. But here she is, 23 hours a day in a cell, isolated for the rest of her life from everyone who loves her. It's hard to accept. That has caused me a lot of stress this last year" ("After the Horror," *Houston Chronicle*, June 6, 2002). In a more recent article appearing in CourtTV.com on July 23, 2004, sensationally entitled, "Lawyer: Yates thinks children are alive," Russell Yates's weekly visits to his wife in prison are mentioned; his support for his wife has clearly continued throughout her incarceration.

2. Feminist sociologist Ruth Frankenberg's expression "racial social geography" is very helpful in distinguishing the radically different social, political, and physical landscapes that situated each woman's actions. According to Frankenberg, a racial social geography "refers to the racial and ethnic mapping of environments in physical and social terms" (Frankenberg 1993, 44).

3. Although I am proffering interpretations of both women's behavior here, I do not mean to suggest that these are the only plausible explanations one could give of either woman's actions. Indeed, there are several possible theoretical frameworks that may be utilized to analyze their respective situations. The possible interpretations I am suggesting are therefore not intended to provide a comprehensive analysis of these two women's situations and their respective responses to them.

4. By horizons I am referring to the broader context within which each woman's actions were situated. These include the temporal horizons of past memories and future anticipations that help to shape the meaning of the present, spatial horizons such as the larger geographical region as well as the immediate locale in which the events unfolded, and the social horizons (such as horizons of race, class, and gender) that help to define the parameters within which everyday life attains its significance.

5. See my 1992 essay "Context and Perspective" for a more comprehensive discussion of how individual perspectives are constructed on the basis of particular contexts of significance.

6. As with other notorious cases of violent bourgeois crime, especially the murder of children by their mother, such as the 1995 South Carolina story of Susan Smith, who sent her car into a local lake, drowning her two sons who were securely strapped into their car seats, this case was tried publicly in the press in the days following the initial deaths. In Susan Smith's case, even her ex-husband David Smith testified that she deserved death for the drownings of their boys, Michael and Alex, a crime compounded, in his and the public's eyes, by her false claim that they had been kidnapped, triggering a 9-day national search for the boys and their abductor (see CNN.com's "U.S. News Year in Review," December 28, 1995, for an overview of the crime and the subsequent trial). Indeed, just as in the case of Susan Smith, Andrea Yates's guilt was reassessed in great detail by the public as well as by the court several months later during the death-penalty trial. Both cases have also been explicitly compared in articles focusing on women who kill their children such as CNN.com's August 8, 2001, article by David Williams entitled "Postpartum Psychosis: A Difficult Defense."

7. Of course, it is not inappropriate to ask why Mrs. Yates's husband did not notice how depressed she was, even if Ms. Yates herself did not recognize the seriousness of her condition. Strangely, there was very little criticism, much less condemnation, of Mr. Yates in the press. The criticism that did occur came primarily from Mrs. Yates's immediate relatives in newspaper articles and media quotes including the following statement by Andrea's brother, Brian Kennedy: "I think that any man and woman whose spouse was that severely down, confused, that sick, that I would do whatever it would take to make sure my other half would get the help that was necessary" ("Yates family members decry husband," CourtTV.com, March 18, 2002). With some minor exceptions, including feminist support by the National Organization for Women (NOW) which organized a candlelight vigil outside the courtroom where the case was being tried (see "NOW Rallies to Mother's Defense," *Washington Post*, September 3,

2001), Andrea Yates was publicly vilified as a criminal who deserved, if not the death penalty, then at least a life sentence for her actions. As one juror stated in the wake of the conviction: "I think she should be punished for what she did considering she did know right from wrong and I think prison's the way to go" ("Jurors: Yates' drowning of her children seemed premeditated," CourtTV.com, March 18, 2002). The lack of blame for Mr. Yates makes sense if we acknowledge the powerful role the (Kantian) notion that we are all autonomous moral agents has in establishing the framework for our societal moral judgments in post-Enlightenment Western civilization. Indeed, if anything, Mr. Yates has been presented as a double victim: first, as a man who was married to a dangerous woman without realizing it; and second, as a man who has suffered, through no fault of his own, the loss of his entire family in one fell swoop. Indeed, Russell Yates has referred to both himself and his wife as victims of the crime, the criminal justice system, and the press: "They've really taken victims and victimized them further. They put our family through hell this past year and unnecessarily. She should have never gone to trial" ("After the Horror," *The Houston Chronicle*, June 20, 2002).

8. I am using this expression "lifeworld" *(lebenswelt)* in the Husserlian sense taken up and elaborated upon by Alfred Schutz with respect to the totality of our social relations with others in *The Phenomenology of the Social World* (1967).

9. I am grateful to Peg Simons for pointing out that Beauvoir offers through the character of Françoise an example of the sincere individual that both preceded and influenced Sartre's own discussion of seriousness, sincerity, and bad faith in *Being and Nothingness*.

10. For a focused discussion of this very point, see the "Myth and Reality" chapter of Beauvoir's *The Second Sex*.

11. See chapter 5 of Sonia Kruks' *Situation and Human Existence* for a detailed account of how Sartre's understanding of freedom and the situation changed from *Being and Nothingness* to the *Critique of Dialectical Reason*. Kruks credits Beauvoir as being a major influence on Sartre in modifying his earlier view and in developing a more robust conception of praxis.

12. Indeed, it is passages such as these that reveal how Beauvoir was already posing significant internal challenges to the ethics of the autonomous for-itself she propounds throughout most of *The Ethics of Ambiguity*.

13. Although it is beyond the scope of this paper to trace out the connections between Beauvoir's existentialist ethics and Sartre's, Margaret A. Simons has provided a compelling analysis of the impact of Beauvoir's early work on Sartre's own concept of situation in the chapter "Beauvoir and Sartre: The Question of Influence" in her book *Beauvoir and The Second Sex: Feminism, Race, and the Origins of Existentialism*.

14. The original reads as follows: "Mon action n'est pour autrui que ce qu'il en fait lui-même: comment donc saurais-je d'avance ce que je fais?" (Beauvoir 1944: 51).

15. See my essay "Freedom, Oppression and the Possibilities of Ethics in Beauvoir's Work."

16. For a fuller description of these "bodily imperatives" and how they function to ground an ethical existence, see chapter 7 of my *Body Images: Embodiment as Intercorporeality*.

17. The reader is unclear by the end of the novel whether Beloved is merely a figment of Sethe's imagination or a real flesh-and-blood human being.

REFERENCES

Beauvoir, Simone de. 1944. *Pyrrhus et Cinéas*. Paris: Gallimard.

———. 1976. *The Ethics of Ambiguity*. Trans. Bernard Frechtman. New York: Citadel Books. [1947. *Pour une Morale de l'ambiguité*. Paris: Gallimard].

———. 1989. *The second sex*. Trans. H. M. Parshley. New York: Vintage Books. [1949. *Le deuxième sexe*, 2 vols. Paris: Gallimard].

———. 1990. *She Came to Stay*. Trans. Yvonne Moyse and Roger Senhouse. New York: W.W. Norton. [1943. *L'Invitée*. Paris: Gallimard].

———. 1999. *America Day by Day*. Trans. Carol Cosman. Berkeley: University of California Press. [1954. *L'Amérique au jour le jour*. Paris: Gallimard].

Bergoffen, Debra. 1997. *The philosophy of Simone de Beauvoir: Gendered phenomenologies, erotic generosities*. Albany: State University of New York Press.

Frankenberg, Ruth. 1993. *White women, race matters: The social construction of whiteness*. Minneapolis: University of Minnesota Press.

Gordon, Lewis R. 2000. *Existentia Africana: Understanding Africana existential thought*. New York: Routledge.

Kruks, Sonia. 1990. *Situation and human existence: Freedom, subjectivity and society*. London: Unwin Hyman.

Merleau-Ponty, Maurice. 1962. *Phenomenology of perception*. Trans. Colin Smith. London: Routledge & Kegan Paul. [1945. *Phénoménologie de la perception*. Paris: Gallimard].

Morrison, Toni. 1987. *Beloved: A novel*. New York: Knopf.

Sartre, Jean-Paul. 1944 [1956]. *Being and nothingness*. Trans. Hazel E. Barnes. New York: Washington Square Press. [1943. *L'Être et le néant*. Paris: Gallimard].

———. 1976. *Critique of dialectical reason*. Trans. Alan Sheridan-Smith. London: Verso. [1960. *Critique de la raison dialectique*. Paris: Gallimard].

Scarry, Elaine. 1985. *The body in pain: The making and unmaking of the world*. Oxford: Oxford University Press.

Schutz, Alfred. 1967. *The phenomenology of the social world*. Trans. George Walsh and Frederick Lehnert. Evanston, Ill.: Northwestern University Press.

Weiss, Gail. 1992. Context and perspective. In *Merleau-Ponty, hermeneutics, and postmodernism*, ed. Thomas W. Busch and Shaun Gallagher. Albany: State University of New York Press.

———. 1999. *Body images: Embodiment as intercorporeality*. New York: Routledge Press.

———. 2002. Freedom, oppression, and the possibilities of ethics in Beauvoir's work. *Simone de Beauvoir Studies* 18 (2001–2002): 9–21.

BETWEEN GENEROSITY AND VIOLENCE: TOWARD A REVOLUTIONARY POLITICS IN THE PHILOSOPHY OF SIMONE DE BEAUVOIR

15

Ann V. Murphy

The ideology of violence and revolution is widely recognized to be one of the most notable touchstones of French existentialism. Of central concern is the consideration of violence as a legitimate course of action in the face of colonialist oppression. While the philosophy of violence that emerges in the work of Frantz Fanon and Jean Paul Sartre has attracted particular notice, Simone de Beauvoir's contributions to the discourse on violence in the French tradition have been largely ignored.

Indeed, even as the current renaissance in scholarship on Beauvoir continues to explore her profundity and importance as a philosopher, sparse attention has been granted to her thinking on violence. This elision is of some importance, for it is around the notion of violence that Beauvoir organizes her thinking on the relationship between ethics and politics. Another ominous consequence is that the neglect of Beauvoir's consideration of violence amounts to the evasion of the issue of race and its influence on Beauvoir's political thought. Finally, given the attention that generosity has received in relation to Beauvoir's ethics, it is strange that her audience has largely ignored the manner in which generosity and violence are linked in Beauvoir's ethical writings.

The themes of gift giving and generosity have figured centrally in politico-philosophic discourse for quite some time. Marcel Mauss's influential *Essay on the Gift* (1950) argued that the gift was, in an important sense, ambiguous. If the structure of the gift is ambiguous, it is because though the gift may appear free and disinterested—an expression of the purest generosity—in reality, it is anything but. In many societies, the reception and reciprocal return of gifts is elaborated and governed within the confines of certain social norms—especially a demand for reciprocation—that obliterate generous intentions and place them on the terrain of exchange and economic calculus. Experientially, then, the gift is plagued by an ambiguity: it may be experienced simultaneously as a refusal of egoistic calculation and as a constraint.

More recently, Jacques Derrida has argued in a familiar move that the conditions for the possibility of the gift are the conditions for its impossibility as well. When the gift is recognized as such, it is annulled, and it becomes an obligation that must be reciprocated.[1] For this reason, Derrida argues that the gift defies the metaphysics of presence to the extent that it must be forgotten—indeed non-present—in order to truly be a gift. The gift thus becomes intimately connected with forgetting, deferral, and erasure.

Feminists writing within the French tradition—particularly Irigaray and Cixous—have been equally as concerned to highlight the manner in which the discourse on the gift has tended to elide considerations of sexual difference, or more precisely, the fact that the exchange economy is predicated on the erasure of women from the position of the giving subject. Both argue that if women were freed from their objectification within the phallocentric economy, the current social order would collapse. And finally, the writers in the existentialist tradition have their own contributions to make to the discourse on the gift, though they have been largely, and lamentably, ignored. In particular, Beauvoir and Sartre were interested in the ways in which generosity could be alienated and enacted as a type of violence and subjugation.

Recent Beauvoir scholarship has largely been dedicated to the identification of Beauvoir as an original and important philosopher in the French tradition. In a number of places Beauvoir's originality as a thinker has been attributed to the theoretical distance she attains from Sartre. The radical divergence between the two when it comes to their respective elaborations of the intersubjective relation has been the object of particular interest. Some scholars have suggested that against and apart from Sartre's early descriptions of intersubjectivity as a savage war of egos, Beauvoir has stressed an ethics of generosity and openness (see Bergoffen 1996). This specific elaboration of the intersubjective relation is justified with particular reference to Beauvoir's text *The Ethics of Ambiguity* (1996).[2]

Attending to the way Beauvoir consistently theorizes generosity and violence together complicates the investigation of generosity in Beauvoir's ethics. While the ethics of generosity that emerges from the text is undoubtedly worthy of the attention it has received, sparse attention has been paid to the ties that bind together generosity and violence in Beauvoir's philosophy. Even as *The Ethics of Ambiguity* gestures toward the importance of generosity for Beauvoir, it is also important in that it contains the outline of a revolutionary politics, a politics that entertains the possibility of violence. Indeed, in *The Ethics of Ambiguity*, Beauvoir takes explicit issue with the embrace of altruism and generosity as political strategies and urges her readers to negotiate the concrete complexities of the situation before coming to judgment on generosity and violence alike.

While Beauvoir by no means advocates violence uncritically in the *Ethics of Ambiguity*, she nevertheless entertains the possibility of violence in certain concrete circumstances. Beauvoir is particularly concerned with those situations in which violence appears as the only recourse against the oppressor. An individual freedom that is occupied with the suppression of the freedom of others is unacceptable, and while the violence exercised in order to rectify this injustice may be no less outrageous, it is, for Beauvoir, a legitimate course of action. There is no way to evade this "obvious" and "bitter" truth: action on behalf of some is always action against others (*EA*, 99/ 143): "A freedom which is occupied in denying freedom is itself so outrageous that the outrageousness of the violence which one practices against it is almost cancelled out" (*EA*, 97/ 141). In refusing to affirm the freedom of all, the oppressor comes to "embody . . . the absurdity of facticity," and insofar as ethics demands the triumph of freedom over facticity, ethics demands the suppression of the oppressor, sometimes by violent means (*EA*, 97/ 140).

Beauvoir is in no way endorsing violence categorically; she appears to be most interested in those situations where violence appears to be unavoidable. Diplomacy and pacifism have their place in politics, but there are moments when the "urgency of struggle" seems to foreclose these options:

> And doubtless it is not a question of backing out of these consequences, for the ill-will of the oppressor imposes upon each one the alternative of being the enemy of the oppressed if he is not that of their tyrant; evidently, it is necessary to choose to sacrifice the one who is the enemy of man; but the fact is that one finds himself forced to treat certain men as things in order to win the freedom of all. (*EA*, 97/ 140)

Hence the ambiguity of violence as Beauvoir understood it. *In fighting for freedom, one must deny it, to the extent that violence is only enacted as body against body.*

This diminution of freedom was, for Beauvoir, the tragedy of violence. The event of violence is only intelligible as human freedom is reduced to brute objectivity. In this respect, violence is cyclical. In enacting violence against another, one denies not only the other's freedom, but one's own as well, to the extent that violence is enacted, for Beauvoir, as immanence. Violence, then, can only be enacted in the deprivation of freedom, not only on the part of the one against whom violence is enacted, but on the part of the perpetrator as well. The tragedy of violence is thus accomplished in the reduction of freedom to facticity, the diminution of free consciousness to the immanence of embodied flesh. On such an account, even those who perpetrate revolutionary violence are sacrificed for the cause. "Every war, every revolution, demands the sacrifice of a generation, of a collectivity, by those who undertake it" (*EA*, 99/ 143).

It is worth pausing to note that Beauvoir's descriptions of violence here foreshadow her later discussions of embodiment in *The Second Sex*. There are two very different bodies inhabiting this later text: the material body, objective and carnal; and the phenomenal and lived body, not a thing but a dynamic and culturally situated locus of meaning.[3] Beauvoir's description of violence as necessarily embodied—and hence confined to the plane of immanence despite its inherently transcendent nature—anticipates her later negotiations with this theme. This is also a point at which her resonance with other existentialist theorists on violence—Fanon in particular—is especially palpable.

Indeed, violence, for Fanon, is powerfully tied to the phenomenon of decolonization, a process that Fanon claims in *Wretched of the Earth* is "always violent" (1963, 35). The violence of decolonization consists in its inauguration of a new humanism, with one notion of humanity coming to replace another (35). Fanon is unequivocal in his claim that the world of the colonized, strewn with prohibitions, can "only be called into question by violence." The interrogation and rejection of the culture of the colonizer is commensurate with a decision made on the part of the colonized to "embody history in his own person" (40). Here Fanon renders violence as an ambiguous movement of immanence and transcendence at once. It is in embodying history that violence is enacted, but violence is equally an attempt at transcendence to the extent that it calls into question—and indeed, alters—the boundaries of the human.

Cognizant of the possibility that "there will never be an *other* future" than war in a world where division and violence define existence, both Fanon and Beauvoir endeavored to envision ethics in such a context. Beauvoir writes:

> The fundamental ambiguity of the human condition will always open up to men the possibility of opposing choices; there will always be within them the desire to be that being of whom they made themselves a lack, the flight from the anguish of freedom; the plane of hell, of struggle, will never be eliminated; freedom will never be given; it will always have to be won. (*EA*, 119/ 171)

Beauvoir's *Ethics of Ambiguity* takes issue with the claim that there is a future peace that promises the possibility of morality. More urgent, for Beauvoir, was the call to elaborate an ethics in a world where violence appeared inescapable. It was necessary that ethics be animated in the concrete world, that it refuse complicity with political abstraction at some level. While ethics were necessarily political for Beauvoir, they were also the last recourse against political tyranny and brutality.

Beauvoir explored the possibility of an ethics that might underlie a revolutionary politics, a politics that was able to refuse complicity with oppression. Today, suspicion still surrounds the adoption of certain liberal discourses on recognition that operate under the pretense that the best way to remedy oppression is to engage the political system as it exists today. Such suspicion is grounded in the worry that battles for rights and recognition do little to refute a regime that is oppressive at its heart. By insisting that ethical decisions always imply a certain politics, but by also noting that ethics could be used as a tool for combating the political status quo, Beauvoir aligns herself with those who would radically challenge the nature of political discourse.

Beauvoir's discussion of the relationship between ethics and politics must be understood with reference to her philosophy of temporality. Because ethics must open to the future, the abstract theorization of certain virtues will never suffice. "Politics is right to reject benevolence to the extent that the latter thoughtlessly sacrifices the future to the present" (*EA*, 136/ 196). There are cases where the evil of an individual seems to demand his subjugation. The universal and abstract embrace of generosity as a political strategy is unsatisfying, for Beauvoir, in that it evades consideration of this circumstance. One cannot simply assent to love all others, to take them as ends, if there are some among them who desire the enslavement and oppression of others. More specifically, Beauvoir was interested in the ways in which generosity could be warped in the hands of the oppressor into an instrument of subjugation. Consequently, if one naively adopts generosity as a political virtue, one risks perpetuating the status quo to the extent that the practice of generosity may only serve to perpetuate power inequities. Beauvoir notes that ethics become contaminated when placed in the hands of the oppressor, and as a consequence, virtues like generosity are not always employed authentically within the confines of an oppressive society. In line with Fanon's suggestion that ethics become "irrevocably poisoned and diseased" when they are in the hands of the colonizer, Beauvoir calls us to pause at the unhesitating embrace of generosity. Thus, Beauvoir's concern with generosity was grounded in her notice of the manner in which ethics were necessarily politicized.

It is this very problematic that Sartre adopts when he writes in *Saint Genet* that "the ethical 'problem' arises from the fact that Ethics is *for us* inevitable and at the same time impossible" (1963, 186). For Sartre, the separation of good and evil could only be abstract; in concrete situations, good and evil could never exist in isolation. "Either morality is stuff and nonsense, or it is a concrete totality which achieves a synthesis of good and evil" (186). Sartre explicitly notes that the synthesis of good and evil that is morality is not meant to be understood in terms of a Nietzschean "beyond," but rather as a Hegelian *Aufhebung*. Any morality that professed to transcend this concrete synthesis of good and evil was, for Sartre, "nonsense" (186). To the extent that it is impossible to be truly moral in an oppressive political climate, ethical decisions are "agony," since one's ethics are formulated in relation to these norms. Ethics, however, are no less inevitable, for their impossibility does nothing to excuse us of our obligation to provide ethical norms for our actions. In a tone that anticipates the Derridean discourse on undecidability, Sartre notes that we are "forced to will and to decide" upon our actions, even with the knowledge that it is impossible that our ethics are wholly good. In the concrete, all action is plagued by the trace of evil (186). In short, ethics is nothing short of paradoxical: concrete ethics are oppressive to the extent that they are situated in reference to the political status quo, but abstract ethics are no less so to the extent that they convince the individual that he or she can be ethical in a fundamentally unethical situation. To relate to individuals through an abstract universal is to alienate them and deny their singularity. Because abstract ethics are complicit in such a ruse, Sartre argues that abstract ethics are formulated in bad faith.

Echoing Beauvoir's resistance to the formalization of ethics, Sartre notes in *Notebooks for an Ethics* (1992) that ethics must evade direction at the abstract universal, perhaps more lucidly rendered as an abstract humanism.[4] Instead, ethics must take up the enigmatic "concrete universal," which Sartre describes as "those men who find themselves in the same historical situation" (*NE,* 7/ 14). Sartre is concerned that abstract ethics assert the value of certain cultural institutions and question only the relationship that one should have to that institution, not the validity of the institution itself (*NE,* 103/ 110).[5] Historically, one's relation to another is always both free and alienated; "there is always both freedom and subjugation" (*NE,* 414/ 430). Thus, the moment of ethics, of creation, of generosity, is in history but always beyond it to the extent that it is dialectically alienated. Free human relations are possible only when the element of the Other is suppressed, but Sartre notes that alienation necessarily binds every concrete situation to the extent that every society is "bound by an Other for which it is Other" (*NE,* 414/ 430). "History," Sartre writes, "will always be alienated" (*NE,* 49/ 54). Our actions as historical agents are "stolen from us." "History is the *Other.* Whatever one does, wherever one does it, the undertaking becomes *other*. It acts through its otherness, and its results are other than what one had hoped for" (*NE*, 46/ 53).

When politicized, this account requires that History be defined as "the sacrifice and devotion of some to the interests of others" (*NE*, 45/ 50). Thus Sartre describes History as "meaningless" to the extent that it cannot explain the suffering and sacrifice of some at the service of others. There is a component to History that is lost without hope of recuperation (*NE*, 34/ 39).

Concretely, the structure explicated above—whereby historical sense comes to contaminate ethical meaning—is exemplified in the existentialist adoption of the discourse on generosity and gift giving. An examination of the theme of generosity in Sartre and Beauvoir forces the acknowledgement that there are moments when the alienation of generosity appears as an instance of subjugation, that is, as an instance of violence.

While marking a departure from his earlier ontology, in his investigations of the politics of the gift in the *Notebooks*, Sartre applies his earlier formulation of bad faith to the realm of ethics in order to betray the manner in which generosity may ultimately appear as a form of subjugation. Because our relationships are always enacted in the presence of a third observer—and, as Sartre claims, "under the sign of oppression"—ethics becomes "poisoned" (*NE*, 9/ 16). Considering generosity, Sartre cautions that the abstract embrace of generosity as a political strategy is enabled by an individual and collective self-deception—bad faith—that generates the illusion that generosity and gift giving may be disinterested, gratuitous, and unrequited, when in reality the concretization of generosity can enact a denunciation of the other.

Sartre and Beauvoir were aligned in their mutual suspicion surrounding the unhesitant embrace of generosity as a political strategy. Even those actions that claim to find their inspiration in the highest virtues may become motivated by the "element of the Other," the realm of political society that informs our ethical acts. When motivated in this way, Sartre claims, an act becomes "rotten—it perpetuates alienation" (*NE*, 417/ 433).[6] Alienation must come to bear on every concrete relation (*NE*, 414/ 430). It follows, then, that even those acts conceived as generous become politically motivated and thus are complicit with the perpetuation of the status quo.

Ontologically, the gift may appear to be "gratuitous, not motivated, and disinterested" (*NE*, 368/ 382). In a culture of alienation, however, the gift becomes a "means of ensnaring the other." My intention in giving is vitiated, and the gift, in being objectified, is inverted, becoming a mechanism of subjugation (*NE*, 370/ 384). Since for Sartre, the original relation to the other is already one of alienation, even acts of generosity become objectified and alienated as well.

The gift economy functions as an exchange between personas in the "element of the Other," or the alienated world where singular humanity is masked by cultural significations. When one is in the element of the Other, "one must accept gifts, for fear of the public admission that one is unable to give in return" (*NE*, 373/ 387). Because the acceptance of gifts is commanded, oppression is sustained. The oppressed are given no choice but to accept, and this acceptance is viewed, not as necessity, but as acquiescence and consent. Sartre examines the ways in which such a concretization of generosity betrays the alienation at the heart of giving, arguing that it is precisely this making-concrete—the event of the gift—that renders generosity as a double movement of alienation and liberation. One gives at the same time "in freedom for freedom" and to enchain the other's transcendence by assigning a destiny (*NE*, 374/ 389). Hence, the notions of friendship and enmity have the same original source. For these reasons, Sartre states, "The bond of friendship is indiscriminately nonfriendship, generosity is indiscriminately subjugation" (*NE*, 368/ 382). The "two simultaneous aspects of the gift"—as a gesture of solidarity and as a manifest structure of reciprocal enslavement—destabilize the boundary between friendship and enmity. Hence, certain situations arise in which one is unable to determine whether the gift is a proposal of friendship or a challenge.

The Ethics of Ambiguity may be read as Beauvoir's critique of the inefficacy of abstract ethics. Her insistence on the concrete nature of ethics situates Beauvoir opposite Kant, Hegel, and Marx, her main interlocutors in the *Ethics*, all of whom she finds deficient in that they proffer problematically abstract or universalist ethics. The two most salient criticisms of existentialism to which Beauvoir responds in *Ethics of Ambiguity* are, first, the accusation that existentialism is unable to furnish the subject with a concrete principle for making choices; and second, that existential philosophy is ultimately a solipsistic philosophy, trapping one within the confines of subjectivism. Her defense of existentialism against the first accusation is largely accomplished in dialogue with Hegel.

Beauvoir argues that the existentialist approach surpasses Hegel's figuring of the dialectic insofar as it refuses to subsume particularity as a moment to be surpassed by the universal (*EA*, 17/ 24). We might read in Beauvoir's critique of this subsumption her own concern for pluralism and for the preservation of the particularity of the individual and the project. "For existentialism, it is not impersonal universal man who is the source of values, but the plurality of concrete particular men projecting themselves toward their ends on the basis of situations whose particularity is as radical and as irreducible as subjectivity itself" (*EA*, 17/ 24). It is the existentialist presupposition of this originary separation that Beauvoir finds redeeming in relation to Hegel. If Hegel can account for particularity only in reference to its subsumption by the universal, then Hegelian pluralism is of an altogether different ilk than the pluralism of the existentialist, which Beauvoir would find superior in that it made the particular originary, and thus managed to avoid the totalizing force of the universal. It is her rejection of the abstract nature of ethics that leads Beauvoir to consider the possibility of violence.[7]

Ethics comes to be situated in the particularity of the project (*EA*, 29/ 40). The myriad ways in which all projects are disrupted necessitates one's essential distance from oneself, a distancing that generates one's ability to judge and weigh options, and the ability to formulate projects. An individual's primary identification as negativity allows for evil to the extent that it accounts for the will's inability to accord with itself.[8] Because of this, Beauvoir claims that existentialism is privileged in that it can truly permit the elaboration of an ethics (*EA*, 34/ 48).

Evil arises, for Beauvoir, through the "possibility of a perverted willing" without which the notion of virtue would be vacant, and without content (*EA*, 33/ 47). The very possibility of evil is predicated on the existentialist understanding of the self as an imperfect and contingent accomplishment; indeed, it is in the acknowledgement of the element of failure involved in the condition of man that lends itself to "the most optimistic ethics" (*EA*, 10/ 13). For Beauvoir, the fundamental lack at the heart of being, the lack that inspires the formulation of our projects, is the gesture that creates the world for consciousness. The structure of the project thus allows for the disclosure of being; in this disclosure there is always inadequation and failure.

For Beauvoir, the ethics that merit the name "existentialist" are ethics that resist previous justifications drawn from civilization and culture; they are an ethics that privileges the future. If there is a rule for the existentialist ethicist, "it is the rejection of every principle of authority," it is to take the risk of inventing an "original solution" to an ethical problem (*EA*, 142/ 205). In this sense, existentialism does not offer the consolations or evasions of an abstract or universalist ethics (*EA*, 148/ 214).

Beauvoir's insistence on the concrete nature of ethics mutually prevents not only her categorical embrace of generosity and altruism as political strategies but also a categorical renunciation of violence. Indeed, Beauvoir is interested not only in generosity as a revolutionary virtue but also in the ways in which the virtues may be distorted within the confines of an oppressive society. It remains true, however, that *The Ethics of Ambiguity* does indeed demonstrate Beauvoir's desire to distance herself from an entirely conflictual model of human relations. This project is accomplished not only via her direct reference to an ethic of generosity but also through the fundamental tenet of *The Ethics of Ambiguity*, namely, the claim that it is inconsistent to will one's own freedom without willing that of others. The authentic willing of one's own freedom necessitates willing the freedom of all.[9] This reduces oppression to a hypocrisy: "If the oppressor were aware of the demands of his own freedom, he himself should have to denounce oppression" (*EA*, 96/ 139). This is perhaps the most important maxim in the text: one must "reject oppression at any cost" (*EA*, 96/ 139).[10]

While it may be legitimate to transform Beauvoir's *ontological* claim that the desire for one's own freedom is bound to the desire for the freedom of all into the *ethical* claim that the only palatable ethics that would result would be an ethic of generosity and care, it is also possible to read Beauvoir differently. It is precisely this imperative, that I respect the freedom of the other, that leads to the possibility of violence and revolution. The ambiguity of human freedom implies violence.

In some moments, it seems as though Beauvoir's negotiations with the theme of violence are tied to an agonistic politics. There was something essential for Beauvoir in the conflict that had come to occupy the political arena, and the rejection of altruism as a political strategy was at the heart of her theorization of the difference, and relation between, politics and ethics. There were too many hesitations regarding such a strategy, not the least of which was the worry that the adoption of generosity as a political strategy would somehow disable the conflictual model of history in the dialectical sense, that it would somehow sacrifice the interests of the future to the politics of the present. It is here that Beauvoir's thinking on history informs her ethical philosophy. The naïve embrace of a virtue like benevolence can become insipid when thoughtlessly employed within the confines of an oppressive society. Such a conception of what it means to be ethical hands the weight of judgment to the past and "sacrifices" the future to historically embedded regimes of oppression. Beauvoir recognized that when generosity is thoughtlessly invoked within the realm of an oppressive society, it can do little to challenge the power structures and hierarchies that are already in place. An abstract ethics that validates the individual's relation to some situation is not adequate to interrogate the institutions that have circumscribed the situation itself. It does not suffice to blindly appeal to some virtue without considering the consequences of its concrete application in a specific circumstance. Beauvoir cautions that when virtues are employed inauthentically, or in bad faith, they certainly do not challenge—and they may even reify—the structures of oppression.

Although she refuses to evade the existential possibilities of violence and war, it is the ethics of existentialism that are the most hopeful to the extent that they refuse to deny the freedom and responsibility of the individual. In the end, the most hopeful analyses are those that are willing to call into question the very virtue of generosity and demand that we be vigilant of the ways in which generosity is concretized. Presumably, the need for this vigilance is now as strong as ever, particularly in our era, where liberalism and its investment in the economy of individualism has managed to conceal the need for institutions that would promote the civic virtues of disinterestedness, devotion, and generosity.

This dilemma is of particular import at a time when radical and revolutionary thought and action are being co-opted by the liberal discourse on rights. Where liberals may acquiesce to the legitimacy of corporate, state, and institutional power, radical discourses on difference may understand oppression as the consequence of capitalism and corporate state interests. Though liberals may denounce the excesses and abuses of the state, they might fail to take up the state as an object of critique. Within this context, revolutionaries are being commodified in a manner that neutralizes the force of their position by making them appear as "loyal" opposition. Given that this centrism remains a dominant political position, radical and revolutionary thought is frequently reconfigured so as to fit comfortably within the confines of modern liberalism. The revival of radicalism would necessitate the engendering of a new ethics that calls for wide-ranging and radical transformation of society as a whole, an ethics that appreciates the complexity of the concrete world and refuses the consolations of abstraction.

NOTES

1. Derrida's distance from Mauss is marked in the claim that the gift and exchange are incompatible. Derrida critiques Mauss for failing to realize that exchange is the annulment of the gift. See *Given Time: I. Counterfeit Money* (1992).

2. Originally published in French as *Pour une morale de l'ambiguïté* (1947), *Ethics of Ambiguity* is hereafter cited as *EA*, with English pagination preceding the French.

3. It is fair to note, however, that Beauvoir encountered difficulties negotiating this tension—a tension that continues to inform her work in *The Second Sex* (1952). For instance, in her discussion of lesbianism in *The Second Sex*, Beauvoir critically interrogates the supposedly "natural" correlation between femininity and femaleness, thus rejecting the charge that lesbians are somehow engaged in an inauthentic endeavor to "imitate the male" (408). And yet she persists in the opinion that lesbianism was an identity to which one could be "cursed" and "doomed" (405, 422). This example illustrates the difficulty that Beauvoir had in reconciling her existentialist and phenomenological loyalties.

4. Originally published in French as *Cahiers pour une morale* (1983), *Notebooks for an Ethics* is hereafter cited as *NE*, with English pagination preceding the French.

5. As an example, Sartre asks, "What relations should one have with the family, assuming that the family exists and that one wants to preserve it (or not change it, which amounts to the same thing)?" (*NE*, 103/ 110).

6. Here Sartre could be no further from Levinas, for whom the introduction of the third was the passage to justice. In Sartre, the presence of the third instigates a culture of alienation: he describes it as "poison" (*NE*, 9/ 16).

7. Beauvoir also critiques the abstract formalism of Hegel's account of recognition. Such an account, Beauvoir argues, recognizes the "*universal* truth of myself" (as I recognize the other as identical to me), "and so individuality is denied" (*EA*, 104/ 150). Beauvoir argues that the Hegelian privileging of the abstract universal renders state and society essentially vacuous: "If the individual is nothing, society cannot be something. Take his substance away from him and the state has no more substance; if he has nothing to sacrifice, there is nothing before him to sacrifice to" (*EA*, 106/ 152). In order that state and society have substance, they must appear as the conglomeration of particular

and concrete projects (*EA*, 106/ 152). Individual freedom, in turn, is only realized through its concretization, that is, as the project is particularly embodied.

8. This is what differentiates existentialist ethics from Kantian ethics, where the autonomous agent is self-identical. Beauvoir, too, identifies ethics as an "adhesion to the self," but this will for adhesion can never be wholly positive, as it is for Kant. At the heart of the individual is a fundamental lack and non-coincidence.

9. It is evident that Beauvoir was not operating with a naïve conception of freedom; freedom she says, "is not the power to do anything you like," but rather, "it is to be able to surpass the given toward an open future" (*EA*, 91/ 131).

10. Fanon and Beauvoir come to markedly similar conclusions regarding the type of ethics they would espouse. The argument at the heart of *Ethics of Ambiguity* holds that one cannot will one's own freedom at the expense of others' without hypocrisy. Fanon concludes *Black Skin, White Masks* with the call "that the enslavement of man cease forever. That is, of one by another" (1967, 231).

References

Beauvoir, Simone de. 1996. *The ethics of ambiguity*. Trans. Bernard Frechtman. New York: Citadel Press. [1947. *Pour une morale de l'ambiguïté*. Paris: Gallimard].

———. *The second sex*. 1952. Trans. H. M. Parshley. New York: Vintage Books. [1949. *Les deuxieme sexe*. 2 vols. Paris: Gallimard].

Bergoffen, Debra. 1996. *The philosophy of Simone de Beauvoir: Gendered phenomenologies, erotic generosities*. Albany: State University of New York Press.

Derrida, Jacques. 1992. *Given time: I. Counterfeit money*. Trans. Peggy Camuf. Chicago: University of Chicago Press. [1991. *Donner le temps*. Paris: Editions Galilée, 1991].

Fanon, Frantz. 1967. *Black skin, white masks*. Trans. Charles Lam Markmann. New York: Grove Press.

———. 1963. *Wretched of the earth*. New York: Grove Weidenfeld. [1961. *Les damnés de la terre*. Paris: François Maspero].

Mauss, Marcel. 1950. Essai sur le don. In *Sociologie et anthropologie*. Paris: Presses Universitaires de France.

Sartre, Jean Paul. 1992. *Notebooks for an ethics*. Trans. David Pellauer. Chicago: University of Chicago Press. [1963. *Cahiers pour une morale*. Paris: Gallimard].

———. 1963. *Saint Genet: Actor and martyr*. Trans. Bernard Frechtman. New York: George Braziller.

CONDITIONS OF SERVITUDE: WOMAN'S PECULIAR ROLE IN THE MASTER-SLAVE DIALECTIC IN BEAUVOIR'S *THE SECOND SEX*

16

Shannon M. Mussett

The treatment of oppression in Simone de Beauvoir's *The Second Sex* offers a unique perspective on the problems plaguing woman's situation. Understood as externally enforced Otherness, oppression is the degradation of freedom into the stagnant life of the *en-soi*.[1] To a large extent, *The Second Sex* is a study of the many ways in which woman suffers oppression through external forces that act to situate, define, and maintain her in an inessential, dependent, and negative position in society. I argue that it is primarily Beauvoir's unusual application of Hegel's master-slave dialectic that allows her access into the perplexity and intricacies of woman's historical oppression.[2] Specifically, Beauvoir characterizes woman as a *kind* of Hegelian slave consciousness in two important ways: (1) woman serves as an instrument of mediation for man; and (2) even though she evades the life-and-death struggle, she nevertheless learns the same lesson of absolute negativity and can thus be emancipated through labor.

In order to show how woman is exemplary of a Hegelian slave, I begin with a brief analysis of the master-slave dialectic, followed by a more elaborate discussion of Beauvoir's woman, and how she (just like Hegel's slave) inhabits the peculiar position of mediator between man and nature and between man and himself. I specifically address the fundamental argument against woman's placement in the master-slave dialectic—namely, her exclusion from a life-and-death battle for recognition with man—as articulated by Eva Lundgren-Gothlin. I argue that if we adhere to Hegel's own description of this particular stage in the dialectic, it is still possible to read Beauvoir's woman as a slave, regardless of her seeming exclusion from the battle for recognition. I conclude by pointing to how woman's experience of absolute negativity and Beauvoir's call for work as liberatory complete woman's placement in the master-slave dialectic.

Lundgren-Gothlin emphasizes the importance of Hegel's influence on Beauvoir by seriously questioning woman's role in the dialectic. The cornerstone of her argument revolves around the notion in Beauvoir's *The Second Sex* that women are destined to give life and not risk it (Lundgren-Gothlin 1996, 74–78). As such, women and men never entered into a life-and-death battle for recognition with each other. She concludes that

> while Beauvoir uses the Hegelian master-slave dialectic to explain the origins of oppression, she does not locate man as master and woman as slave in this dialectic. Instead, woman is seen as not participating in the process of recognition, a fact that explains the unique nature of her oppression. (72)

I call into question this claim that woman is not a slave and is therefore not trapped in a master-slave relationship with man. In actuality, not only does Beauvoir's woman fulfill all of the necessary requirements of a slavish consciousness, but the relationship between man and woman is almost a *perfection* of this Hegelian stage, which explains the tenacity of woman's oppression. I am more sympathetic to Margaret Simons, who writes:

> Turning Hegel against himself, Beauvoir argues that his description of the relationship of men, whose warfare and inventions create values that transcend the mere repetition of Life, and women, whom biology destines to immanence, the passive and dependent reproduction of Life, is more reflective of the absolute opposition of the master/slave relationship than any relationship between men. (Simons 1995, 151)

Although I agree with Simons that the master-slave opposition is crystallized in the woman-man relationship, my emphasis is on woman's role as a tool of mediation for man as well as her experience of absolute negativity, rather than on her destiny as maintainer and nurturer of life.

As Lundgren-Gothlin points out, one of the strongest objections against the participation of men and women in the master-slave dialectic is Beauvoir herself: whereas the warrior risked his life to assert human values over the animal, she writes, "the worst curse that was laid upon woman was that she should be excluded from these warlike forays. For it is not in giving life but in risking life that man is raised above the animal" (1989, 64; [1976, I:113]). Women, who are confined to giving life, would thus never enter into a life-and-death struggle with men and consequently would be excluded from the Hegelian narrative. Even more to the point, Beauvoir writes that between man and woman, "there has been no combat" (1989, 64; [1976, I:114]).³ Regardless of the instances where Beauvoir argues against a *literal* battle to the death between man and woman, I maintain that in two important senses, woman is trapped in the master-slave dialectic. On the one hand, the descriptions of woman as a free being that is nonetheless trapped as a mediator between man and nature and between man and himself fits very closely with Hegel's description of the slave who mediates for the master in the same way. On the other hand, the vital lesson that the slave learns through his near encounter with death—namely that self-consciousness is absolute negativity—is a lesson that woman learns as well, although through a different route than in a direct confrontation with man in battle.

FROZEN SLAVES: THE MASTER-SLAVE DIALECTIC AND ITS APPLICATION TO WOMAN

In order to elaborate the role of mediation in Beauvoir's study of the master-slave dialectic, I first turn to Hegel's discussion of this rich and complex dynamic in the *Phenomenology of Spirit*. Two of the most important elements of mediation are its role in the *becoming-other* of the self, and the insight into the nature of the self (or "I") as *pure negativity*.⁴ For the purposes of this essay, I focus primarily on the ways in which mediation functions in the master-slave dialectic.

The master-slave dialectic is found in the first stages of *self*-consciousness. Noteworthy of this particular stage in the development of consciousness is that self-consciousness is defined as desire in general.[5] Desire is not a blind impulse toward the outside world, but rather, "the object of immediate desire is a *living thing*" (Hegel 1977, 106; [1996, 139]). This desire is not satisfied with attempts at the mere consumption of life in general, because simple negation only leads to a furthering of desire and not to a satisfaction of it. As such, self-consciousness comes to realize that it will only achieve satisfaction in another self-consciousness. In other words, self-consciousness will exist in and for itself only when it is acknowledged (mediated) by another independent self-consciousness (1977, 111; [1996, 145]). However, this recognition is neither easily granted nor guaranteed.

Each self-consciousness tries to assert itself as subject by ridding itself of objectivity. This requires reducing the other into a *negativity*—an object to be destroyed and reabsorbed back into the self (Hegel 1977, 113; [1996, 148]). Objectification of the other results not only from the inability of each self-consciousness to recognize the other as an independent self-consciousness, but the *necessity* of each, in order to define itself as subject, to posit and attempt to overcome the seeming objectivity of the other. Self-consciousness thus requires an originally antithetical "other" that must be objectified. This objectification, as Hegel claims above, requires positing the other as a negativity (an object) that must itself be negated.

In the struggle that follows, both self-consciousnesses engage in a life-and-death battle for the recognition of selfhood over mere animal existence. The victor is the self-consciousness that is willing to lose its life to prove its subjectivity. The defeated becomes the servile consciousness that clings to life rather than risk its loss. As a result of his victory in the battle for recognition, the master is *mediated* by another consciousness—that is, "through a consciousness whose nature it is to be bound up with an existence that is independent, or thinghood in general" (Hegel 1977, 115; [1996; 150]). In one sense, the master uses the slave to mediate himself in order to recognize himself *as* a self. Hegel continues, "The lord puts himself into relation with both of these moments, to a *thing* as such, the object of desire, and to the consciousness for which thinghood is the essential characteristic" (1977, 115; [1996; 150–51]).[6] This is a crucial moment—the master's mediation through the slave to relate to *both* nature and himself—in understanding the role that woman will come to play in this dialectic for Beauvoir.

At this point, the master is in a double relation: on the one hand, he desires to negate a *thing as such,* that is, something that has objective being and is not self-consciousness. On the other hand, he places himself into a relation with a consciousness whose essential characteristic is *thinghood,* that is, one that is an unessential, object-consciousness. In short, the master desires *both* the object (in nature) and the object-consciousness (as projected onto the slave). In fact, he desires the slave because the slave is the mechanism of mediation not only in the affirmation of the master's self-consciousness but also because the slave labors on nature. For Beauvoir, this double mediating role becomes grafted onto woman. Just as the slave serves the dual role as mediator between the master and nature *and* the master with himself, so too does woman act as a buffer between man and an alien and hostile nature as well as a mirror to reflect man's own image back to himself.

As with Hegel, Marx, and Kojève, Beauvoir maintains that nature at first appears as an overwhelming and alien force that must be conquered or at least managed in order for humanity to overcome its animality.[7] Strongly influenced by the aforementioned philosophers, Beauvoir locates the struggle between the sexes as somewhat rooted in this natural setting. She explains that early humans experienced nature with a mixture of awe and dread:

> Man encounters Nature; he has some hold upon her, he attempts to appropriate her. But she cannot fulfill him. Either she appears simply as a purely impersonal opposition, she is an obstacle and remains a stranger; or she submits passively to man's desire and permits assimilation by him; so that he takes possession of her only through consuming her—that is, through destroying her. In both cases he remains alone. (1989, 139; [1976, I:237]; translation modified)

Mirroring Hegel, the master's (man's) desire is thwarted in his attempts to consume nature through his inability to assimilate, negate, or destroy it, thus leaving him in a constant state of renewed need. Frustrated by the conditions of alienation and unfulfilled desire, man began associating the mystery of woman with the mystery of nature, which resulted in an interesting amalgam. Not only were the two similar, but "in woman was to be summed up the whole of alien nature" (1989, 69; [1976, I:120]).[8]

Man's technological advances spurred his attempts to be rid of his ties to nature. These moments were paralleled by his wishes to be rid of his ties to woman, whom he had already equated with nature. According to Beauvoir, "in woman are incarnated the disturbing mysteries of nature, and man escapes her hold when he frees himself from nature" (1989, 75; [1976, I:127]). In other words, the more that man becomes the master of nature (the more he enslaves what he claims to be natural forces), the more he gains mastery over woman.

In a peculiar doubling, woman not only acts as the embodiment of nature for man (thus making his separation from nature *and* woman easier) but because she cannot possibly *be* the totality of nature, woman can act as a mediating tool *between* man and nature. Beauvoir writes that "she is the privileged object through which he subdues Nature" (1989, 156; [1976, I:262]). As a "natural being," she provides a midpoint through which man may safely pass to access and dominate the once-threatening nature. Indeed, this double life makes woman a unique kind of slave because both woman and nature are objects of man's desire through a confusion and fusion of the two. Man, like self-consciousness in Hegel's *Phenomenology*, seeks to overcome and master nature through the negation and annihilation of it. However, according to Beauvoir, man's attempts to consume nature are thwarted unless it takes on a subjective face through woman. Woman, like Hegel's slave, will come to be associated with nature in order that man may have access to one of his desires: the consumption of nature. Additionally, because woman is not usually destroyed in her consumption, man's desire is partially fulfilled and indefinitely prolonged. Perhaps woman mediates even better than Hegel's slave, who simply *works* on nature, because woman comes to *embody* it.[9] This makes the appropriation of nature by man much easier and more satisfying. It remains to be seen how woman, as object, serves the same role for man that the object-being of the slave serves for the master.

As the being who must fulfill the role of combining nature and artifice, woman is also forced into the role of an object. For example, Beauvoir tells us that, whereas the ideal of feminine beauty is variable, *certain demands remain constant:* "Since woman is destined to be possessed, her body must present the inert and passive qualities of an object" (1989, 157; [1976, I:263–64]). *The Second Sex* is filled with descriptions, from ornamentation to lifestyle, of how women come to take on and embody the role of the objectified other.[10] In line with Hegelian logic, consciousness objectifies what is other to it and then tries to overcome or negate this objectivity by taking it back into itself. This objectification of otherness is necessary for the subject to find its limits and define its subjectivity. Thus, according to the needs of masculine self-definition, "the 'true woman' is required to make herself object, to be the Other" (1989, 262; [1976, I:407]) in order that man may define himself as subject.

Why is this positing of the other a necessary step in the setting up of identity? The answer, for Beauvoir, is through a Hegelian analysis of consciousness. She explains that "otherness is a fundamental category of human thought" and that each consciousness struggles to set itself up as the essential subject by making the other the inessential object (1989, xxiii; [1976, I:16]).[11] Clearly, this movement precipitated in the master-slave dialectic in which the master actually *won* the ability to objectify the other as Other. Although the beginnings of humanity are shrouded in mystery, Beauvoir hints that man won this right over woman long ago.[12] Ironically, this "freedom to objectify" that man performs on woman is actually an attempt to escape his own freedom. Man wants to possess woman-the-other as an object since he himself actually desires to *be* an object, thus escaping his own existential freedom. Beauvoir tells us that "he never succeeds in abolishing his separate ego, but at least he wants to attain the solidity of the in-itself . . . to be petrified into a thing" (1989, 269; [1976, II:15]). For man, woman-as-object thus makes the perfect object-being into which man may alienate his desire to be an object. Because he cannot take her otherness back into himself (in other words, negate his own desire for objectivity as transferred onto woman) without literally destroying her, the movement is inhibited, and she remains the objectified Other for an exceptionally long time.

We now have woman fulfilling the role of slave in two ways; on the one hand, she is the perfect mediator between man and nature, and on the other, she fulfills the role of object-being for man's own self-definition. But there remains one last crucial element that woman must fulfill in order to be truly considered a "slave" in the master-slave dialectic. She must also be a self-consciousness, or in Beauvoirean terms, a transcendent existent.

Woman is an "ambiguous idol" for man; he finds that although he may objectify her, she must be a subject by necessity. Beauvoir writes, "When woman thus appears as the associate of man . . . she is of necessity endowed with a consciousness, a soul. He could not depend so intimately upon a creature who did not participate in the essence of humanity" (1989, 170; [1976, I:281]; translation modified).[13] Therefore, woman is not simply an object—she is a conscious ego. Similarly, the slave is not simply an object but is, as Hegel tells us, a "consciousness in the form of thinghood" (1977, 115; [1996, 150]). The master, in objectifying the slave, still realizes that the slave is not merely an object—only that he is simply the inessential consciousness whose being is bound up with thinghood. In the same way, man, in objectifying woman, does not mistake her for a thing, but places her in the category of Other—whose essence is to be simultaneously object *and* subject. Woman's ontological freedom is a necessary constituent in the struggle between her and man.

Thus, the first phase of the argument as to woman's place in the master-slave dialectic has come full circle. Woman fulfills all the necessary requirements for a perfect mediatrix/slave to man-the-master. Beauvoir emphasizes this when she writes that man

> aspires in contradictory fashion both to life and to repose, to existence and to merely being . . . he dreams of quiet in disquiet and of an opaque plenitude that nevertheless would be endowed with consciousness. This dream incarnated is precisely woman; she is the wished-for intermediary between nature, the stranger to man, and the fellow being who is too closely identical. (1989, 140–41; [1976, I:239])

Woman is thus the perfect synthesis of all that the master wishes: intermediary between man and nature, yet endowed with the inessential and dependent object-consciousness so desperately desired in a vassal. However, unlike Hegel's slave, who eventually overcomes his servitude, woman's journey through this stage is constrained and brought to an end prematurely. How does Beauvoir's woman become trapped as the tool of mediation for man? How is it that "woman thus seems to be the inessential who never goes back to being the essential, to be the absolute Other, without reciprocity" (1989, 141; [1976, I:239])? The slave and master eventually invert their roles in Hegel's dialectic. Why, then, haven't men and women inverted their roles or moved past this frozen moment of development?

The answer lies to a great extent in the role of absolute negation. Beauvoir tells us that woman offers respite from the "implacable dialectic" between men, who enter into the life-and-death struggle with each other (1989, 141; [1976, I:239]). If woman's unique type of slavery allows man to use her as a slave without ever engaging in a life-and-death battle, then perhaps she travels through this stage of consciousness via a different route than Hegel's narrative prescribes. This trajectory has arguably prohibited her from overturning her servitude until recently. I maintain that although her passage through this moment of the dialectic is different, the essential lesson is identical. In other words, woman undergoes the same education as the slave—namely, that the essence of self-consciousness is pure negativity—without having to enter into a life-and-death conflict.[14] Because Beauvoir has her learning the same lesson, it only makes sense that her liberation will emerge, just as it does for Hegel's slave, out of productive labor.

THE LESSONS OF NEGATIVITY AND THE MOVE TOWARD WORK

The centrality of the fear of death and the role of work cannot be overemphasized in Hegel's account of the passage into and out of the master-slave dialectic. Death functions as the instigator in the struggle for recognition as each self-consciousness stakes its own life in order to prove its humanity over its animality.[15] However, the slave, in discerning the real possibility of the loss of its life, experiences true terror. Hegel explains that "this consciousness has been anxious, not of this or that particular thing or just at odd moments, but its whole being has been seized with fear; for it has experienced the fear of death, the absolute Master." In its confrontation with the possibility of its own nonexistence, the soon-to-be slave experiences a substantial lesson into the nature of self-consciousness because the experience of this fear actually indicates "the simple, essential nature of self-consciousness, absolute negativity, *pure being-for-self*, which consequently is *in* this consciousness. This moment of pure being-for-self is also *for* the slave, for in the master it exists for him as his *object*" (1977, 117;

[1996, 153]; translation modified). The master, as the essential consciousness, is the *explicit* expression of the slave's being-for-self.

The parallel between the master and slave and Beauvoir's man as the essential (the One) as opposed to woman the unessential (the Other) is clear. Both the master and man exist *for* the slave and woman respectively as the external manifestation of self-consciousness's being-for self. What is not so clear is the *implicit* experience of pure being-for-self that the slave experiences through the confrontation with his own mortality. Through the fear of death, the slave experiences the truth of self-consciousness in the form of an existential moment of absolute negativity (what will come to be understood as *freedom*). In order to uphold the argument that Beauvoir's woman is constituted as a slavish consciousness then, she must somehow suffer the same kind of experience. I argue that the threat of death, which is described by Hegel as an experience of absolute negativity, is undergone by woman but in a different fashion. Both the slave and woman experience the explicit understanding of self-consciousness in the master and/or man. However, what the slave learns implicitly through confronting death, woman learns through oppression.

Beauvoir writes that woman has been externally defined as the Other to man, who is defined as the Self: "He is the Subject, he is the Absolute—she is the Other" (1989, xxii; [1976, I:15]). As stated above, for both Hegel and Beauvoir, self-consciousness desires to reduce the other into a negativity or an object. This insight into human interaction allows Beauvoir access into one of the reasons why woman is an objectified (negative) consciousness: man needs woman to mediate himself so as to define himself. In order to accomplish this desired mediation, man defines woman as all that is not-man (Other) so that he can define what he *is*.

Although there is no simple definition of what defines the Other, Beauvoir writes throughout the text that woman is defined as the *negative* of man, that is, all that man is *not*. For example, Beauvoir explains that "the relation of the two sexes is not quite like that of two electrical poles, for man represents both the positive and the neutral . . . whereas woman represents only the negative . . . without reciprocity" (1989, xxi; [1976, I:14]). Woman's negativity is absolute for Beauvoir because man casts her as the "Absolute Other" and not simply as an other: "To the precise degree in which woman is regarded as the absolute Other . . . it is impossible to consider her as another subject" (1989, 71; [1976, I:122]; translation modified). Woman is never considered a subject, because she is defined as the essence of absolute alterity. The affinity between Otherness and negativity runs throughout *The Second Sex* from history, myths, and lifestyle.[16] Consequently, I read Beauvoir's constant references to woman as Other as strongly enmeshed in an understanding of woman as the absolute negative of man's positive assertion of self. This is because her otherness never returns to herself and remains absolute alterity.[17]

Although Beauvoir provides numerous aspects of woman's negativity, there is perhaps no stronger evidence of woman as negative than in her direct association with death. For example, speaking of man's ambiguous and uneasy ties to his own mortality and to woman, Beauvoir writes that "what man cherishes and detests first of all in woman . . . is the fixed image of his animal destiny; it is the life that is necessary to his existence but that condemns him to the finite and to death" (1989, 165; [1976, II:274]). The fear of death that all human beings experience gets translated onto woman because of her role in giving birth. Because she brings life into the world, she must somehow be responsible for taking it away. Death is not accepted as natural or necessary by man, and he revolts against his impermanence: "Horrified by needlessness and death, man feels horror at having been engendered" (1989, 146; [1976, I:246]). Because death is the absolute negation of life (or the negative in general) woman, as the harbinger of man's mortality, accordingly takes on this horror.[18] Nonexistence is precisely that before which Hegel's slave trembled, and here we see woman being alloyed with death. Is it therefore possible to see Beauvoir's woman as experiencing the same lesson of absolute negativity learned *implicitly* by the slave, but as a lesson *externally* enforced by man, who defines her as the absolute Other?

In the first section of this chapter I explored the ways in which Beauvoir's woman became amalgamated with nature in order to provide man access to nature. Now we see that woman also becomes fused with death, because man fears his own mortality and so translates that fear onto woman. Just as the oppression of woman was more puissant than that of Hegel's slave because rather than merely working on nature she *became* all of nature, so her affinity with the negative is arguably more powerful because rather than choosing to face death, she *becomes* it. The remaining task is to elucidate the way woman internalizes this negativity as an implicit experience of pure being-for-self.

Sonia Kruks argues that Beauvoir's analysis of oppression contains the insight that to be oppressed is to be externally forced to internalize the oppressor's judgment of who or what one is. Pointing to Beauvoir's discussion in *The Ethics of Ambiguity*, Kruks writes that Beauvoir "suggests that oppression can permeate subjectivity to the point where consciousness itself becomes no more than a product of the oppressive situation" (Kruks 1992, 100). In other words, an ontologically free consciousness can internalize an externally enforced situation of oppression and become an *oppressed* consciousness. This understanding of internalizing the external is crucial to seeing how woman in *The Second Sex* learns the same lesson as the slave, namely, the negativity at the heart of self-consciousness.

Although I would argue that, for Beauvoir, woman never made a choice to accept her definition as absolute Other, there are passages where we find woman coming to accept or *internalize* this definition. For example, Beauvoir explains that

> it is not the Other who, in defining himself as the Other, establishes the One. The Other is posed as such by the One in defining himself as the One. But if the Other is not to regain the status of being the One, *he must be submissive enough to accept this alien point of view.* (1989, xxiv; [1976, I:17]; emphasis mine)

This passage illustrates not only man's external imposition of absolute alterity onto woman, but woman's consequent internalization of that Otherness. Beauvoir later writes that "with woman, dependency is interiorized: she *is* a slave even when she behaves with apparent freedom" (1989, 481; 1976, II: 327–28).[19] Woman thus becomes, ironically, *more* trapped than Hegel's slave because she internalizes the outward definition of herself as Other without ever actually choosing to do so. And precisely because the Other is the negative of the self, woman has internalized the same lesson as the slave. Thus, admittedly through a different track than Hegel's slave, woman has experienced the slave's encounter with the truth of self-consciousness.

The problem for woman is that the aforementioned lesson of negativity has been externally enforced. Hegel's slave, before it entered into its slavery, was given two crucial choices: it chose to enter into the battle, and it chose to preserve its life in servitude rather than lose it. It is true that woman, for Beauvoir, never had a choice and never entered into battle. But the experience of negativity as what is at the heart of self-consciousness remains the same, and as such, it is through her definition as Other that she will learn the truth of self-consciousness, or *freedom*. Again, I am arguing that Beauvoir's woman is a kind of slave-consciousness in the Hegelian sense, not an exact manifestation of it. Lacking the internal experience of choice in two ways, woman has therefore not been able to sublate her servitude. However, the experience of negativity is still present, and thus the lesson is theoretically the same. Because she did not choose this experience, her passage out of her servitude has been historically more stubborn and stagnant than Hegel's slave. But because she does know absolute negativity, she can and will benefit from work.

If Beauvoir's woman experiences the same lesson as the slave, namely, that self-consciousness is absolute negativity, then her liberation through work is also in line with Hegelian logic. In *The Second Sex* Beauvoir clearly believes that woman's liberation centers on her admission into the public sphere through productive labor. Hegel writes that it is through work that the slave turns its purely negative relationship to nature into something that is formative of the slave's self-consciousness (1977, 118; [1996, 153]). Working on the independent object gives the slave an awareness of the human power to create. However, Hegel explains that labor, to be self-affirming, must be undergone after the experience of the absolute fear of death:

> If consciousness fashions the thing without that initial absolute fear, it is only an empty self-centered attitude; for its form or negativity is not negativity *per se*, and therefore its formative activity cannot give it a consciousness of itself as essential being. If it has not experienced absolute fear but only some lesser dread, the negative being has remained for it something external, its substance has not been infected by it through and through. (Hegel 1977, 119; [1996, 154–55])

At first glance, it appears quite obvious that woman, because she has not entered into the violent battle with man for sovereignty, could only be trapped in experiencing a "lesser dread" than the loss of life. However, as I have argued, woman has experienced absolute negativity in her situation as the "absolute Other without reciprocity." This externally enforced alterity does not simply remain external but comes to be internalized by woman herself in her own self-definition and self-understanding.

Because there is a discrepancy in Hegel between the experience of absolute negativity (confronting death in battle) and the beginnings of formative activity (working on nature), a space is opened up for the possibility of woman being arrested between the two stages. Beauvoir is clear that work is the only guarantor of concrete liberty for women (1989, 679; [1976, II:597]). However, women have been trapped in the negative for thousands of years by being denied access to transcendent work (which for Beauvoir means work *not* associated with the domestic sphere or maternity). But simply because they have not had access to productive labor does not mean that they are not slaves in the Hegelian sense. In fact, trapped between negativity and the creative employment of that negativity, they are *detained* at this stage. Addressing the vast distance between the experience of negativity and the participation in productive work finalizes Beauvoir's appropriation of Hegel's master-slave dialectic and completes her explanation of why woman's oppression has been so insidious and longstanding.[20]

CONCLUSION

Is woman's servitude exactly the same as Hegel's slave? No, the dialectic between men for Hegel cannot be seamlessly applied to the dialectic between man and woman. However, it has been my argument that, although it is not the same, for Beauvoir it is paradoxically an arrestment and therefore a perfection of it—so much so that neither master nor slave has sought to overcome this stage until recently. Thus, contrary to Lundgren-Gothlin's claim, man and woman not only experience a dialectic of mastery and servitude with each other, but they are in fact *trapped* in one.

Hegel's slave fulfills the role of mediator between the master and nature, and the master and himself. Woman, by taking on the role of nature, gives man the perfect tool for his mediation with nature. It is much easier to appropriate the foreign when it wears a human mask. But woman, posited as the inessential Other, does not resist man with the same force as another male consciousness does, thus offering the ideal midpoint between man as subject and nature as object. Forced to take on object-being while maintaining basic ontological freedom, woman also allows man almost unlimited powers of self-definition. Taking the place of the natural object by which man realizes the limits of his subjectivity, and serving as the inessential subject who recognizes him as essential, woman is the ideal slave.

In addition, woman, like Hegel's slave, learns the lesson of the essence of self-consciousness: at its heart, self-consciousness is absolute negativity. For both Hegel and Beauvoir, this negativity allows us to conceive of the subject as freedom and transcendence in its highest activities. Although Hegel's slave experiences negativity through choice, Beauvoir's woman learns negativity through internalizing absolute Otherness. Regardless of their different paths, both have an implicit understanding of the essence of self-consciousness, and both have the possibility of achieving freedom through labor. Beauvoir clearly puts an original spin on Hegel's most famous stage of consciousness in her analysis of woman's servitude. Trapped at the intersections of nature, object-consciousness, and the negativity at the heart of freedom, woman's oppression proves to be a historical arrestment of the master-slave dialectic that is much more deleterious and obstinate than is Hegel's own formulation.

NOTES

A version of this paper was first presented at the 2001 meeting of the Society for Phenomenology and Existential Philosophy.

1. Beauvoir describes oppression as a condition of externally enforced alterity in *The Ethics of Ambiguity* (1996, 81–83).

2. I am in agreement with Nancy Bauer, who argues that Beauvoir's appropriation of Hegel, although not an exact mirroring of Hegelian philosophy, is in fact essential to her philosophical method (2001, 78–85).

3. However, this is not to say that Beauvoir is not aware that there are many instances in history of women actually participating in battle (see 1989, 62; [1976, I:110]). Margaret Simons (1983, 63) points out that key passages on female *condottieres* who "took up arms like men" have been deleted in the English translation. Taking a different approach, Jeffrey Gauthier (1997, 131–36) points out that Beauvoir was implicitly aware of the components of aggression, conquering, and violence evident in masculine sexuality and argues that this opens up the possibility of a Hegelian confrontation between man and woman.

4. Hegel describes mediation as a process of the Absolute (also referred to as Self or Subject) that "implies a *becoming-other* that has to be taken back." In addition, he explains that mediation is "the moment of the 'I' which is for itself pure negativity" (1977, 11; [1996, 25]).

5. Desire and negativity denote the fundamental lack of coincidence of the self, or *freedom*—something that Beauvoir's woman will experience despite evading violent battle. In reference to desire, Lundgren-Gothlin (1996, 56–66) masterfully discusses the influence of Alexandre Kojève on Beauvoir's Hegelianism. Judith Butler (1987, 9–10), although not addressing Beauvoir's philosophy directly, provides an important study of the negative and desire in French Existentialism that is strongly influenced by Hegel and Kojève.

6. For the importance of this double-relation, see Kojève (1980, 17).

7. See Kojève (1980, 11), and Marx and Engels (1995, 51).

8. Beauvoir asserts that woman's body appeared more natural to early man because her cycles mimic the moons and the seasons. In addition, because of her role in maternity, early man believed that "the land is woman and in woman abide the same dark powers as in the earth" (1989, 68; [1976, I:118]). For a treatment of how Beauvoir ties the discussion of woman and nature into the production of myths, see Scholz (2000, 52–54).

9. For Beauvoir's main discussion of woman as mediatrix, see in particular the chapter entitled in English, "Dreams, Fears, Idols" (1989, 157, 180, 197; [1976 I:263, 295–96, 318]).

10. For only one among many such discussions, see Beauvoir (1989, 157–60; [1976, I:263–67]).

11. And of course, Beauvoir's famous claim that "things become clear . . . if, following Hegel, we find in consciousness itself a fundamental hostility toward every other consciousness; the subject can be posed only in being opposed—he sets himself up as the essential, and constitutes the other as the inessential, the object. But the other consciousness sets up a reciprocal claim" (1989, xxiii; [1976, I:17]; translation modified).

12. See, for example, Beauvoir's claim that man became master of woman with the onset of the patriarchy (1989, 154; [1976, I:259]).

13. In addition, "Man seeks in woman the Other as Nature *and* as his fellow being" (1989, 144; [1976, I:243]; emphasis added).

14. Lundgren-Gothlin concludes that "man is the master, the essential consciousness in relation to woman, the woman is not a slave in relation to him. This makes their relationship more absolute, and *non-dialectical,* and it explains why woman is the *absolute Other*" (1996, 72). As it has been my argument that women are *already in* the master-slave dialectic with men, there must be some way in which women can elude this violent engagement and still learn the same lessons. Bauer (2001, 191) does a nice job highlighting the inconsistencies in Lundgren-Gothlin's claim that men are masters but women are not slaves.

15. The staking of one's life to elevate oneself over the natural or animal is central to Kojève's reading of Hegel as well. See Kojève (1980, 6–8) and Lundgren-Gothlin (1996, 63).

16. For examples of woman and negativity in *The Second Sex*, see: woman defined negatively to man (1989, 143; [1976, I:242–43]); woman as private property established in negative fashion (1989, 154; [1976, I:259]); woman experiencing only negative lib-

erty (1989, 106, 130, 188; [1976, I:179, 223, 306]); and housework as negative time (1989, 451; [1976, II: 268]).

17. Kimberly Hutchings argues that when Beauvoir writes of woman as the absolute Other, "the relation between man and woman is subsumed under the relation between subject and object, between which there is a fundamental and intractable alienation." In other words, woman as Other becomes the object-consciousness that never returns to the self and is therefore "the target of pure negativity" (Hutchings 2001, 25). For an example of the lack of a return to the self in woman, see Toril Moi's discussion of the incomplete circuit of sexual alienation and recovery (Moi 1994, 148–78). Although highly critical of Beauvoir's Freudian and Lacanian treatment of female sexuality, Moi clearly articulates Beauvoir's claims that woman's alienation never gives her back herself or her body in any *positive* sense.

18. One must be careful of overemphasizing the association between woman and death and always remember that it is a *critique* of woman's place in Western thought and history. For example, Debra Bergoffen emphasizes the distinctly "un-Hegelian" themes of the erotic, passionate, and sexual in Beauvoir (1997, 202).

19. See also Moi's discussion of the internalization of patriarchal ideology in Beauvoir (Moi 1994, 173). The question as to whether Beauvoir's woman accepts her servitude or is utterly mystified into thinking her situation is natural (as does the slave in *The Ethics of Ambiguity* [1997, 37, 85, 98]) although critical to understanding how far woman *chooses* her oppression, lies outside the scope of this particular argument. Here I am dedicated solely to elucidating the way Beauvoir's woman internalizes this originally externally enforced negativity.

20. Jennifer Purvis argues that Beauvoir's primary discussion of labor takes place in her treatment of the married woman who is engaged in merely repetitive activities (e.g., housework) and concludes that woman's situation cannot be rectified by labor; consequently, liberation "cannot be achieved within the Hegelian narrative" (2003, 150). I agree with Purvis that domestic labor is no solution for Beauvoir's oppressed woman; however, given that labor is treated more broadly in the context of productive or creative labor, I disagree with her that liberation cannot be attained within the Hegelian model.

References

Bauer, Nancy. 2001. *Simone de Beauvoir, philosophy, and feminism.* New York: Columbia University Press.

Beauvoir, Simone de. 1976 [1949]. *Le deuxième sexe.* 2 vols. Reprint, Paris: Gallimard.

———. 1989. *The second sex.* Trans. H. M. Parshley. New York: Vintage.

———. 1997. *The ethics of ambiguity.* Trans. Bernard Frechtman. Secaucus, N.J.: Carol Publishing Group.

Bergoffen, Debra B. 1997. *The philosophy of Simone de Beauvoir: Gendered phenomenologies, erotic generosities.* Albany: State University of New York Press.

Butler, Judith. 1987. *Subjects of desire: Hegelian reflections in twentieth-century France.* New York: Columbia University Press.

Gauthier, Jeffrey. 1997. *Hegel and feminist social criticism.* Albany: State University of New York Press.

Hegel, G. W. F. 1996 [1986]. *Phänomenologie des geistes.* Reprint, Frankfurt am Main: Suhrkamp.

———. 1977. *Phenomenology of spirit.* Trans. A. V. Miller. Oxford: Oxford University Press.

Hutchings, Kimberly. 2001. De Beauvoir's Hegelianism: Rethinking *The second sex. Radical Philosophy* 107: 21–31.

Kojève, Alexandre. 1996. *Introduction to the reading of Hegel.* Trans. James H. Nichols Jr. Ed. Allan Bloom. Ithaca, N.Y.: Cornell University Press.

Kruks, Sonia. 1992. Gender and subjectivity: Simone de Beauvoir and contemporary feminism. *Signs* 18 (1): 89–110.

Lundgren-Gothlin, Eva. 1996. *Sex and existence: Simone de Beauvoir's* The second sex. Hanover, N.H.: Wesleyan University Press.

Marx, Karl, and Friedrich Engels. 1995. *The German ideology.* Ed. C. J. Arthur. New York: International Publishers.

Moi, Toril. 1994. *Simone de Beauvoir: The making of an intellectual woman.* Cambridge, Mass.: Blackwell.

Purvis, Jennifer. 2003. Hegelian dimensions of *The second sex:* A feminist consideration. *Bulletin de la Société Américaine de Philosophie de Langue Française* 13 (21): 128–56.

Scholz, Sally J. 2000. *On de Beauvoir.* Belmont, Calif.: Wadsworth.

Simons, Margaret A. (1983) 1999. The silencing of Simone de Beauvoir: Guess what's missing from the "The Second Sex." In *Beauvoir and the second sex: Feminism, race, and the origins of existentialism.* Lanham, Md.: Rowman and Littlefield.

———. (1995) 1999. "The second sex" and the roots of radical feminism. In *Beauvoir and the second sex: Feminism, race and the origins of existentialism.* Lanham, Md.: Rowman and Littlefield.

Contributors

Nancy Bauer is Associate Professor of Philosophy at Tufts University. She is author of *Simone de Beauvoir, Philosophy, and Feminism* and is working on a new book, *How to Do Things with Pornography.*

Debra B. Bergoffen is Professor of Philosophy and Women's Studies at George Mason University. She is author of *The Philosophy of Simone de Beauvoir: Gendered Phenomenologies, Erotic Generosities* and editor of several anthologies.

Suzanne Laba Cataldi is Professor of Philosophy at Southern Illinois University Edwardsville. Author of *Emotion, Depth and Flesh: A Study of Sensitive Space,* she has published essays in ethics, feminism, and existential phenomenology.

Edward Fullbrook, University of the West of England, is author (with Kate Fullbrook) of *Simone de Beauvoir and Jean-Paul Sartre: The Remaking of a 20th Century Legend* and *Simone de Beauvoir: A Critical Introduction.*

Eva Gothlin, Associate Professor of History of Ideas and Science, and Lecturer in Gender Studies at the University of Göteborg, Sweden, is author of *Sex and Existence: Simone de Beauvoir's* The Second Sex.

Sara Heinämaa is Senior Lecturer in Theoretical Philosophy at the University of Helsinki, and Professor of Humanist Women's Studies at the University of Oslo. Her latest book is *Toward a Phenomenology of Sexual Difference: Husserl, Merleau-Ponty, Beauvoir.*

Laura Hengehold teaches at Case Western Reserve University in Cleveland, Ohio. She has published essays exploring the relationship between language, desire, and the lived experience of women's embodiment.

Stacy Keltner is Assistant Professor of Philosophy in the Department of History and Philosophy at Kennesaw State University in Kennesaw, Georgia. She has published articles on Irigaray, Kristeva, and Levinas.

Michèle Le Doeuff is Director of Research in Philosophy at the Centre National de la Recherche Scientifique in Paris. Her books include *The Philosophical Imaginary; Hipparchia's Choice, An Essay Concerning Women, Philosophy, Etc.;* and *The Sex of Knowing.*

Ann V. Murphy is New South Global Postdoctoral Fellow in the School of Philosophy at the University of New South Wales in Sydney, Australia. Her research focuses on the relationships between violence, sexuality, race, and group identity.

Shannon M. Mussett is Assistant Professor of Philosophy at Utah Valley State College in Orem, Utah. She is co-editor (with Sally Scholz) of *The Contradictions of Freedom: Philosophical Essays on Simone de Beauvoir's* The Mandarins.

Margaret A. Simons is Professor of Philosophy at Southern Illinois University Edwardsville. She is author of *Beauvoir and* The Second Sex: *Feminism, Race, and the Origins of Existentialism* and editor (with Sylvie Le Bon de Beauvoir) of *Philosophical Writings,* the first in a seven-volume series of Beauvoir's works in English translation.

Ursula Tidd teaches French studies at the University of Manchester in Manchester, England. She has written an introduction to Beauvoir's thought in the Routledge Critical Thinkers series and several articles on Beauvoir's novels.

Andrea Veltman is Assistant Professor of Philosophy at York University in Toronto. She is working on a new anthology in social and political philosophy and on a book developing a non-subjectivist account of meaningful work.

Karen Vintges is Senior Lecturer in Political and Social Philosophy in the Department of Philosophy at the University of Amsterdam. She is co-editor of *Feminism and the Final Foucault* and author of *Philosophy as Passion: The Thinking of Simone de Beauvoir.*

Julie K. Ward is Associate Professor of Philosophy at Loyola University, Chicago. She is editor of *Feminism and Ancient Philosophy* and (with Tommy Lee Lott) *Philosophers on Race: Critical Essays.*

Gail Weiss is Director of the Human Sciences Graduate Program and Associate Professor of Philosophy at The George Washington University. She is author of *Body Images: Embodiment as Intercorporeality* and co-editor of *Thinking the Limits of the Body.*

Index

9 780253 218407